Praise for

AMERICA VS. THE OVERCLASS

"The thesis of Stephen Young's book is a simple one: America was created by a covenant. That covenant gave the country internal coherence and facilitated its growth and prosperity right up to the period after the Second World War. This covenant was progressively lost in the 1960s. Since then, America has been taken over by an elite, rent-seeking Overclass which lost its inner compass. The Trump phenomenon (both Trump One and Trump Two) was a mass reaction against this Overclass. Restoring a Covenantal America, however, requires the inner direction of Americans and their leaders to be reset. This is an arduous struggle which must be waged with persistence. The future of America depends on it. Young's book provides historical and intellectual underpinnings for a movement of revival in America which is gathering force but still lacks clarity."

GEORGE YEO, former Singapore foreign minister

"In *America vs. the Overclass*, Stephen Young takes us on an intellectual and experiential journey that examines what is fundamentally ailing our country and what it will take to heal it. He shows his work—laying out the path that led us to our current challenges and then offering thoughtful solutions rooted in faith, personal responsibility, and a return to inner-directed values. As someone who has spent a career in criminal justice, I have seen firsthand how other-directed thinking—seeking external validation, blaming others, and waiting for systems to 'fix' us—keeps people trapped in cycles of harm. Stephen Young's message is clear: We must restore inner-directed values that teach each of us we have value and that honest, respectful stewardship of our own talents can strengthen our families, communities, and nation. Regardless of whether we concur with his conclusions, this book encourages readers to present their own intellectual and experiential insights and suggest solutions that will genuinely advance the well-being of humanity. This is a timely, courageous book that calls us to reflect daily, remain humble, and pursue greatness by first improving ourselves and those who depend on us."

MATT BOSTROM, PhD, president, Center for Values-Based Initiatives; former sheriff of Ramsey County, Minnesota; and former assistant chief of operations of the Saint Paul, Minnesota, police department

"In *America vs. the Overclass*, Stephen Young delivers a road map for us to push past mere complaints and gain control of our own lives to contribute in a positive way. After nearly twenty years, I took the leap to leave the comforts of corporate media to tell the truth about the George Floyd lies that have led to untold damage to the police profession and to the once great Midwest city of Minneapolis. I commend Steve Young for having the courage to also be a truthteller and to give every reader the tools to do the same. As Young points out, if we recognize the power we all have to push past the fake divide, our country's greatest days are ahead. It's time we transform blame into responsibility."

LIZ COLLIN, journalist, Alpha News, and producer, *The Fall of Minneapolis*

"*America vs. the Overclass* exposes why so many of our institutions falter despite being guided by capable, well-educated professionals. Stephen Young argues that higher education has largely stopped forming leaders and instead produces managers—individuals trained to assess risk and reach decisions but not inwardly prepared to act when responsibility carries personal cost. By framing leadership as a covenant rather than a contract, Young underscores why courage and interior formation are indispensable: covenants bind the self to responsibility, especially when action requires risk. The challenge Young delivers to the reader is not to do something first but to become someone capable of doing something— to reckon with one's own ethical responsibility for the institutions one inhabits and the future one is shaping. From my work in ethical leadership and human development, I recognize how this deficit of an examined self fuels moral outsourcing and institutional paralysis, even when the right course of action is widely understood. Without inwardly formed leaders willing to bear responsibility, our social, economic, and democratic systems cannot remain sustainable."

MICHAEL LABROSSE, psychotherapist; president, Leadership Solutions Internationale; former ethics and corporate social responsibility officer, First Bank System (now U.S. Bank)

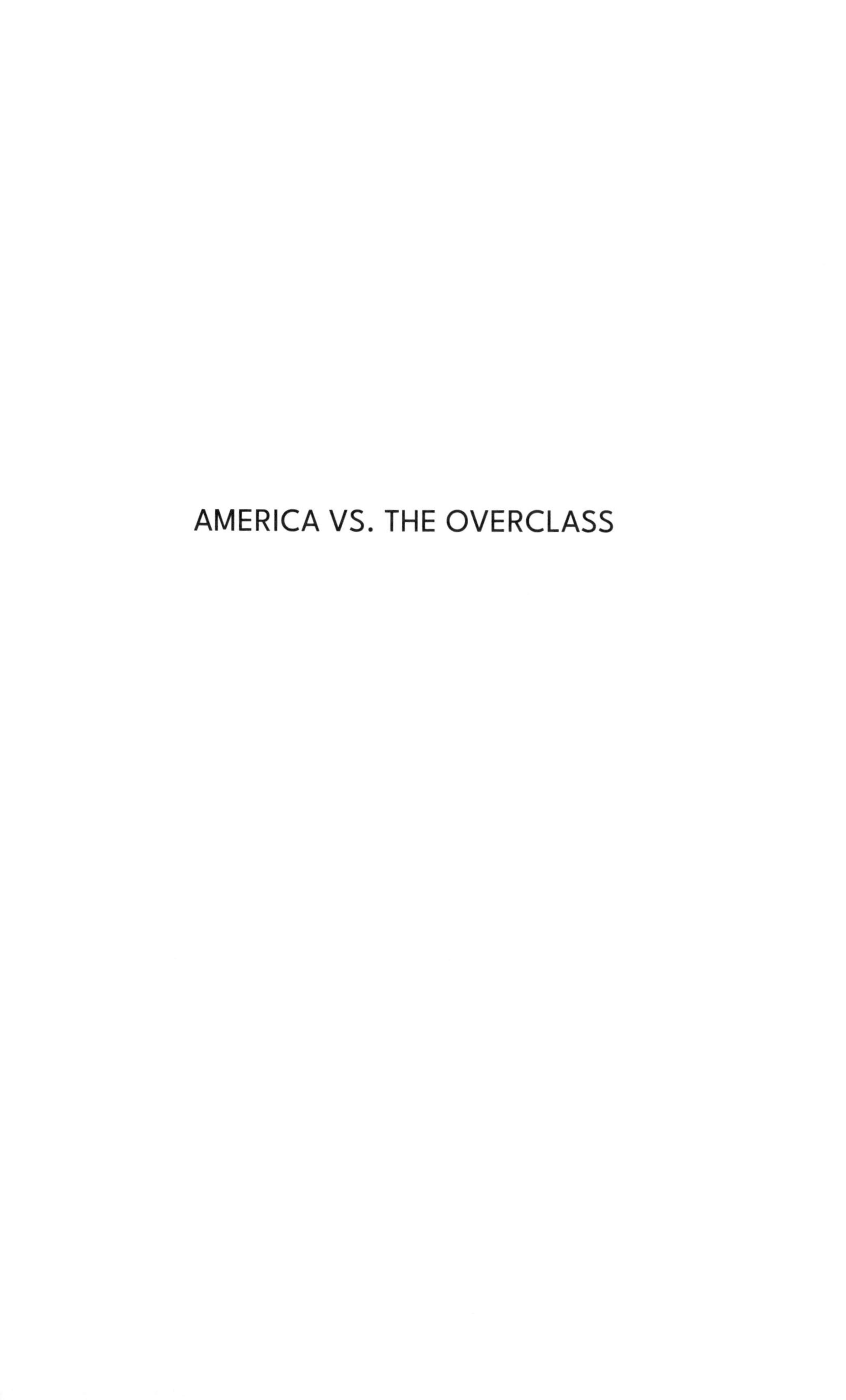

AMERICA VS. THE OVERCLASS

AMERICA vs. THE OVERCLASS

How a New Elite Corrupted Our Nation and What We Can Do to Stop Them

STEPHEN B. YOUNG

RealClear
Publishing

RealClear
Publishing

www.amplifypublishinggroup.com

*America vs. the Overclass: How a New Elite Corrupted Our Nation
and What We Can Do to Stop Them*

For more information, please contact:
RealClear Publishing, an imprint of Amplify Publishing Group
620 Herndon Parkway, Suite 220
Herndon, VA 20170
info@amplifypublishing.com

Library of Congress Control Number: 2025915566

CPSIA Code: PRV0126A

ISBN-13: 979-8-89138-468-2

Printed in the United States

*To those Americans who have raised a standard
of patriotic excellence to which
the wise and the honest have repaired.*

*To those in my family who, since 1776,
have upheld such a standard
but with anxious trepidation for the secure well-being
of my grandchildren—Tamir, Odin, Maceo,
Astrid, Ezra, Allaire, and Claudia—
and for their descendants.*

For within Wisdom is a spirit intelligent, holy, unique, manifold,
subtle, mobile, incisive, unsullied, lucid, invulnerable,
benevolent, shrewd, irresistible, friendly to humanity,
steadfast, dependable, unperturbed, all-surveying . . .

—Book of Wisdom 7:22

CONTENTS

AUTHOR'S NOTE

My first intimations about the topic of this book—how Americans came to be subordinated to a professional elite of managers and influencers—came as I was preparing to leave for Vietnam to work for the U.S. Agency for International Development in Civil Operations Rural Development Support. My mission was to assist local villagers and their elected officials in the villages of South Vietnam in defending themselves against an insurgency instigated and directed by the Vietnamese Communist Party, which ruled North Vietnam.

As I was about to leave, I wrote the following letter to my friend and mentor, Harvard professor David Riesman:

August 12, 1968
Wellfleet

Dear Professor Riesman,

Tomorrow I leave for Vietnam after one week here with my family and one year's training. I expected the federal bureaucracy to be frustrating, but I am surprised to feel physically dirty after this year in the Vietnam Training Center. Contrasted with even a reasonable ideal, that institution is a disgrace. However, I am looking forward to the next two years, more on the basis of an instinct that some good will come of it, that a corner has been established around which we might be able to turn, than on a close analysis of the situation—muddled as usual.

In fact I am more concerned about my own country's political development than the future of Vietnam. There, some goals and methods are fairly widely accepted as worthy of attempt, but here, we seem caught in the doldrums of unknown latitudes. And I am not so distressed by the rising conservative ferment as by the failure of American liberals. It is failure, I feel, to perceive the primary problem and consequently a failure to build a progressively motivated power structure.

They do not have an incisive analysis of the American people—their desires, fears, social strata, or other characteristics which mark the atoms of our national molecule. Restructuring the arrangement and direction of national energies demands the rearrangement of national atoms. And we must know the elements before we attempt the chemistry.

This absence of hard analysis results from the American liberal's fascination with his emotions. He reacts so much from conscience that I fear he is easily led to the superficial, the temporary, the dramatic, and away from a sense of responsibility which those who aspire to power must have.

This political immaturity, I am sure, has roots far into the American past. But since historical awareness lies shamefully far from my perspective, current structural considerations strike me as significant. Many contemporary liberals compose what I take as the New American Elite—the college educated. This part of the middle class—those whose status as well as economic role is a direct consequence of a college degree—is looked up to, respected, and proud of its intellectual abilities. Yet they do not have a crucial voice in that allocation of national resources which is the domain of the power structure. Feeling themselves superior, the New Elitists do not have power. Senior executives, the "old" politicians, labor unions, big city lawyers, still lead the institutions which ration the wealth and energy of the nation. The New Elite rejects these segments of society and calls for a New Politics, a politics of participation or rather *their* participation. The institutional basis for the elite seems to be the university, and their vanguard is their youngest generation—this year's active and upset students.

The surface badge of identity which places one in the New Elite is a McCarthy sticker. The passwords of the Elitists follow from the issues McCarthy has raised and are well known. Structurally speaking, I find three ways to distinguish this New Elite. Their most important rite of passage is graduation from college buttressed in some cases by further study. Successful graduation buys them a first class ticket into the middle class. Their function is to manage our technology, to organize knowledge and information so that some degree of rationality prevails in our economic arrangements and to a lesser degree in our social and political structures. They do not seem to determine fundamental directions but make the journey as efficient as possible. They are the intelligentsia of the postindustrial American Technocracy. Finally their lifestyle is that of suburbia, a mixed heritage of individualism and conformity. To me the key factor here is that their life can be seen as revolving around academic achievement. They struggled through childhood to get in, they worked there and afterward built on that college experience. They are not really in business as we have understood it, they are not in politics, they are the embryonic ruling class angry at their lack of power.

However it is not clear to me whether they want power in the traditional sense. Rather than actually occupy positions of authority and spend their days bothered by making decisions and then executing them, the New Elite may only demand inclusion for some form of moral or intellectual veto. The kind of power they seek probably derives from their class position in the structure, but I have not thought enough about their position and its implications to make a reasonable analysis.

Yet we have always had education people in the middle class and in the elite without the agitation which the Graduated are showing today. In the past, I guess, higher education was a desirable attainment of people whose role in society was primarily determined by other factors, such as inherited wealth, family, business, farm. In other words, the path to a livelihood was not solely dependent on the degree. Now it seems to me that college education has become the preeminent generator of our upper echelons. This fact of its paramount importance not only gives it great status but increasingly focuses attention on this process and its benefits. Secondly, we now live with the quantum leap in numbers of college graduates produced by the education industry since World War II. Thirdly, the kinds of jobs which educated specialists attain have become more important to the society and higher paid. They have now come into their own.

And then we must ask what kind of society will flourish under this New Elite. They seek a new politics; capitalistic business pursuits do not interest them; instrumental politics probably bores them, while discussion of ideas and the "correct" approach delights them. But the Elite has produced many of our Peace Corps Volunteers and Vista workers along with the young who find enjoyment in serving. Here obviously in an advantage to our society.

Unfortunately though, because of the nature of our educational system in the universities, this New Elite has emerged with certain biases. That the most crucial part of their education, which they struggled for and now rest upon, did not give them good judgment—the ability to think rigorously, to put things in perspective, to attain a posture of balance and tolerance, because it gave them training only as more sophisticated technicians. We have taken the institution of higher education, or formalized training for an elite, and transformed it into merely another part of our technocracy—producing experts to fit into some corner of our postindustrial order. We have taken the soul out of higher education by developing "diploma mills" which are not much more than ten-cent stores offering a variety of tickets into the desired realms of suburban bliss. We emphasize specialization, the master of small bits, of the techniques relevant to a particular field. Further, graduates feel their competence has, by virtue of their college experience, given them an omnicompetence, that universalism attained in previous days. They leave their school with a sense of righteousness and pride which is rather impressive though highly undeserved. We have given them a gown with which to parade their still uneducated sensibilities and emotions as the dictates of the highest reason.

And [now] we have a New Elite—trained as technocrats, acting as universalists, important to our society yet alienated from it. And I am worried about it. Please don't take the time to answer my thoughts at length, but I would like to know if you think there might be some truth to all this.

I hope your work continues to be satisfying and that all goes well in Cambridge.

Sincerely Yours,
Stephen B. Young

AMERICAN DESTINY

The writing of this book on America—its post-modern travails and contested political evolution—might have been fated by family destiny.

Growing up in Washington, DC, I was the first grandchild. My maternal grandparents, George and Miriam Morris, lived in a big house on Kalorama Road that was originally built in Danvers, Massachusetts, in the eighteenth century and which my grandparents moved to Washington (where Grandfather was a lawyer) because Grandmother loved American history and collected eighteenth-century American Chippendale furniture.

Grandmother took a special interest in me and made sure I sat still and listened to her talk about history and—especially—about the Morris family. She gave me a mind to walk in the ways of my forebears and do well by my country. My dad and uncles had recently served in World War II, so it was easy for me to internalize standing up for the best in American values. Later, with that very much in mind, I would join the march from Selma to Montgomery as part of the Civil Rights Movement and volunteer to serve with the United States Agency for International Development in South Vietnam in village self-development, self-government, and self-defense.

But (and Grandmother did not stress this at the time) our branch of the Morris family lived in New Jersey, not in Morrisania, New York City, in what is today the Bronx, where the famous Morrises had a large estate. My ancestors were cousins of the prominent Morrises.

The first Morris to leave a mark on what would become the American Republic was Lewis Morris.

To oppose the colonial governor of New York appointed by the British Crown, in the early 1700s, he funded the journalist and printer John Peter Zenger in publishing a politically partisan newspaper complaining about the governor. The governor issued a proclamation condemning Zenger's newspaper for "divers scandalous, virulent, false and seditious reflections." Today Americans stress out over what we call "misinformation", "disinformation", and politically incorrect thoughts and speech. As Grandmother Morris used to tell me: "There is nothing new under the sun."

Zenger was sued for libel, but the jury acquitted him, establishing the principle of freedom of speech and the press in the British colonies. The case established the foundational principle that telling the truth is not libelous.

On July 4, 1776, the grandson of this Lewis Morris (also named Lewis Morris) signed the Declaration of America's Independence. Here is his signature:

With his signature, he contracted that: "And for the support of this Declaration, with a firm reliance on the protection of divine Providence, we mutually pledge to each other our Lives, our Fortunes and our sacred Honor."

This was not the language of a Donald Trump or a Joseph Biden.

Most importantly for Americans until today were the words my collateral ancestor promised to live by:

> We hold these truths to be self-evident, that all men are created equal, that they are endowed by their Creator with certain unalienable Rights, that among these are Life, Liberty and the pursuit of Happiness. --That to secure these rights, Governments are instituted among Men, deriving their just powers from the consent of the governed, --That whenever any Form of Government becomes destructive of these ends, it is the Right of the People to alter or to abolish it, and to institute new Government, laying its foundation on such principles and organizing its powers in such form, as to them shall seem most likely to effect their Safety and Happiness.

All my life, every time I have read this, I have thought of my family (see the hereditary Morris family crest to the right, which was affixed to the inside cover of a 1713 book owned by Lewis Morris, which—by good fortune—I now have in my home office) and our dedication over the generations to our country.

But the Morris story did not end with the Declaration. In 1787 at another gathering of leaders in Philadelphia, Gouverneur Morris—the half-brother of Lewis—would sign the proposed constitution for the new Republic of the United States of America.

Here is his signature:

Much more important to my country than his signature was the preamble he wrote for that Constitution:

> We the People of the United States, in Order to form a more perfect Union, establish Justice, insure domestic Tranquility, provide for the common defence, promote the general Welfare, and secure the Blessings of Liberty to ourselves and our Posterity, do ordain and establish this Constitution for the United States of America.

And so a fortuitous destiny, I suppose, has put me in a position to write a book dedicating my intellectual integrity to the defense of that inspired vocation for the people of America, my country, 250 years after my country declared before the peoples of the world its independent right to provide and protect life, liberty, and the pursuit of happiness for its citizens (and by implication for the peoples of every other country as well).

CHAPTER 1

ONCE A COVENANTAL PEOPLE

Things fall apart; the centre cannot hold;
Mere anarchy is loosed upon the world,
The blood-dimmed tide is loosed, and everywhere
The ceremony of innocence is drowned;
The best lack all conviction, while the worst
Are full of passionate intensity.

William Butler Yeats, "The Second Coming"

How long can one people sustain itself as a great nation?

The United States of America is 250 years old. How many more years of civic health, economic prosperity, and existential stamina does it have left?

My forebearers were part of the founding. In April 1776 Winthrop Young took the association oath in New Hampshire to "oppose with arms the operations of His Majesty's Armies in the North American Colonies." Lewis Morris signed the Declaration of Independence. His half brother, Gouverneur, wrote the preamble to the federal Constitution.

Benjamin Franklin put the case of national survival this way: when asked upon completion of the draft Constitution, "What kind of government have you given us?" Franklin replied, "A republic, Madame, if you can keep it." His reference to "keeping" it invoked the need for virtue. He believed that no republic can stand if its citizens lack virtue.

We Americans must now ask ourselves, "What has happened to our virtue? How much remains?"

On January 15, 2025, Joseph R. Biden spoke to the American people in his last speech as their president. Ominously, he warned them, "Today, an oligarchy is taking shape in America of extreme wealth, power, and influence that literally threatens our entire democracy, our basic rights and freedoms, and a fair shot for everyone to get ahead."[1] But in character, the hapless Biden once again got his facts wrong. He was correct in saying that an oligarchy has taken over managing much of American life, but he was very wrong in pointing out who actually belongs to that Overclass.

Biden spoke of a "disastrous rise of misplaced power," of a "tech-industrial complex," and of "truth smothered by lies for power and profit." But he misspoke in not correctly revealing that oligarchy to be one of salaried managers, expensively educated in American colleges and universities, who have now arrogated unto themselves the cultural and social authority, along with the requisite institutional offices, to tell Americans how to behave and what to think, all while happily extracting financial rents from the economy.

President Biden thus left Americans with this question: "How far have we fallen since September 1787?"

In 1976 a real man of empire, Sir John Bagot Glubb (also known as Glubb Pasha) examined the lifespans of different empires over the past 4,000 years in his little-known book *The Fate of Empires and Search for Survival*. What he saw was an average lifespan of 250 years, or only ten generations, from rise to fall.[2]

Glubb did not consider the Chinese experience with the rise and fall of dynasties, but each Chinese dynasty, from the Han to the Qing, also completed its rise and fall in roughly 250-year cycles.

As a general rule for all peoples and nations, Glubb concluded, "It has been shown that, normally, the rise and fall of great nations are due to internal reasons alone. Ten generations of human beings suffice to transform the hardy and enterprising pioneer into the captious citizen of the welfare state."

THE NATION	DATES OF RISE AND FALL	DURATION IN YEARS
Assyria	859–612 BC	247
Persia	538–330 BC	208

(Cyrus and his descendants)

THE NATION	DATES OF RISE AND FALL	DURATION IN YEARS
Greece	331–100 BC	231

(Alexander and his successors)

THE NATION	DATES OF RISE AND FALL	DURATION IN YEARS
Roman Republic	260–27 BC	233
Roman Empire	27 BC–AD 180	207
Arab Empire	AD 634–880	246
Mameluke Empire	1250–1517	267
Ottoman Empire	1320–1570	250
Spain	1500–1750	250
Romanov Russia	1682–1916	234
Britain	1700–1950	250

Glubb had no illusion that Americans could avoid this fate of regime collapse. He wrote in 1976, "The United States arose suddenly as a new nation, and its period of pioneering was spent in the conquest of a vast continent, not an ancient empire. Yet the subsequent life history of the United States has followed the standard pattern which we shall attempt to trace—the periods of the pioneers, of commerce, of affluence, of intellectualism and of decadence."

Pioneers build and expand their people's rule with wild courage and energy. Then in an age of commerce, the community grows rich and reaches its high noon. But then money has a baleful influence. According to Glubb,

> There does not appear to be any doubt that money is the agent which causes the decline of this strong, brave and self-confident people. The decline in courage, enterprise and a sense of duty is, however, gradual.
>
> The first direction in which wealth injures the nation is a moral one. . . . But, beneath the surface, greed for money is gradually replacing duty and public service. Indeed the change might be summarized as being from service to selfishness.

After high noon, civil dissensions usher in an age of decline with the intensification of political hatreds. The community is penetrated by foreigners. Glubb continues,

> One of the oft-repeated phenomena of great empires is the influx of foreigners to the capital city. . . . The immigrants are liable to form communities of their own, protecting primarily their own interests, and only in the second degree that of the nation as a whole. . . .
>
> As the nation declines in power and wealth, a universal pessimism gradually pervades the people, and itself hastens the

decline. . . . A community of selfish and idle people declines, internal quarrels develop in the division of its dwindling wealth, and pessimism follows, which some of them endeavour to drown in sensuality or frivolity. In their own surroundings, they are unable to redirect their thoughts and their energies into new channels.

In this final phase of communal decadence, the people lose their virtue and, in its place, enthrone defensiveness, pessimism, materialism, frivolity, welfare-state dependency and entitlements, and a weakening of religion. When decadence sets in, citizens mutate into subjects under management, refusing responsibility while demanding dutiful patronage from their superiors; moral intelligence atrophies; leadership becomes performative only; beneath behavioral surfaces is emptiness; and solidity is illusory.

From an engineering design perspective, a kingdom, a nation, or a regime in its final stage of decadence has become "fracture critical"—the failure of just one part under accumulating stress may quickly result in the collapse of the entire bridge or other structure. As Hemingway quipped about financial collapse, "gradually, then all at once." A system that is "fracture critical" has no redundancy, where, when one component fails, no others step up to withstand the accumulated stress, or no resiliency, where its parts, with flexibility and elasticity, jointly share in stress management and bring forth new strengths in times of need. In human systems the fracture-critical component is often the ruling elite or, for individuals, the ego-identity, either of which loses its will or purpose for living. It is widely said that "a fish rots from the head."

Most likely not by coincidence, Glubb's thinking was paraphrased on American television. In the 2023 show *Special Ops: Lioness*, one character rants about the coming decline and fall of the American empire. Cultural commentator Rick Marin writes,

The money launderer's daughter, a member of the Lioness squad, has been tasked with turning her father on his cartel-boss brother. Her cover is a fake dishonorable discharge from the Army, news that precipitates his rant. Which it turns out is just a warm-up for a peroration on the decline and fall of the American empire. . . .

"The first sign an empire is failing is when its people question the institutions the empire was built on. The structure of government, the churches, the schools. They reject God because the emperors believe they are God. And the people become so rich, everyone believes they are an emperor as well. And too good to do the jobs that built the empire in the first place. So they outsource those jobs. And they open their borders to allow people desperate to do all the other jobs the other people are too rich to do. Then comes the guilt for all this wealth. But still the empire thrives. And now everyone questions their wealth. Then they question themselves. And then they reject everything that built the empire to begin with. They destroy their own symbols, attack themselves like a cancer, attack the people who protect the empire, attack you for protecting it. Then the wolves come. And all the people who lived like emperors will know the suffering they blamed themselves for creating. And they will be slaughtered. And a new empire will rise from its ashes. Then the cycle begins again."[3]

More seriously, Glubb's analysis was given substantial affirmation by Professors Daron Acemoglu and James Robinson in their 2012 book *Why Nations Fail*, which was to receive the 2024 Nobel Prize in economics.[4] Acemoglu and Robinson argued that for nations, societies, and regimes, the quality of their institutions makes for success or failure. Good institutions bring about political, cultural, social, and economic well-being. Bad institutions bring about failure—poverty, oppression, systemic unhappiness, and overthrow. And they note institutions are created and maintained by elites. So the failures of empires, dynasties, regimes, and nations, as documented by Glubb, would necessarily have come from the failures of their respective elites.

Whether America is in failure mode today will be determined by the quality and competence of our current elite, those with college and postgraduate degrees, whom I worried about in 1968 as I was leaving my country to fight for the ideals of human dignity in South Vietnam. If that elite fails, the American experiment in ordered liberty will come to an end on schedule, and possibly, the American people will thus come under the superintendence of one or more greater rising powers in a new world order of dog-eat-dog.

The Evolution of the Covenant

Americans first came together as a covenantal people.

A covenant creates a social structure based on a shared sense of history and destiny. It gives deep meaning to one's life on earth.

A covenant creates a partnership, reciprocal dependencies that lower our risks and increase the probability of securing better outcomes in our lives. Covenants create social capital through the reciprocal granting of rights and the acceptance of responsibilities. Covenants unite self and other—husband with wife and wife with husband, friend with friend, individual with the state. In a covenant the self gains rights as another assumes obligations, and the other gains rights as the self assumes obligations. The duties of one are balanced against the duties of the other in a commonwealth of achievement and security.

Covenants differ from contracts in that, under a covenant, there is a coming together of lives in serious, consequential relationship, while in a contract, there is most often only a stand-alone transaction to perform with a parting of ways upon completion of the task. Covenants imply fiduciary concern for the other, as well as stewardship and ministry. Covenants presume a willingness to sacrifice come what may to stalwartly succor one's confederates. Breaking a covenantal obligation is far more serious than failure to perform under a contract.

Consider the overtones of sanctity expressed in traditional marriage vows: "In the name of God, I take you to be my (husband/wife), to have and to hold from this day forward, for better, for worse, for richer, for poorer, in sickness and in health, to love and to cherish, until we are parted by death. This is my solemn vow."

Making such a covenant provides spiritual goodness and honor, a sense of purpose, to those who accept its terms and who pledge themselves in loyalty one to another.

Our founders made this covenant explicit in our Declaration of Independence, including in its terms the ideals to which Americans would devote themselves.

> We hold these truths to be self-evident, that all men are created equal, that they are endowed by their Creator with certain unalienable Rights, that among these are Life, Liberty and the pursuit of Happiness. . . . And for the support of this Declaration, with a firm reliance on the protection of divine Providence, we mutually pledge to each other our Lives, our Fortunes and our sacred Honor.

We also find covenant much earlier in our history, in the first notable expression of a unique and exceptional American destiny: the Mayflower Compact, which forty-one Pilgrim passengers signed at sea before reaching Cape Cod.[5] Its exact author or authors are unknown, but its pledge of mutual responsibility before God in establishing governing institutions is clear.

> Having undertaken for the Glory of God, and Advancement of the Christian Faith, and the honour of our King and

Country, a voyage to plant the first colony in the northern parts of Virginia; do by these presents, solemnly and mutually in the Presence of God and one of another, covenant and combine ourselves together into a civil Body Politick, for our better Ordering and Preservation, and Furtherance of the Ends aforesaid; And by Virtue hereof to enact, constitute, and frame, such just and equal Laws, Ordinances, Acts, Constitutions and offices, from time to time, as shall be thought most meet and convenient for the General good of the Colony; unto which we promise all due submission and obedience.

John Winthrop further affirmed this covenantal relationship in his sermon on board the ship *Arbella* as his Puritans sailed in to their new "homeland," the British colony in Massachusetts Bay. Winthrop wrote,

Thus stands the cause between God and us. We are entered into covenant with Him for this work. We have taken out a commission. The Lord hath given us leave to draw our own articles. We have professed to enterprise these and those accounts, upon these and those ends. We have hereupon besought Him of favor and blessing. Now if the Lord shall please to hear us, and bring us in peace to the place we desire, then hath He ratified this covenant and sealed our commission, and will expect a strict performance of the articles contained in it; but if we shall neglect the observation of these articles which are the ends we have propounded, and, dissembling with our God, shall fall to embrace this present world and prosecute our carnal intentions, seeking great things for ourselves and our posterity, the Lord will surely break out in wrath against us, and be revenged of such a people, and make us know the price of the breach of such a covenant. . . .

For we must consider that we shall be as a city upon a hill. The eyes of all people are upon us. So that if we shall deal falsely with our God in this work we have undertaken, and so cause Him to withdraw His present help from us, we shall be made a story and a by-word through the world. . . .

And to shut this discourse with that exhortation of Moses, that faithful servant of the Lord, in his last farewell to Israel, Deut. 30. "Beloved, there is now set before us life and death, good and evil," in that we are commanded this day to love the Lord our God, and to love one another, to walk in his ways and to keep his Commandments and his ordinance and his laws, and the articles of our Covenant with Him, that we may live and be multiplied, and that the Lord our God may bless us in the land whither we go to possess it. But if our hearts shall turn away, so that we will not obey, but shall be seduced, and worship other Gods, our pleasure and profits, and serve them; it is propounded unto us this day, we shall surely perish out of the good land whither we pass over this vast sea to possess it.[6]

Years later the first agreement of a national character among the several British colonies in North America would take a covenantal form. In September 1774 the first Congress of representatives of the British colonies met in Philadelphia. The Congress adopted Articles of Association on October 20. Those articles affirmed a boycott of goods imported from Great Britain as a response to acts passed by the British Parliament that were inimical to the interests of the colonists and concluded with a covenantal pledge.

And we do solemnly bind ourselves and our constituents, under the ties aforesaid, to adhere to this association, until such parts of the several acts of parliament passed since the close of the last war . . . are repealed.[7]

Of considerable interest in revealing the aspirational values of the emerging American nation, the Articles of Association in Article 2 called for an end to the slave trade.

> We will neither import nor purchase, any slave imported after the first day of December next; after which time, we will wholly discontinue the slave trade, and will neither be concerned in it ourselves, nor will we hire our vessels, nor sell our commodities or manufactures to those who are concerned in it.

The Preamble to the American Constitution of 1787 took a covenantal form.

> We the People of the United States, in order to form a more perfect Union, establish Justice, insure domestic Tranquility, provide for the common defence, promote the general Welfare, and secure the Blessings of Liberty to ourselves and our Posterity, do ordain and establish this Constitution for the United States of America.

During the convention in Philadelphia, which drafted the Constitution to be presented to the American people for ratification, George Washington framed the work before the delegates in the covenantal tradition.

> Let us raise a standard to which the wise and the honest can repair. The rest is in the hands of God.

In his address of April 30, 1789, when accepting the office of president of the United States of America, George Washington described the new political community as something special.

No people can be bound to acknowledge and adore the Invisible Hand which conducts the affairs of men more than those of the United States. Every step by which they have advanced to the character of an independent nation seems to have been distinguished by some token of providential agency.

When faced with the prospect of a civil war ending the national covenant, the new president, Abraham Lincoln, used covenantal language to affirm his right to wage war to prevent the secession of the Southern states from the constitutional union.

Descending from these general principles, we find the proposition that in legal contemplation the Union is perpetual confirmed by the history of the Union itself. The Union is much older than the Constitution. It was formed, in fact, by the Articles of Association in 1774. It was matured and continued by the Declaration of Independence in 1776. It was further matured, and the faith of all the then thirteen States expressly plighted and engaged that it should be perpetual, by the Articles of Confederation in 1778. And finally, in 1787, one of the declared objects for ordaining and establishing the Constitution was "to form a more perfect Union."

But if destruction of the Union by one or by a part only of the States be lawfully possible, the Union is less perfect than before the Constitution, having lost the vital element of perpetuity.

It follows from these views that no State upon its own mere motion can lawfully get out of the Union; that resolves and ordinances to that effect are legally void, and that acts of violence within any State or States against the authority of the United States are insurrectionary or revolutionary, according to circumstances.[8]

He concluded by again using the moral language of covenantal fiduciaries.

> In your hands, my dissatisfied fellow-countrymen, and not in mine, is the momentous issue of civil war. The Government will not assail you. You can have no conflict without being yourselves the aggressors. You have no oath registered in heaven to destroy the Government, while I shall have the most solemn one to "preserve, protect, and defend it."

The Southern states did not agree to Lincoln's plea for them to keep the national covenant. During the ensuing Civil War of 1861 through 1865, Lincoln continued to use covenantal analogies to justify that war to end slavery and save America as a united constitutional republic. In his short but emotionally stirring Gettysburg Address, he affirmed,

> But, in a larger sense, we can not dedicate—we can not consecrate—we can not hallow—this ground. The brave men, living and dead, who struggled here, have consecrated it, far above our poor power to add or detract. The world will little note, nor long remember what we say here, but it can never forget what they did here. It is for us the living, rather, to be dedicated here to the unfinished work which they who fought here have thus far so nobly advanced. It is rather for us to be here dedicated to the great task remaining before us—that from these honored dead we take increased devotion to that cause for which they gave the last full measure of devotion— that we here highly resolve that these dead shall not have died in vain—that this nation, under God, shall have a new birth of freedom—and that government of the people, by the people, for the people, shall not perish from the earth.

In November 1861, Julia Ward Howe wrote a "hymn" ("The Battle Hymn of the Republic") for Union soldiers to sing as they fought Confederate armies in a war to save the American union and end slavery. Howe used the metaphor of covenantal duty to justify such service and inspire dedicated faithful execution of its military office:

> [God] hath loosed the fateful lightning of His terrible swift sword:
> His truth is marching on. . . .
> He has sounded forth the trumpet that shall never call retreat;
> He is sifting out the hearts of men before His judgment-seat:
> Oh, be swift, my soul, to answer Him![9]

Echoes of covenant also can be heard in John F. Kennedy's 1961 inaugural address.

> And so, my fellow Americans: ask not what your country can do for you—ask what you can do for your country. . . .
> With a good conscience our only sure reward, with history the final judge of our deeds, let us go forth to lead the land we love, asking His blessing and His help, but knowing that here on earth God's work must truly be our own.[10]

President Kennedy would be assassinated in November 1963. As the 1960s continued to unfold, more and more Americans would turn away from their nation's covenantal heritage.

A Tragic Exception

From the start, the American covenant was not extended to African slaves and indigenous peoples. That discriminatory separation has yet to be fully rectified.

Most African slaves were confined to plantations in the tidewater and coastal lowlands of Virginia, the Carolinas, and Georgia. The Southern colonial population was not associated with the Puritan tradition of covenantal dedication. The Southern colonies had been founded by more socially elite families adhering to the Church of England in theology and lifestyles.[11] They were not prone to building out covenantal communities.

The hills and mountains to the west of the plantation lowlands were settled by Scotch-Irish immigrants, very clannish and standoffish in their manners and family orientations. They had no interest in mingling with outsiders and were not at all hospitable to indigenous communities or African slaves.[12]

After the Civil War was won by the Union, slavery was abolished, and former slaves were given full legal rights of citizenship. But socially and culturally, the former slaves were not welcomed into the covenant of those chosen to build in this country a "city upon a hill." This continued exclusion from community was ratified by the United States Supreme Court in its 1896 opinion in the case of *Plessy v. Ferguson*.[13]

In the case, a person with one-eighth Negro ancestry was barred from sitting in a railroad car reserved for members of the "White race" and was taken into custody by the police for his effrontery in violating a law of Louisiana that mandated separate cars for the separate races.

In that case the court agreed that, under the Fourteenth Amendment to the Constitution, former slaves had been given "legal rights" equal to those of White citizens. But, the court continued, the Amendment had not conferred upon "Negroes" the social and cultural rights to comingle with Whites against the wishes of White citizens.

The court continued,

> The [Plaintiff's] argument also assumes that social prejudices may be overcome by legislation, and that equal rights cannot be secured to the negro except by an enforced commingling of the two races. We cannot accept this proposition. If the two

races are to meet upon terms of social equality, it must be the result of natural affinities, a mutual appreciation of each other's merits, and a voluntary consent of individuals. . . .

. . . So far, then, as a conflict with the Fourteenth Amendment is concerned, the case reduces itself to the question whether the statute of Louisiana is a reasonable regulation, and, with respect to this, there must necessarily be a large discretion on the part of the legislature. In determining the question of reasonableness, it is at liberty to act with reference to the established usages, customs, and traditions of the people, and with a view to the promotion of their comfort and the preservation of the public peace and good order. Gauged by this standard, we cannot say that a law which authorizes or even requires the separation of the two races in public conveyances is unreasonable. . . .

Laws forbidding the intermarriage of the two races may be said in a technical sense to interfere with the freedom of contract, and yet have been universally recognized as within the police power of the State.

Thus did the Supreme Court leave to the people the power to decide who was to be included in and who was to be excluded from the covenant setting forth American national purpose and identity.

The 1954 Supreme Court opinion in *Brown v. Board of Education* overturned *Plessy*, but again, courts have no authority to write the terms of a people's cultural covenant.

In the historic 1963 March on Washington, the Rev. Martin Luther King Jr. proposed to the American people just such an amendment to their covenant of national identity and purpose. He insisted that all Americans not be judged by the color of their skins but only by the content of their character, implying that anyone of good character was qualified to affirm and keep the American covenant to build a city upon a hill, accepting all the responsibilities thereunto appertaining.

King drew on America's covenantal heritage of a collective effort to build that city upon a hill with these words:

> When we allow freedom ring, when we let it ring from every village and every hamlet, from every state and every city, we will be able to speed up that day when all of God's children, black men and white men, Jews and Gentiles, Protestants and Catholics, will be able to join hands and sing in the words of the old Negro spiritual: Free at last! Free at last! Thank God Almighty, we are free at last![14]

In 1968 King would be assassinated.

The Civil Rights Movement of the 1960s led to Congress adopting the Civil Rights Acts of 1964 and 1965. These acts would, by law, abolish the post–Civil War segregation by race imposed by Southern states on their citizens. But again, laws are limited in their power to change hearts and soften souls so that all are welcomed into the beloved community.

The Covenantal Tradition

The American covenantal tradition derives first from Hebrew Scripture and then from the teachings of Jesus in the New Testament of the Christian Bible.

In the book of Genesis, we are told that God, Yahweh, makes a covenant with Noah after the flood and then another with Abraham. Yahweh's covenant with Noah was for him and his descendants to populate the earth and live rightly. That covenant also embraced "all living things."[15] The rabbinical tradition holds that associated with Yahweh's covenant is for all people after the flood to live by these particular precepts: not to worship idols, not to curse God, not to commit murder, not to commit adultery or other sexual immorality, not to steal, not to eat flesh torn from a living animal, and to establish courts of justice.

Later, Yahweh blesses Abraham and promises to make of him a great nation. Still later, Yahweh made a covenant with Abraham to give him and his descendants the land "from the river of Egypt to the great river."[16] But Yahweh did not take Abraham's fidelity for granted. To partake of a covenant requires obedience, as well as enjoyment of advantages. Abraham's test was to offer his son Isaac in sacrifice to Yahweh. Abraham complied, and Yahweh did not permit harm to come to the boy, saying to the father, "Do not harm him, for now I know you fear God. You have not refused me your own beloved son."[17]

Most importantly, in the Hebrew scriptures, covenant becomes foundational for the Israelites after they return to Canaan from exile and slavery in Egypt. The book of Deuteronomy tells us that before they crossed the river Jordan into the land that Yahweh was giving them for a homeland, Moses instructed the future Israelites:

> If you fully obey the Lord your God and carefully follow all his commands I give you today, the Lord your God will set you high above all the nations on earth. All these blessings will come on you and accompany you if you obey the Lord your God: You will be blessed in the city and blessed in the country.
>
> The fruit of your womb will be blessed, and the crops of your land and the young of your livestock—the calves of your herds and the lambs of your flocks.
>
> Your basket and your kneading trough will be blessed.
>
> You will be blessed when you come in and blessed when you go out.
>
> The Lord will grant that the enemies who rise up against you will be defeated before you. They will come at you from one direction but flee from you in seven.
>
> The Lord will send a blessing on your barns and on everything you put your hand to. The Lord your God will bless you in the land he is giving you.

The Lord will establish you as his holy people, as he promised you on oath, if you keep the commands of the Lord your God and walk in obedience to him. Then all the peoples on earth will see that you are called by the name of the Lord, and they will fear you. The Lord will grant you abundant prosperity—in the fruit of your womb, the young of your livestock and the crops of your ground—in the land he swore to your ancestors to give you.

The Lord will open the heavens, the storehouse of his bounty, to send rain on your land in season and to bless all the work of your hands. You will lend to many nations but will borrow from none. The Lord will make you the head, not the tail. If you pay attention to the commands of the Lord your God that I give you this day and carefully follow them, you will always be at the top, never at the bottom. Do not turn aside from any of the commands I give you today, to the right or to the left, following other gods and serving them.[18]

But to earn the benefits of Yahweh's covenant from generation to generation, the Israelites must walk in the way of their Lord as he expects. The prophet Micah explained,

What does the Lord your God ask of you but to fear the Lord your God, to walk in obedience to him, to love him, to serve the Lord your God with all your heart and with all your soul, and to observe the Lord's commandments and decrees that I am giving you today for your own good?[19]

In later generations, when the people and their leaders did not fulfill their responsibilities under the covenant with Yahweh, Yahweh called on prophets to speak out and call the wayward back to the path of duty. The prophet Micah asked, "What does the Lord require of you? To act justly and to love mercy and to walk humbly with your God."

The prophet Ezekiel castigated those who ruled Israel.

> The word of the Lord came to me: "Son of man, prophesy against the shepherds of Israel; prophesy and say to them, this is what the Sovereign Lord says: 'Woe to you shepherds of Israel who only take care of yourselves! Should not shepherds take care of the flock?' . . .
>
> ". . . This is what the Sovereign Lord says: 'I am against the shepherds and will hold them accountable for my flock. I will remove them from tending the flock so that the shepherds can no longer feed themselves. I will rescue my flock from their mouths, and it will no longer be food for them.'"[20]

The reciprocal responsibilities created by Yahweh's covenants with Abraham and the Israelites were limited to a people—the Israelites. More generous access to the benefits of that covenant was provided by Jesus Christ as related in the books of the New Testament. Jesus provided instruction in how anyone could "walk in the way of the Lord." He said of his ministry, "I am the way and the truth and the life. No one comes to the Father except through me."[21]

The Bible relates that even Jesus was tested for his faith. When he was hungry after fasting, the devil tempted him to make bread. Jesus replied that the way of living faithfully with God was not by bread alone "but by every word of God." When the devil offered him worldly pomp and circumstance, Jesus refused, saying, "Away from me, Satan!"[22]

In his Sermon on the Mount, Jesus set forth the behaviors—the dao—acceptable to the Lord God: Be meek; thirst after righteousness; show mercy; be pure in heart; fear not persecution for being righteous; do not hide your talents or your good works from the eyes of others; judge not that you be not judged; do unto others as you would have them do unto you; do not try to serve both God and the tempting idols of this world; and think of yourself as a city upon a hill, visible to all.[23]

Later, Jesus would add teachings on turning the other cheek, feeding the hungry, giving drink to the thirsty, taking in a stranger, visiting the sick, and providing clothes for the naked.[24]

At the Last Supper, Jesus provided a means for any individual who seeks to live in God's trust to enter into a covenantal relationship with him through the ritual of the Eucharist, affirming divine acceptance of his personhood. Partaking of bread was to ingest Christ, binding the supplicant to divine purpose. Drinking of wine was also to ingest Christ and also to fuse the personhood of the supplicant with a divine personhood.

The Early Christian Church Fathers accordingly refocused the Hebrew covenantal tradition on individual covenants with God for personal salvation. After the passing of Jesus, his disciples organized congregations of the faithful, which became a church. The covenantal practice of this new Christian church was managed by intermediaries—literate clerics chosen by church leaders and held in esteem by the people—who, for individual believers, brokered the formation of their covenants with God (baptism, the Eucharist) and managed the complexities that came with the faithful execution of their trust responsibilities under their personal covenants (confession and absolution).

With the Protestant Reformation, the church as intermediary between believers and God was deemphasized as the individual's direct personal relationship with God through faith and associated good works became the centerpiece of every personal covenant with divine authority.

In American covenantal practice, those following Calvinist Protestant teachings looked more to the legalistic covenantal practices described in the Torah and the Old Testament. Those who were Catholic, members of the Church of England, Methodists, and some Baptists took the covenant to be more personal and spiritual to be ratified with celebration of the Eucharist and personal devotions.

A further expansion of covenantal possibilities was proposed by John Locke in his *Second Treatise on Civil Government.*[25] Locke secularized the process of making covenants and living by their terms. Locke replaced God as the authority in command by the law of nature. That law, said Locke, created human persons with the will and moral competence to "order their actions and dispose of their possessions and persons as they see fit." This natural liberty was a human right: "The natural liberty of man is to be free from any superior power on earth, and not to be under the will or legislative authority of man, but to have only the law of nature for his rule. The liberty of man, in society, is to be under no other legislative power, but that established, by consent, in the commonwealth."[26] Locke thus used covenant as the means of establishing political community and giving it legitimacy. Under the covenant creating a "commonwealth," the political authority of the community, which protects the inherent rights of its citizens, could enact laws binding on members of the community and then enforce such laws on those members, and reciprocally, members of the commonwealth bound themselves to obedience before those laws. The Lockean model of secular covenant was used in the American Declaration of Independence and later for the adoption by the American people of a written constitution for their federal government.

Locke proposed,

> Wherever, therefore, any number of men so unite in one society, as to quit everyone his executive power of the law of nature, and to resign it to the public, then, and there only, is a political or a civil society. . . .
>
> And this puts men out of a state of nature into that of a commonwealth, by setting up a judge on earth with authority to determine all the controversies and redress the injuries that may happen to any member of the community.[27]

In the covenantal practices of the American people's experiment in ordered liberty, the covenantal tradition of the Old and New Testaments, on one side, and the Lockean proposal for using covenant in secular, civil society, on the other, complemented each other, each providing succor for the other and reinforcing its pride of place in quintessential American habits of the heart.

Covenantal Responsibility

The effect of making a covenant is to assume responsibility. Without a covenant, we are free to ignore others and may use our powers capriciously, pursuing no cause other than our own willful truth. When we promise, we assume duties. In a covenantal promise, we most always assume responsibilities to behave well. We agree to act as an agent or to execute a trust. These responsibilities are known in the law as fiduciary duties of loyalty and due care. Supporting this assumption of responsibility must be the deployment of capabilities to execute faithfully the office we have accepted.

So when one becomes president of the United States of America, an oath must be sworn to "faithfully execute the Office of President of the United States, and will to the best of my ability, preserve, protect and defend the Constitution of the United States."

Entering into a covenantal relationship creates what Martin Buber called an "I-Thou" relationship. In a covenant a person is called to engage morally with another or with others by accepting a role or an office. Fulfilling the obligations associated with such a role or office brings forth capabilities that provide us with purposeful energies and a sense of direction in our life. We have a vocation that makes us important to another or to others.

We might therefore say that making a covenant gives us a "dao" or way of living.

The terms of the covenant provide us with direction and purpose. After making a covenant, we know there is meaning and consequence to our lives. Our personhood has become more important to history; we have agreed to listen to the "better angels of our nature," as Lincoln phrased it. In a covenant we put narcissism behind us and start to live for others, building a better future in collaboration with others, serving the common good.

Under the American covenant, the personal capabilities and life orientation—the dao—that we as individuals adopt for our personal practice have been called the "Protestant Ethic" or the "Protestant Work Ethic."[28]

Benjamin Franklin made a list of these virtues in his autobiography as follows:

1. TEMPERANCE. Eat not to dullness; drink not to elevation.
2. SILENCE. Speak not but what may benefit others or yourself; avoid trifling conversation.
3. ORDER. Let all your things have their places; let each part of your business have its time.
4. RESOLUTION. Resolve to perform what you ought; perform without fail what you resolve.
5. FRUGALITY. Make no expense but to do good to others or yourself; i.e., waste nothing.
6. INDUSTRY. Lose no time; be always employ'd in something useful; cut off all unnecessary actions.
7. SINCERITY. Use no hurtful deceit; think innocently and justly; and, if you speak, speak accordingly.
8. JUSTICE. Wrong none by doing injuries, or omitting the benefits that are your duty.
9. MODERATION. Avoid extreams; forbear resenting injuries so much as you think they deserve.
10. CLEANLINESS. Tolerate no uncleanliness in body, cloaths, or habitation.
11. TRANQUILLITY. Be not disturbed at trifles, or at accidents common or unavoidable.

12. CHASTITY. Rarely use venery but for Health or Offspring, Never to Dulness, Weakness, or the Injury of your
own or another's Peace or Reputation.

13. HUMILITY. Imitate Jesus and Socrates.[29]

Franklin, practical man that he was, also made a list of those virtues a community would attain if composed of individuals animated by the Protestant Ethic of personal capabilities. Those virtues are generosity, magnificence, splendor, honor, power, glory, reputation, equality, and liberty.[30]

Ironically, the Protestant Ethic does not vindicate selfish individualism. Since it flows from a tradition of covenantal association, the Protestant Ethic effectively guides individuals toward "self-interest properly understood,"[31] or "self-interest understood upon the whole,"[32] or "enlightened" self-interest.[33] After his 1835 visit to America, de Tocqueville explained that Americans supported their decentralization of political power with certain "habits of the heart," which led them to join associations and work collectively.

On a practical basis, de Tocqueville explained that in a democracy, citizens are individually independent and so weak—"They can hardly do anything for themselves, and none of them is in a position to force his fellows to help him. They would all therefore find themselves helpless if they did not learn to help each other voluntarily." In other words, they must come together in covenant for common purposes.[34] He asserted, "Feelings and ideas are renewed, the heart enlarged, and the understanding developed only by the reciprocal action of men one upon another."[35]

Following self-interest narrowly understood keeps one outside the covenant. This reality served the novelist Herman Melville well in his novel *Moby Dick*, the tragic story of a whaling ship captain, Ahab, obsessively seeking revenge on a white whale—Moby Dick. At the end of this fable about human purpose, the whale wins, sinking the ship, and Ahab and his crew all drown, save for one bystander who survives to tell us the tale.

Importantly, de Tocqueville concluded that in America "religion" made possible a democratic political society. "America is still the place where the Christian religion has kept the greatest real power over men's souls . . . the country where it now has widest sway is both the most enlightened and the freest."[36] This beneficial religion, he added, "reigns supreme in the souls of women, and it is women who shape mores."[37]

"The religious atmosphere of the country was the first thing that struck me on arrival in the United States."[38]

Franklin was not the only American to crystallize the Protestant Ethic in maxims of good character as the duty of one bound by covenant with destiny.

There were the Boy Scouts. A Boy Scout took an oath (similar to a covenant but binding oneself rather than two parties) as follows:

"On my honor I will do my best to do my duty to God and my country and to obey the Scout Law; to help other people at all times; to keep myself physically strong, mentally awake, and morally straight."

Under the Scout Law, a faithful Scout would be as follows:

TRUSTWORTHY. Tell the truth and keep promises. People can depend on you.

LOYAL. Show that you care about your family, friends, Scout leaders, school, and country.

HELPFUL. Volunteer to help others without expecting a reward.

FRIENDLY. Be a friend to everyone, even people who are very different from you.

COURTEOUS. Be polite to everyone and always use good manners.

KIND. Treat others as you want to be treated. Never harm or kill any living thing without good reason.

OBEDIENT. Follow the rules of your family, school, and pack. Obey the laws of your community and country.

CHEERFUL. Look for the bright side of life. Cheerfully do tasks that come your way. Try to help others be happy.

THRIFTY. Work to pay your own way. Try not to be wasteful. Use time, food, supplies, and natural resources wisely.

BRAVE. Face difficult situations even when you feel afraid. Do what you think is right despite what others might be doing or saying.

CLEAN. Keep your body and mind fit. Help keep your home and community clean.

REVERENT. Be reverent toward God. Be faithful in your religious duties. Respect the beliefs of others.[39]

The movie and TV singing cowboy character Roy Rogers provided young Americans with these rules of conduct:

1. Be neat and clean.
2. Be courteous and polite.
3. Always obey your parents.
4. Protect the weak and help them.
5. Be brave but never take chances.
6. Study hard and learn all you can.
7. Be kind to animals and take care of them.
8. Eat all your food and never waste any.
9. Love God and go to Sunday School regularly.
10. Always respect our flag and our country.[40]

Real-life Hollywood actor Gene Autry, who played many a cowboy on the silver screen, also had his recommendations for how to live with honor and dignity.

1. The Cowboy must never shoot first, hit a smaller man, or take unfair advantage.
2. He must never go back on his word or a trust confided in him.

3. He must always tell the truth.
4. He must be gentle with children, the elderly, and animals.
5. He must not advocate or possess racially or religiously intolerant ideas.
6. He must help people in distress.
7. He must be a good worker.
8. He must keep himself clean in thought, speech, action, and personal habits.
9. He must respect women, parents, and his nation's laws.
10. The Cowboy is a patriot.[41]

American patriotism has been distinguished by a devotional embrace of a communal idealism—a vocational calling of service that is covenantal in its spirit of mutual obligation.

The behaviors expressing the Protestant Ethic noted above manifest each and every one an "I-Thou" ethic of relationships with others. In this way they manifest a dao seeking covenantal sincerity in our interactions with community and others. Another traditional American way of conceptualizing this covenantal dao has been to speak of good character.

Public schools were instituted starting in the late 1830s to bring children, especially the children of immigrants, into the American covenantal tradition, making them both citizens accepting personal responsibility for self and community and persons of good character in all that they do.

More recently Stephen Covey in his *The 7 Habits of Highly Effective People* and Jordan Peterson in his *12 Rules for Life* carried forward the "I-Thou" ethic of America's covenantal tradition.

Covey's seven recommended good habits are as follows:

1. Be proactive—have a personal vision.
2. Begin with the end in mind—be centered so that you can engage with others.
3. Put first things first—be disciplined so that you can respect what comes to you from reality.

4. Think win-win—seek mutual benefit in all your relationships.
5. Seek first to understand, then to be understood—use empathetic communication.
6. Synergize—cooperate.
7. Sharpen the saw—renew day in and day out your physical, mental, social/emotional, and spiritual assets.[42]

Jordan Peterson's 12 Rules are as follows:

1. Stand up straight with your shoulders back.
2. Treat yourself like someone you are responsible for helping.
3. Make friends with people who want the best for you.
4. Compare yourself to who you were yesterday, not to who someone else is today.
5. Do not let your children do anything that makes you dislike them.
6. Set your house in perfect order before you criticize the world.
7. Pursue what is meaningful (not what is expedient).
8. Tell the truth—or, at least, don't lie.
9. Assume that the person you are listening to might know something you don't.
10. Be precise in your speech.
11. Do not bother children when they are skateboarding.
12. Pet a cat when you encounter one on the street.[43]

Americans Have Walked Away from Their Covenantal Tradition

By and large, today's Americans have replaced covenantal responsibility with narcissism. Our culture, society, economy, and politics are now about the "me," not about the "us."

As mentioned earlier, the abandonment of the covenantal tradition began in the mid-1960s. In 1963, when President John F. Kennedy was assassinated, the event destabilized the conscience of the country just as the biblical Job was dumbfounded when fortune turned completely against him. He could not comprehend how his covenantal God could fail to keep the terms of their agreement when he had been upright and faithful.

After President Lyndon Johnson sent American combat forces to defend South Vietnamese nationalists against an illegal invasion from Communist North Vietnam, many sons of elite White families did not want to serve their country in that cause, though their fathers had served bravely without complaint in World War II. President Johnson defended his decision in terms of moral responsibility: "We did not choose to be the guardians of the gate, but there is no one else."[44]

There were some 1,200 young men in my 1967 graduating class at Harvard College. My best estimate is that not many more than 10 served in Vietnam and not many more than 50 in the military in any capacity.

In a brutally honest comment, Senator William Fulbright, a leading light in the growing antiwar movement objecting to the defense of the South Vietnamese, in a personal meeting with the president, once demanded that Johnson abandon the South Vietnamese, saying, "But, Lyn, they're not our kind."[45]

For Fulbright, if you were not part of the covenant, you just didn't count.

In 1968 the April assassination of Martin Luther King Jr., followed two months later by the June assassination of Robert F. Kennedy when he sought to be elected president, aggravated the Joblike angst of many Americans: What had gone wrong?

The American failure to prevent the Communist capture of South Vietnam in April 1975 was an inflection point for many Americans. That failure of national purpose was used by more and more Americans to justify the rejection of their inherited covenantal tradition because, according to that tradition, only truly worthy people deserve victory, and now their country was a loser. Why stick with a tradition if it makes you feel unworthy?

By the opening years of the twenty-first century, a new ethic was finding adherents among Americans, an ethic of power more aligned with the teachings of Friedrich Nietzsche than with the moralism of the Puritans. A win/lose dichotomy of oppressor and oppressed was preached as the "truth" about America, where the oppressors—mostly White and male—excluded the "oppressed"—mostly people of color and women—from enjoying the privileges of being in a covenantal relationship with divine goodness.

A term—"privilege"—was found and conceptually manipulated to stigmatize and delegitimate the covenantal tradition. Those Americans who had endeavored to keep their covenantal obligations were belittled for having achieved or enjoyed life outcomes that they did not deserve. According to Dr. Sherita Golden, the chief diversity officer at Johns Hopkins Medicine,

> Privilege is characteristically invisible to people who have it. People in dominant groups often believe they have earned the privileges they enjoy or that everyone could have access to these privileges if only they worked to earn them. In fact, privileges are unearned and are granted to people in the dominant groups whether they want those privileges or not, and regardless of their stated intent.[46]

The covenantal Protestant Ethic has been widely rejected and marginalized on the grounds that it privileges a particular race. A twelve-page *Diversity, Equity, and Inclusion Glossary of Terms* published by the California Community Colleges System makes this case. The glossary instructs that "merit" as "a concept . . . is embedded in the ideology of Whiteness and upholds race-based structural inequality. Merit protects White privilege under the guise of standards."[47]

Another delegitimation of covenantal responsibilities is provided by the definition of "White supremacy": "a historically based, institutionally perpetuated system of exploitation and oppression of continents, nations and peoples of color by White peoples and nations of the European continent for the purpose of maintaining and defending a system of wealth, power and privilege."[48] From this perspective, covenant in the American tradition was no more than a fictive, socially constructed narrative authored to exploit and oppress those who did not measure up to what was expected as a moral norm of responsibility.

The National Museum of African American History and Culture of the Smithsonian Institution posted on its website for a while a declaration that following values and behaviors of the American covenantal tradition embodied "Whiteness" and so deserved no allegiance from right-minded people.

- First, in 2020, according to the museum, self-reliance, personal independence and autonomy, control of your life chances, and a you-deserve-to-get-what-you-work-for attitude were isolated as particular to a Whiteness persona.
- Second, in thinking about the world and one's life, objective, rational, linear thinking, a belief in cause-and-effect relationships, and comfort with quantitative approaches are compartmentalized among those afflicted with Whiteness.
- Third, the psychosocial orientation of Whiteness prioritizes hard work as the key to success, so "if you didn't meet your goals, you didn't work hard enough."
- Fourth, it is Whiteness foolishness to believe that no one has to be a victim, as you can plan for your future and delay indulgence and gratification, confident that "tomorrow will be better."
- Fifth, writing and reading are Whiteness methodologies, and their cultural history—Christianity, Athens and Rome, Western Europe, the "King's" English—is important to Whiteness-inclined Americans. Thus, Whiteness people

have an action orientation; they feel a need to "do something" about a situation. They make decisions.
- Sixth, in Whiteness thinking, wealth determines your
worth; your job is who you are; owning goods and property,
controlling space, give you authority.[49]

Thus, attributes of American covenantal responsibility were transformed from admired psychosocial orientations into unworthy, even
unjustifiable, rationalizations that served the needs of an oppressive power
structure legitimatized by racism.

In 2024 a new "narrative" emerged to more directly delegitimize and
marginalize the American covenantal tradition. A discourse around
"Christian Nationalism" emerged to denigrate that tradition as offering
only mean sectarianism and unenlightened parochialism.

The covenantal "I-Thou" ethic has thus been superseded by an "I-It"
ethic, where what we respond to is seen only as "objects," and where
other persons have become impersonal and conceptually constituted
social "facts." There is no "Thou" there anymore.

Relationships among Americans today are so often self-serving. The
moral sense that grounds community is missing in action. Americans have
individually gone off on their own with no covenant to sustain them as a
people.

As a result, Americans today are, largely speaking, lonely, depressed,
and mistrustful. They regularly rely on coping behaviors, many of which
are self-destructive or abusive, to get through their days and nights. Too
many Americans are dysphoric—disconcerted about who they are. They
have unknowingly depleted their social capital but wonder why nothing
seems to work well or bring palpable happiness.

A proxy affirmation of the American covenant by Americans today is
the conviction that the American Dream—if you work hard, you will get
ahead—is within the reach of American citizens as a kind of birthright.

Tellingly, in a July 2025 poll, 69% of those Americans asked did not believe that such a covenantal promise still holds true or that it ever did.[50]

Americans today are no longer a covenantal people.

CHAPTER 2

THE UNRAVELING OF A FREE SOCIETY

When sorrows come, they come not single spies.
But in battalions!

William Shakespeare, *Hamlet*

Those whom the gods would destroy,
they first deprive of reason.[1]

Sophocles, *Antigone*

In my own studies, the best precedent I can think of for what has happened and is happening to the American Republic is what happened to the Roman Republic, which caused its collapse and replacement by an imperial autocracy. The elite, patrician families of the Republic lost their way.

Cicero provided a key insight into the fall of the Republic's constitutional arrangements in a letter he wrote to his dear friend Atticus in June 59 BCE.

Atticus was in Greece on a business trip. Cicero wrote to bring him up to date on happenings in Rome. He described an aberration in political leadership with just three powerful individuals—Pompey with personal support from the men in his legions, Crassus with great wealth, and Julius Caesar with skillful instincts—calling the shots. Caesar had been elected consul, Crassus rigged elections and fixed jury outcomes with money exchanged for compliance with his wishes, and Pompey had his legions on hand, just in case things got out of control.

Cicero wrote to his friend that when Caesar entered the theater, no one clapped and that when a playwright included a pun on Pompey's name, the audience responded with a dozen "Encores!" He reported that young Curio was the only one to speak out in opposition.

His conclusion, however, which illuminated the road leading to the collapse of the Republic some fifteen years later, was insightful: "All this doesn't make one more hopeful, but only sadder, to see that the sentiment of the community is free while its virtue is in chains."[2]

What his Republic had stopped promoting, he wrote just before its fall, was good governance: "Just as a fair voyage is the object of the pilot, health of the physician, victory of the general, so our statesman's object is the happiness of his countrymen—to promote power for their security, wealth for their abundance, fame for their dignity, virtue for their good name."[3]

The De-Enlightening of America:
The Onset of Systemic National Identity Dysphoria

Americans today are not well disposed.

In September 2025, Echelon Insights reported that 74% of Americans thought that the biggest threats to their country come from other Americans in the form of polarization, corruption in government, or dysfunctional cultural trends. Only 22% thought that the biggest threats to the United States come from outside their country—adversaries such as Russia, China, and Iran. Those unsure where the most dire dangers lurked represented 5%.[4]

A Quinnipiac University poll July 16, 2025, found that Americans gave congressional Democrats a 19% approval rating, while 72% disapproved. At the same time, one-third of voters (33 percent) approved of the way Republicans in Congress were handling their jobs, while 62 percent disapproved and 5% did not offer an opinion. Joining a new third party was supported by 49% of American voters.

Americans couldn't seem to approve of anything. Half of those questioned thought that the American Dream was unattainable, with 43% thinking that the American Dream is alive and well. Respondents disapproved of President Trump by 54%, with 40% approving. They disapproved of the Supreme Court by 53%, with 40% approval. And by 63% to 30%, they thought the Court was driven more by politics than by the law.[5]

In April 2024 ABC News reported, "Most Americans think the country is on the wrong track. Poll after poll has shown it: 65% in a Reuters/Ipsos poll, 58% in a Harvard-Harris poll, 65% in a *USA Today/Suffolk* survey, 64% in a Yahoo News survey, 65% in a *New York Times/Siena* poll, and 69% in a *Wall Street Journal* survey."[6]

Lance Morrow, writing in the *Wall Street Journal* on December 25, 2023, wrote,

> America feels like an alcoholic household—crazy with grievance, accusation, irrational rage, screaming in the middle of the night. The children lie in the dark, wide-eyed, listening. In the morning, the family comes downstairs trying to pretend that everything is normal. There's a lot of pretending: The southern border isn't wide open; unpunished crime is social justice; the president of Harvard deserves her job. Things aren't normal. Everyone knows it. The country doesn't quite recognize itself. America has gone astray in a strange new landscape. It's a different America all right. In an alcoholic household, the one you thought you could trust becomes a stranger—suddenly dangerous. Trust is the first casualty. A baffled country can neither grasp nor admit what it has become.[7]

Dysphoria is defined as a mental state in which a person has a profound sense of unease or dissatisfaction because of an identity crisis. Identity dysphoria is a disease of the self-concept, where one's sense of self is in disequilibrium, restless, unsettled, and which, therefore, disturbs one's thoughts, emotions, and relationships.

Identity dysphoric personalities, more likely than not, have a need for "safe spaces" and feel compelled to shun ("cancel") those who think differently. Such personalities seek to change the culture and revise social conventions the better to like themselves.

The first national leader to comment publicly on the emergence of identity dysphoria among Americans was President Jimmy Carter in his televised speech of July 15, 1979, a speech that was quickly denigrated as the "Malaise Speech."

Carter said,

> I want to speak to you first tonight about a subject even more serious than energy or inflation. I want to talk to you right now about a fundamental threat to American democracy.
>
> I do not mean our political and civil liberties. They will endure. And I do not refer to the outward strength of America, a nation that is at peace tonight everywhere in the world, with unmatched economic power and military might.
>
> The threat is nearly invisible in ordinary ways.
>
> It is a crisis of confidence.
>
> It is a crisis that strikes at the very heart and soul and spirit of our national will. We can see this crisis in the growing doubt about the meaning of our own lives and in the loss of a unity of purpose for our nation. . . .
>
> In a nation that was proud of hard work, strong families, close-knit communities, and our faith in God, too many of us now tend to worship self-indulgence and consumption. Human identity is no longer defined by what one does, but by what one owns. But we've discovered that owning things and consuming things does not satisfy our longing for meaning. We've learned that piling up material goods cannot fill the emptiness of lives which have no confidence or purpose.

The symptoms of this crisis of the American spirit are all around us. For the first time in the history of our country a majority of our people believe that the next five years will be worse than the past five years. Two-thirds of our people do not even vote. The productivity of American workers is actually dropping, and the willingness of Americans to save for the future has fallen below that of all other people in the Western world.[8]

Our identity dysphoria has only intensified since July 1979. According to a November 2023 *Wall Street Journal*/NORC survey,

- 36% of voters think the American Dream still holds true.
- In 2016 it was 48,% and in 2012 it was 53%.
- 45% think it once was true but not now.
- 19% said it was never true, up from 3% in 2012.
- Only 28% of those under 50 said hard work will lead to advancement. [9]

Half the voters said life in America is worse than it was fifty years ago, while 30% said it had gotten better.[10]

America's mental health crisis drove suicides to a record high in 2022. Nearly 50,000 people in the United States lost their lives to suicide, according to a provisional tally from the National Institute on Drug Abuse. The agency said the final count would likely be higher. The suicide rate of 14.3 deaths per 100,000 people reached its highest level since 1941.[11]

More than 100,000 Americans died from drug overdoses between May 2020 and April 2021—the most ever recorded in a single year—according to the National Center for Health Statistics. The number of drug overdose deaths was up almost 30% from the 78,000 deaths in the prior year and was nearly three times that of traffic-accident deaths and twice that of gun deaths during the same period. Most of the deaths were due to opioids, fueled by the powerful drug fentanyl, which is often added to illegal drugs to enhance their potency.[12]

Figure 1. National Drug Overdose Deaths*, Number Among All Ages, by Sex, 1999-2022

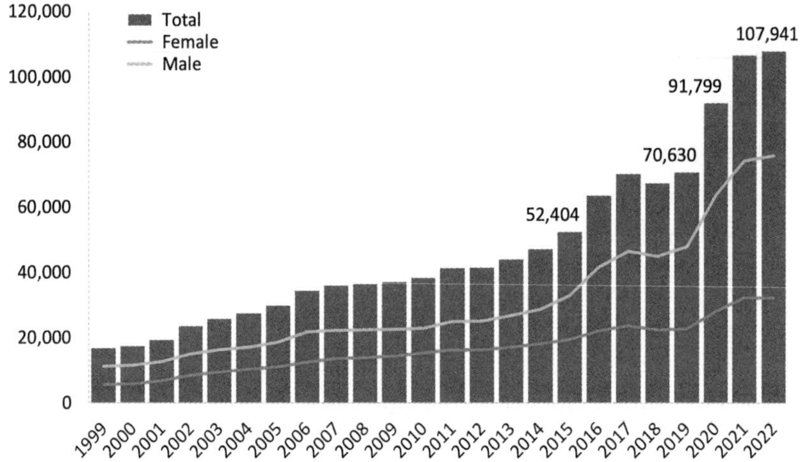

*Includes deaths with underlying causes of unintentional drug poisoning (X40–X44), suicide drug poisoning (X60–X64), homicide drug poisoning (X85), or drug poisoning of undetermined intent (Y10–Y14), as coded in the International Classification of Diseases, 10th Revision. Source: Centers for Disease Control and Prevention, National Center for Health Statistics. Multiple Cause of Death 1999-2022 on CDC WONDER Online Database, released 4/2024.

Among Americans aged 12 years and older, more than 37 million were current illegal drug users (used within the last thirty days) as of 2020.

- 13.5% of Americans 12 and over used drugs in the last month, a 3.8% increase year-over-year (YoY).
- 59.277 million or 21.4% of people 12 and over have used illegal drugs or misused prescription drugs within the last year.
- 138.543 million or 50.0% of people aged 12 and over have illicitly used drugs in their lifetime.
- 138.522 million Americans 12 and over drink alcohol.

- 28.320 million or 20.4% of them have an alcohol use disorder.
- 57.277 million people use tobacco or nicotine products (vape).
- 25.4% of illegal-drug users have a drug disorder.
- 24.7% of those with drug disorders have an opioid disorder; this includes prescription pain relievers or "painkillers" and heroin.[13]

"Less than half (47%) of Gen Z Americans are thriving in their lives—among the lowest across all generations in the U.S. today and a much lower rate than millennials at the same age," a September 2023 report from Gallup and the Walton Family Foundation said.[14]

Researchers surveyed more than 3,000 people aged 12–26. Only 41% of Gen Z members aged 18 to 26 are thriving, according to the study, while millennials, at the same age, were thriving at a rate of about 60%.

Asked to describe their current mental health or well-being, only 15% of Gen Z members aged 18–26 said it was excellent. That's a steep drop compared with a decade ago, the study found, when 52% of millennials in that same age range said their mental health was excellent.

Mental health isn't the only issue the study explored. Other findings include the following:

- About half (53%) of Gen Z students who want to pursue higher education believe they'll be able to afford it.
- 40% of Gen Z students said they worried a lot or somewhat about gun violence at their school.
- Making "enough money to live comfortably" is Gen Z's "most frequently cited hope for the future," with 69% of those surveyed ranking it among their top wishes.[15]

Next, about 40% of adults admit to still sleeping with a stuffed animal or blanket from their childhood, according to a survey conducted by Build-A-Bear Workshop. To quote the report: Experts say it's OK to sleep with your stuffed animal every night—even if you no longer sleep in your childhood bed. However, if your attachment to your stuffed animal affects your work or relationships, that's usually a sign of a deeper issue that needs to be addressed.[16]

Parenting has become a source of dysphoria. In August 2024 the surgeon general of the United States published a report titled *Parents Under Pressure*. In his introduction, Surgeon General Vivek Murthy wrote,

> . . . there are new stressors that previous generations didn't have to consider. These include the complexity of managing social media, parents' concerns about the youth mental health crisis, and an epidemic of loneliness that disproportionately affects young people and parents, just to name a few. One response . . . has been an intensifying culture of comparison—often propagated by influencers and online trends—with unrealistic expectations around the milestones, parenting strategies, achievements and status symbols that kids and parents must pursue. Chasing these unreasonable expectations has left many families feeling exhausted, burned out, and perpetually behind. Given all these factors, it's no wonder that so many parents are struggling. In my conversations with parents and caregivers across America, I have found guilt and shame have become pervasive, often leading them to hide their struggles, which perpetuates a vicious cycle where stress leads to guilt, which leads to more stress.

His report included these statistics:

1. "41% of parents say that most days they are so stressed they cannot function and 48% say that most days their stress is

completely overwhelming compared to other adults (20% and 26%, respectively)."

2. "Nearly 3-in-4 parents are extremely or somewhat worried that their child will struggle with anxiety or depression."

3. "School shootings, or the possibility of one, are a significant source of stress for nearly three-quarters of parents (74%)."

4. "In a 2021 survey, approximately 65% of parents and guardians, and 77% of single parents in particular, experienced loneliness, compared to 55% of non-parents."

5. "Nearly 70% of parents say parenting is now more difficult than it was 20 years ago, with children's use of technology and social media as the top two cited reasons."

6. "A majority of parents of adolescents say they are somewhat, very, or extremely worried that their child's use of social media could lead to problems with anxiety or depression (53%), lower self-esteem (54%), being harassed or bullied by others (54%), feeling pressured to act a certain way (59%), and exposure to explicit content (71%)."

7. "Further, a modern practice of time-intensive parenting and contemporary expectations around childhood achievement may contribute further to the stressors faced by parents."[17]

The tensions and unpleasantness of parenting show up in the phenomenon of "Mom Rage," the subject of Minna Dubin's book *Mom Rage: The Everyday Crisis of Modern Motherhood.*

Colleen Seto wrote in *Today's Parent*,[18]

It's a weekday morning and I'm making breakfast. My eight-year-old daughter sits down to eat, but my five-year-old son is MIA. Suddenly, a gruesome wail echoes through the house. I dash to my son's room to find him star-fished on the floor in his underwear, clothes strewn everywhere.

"What's happening?" I ask. "Are you hurt?"

"My pants feel weird!" he shrieks.

I can't help but groan. This is day three that his pants don't "feel right." I calmly suggest different pairs, but none will do—too tight, too loose, have pockets, or otherwise somehow offensive. After kicking off a fourth pair, he throws himself back to the floor.

That's when my hands start to shake. My heart starts to pound and my face grows hot. I hurl all the pants on his bed, shout that he's going to school in his goddamn underwear, and storm out.

It was not my finest moment.

I'm not actually an angry person—friends have even referred to me as Zen. And yet, since becoming a mother, particularly once my second child hit his toddler years, I've experienced more moments of outright rage than I care to admit. I've had to flee to my bedroom, shut the door and scream or cry or both. Sometimes, I feel generally pissed off at everyone and everything, and even the smallest infraction will incite rage.

This is not the mom I want to be.

What has gone wrong with American families? Why are American women experiencing identity dysphoria with motherhood?

My wife didn't, but she is Vietnamese, and Vietnamese mothers are very proud of who they are and the contributions they are making as mothers. Starting at two years, they insist on inner-direction for their children—control of emotions, showing respect for others, speaking to the point, and learning.

I can't remember my mother ever succumbing to mom rage. Nor can I imagine my grandmothers and two great-grandmothers so succumbing.

They were matrons and matriarchs who were very much in control of their families.

Mom rage seems to be triggered by a sudden loss of control over young children. And a need for control is symptomatic of people without a strong identity, people who are not certain of who they are and so easily perceive emotional dangers and ego threats in the routines of daily living.

Seto reports that triggers could be when your kids don't listen, when they hurt their sibling, or if plans go sideways. Megan Helm first began experiencing mom rage four months after her second child was born. "I felt so angry," she recalls. "I was yelling at my kids for being the way they're supposed to be."

That's not unusual. Experts say rage triggers can be things that, intellectually, you know shouldn't bother you. Other times you might find yourself screaming at your kids when they literally did nothing at all. "Often, triggers have nothing to do with the child," says Laura Markham, a New York–based clinical psychologist, parenting coach, and author of *Peaceful Parent, Happy Kids.* "It could be from fighting with your partner, a bad day at work or unresolved issues from childhood."[19]

Stressful parenting and anxious adults have contributed to a decline of trust among Americans. Lack of trust in others contributes to feeling alone, which inculcates identity dysphoria.

Americans have little confidence in their institutions. In 2022, according to a Gallup survey, the percentage of Americans who had a "great deal or quite a lot" of trust was as follows: 7% in Congress, 11% in television news, 14% in big business, 14% in the criminal justice system, 16% in newspapers, 23% in the presidency, 25% in the Supreme Court, 27% in banks, 28% in public schools, 28% in labor unions, 31% in religious organizations, 38% in the health care system, and 45% in the police. No major institution was trusted by a majority of the American people. That fact exposes a nation in decline.[20]

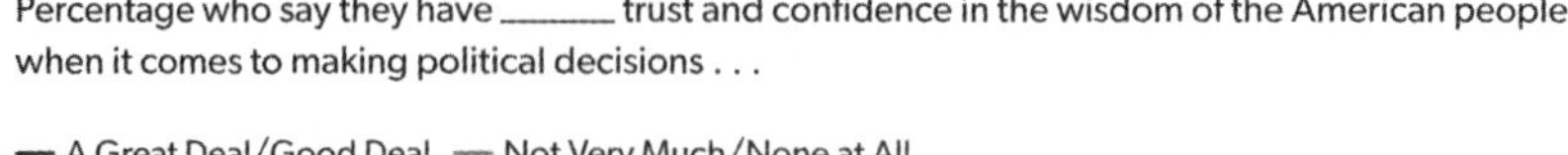

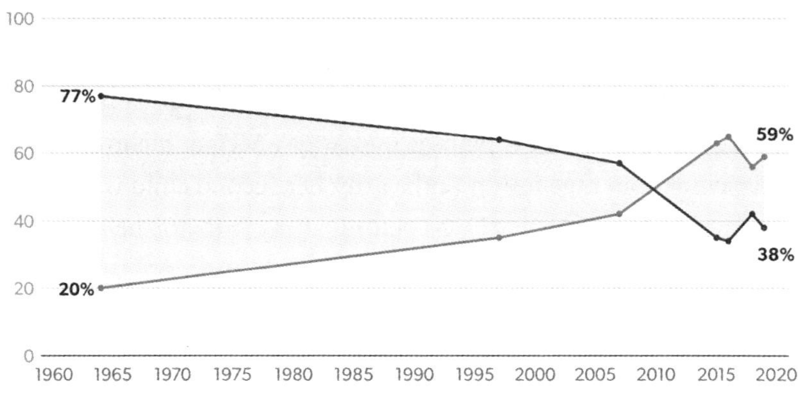

Furthermore, 22% of millennials in the poll said they had zero friends, 27% said they had "no close friends," 30% said they have "no best friends," and 25% said they have no acquaintances. In comparison, just 16% of Gen X and 9% of baby boomers say they have no friends.[21]

Nearly 30% of American households comprise a single person, a record high. The U.S. Census shows that "solitaries" made up 8% of all households in 1940. The share of solo households doubled to 18% in 1970 and more than tripled, to an estimated 29%, by 2022.[22] Nearly half of all young adults are living with their parents, according to a new survey by Harris Poll for Bloomberg, roughly the same level as it was in the 1940s.[23]

The percentage of U.S. adults who report having been diagnosed with depression at some point in their lifetime has reached 29.0%, nearly 10 percentage points higher than in 2015. The percentage of Americans who currently have or are being treated for depression has also increased to 17.8%, an increase of about 7 points over the same period. Both rates are the highest recorded by Gallup since it began measuring depression using the current form of data collection in 2015.[24]

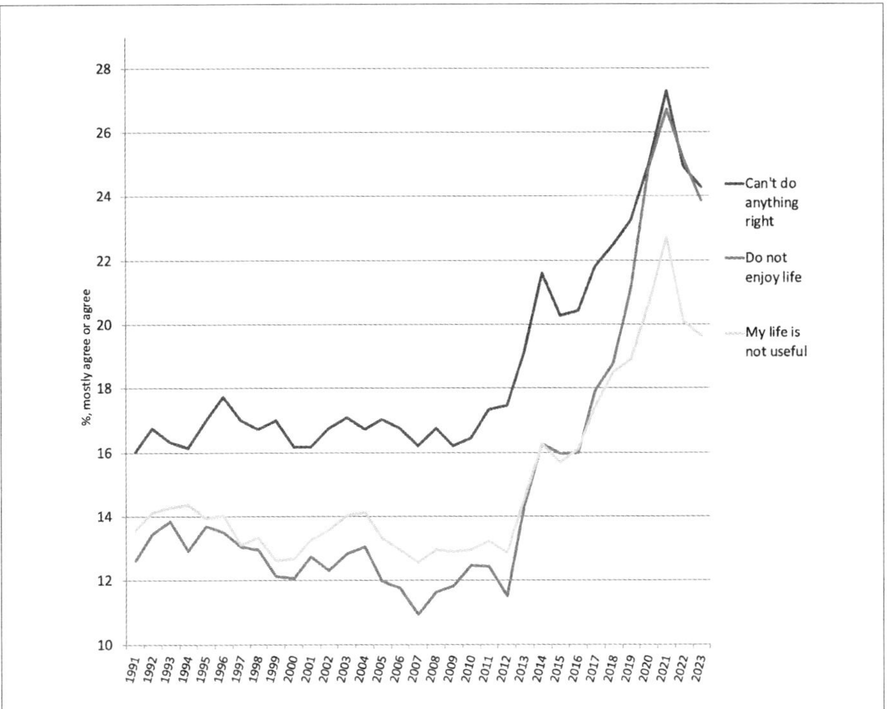

Percent of 13- to 18-year-olds who agree with "I can't do anything right" or "My life isn't useful," or who disagree with "I enjoy life as much as anyone," 1991–2023. Source: Monitoring the Future surveys of 8th, 10th, and 12th graders. Note: The 2020 data were collected in February and early March before COVID lockdowns.

In another poll, 50% agreed that "the economic and political systems are stacked against people like me." The Country Financial Security Index found that 27% of Americans said they've had to take money out of savings, and 54% said that they used such money to pay for everyday expenses.[25] A total of 63% of American employees can't come up with $500 for an emergency, according to the SecureSave report.[26] Credit card balances shot up by $45 billion between the first and second quarters of 2023, a 4.6% increase that pushed total credit card debt beyond the $1 trillion mark, according to the Federal Reserve Bank of New York. Many employees don't have enough savings to cover one month of their expenses.[27] Over one-third of employees earning $100,000 or more live paycheck to paycheck.[28]

Because of inflation, income does not buy what it used to.

Consumer Price Index for All Urban Consumers: Purchasing Power of the Consumer Dollar in U.S. City Average

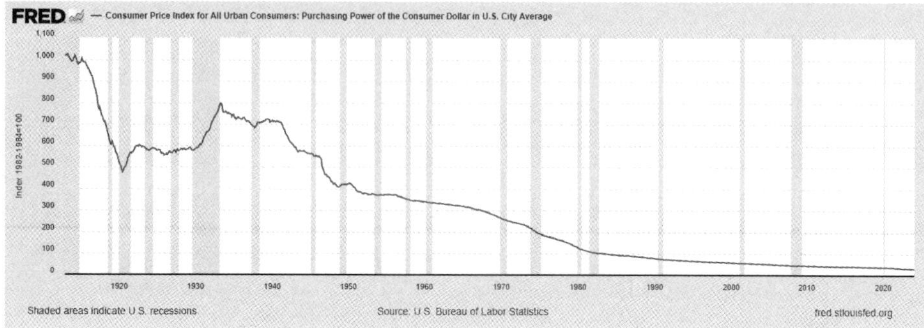

The U.S. Census Bureau recently released estimates showing there were 10.9 million one-parent family groups with a child under the age of 18 in 2022. Data from the annual release of America's Families and Living Arrangements also show that 80% of one-parent family groups were maintained by a mother.

In 2019, of 130 countries and territories, the United States had the world's highest rate of children living in single-parent households. Almost a quarter of U.S. children under the age of 18 live with one parent and no other adults (23%), more than three times the share of children around the world who do so (7%).

According to the America's Families and Living Arrangements report, more than half (51.2%) of all Black children lived with one parent in 2022, compared with about one in five (21.3%) of White children.

Moreover, between 1980 and 2022, the proportion of children living in two-parent families declined for White youth (82.7% to 75.6%) and Hispanic youth (75.4% to 67.5%). For Black youth, the proportion of children living in two-parent families in 2022 (43.0%) was about the same as in 1980 (42.2%).

Additionally, between 1970 and 2022, the proportion of children living with their mothers in single-parent households increased from 7.8% to 16.7% for White youth and from 29.5% to 45.6% for Black youth. For children of

Hispanic ethnicity, the proportion living with their mother in single-parent households increased from 19.6% in 1980 to 24.5% in 2022.[29]

All this data points to the fact that a significant and increasing proportion of American children are growing up without the same level of paternal support and nurturing that conferred advantage on the majority of their peers and the vast majority of their forebears. The diminution of love, caring, and responsibility inherent in many of these single-parent families can only be a source of social and moral instability given the profound importance to society of the institution of family.

Another sign of the crumbling of covenantal America is disdain for military service despite the proud military traditions that once held sway. A poll by the research institute Echelon Insights of 1,029 likely voters, conducted between October 23 and 26, 2023, found that 72% of those asked would not be willing to volunteer to serve in the armed forces if America were to enter a major conflict, compared with 21% who would. The remainder were unsure.

The poll was conducted after Hamas led an unprecedented terrorist attack on Israel on October 7, which brought to the fore the possibility of an existential war against Nazi-like evil.

In fiscal year 2023, the army came up about 10,000 new enlistments short of a goal of 65,000 new active duty soldiers. The Army Reserve also had dire recruiting numbers, gaining just 9,319 reservists of the 14,650 it needed, a shortfall of about 36%. The Air Force missed its enlisted active duty recruiting goals for the first time since 1999, getting only 24,100 of the 26,877 airmen it needed. It did manage to reach its active duty officer goal of 967.

The Air Force Reserve and the Air National Guard faced an even larger enlisted shortfall. The reserve component pulled in 5,288 of the 7,765 new enlisted airmen it needed, more than 30% behind its goal. It also filled only 1,195 of the 1,535 officer spots it needed, about 23% short. The Air National Guard filled 7,120 of the 11,745 spots needed for its enlisted guardsmen, or nearly 40% short. The Guard did, however, outperform on its officer numbers, reaching 1,421 officers, with only 1,196 needed.

For active duty enlisted sailors, the Navy reached 30,236 of its 37,700 goal, almost 20% short. It also recruited 2,080 officers, almost 18% short of its goal of 2,532 officers. It also missed its reserve goals by a wide margin, hitting 3,000 enlisted reservists or almost 45% short of the 5,390 it wanted. Reserve officers also fell short by 40%, hitting 1,167 of the 1,940 sought.[30]

However, after the election of Donald Trump as president in 2024, more Americans were willing to join the country's armed forces, in a change of values reverting to more traditional covenantal norms.

In September 2023 Rasmussen conducted an opinion survey for the Committee to Unleash Prosperity. Survey results were published as a report with the title "Them vs. U.S.: The Two Americas and How the Nation's Elite Is Out of Touch with Average Americans." This report is based on two separate surveys of 1,000 members of the Elite, defined as those having a postgraduate degree, a household income of more than $150,000 annually, and living in a zip code with more than 10,000 people per square mile. Approximately 1% of the total U.S. population meets these criteria.

Some of the profound attitudinal differences between elites and average Americans were as follows:

- In a time when most Americans have suffered a loss of real take-home pay, 74% of elites say they are financially better off today than in the past versus 20% of all Americans.
- Nearly six in ten elitists say there is too much individual freedom in America—double the rate of all Americans.
- More than two-thirds (67%) favor rationing of vital energy and food sources to combat the threat of climate change. [Asked if they would favor "rationing of gas, meat, and electricity" to fight climate change, 89% of Ivy Leaguers said yes, as against 28% of regular people. Asked if they would personally pay $500 more in taxes and higher costs to fight climate change, 75% of the Ivy Leaguers said yes, versus 25% of everyone else.]

- In stark contrast to the rest of America, 70% of the elites trust the government to "do the right thing most of the time."
- Two-thirds (67%) say teachers and other educational professionals should decide what children are taught rather than letting parents decide.
- Somewhere between half and two-thirds favor banning things like SUVs, gas stoves, air conditioning, and nonessential air travel to protect the environment.
- About six in ten elitists have a favorable opinion of the so-called talking professions—lawyers, lobbyists, politicians, and journalists.
- President Joe Biden enjoyed an 84% job approval rating from this advantaged group—roughly twice as high as in the general public.[31]

Criminal behavior is another consequence of identity dysphoria. While some degree of sociopathology or psychopathology is implicit in behaviors that break the normal social contract between person and person, a personhood inclined toward criminal abuse of others and knowingly wrongful appropriation of their property is most likely suffering from inner desperation and dysfunction. What made Raskolnikov kill the old lady in Dostoevsky's novel *Crime and Punishment*? What made Adam Lanza kill his mother and then 26 others at the Sandy Hook Elementary School in Connecticut, 20 of them children ages 6 and 7? Their ego-identities were not healthy.

In recent years successful criminality in America has been rising.

In American cities with over 1 million people, the arrest rate for reported violent crimes averaged 41% in the years from 1996 to 2019 but dropped to 20.3% in 2022. The arrest rate of those who committed murder fell by 37%, rape by 58%, robbery by 50%, and aggravated assault by 54%.

The average arrest rate for reported property crime fell from an average of 13% in the years from 1996 to 2021 to 4.5% in 2022—a 64% drop.

The drop in reported larceny theft, the largest property crime category, fell from an average arrest rate of 14.6% to just 3.8%—a 75% drop.

If you look at arrests as a percentage of all crime (reported and unreported), in large cities only 8% of all violent crime and 1% of all property crime result in an arrest.[32]

On August 27, 2025, during a celebration of Mass in the chapel of Annunciation Catholic School in Minneapolis, Minnesota, Robin (née Robert) Westman shot at worshippers, killing two children and wounding eighteen others before killing her/him self. Apparently, Westman suffered from identity dysphoria. Before the shooting, Westman had written in a notebook which he had shared on YouTube that he regretted his decision to transition from a male identity and persona to a female identity and persona.

He wrote: "I only keep [the long hair] because it is pretty much my last shred of being trans. I am tired of being trans. I wish I never brain-washed myself. . . . I can't cut my hair now, as it would be an embarrassing defeat and it might be a concerning change of character that could get me reported. It just always gets in my way. I will probably chop it on the day of the attack." Seemingly, he now wanted to abandon his new identity, scribbling on another page of the notebook: "I don't want to dress girly all the time, but I guess sometimes I really like it. I know I am not a woman, but I definitely don't feel like a man."

Whichever gender persona—male or female—Robin was (or was this unhappy person once again more Roger than Robin?), she (or he) was not emotionally and intellectually secure in their presentation of self. So, who indeed was Robin or Roger, with their identity dysphoria? Out of chaotic inability to secure self-acceptance came death.[33]

Coping with Dysphoria

If we cannot change whatever disturbs us, whatever depresses us, or whatever triggers fear and flight, we enable coping mechanisms—intellectual, behavioral, and psychological. We seek the support of enablers. We change our metabolisms with stimulants and depressants.

But it seems that Americans have found a new coping mechanism by just getting away from it all—seeking solitude where what is out of sight and out of mind can't bring us down.

American men who watch television now spend seven hours in front of the TV for every hour they spend with another person outside their home.[34] Derek Thompson worries that "[t]he individual preference for solitude, scaled up across society and exercised repeatedly over time, is rewiring America's civic and psychic identity."[35] From 2003 to 2023, face-to-face socializing declined by 38% for those with no high school diploma, by 40% for African Americans, and by 36% for unmarried men. Men spend more time alone than women, and young men are increasing their alone time faster than any other group.[36]

Many Americans can't cope anymore with the culture and society that has been imposed upon them. They lean more and more toward dysphoria. Solitude, not society, becomes the preferred setting for finding safe spaces and psychosocial refuge.

Is America facing a doom loop where dysphoria encourages depression and searching for solitude, both of which reinforce feelings of dysphoria, which then further exacerbates depression and intensifies the search for solitude?

What Has Gone Wrong?

The root cause of American identity dysphoria is sociological. An Overclass has emerged over the past century to dominate our economy, culture, society, and, most divisively, our politics.

The "new class" has been the term used for this power elite by social commentators and intellectuals for several decades, but we should really be talking about an Overclass that seeks to bring other segments of society under its control at the expense of the classical virtues such as resilient character and courage, which have historically sustained our society as a covenantal community.

This Overclass has put our virtue in such chains that we can no longer sustain a vibrant constitutional republic. The short-term selfishness and self-righteousness baked into the personal identities of the Overclass, with much hubris, have propelled them, without thinking carefully, to break the founding American covenant with Providence just as the wayward "shepherds" of Israel broke their covenant so many centuries before.

In his first inaugural address, George Washington spoke of this very eventuality.

> I dwell on this prospect with every satisfaction which an ardent love for my country can inspire, since there is no truth more thoroughly established than that there exists in the economy and course of nature an indissoluble union between virtue and happiness; between duty and advantage; between the genuine maxims of an honest and magnanimous policy and the solid rewards of public prosperity and felicity; since we ought to be no less persuaded that the propitious smiles of Heaven can never be expected on a nation that disregards the eternal rules of order and right which Heaven itself has ordained; and since the preservation of the sacred fire of liberty and the destiny of the republican model of government are justly considered, perhaps, as deeply, as finally, staked on the experiment entrusted to the hands of the American people.

And so the question before the American people becomes: Has this new Overclass so badly abused the republic entrusted to the hands of the American people that we must now pay for that abuse through societal collapse?

At the Root of It All—Karl Marx

Karl Marx made himself famous, and thereby made human history darker and bloodier, with his concept of how power works in societies. Marx assumed that material realities determine culture and values. The events of history rest on economics—the mode of production of goods and services and the taking care of tangible human needs and desires. The mediating mechanism between economics and compatible cultural and political dynamics is class structure—peasant, worker, aristocrat, capitalist, and bureaucrat.

For Marx, every economic system—feudalism, mercantilism, capitalism, socialism, Communism, and so on—brings forth a specialized class that rationalizes and manages the production of goods and services. In feudalism, landed aristocrats exploiting peasants drove culture and politics. In capitalism, the middle class—a bourgeoisie or "capitalists" (whom Marx denigrated as just a bunch of greedy "Mr. Moneybags")—funded and managed factory enterprises and thereby determined social norms and government laws and policies. In Communism, he theorized that the workers—the proletarian class—would abolish the capitalist mode of production, giving the former capitalists no place to hang their hats, and so bring about the "withering away" of the state apparatus.

The British and Dutch colonies of North America had neither peasants nor aristocrats. New England and the central colonies were home to middle-class families, both on farms and in towns and cities. The Pilgrims and the Puritans were middle-class Protestants.[37] And their Protestant Ethic (think of Ben Franklin's maxims—"A penny saved is a penny earned" and "Early to bed and early to rise makes a man healthy, wealthy, and wise"), according to German sociologist Max Weber, was quintessentially bourgeois and "capitalist." In fact, Weber credited the Protestant Ethic with giving rise to capitalist behaviors and successful small-scale business enterprises.

The southern North American colonies were different. They were founded by gentry families more socially aligned with the English royalty and aristocracy.[38] In the Southern colonies, the mode of production was the plantation, which became very profitable in growing cotton after the invention of the cotton gin and the spinning jenny, which industrialized the making of cotton cloth. To work plantations, slavery was adopted from Spanish and Portuguese precedents, which in turn had their roots in Muslim practices brought to Spain by the conquering Moors and via sugarcane production in Africa and the Azores.

Slaves in the American Southern colonies were a special case of serfdom, one legitimated by racist stereotyping. Southern gentry families lived aristocratically in great mansions indulged by obedient servants, as notoriously portrayed in the movie *Gone with the Wind*.

Until the Industrial Revolution, the American colonies—and later the several states united under a federal constitution—had no Marxist proletariat of factory workers.

Today America no longer has a socioeconomic class of farmers. In 2022 direct on-farm employment accounted for about 2.6 million American jobs, or 1.2% of U.S. employment.[39]

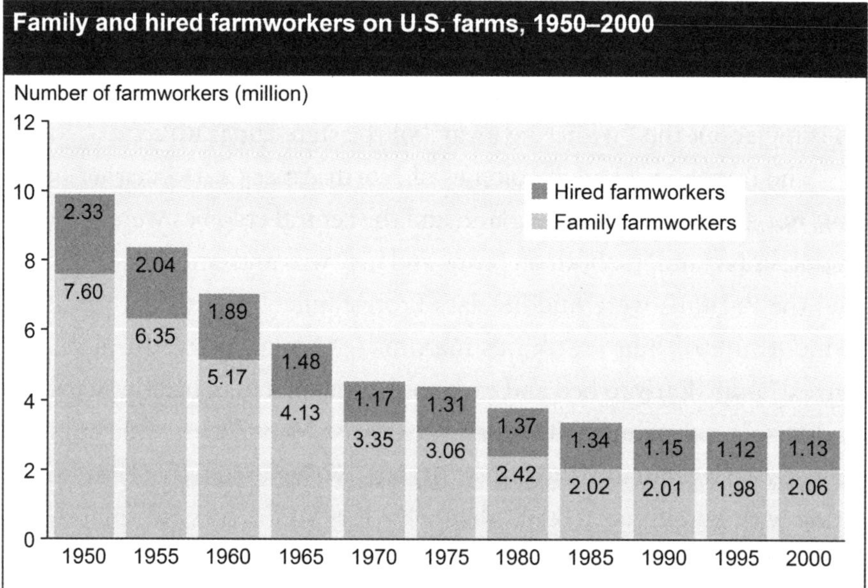

Note: Family farmworkers include self-employed farmers and unpaid family members. Hired farmworkers include direct hires and agricultural service workers employed by farm labor contractors.
Source: USDA, Economic Research Service using data from USDA, National Agricultural Statistics Service, Farm Labor Survey (FLS).

Those who work farms today are mostly small capitalists. Farming has been industrialized. As of May 2022, the John Deere X9 1100 combine sold for an amount ranging from $900,000 to over $1,000,000. No traditional "farmer" could ever afford to buy and use such a machine. John Deere promotes its X9 1100 as follows:

> You need maximum productivity for maximum profitability, you need an X9 Combine. These rugged combines deliver an average of 45% more harvesting capacity across all crop types, with no sacrifice in grain quality—all while using 20% less fuel. The X9 1100 can harvest up to 30 acres an hour in wheat: in high-yielding corn it delivers up to 7,200 bushels (253,721 liters) per hour, which means you can fill up to 7 semi-trailers per hour.

This is the language of business.

In 2023 the median total farm household income was forecast at $99,523, according to the United States Department of Agriculture. The median household income in the United States in 2023 was $80,610.

In the 1880s large corporations and financial combinations of corporations were leading economic growth. This was the era of John D. Rockefeller and J. P. Morgan, the trusts and the robber barons of maturing American capitalism. By the 1920s, with the introduction of production lines in great factories—think of Henry Ford and his River Rouge Plant in Detroit—the American mode of production supported consumerism for the middle class.[40] Buying stock ownership interests in corporations gave Americans the opportunity to share in the profits made by these great firms.

Starting as a response to the inequalities of the robber barons, a political movement arose, importing the welfare state policies of Otto von Bismarck's Germany to increase the role of government in the economy to limit monopoly power, provide a central bank, and supply a check on the discretion of business decision-makers. Both corporations and government began developing bureaucratic staffs. New administrative agencies, independent from regular departments, were created. In time new departments of the federal government would be established. An income tax was adopted to fund the expanding federal government. Labor unions were organized to equalize the power of workers and owners in setting wages and factory working conditions.

Blue-collar employment—our Marxist proletariat—has been shrinking as a proportion of employed Americans. Dominance in all American institutions has gravitated to white-collar, salaried, college-educated men and women.

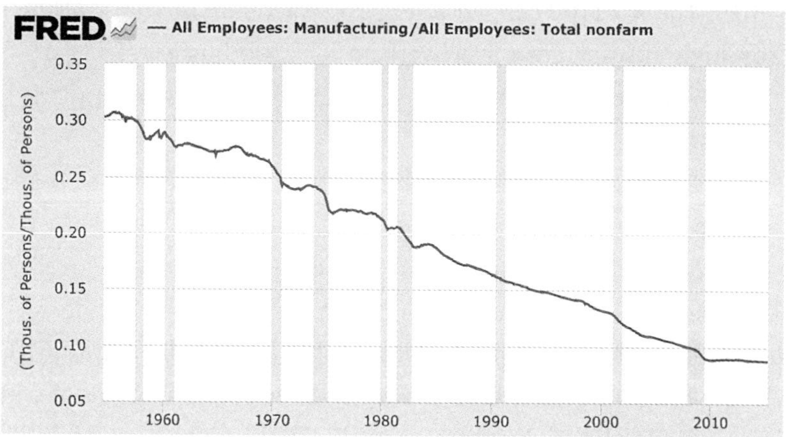

The Percentage of Americans with College Degrees

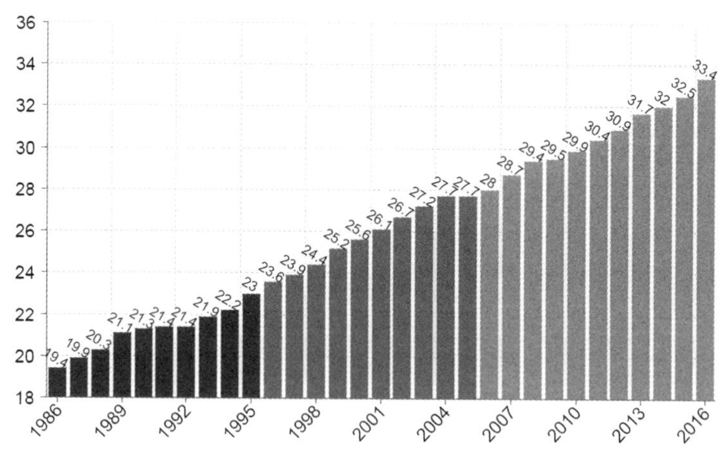

These workers—managers—are necessary for postindustrial private enterprises, public administrations, and nonprofits (foundations, hospitals, colleges, and universities) to thrive.

This is the Marxist substructure of America's contemporary economy—an Overclass of administrators, influencers, and knowledge workers. The relation of this Overclass to the means of production is salary, the buying of their skills in delivering rational-legal functionality to private and public institutions and managing the production of symbolic goods for the general culture.

In Marxist terms, the Overclass is neither capitalist nor proletarian. Unlike Marx's capitalists, members of the Overclass are not owners of private companies but managers of businesses or perhaps investors in those businesses who rely on managers to keep company stock prices high and rising. Also, members of the Overclass manage nonprofits—foundations, charities, churches, museums, colleges, universities, etc. And unlike Marx's salaried employees—his proletarian workers—members of the Overclass can give orders to those they supervise. They are trained experts and managers holding legal authority to run organizations.

CHAPTER 3

THE PSYCHOSOCIAL ORIENTATION OF THE OVERCLASS

"When I use a word," Humpty Dumpty said
in rather a scornful tone, "it means just
what I choose it to mean—neither more nor less."
"The question is," said Alice, "whether you can
make words mean so many different things."
"The question is," said Humpty Dumpty,
"which is to be master—that's all."

Lewis Carroll, *Through the Looking-Glass, and What Alice Found There*

As Marx provided for a substructure of materialism for his theory of human strivings, he also married that objective reality to an intangible world of beliefs and values—class ideology. Each class, Marx proposed, would have a culture and social mores of its own, which would be suitable stimulants energizing its functional contributions to the means of production in its time. This intangible realm of motivation and legitimation, of self-concepts that would bring meaning and purpose to lives, was called by Marxists the "superstructure" of human societies.

Feudalists would devise codes of honor, valor, and nobility. Capitalists would have the Protestant Ethic or its neo-Confucian equivalent in personal discipline and educational achievement. Proletarians would see the world through a lens of oppression.

But what would be the mental superstructure of the American Overclass?

In his 1950 book *The Lonely Crowd*, David Riesman accurately identified and described the superstructure mindset that would emerge from the Overclass. This is Riesman's concept of an "other-directed" personality.

Riesman contrasted the new other-directed personality with the older one, which he called "inner-directed."[1] Riesman modeled his inner-directed personality ideal on those persons inspired by the Protestant Ethic and in tune with the "rugged individual" ideal of pioneers, frontiersmen, mountain men, and cowboys. "Inner-direction" was particularly characteristic of the Scotch-Irish, the poor immigrants who came from Scotland via Ireland starting in the 1720s and who bypassed the coastal cities to stake out claims in and on the far side of the Appalachian Mountains. From this community came men such as Daniel Boone, Davy Crockett, and Andrew Jackson.

Inner-direction and other-direction are modal personalities. They shape who a person is, how they think, rationalize, make choices, adopt values, make friends, raise children, act as coworkers and citizens, and engage in culture, society, and politics.

Inner-Directed: Foot on the Gas, Hands on the Wheel, Open Road Ahead

An early example of an inner-directed person, and naturally enough in the Protestant traditions, was Martin Luther. When Luther was asked in 1521 to recant before the Holy Roman emperor Charles V his belief that we can be justified before God by faith alone, he said, "Here I stand; I can do no other."

Long before Martin Luther stood his ground, in what I prefer to call the parable of temptation, the Christian New Testament (Matthew 4) recounts that Satan put Jesus to a test of character: taking Jesus up to a very high mountain, Satan showed him "all the kingdoms of the world and their splendor." And he said to him, "I will give you all these, if you fall at my feet and do me homage."

Jesus stood on his identity and refused to take direction from Satan, saying only, "Away with you." We read, "Then Satan left him and suddenly angels appeared and looked after him."[2]

In a very different cultural context, Confucius compared our inner virtue to the North Star, "which keeps its place and all the stars turn towards it."[3] He affirmed that what the virtuous person seeks is in himself, while, to the contrary, what a mean, petty, weak person seeks is in others.[4]

He also advised, "See what a person does. Mark their motives. Examine in what things they rest. How can a person conceal their character?"[5] He also added, "To see what is right and not do it is want of courage."[6]

The Chinese moral philosopher Mencius refused to be ordered around by a king.

> Mencius went to see King Hui of Liang. The king said, "Venerable sir, since you have not counted it far to come here, a distance of a thousand li, may I presume that you are provided with counsels to profit my kingdom?"
>
> Mencius replied, "Why must your Majesty use that word 'profit?' What I advocate is only to have a benevolent and humane personality and right relationships."

Mencius understood "profit" as the seeking of what others fear and desire.

> If your Majesty says, "What is to be done to profit my kingdom?" the great officers will say, "What is to be done to profit

our families?" and the inferior officers and the common people will say, "What is to be done to profit our persons?" Superiors and inferiors will try to snatch this profit the one from the other, and the kingdom will be endangered. . . . Let your Majesty also say, "Benevolence and righteousness, and let these be your only themes." Why must you use that word—"profit?"[7]

In 1588, at Tilbury, as her forces gathered to repel a Spanish invasion, Elizabeth, the Protestant queen of England, proclaimed,

My loving people,

We have been persuaded by some that are careful of our safety, to take heed how we commit ourselves to armed multitudes, for fear of treachery. But I assure you, I do not desire to live to distrust my faithful and loving people.

Let tyrants fear. I have always so behaved myself that, under God, I have placed my chiefest strength and safeguard in the loyal hearts and good-will of my subjects; and therefore I am come amongst you, as you see, at this time, not for my recreation and disport, but being resolved, in the midst and heat of the battle, to live and die amongst you all; to lay down for my God, and for my kingdom, and my people, my honour and my blood, even in the dust.

I know I have the body of a weak and feeble woman; but I have the heart and stomach of a king, and of a king of England too, and think foul scorn that Parma or Spain, or any prince of Europe, should dare to invade the borders of my realm; to which rather than any dishonour shall grow by me, I myself will take up arms, I myself will be your general, judge, and rewarder of every one of your virtues in the field.[8]

In 1799, in a letter to her sister, the Protestant Abigail Adams, wife of revolutionary leader John Adams, wrote,

I send my little Niece a Book. I did not Read it untill I bought it, there is no harm in it, many useful lessons, but some which I do not assent to or approve of—I will never consent to have our sex considered in an inferiour point of light. Let each planet shine in their own orbit. God and nature designd it so—If man is Lord, woman is Lordess. That is what I contend [. . .] for, and if a woman does not hold the Reigns [*sic*] of Government, I see no reason for her not judging how they are conducted.[9]

A touching and eloquent example of inner-direction was written by Major Sullivan Ballou of the Second Rhode Island Regiment during the American Civil War in his last letter to his wife. Major Ballou was killed on the battlefield on July 21, 1861, during the first battle along the Bull Run in Northern Virginia.

If it is necessary that I should fall on the battle-field for any country, I am ready. I have no misgivings about, or lack of confidence in, the cause in which I am engaged, and my courage does not halt or falter. I know how strongly American civilization now leans upon the triumph of government, and how great a debt we owe to those who went before us through the blood and suffering of the Revolution, and I am willing, perfectly willing to lay down all my joys in this life to help maintain this government, and to pay that debt. . . .

Sarah, my love for you is deathless. It seems to bind me with mighty cables, that nothing but Omnipotence can break; and yet, my love of country comes over me like a strong wind, and bears me irresistibly on with all those chains, to the battlefield. The memories of all the blissful moments I have spent with you come crowding over me, and I feel most deeply grateful to God and you, that I have enjoyed them so long.[10]

The emotional and psychological "stuff" of an inner-directed person was well captured by William Ernest Henley in his 1888 poem "Invictus."

> Out of the night that covers me,
> Black as the pit from pole to pole,
> I thank whatever gods may be
> For my unconquerable soul.
>
> In the fell clutch of circumstance
> I have not winced nor cried aloud.
> Under the bludgeonings of chance
> My head is bloody, but unbowed.
> Beyond this place of wrath and tears
> Looms but the Horror of the shade,
> And yet the menace of the years
> Finds and shall find me unafraid.
>
> It matters not how strait the gate,
> How charged with punishments the scroll,
> I am the master of my fate,
> I am the captain of my soul.[11]

Inner-direction has also been well expressed by Rudyard Kipling in his 1895 poem "If."

> If you can keep your head when all about you
> Are losing theirs and blaming it on you,
> If you can trust yourself when all men doubt you,
> But make allowance for their doubting too; . . .
> Or being lied about, don't deal in lies,
> Or being hated, don't give way to hating, . . .

If you can meet with Triumph and Disaster
And treat those two impostors just the same; . . .
If you can force your heart and nerve and sinew
To serve your turn long after they are gone,
And so hold on when there is nothing in you
Except the Will which says to them: "Hold on!"

If you can talk with crowds and keep your virtue,
Or walk with Kings—nor lose the common touch,
If neither foes nor loving friends can hurt you,
If all men count with you, but none too much;
If you can fill the unforgiving minute
With sixty seconds' worth of distance run,
Yours is the Earth and everything that's in it,
And—which is more—you'll be a Man, my son![12]

A third poem that conveys a conviction about being inner-directed is Robert Frost's "The Road Not Taken."

Two roads diverged in a yellow wood,
And sorry I could not travel both
And be one traveler, long I stood
And looked down one as far as I could
To where it bent in the undergrowth;

Then took the other, as just as fair,
And having perhaps the better claim,
Because it was grassy and wanted wear;
Though as for that the passing there
Had worn them really about the same,

And both that morning equally lay
In leaves no step had trodden black.
Oh, I kept the first for another day!
Yet knowing how way leads on to way,
I doubted if I should ever come back.

I shall be telling this with a sigh
Somewhere ages and ages hence:
Two roads diverged in a wood, and I—
I took the one less traveled by,
And that has made all the difference.[13]

Riesman's observation was that by 1950 such "rugged individualism" among Americans had effectively been replaced by a compliant collectivism whereby others could give directions to one's soul. For Riesman the values professed by peer groups successfully marginalized the virtues of individuals, the traits of character that provided autonomous direction and resilience in the face of events.

Riesman defined inner-direction as that inner voice that "channels choice through a rigid though highly individualized character."[14]

In 1918 German sociologist Max Weber, with forebodings about the future of the new German constitutional republic seated in Weimar, gave a lecture at Munich University on "Politics as a Vocation." He made a case for moral leadership, not demagoguery or a closed-minded emotional embrace of a "juristic rationalism" that legitimated a dictatorial state. He called for an "ethic of responsibility," a personal orientation to inner-direction, saying, "The honor of the political leader . . . lies precisely in an exclusive personal responsibility for what he does, a responsibility he cannot and must not reject or transfer."[15]

Weber insisted that the "decisive psychological quality of the politician [is] his ability to let realities work upon him with inner concentration and calmness." The responsible leaders must differentiate themselves by a "firm taming of the soul."

One effective distinction between the inner-directed person and the other-directed one is their ability to stand on principle. The inner-directed person is more capable of taking a stand on principle, while the other-directed person prefers to adjust their principles to the views of others. The other-directed are on alert about which way the wind of socially important opinion is blowing at any given moment. In contemporary terms other-directed people are fearful of being canceled, of being ostracized by those whose opinions guide their thinking and provide them with social inclusion.

In his 1988 book *In Pursuit of Happiness and Good Government*, exploring what it is that can make government "good" for people, Charles Murray centered on the promotion of inner-direction, what he called an internal "locus of control."[16] He concluded that "people vary in the degree to which they see themselves as being responsible for what happens to them." The variations align with Riesman's inner-direction (internal control for Murray) and other-direction (external control for Murray). Murray writes, "To be an internal is to assume self-possession, the key psychological attribute of self-respect."

Self-respect wards off low self-esteem. Low self-esteem is associated with traits often derived from other-direction: submissiveness, general maladjustment, lack of imagination, dependence on others, reduced creativity and flexibility, and a tendency to be more authoritarian when feeling in the right.

Murray thinks that self-respect is about measuring up to standards—those originating with you or those you appropriate from others.[17] Murray concludes that good public policies should let people find self-respect through the acquisition of self-possession—"that they take a high degree of responsibility for their lives and act on that responsibility. . . . The threshold condition of self-respect is that one feel, not in one's public protestations but in one's heart, that [one] is a net contributor to the world."[18]

We might helpfully think of inner-direction as a welcome form of human capital—an asset which empowers us to seek prosperity and happiness. It turns out that lifetime earnings vary with attachment to working.[19] Differences among people as to hours worked over a lifetime are large. Those who attach themselves to work end up with more accumulated earnings over their working life. Those less attached to work end up with lower cumulative earnings. The inference to me is that attachment to work derives from a personality orientation—when work is conceptualized as a vocation giving one's life a higher and more sustaining meaning and not felt to be an imposition, a burden, a "labor" not of love but of something to be minimized, even shunned if possible. The source of such a personalized commitment to work would come from inner-direction. The closer work aligns with one's innermost sense of self-assurance and moral value, the more one will appreciate being attached to one's work.

This connection between one's inner-direction and one's work brings to mind the insight of Heraclitus that "character is destiny," or *ethos anthropos daimon*—a spirited sense of self within us (our *daimon*) sets our course in life for better or worse. The course—the work—which such spirit chooses for us brings forth our individual destinies.

One might think of inner-direction as a searchlight shining from within out onto the world and other-direction as looking into a kaleidoscope as we turn the outer cylinder around and around, seeing shifting patterns of shining, pretty little pieces of plastic falling into place and then disappearing as another montage moves into view. With inner-direction we build a relationship with truth. With other-direction we are enthralled by changing superficials.

The inestimable value of inner-direction from a theological perspective on the nature of the human experience is revealed in the parable of Job in the Old Testament. Job is introduced as a "sound and honest man who fears God and shuns evil." Job describes himself as one who has "walked in the way of the Lord without swerving," having within him a charism that centers his ego-identity with firm and fixed meaning and purpose.

But Satan then challenges Yahweh, Job's God, to test the quality of Job's inner-direction, saying that Job measures his self-worth by his wealth. Yahweh then gives Satan power over Job. Satan arranges for Job's donkeys and camels to be stolen and for his servants, sons, and daughters to be killed. But Job had committed no sin, and his character remained true to its inner-direction, so he did not reproach Yahweh. Satan then "struck Job down with malignant ulcers." Job's wife asked, "Why persist in this integrity of yours?" She proposed, "Curse Yahweh and die."

Job's three friends then urge him with reasons to admit his sinfulness and beg God for forgiveness—in other words, to become other-directed and subordinate his integrity under the direction of others, to curry favor with Yahweh. One's suffering arises from one's iniquity, they insisted. The conformists with downcast eyes are rewarded, while the proud are punished. "It is people who breed trouble for themselves." If Job's integrity were real, they inferred, God would not have spurned him.

Job stands his ground and refuses to confess any sinfulness of heart or mind, calling on Yahweh to "test me in the crucible," adding, "In my heart I need not be ashamed of my days."

Then Yahweh speaks to Job, pointing out the limitations of his knowledge—that Job knows not the realities of heaven and earth, the scope of the Creator's powers.

Job admits to Yahweh that his words have been "frivolous," but he does not go farther than that in taking upon himself any guilt or blame. He repents of his ignorance in humility, retracting words inspired only by that limited understanding of a larger truth. He does not ask to be forgiven for any flaw of character.

Yahweh then restores Job's wealth and rebukes his friends for "not having spoken about me correctly."

The lesson here is to ground your character in wisdom—which is fear of the Lord, coupled with an intuitive awareness of human shortcomings—and not to seek hither and yon for your own personal truth, for that is the course of narcissism and even make-believe. Take your course, therefore, directly from the kingdom of heaven rather than from humanly contrived kingdoms of powers and principalities.

The importance of internalizing wisdom is also advocated by the "Great Learning" text in the Chinese Confucian tradition, which admonishes us as follows: to cultivate your person, first rectify your heart; to rectify your heart, first seek to be sincere in your thoughts; to be sincere in your thoughts, extend to the utmost your knowledge; to extend your knowledge, investigate things. (In other words: Think hard for yourself; don't just take in what others say and think.)[20]

Other-Directed: Running on Empty

Riesman perceived that other-directed people were emerging in the upper middle class of larger cities.[21] He said it was the "typical character of the 'new' middle class—the bureaucrat, the salaried employee in business," those engaged in white-collar work and the service trades.[22]

> What is common to all other-directed people is that their contemporaries are the source of direction for the individual—either those known to him or those with whom he is indirectly acquainted, through friends, through the mass media. This source is of course "internalized" in the sense that dependence on it for guidance in life is implanted early. The goals towards which the other-directed person strives shift with that guidance: it is only the process of striving itself and the process of paying close attention to the signals from others that remain unaltered throughout life. This mode of keeping in touch with others permits a close behavioral conformity . . . through an exceptional sensitivity to the actions and wishes of others.[23]

Riesman believed that other-directed people had an insatiable psychological need for approval by others.

This way our inner sense of well-being flows as a narrative from influencers to us, from the objective dominant psyche outside to the subjective, subordinate, and malleable ego-identity inside. Other-direction is a form of appropriation of that outside narrative whereby the other becomes the self. We surrender our agency to the other on the assumption that they are superior, expert, insightful, and hip.

An inner-directed person is an author. An other-directed person just reads.

But some object to inner-direction on principle. Alissa Quart, author of *Bootstrapped: Liberating Ourselves from the American Dream*, writes: "For too long stability has been framed as a psychological characteristic, a mental steadiness cultivated from within. By the same token, instability has been viewed as a psychological failing that comes from low self-esteem, a history of abuse, or a failure to work on oneself. But in the time of terra infirma, a certain degree of anxiety about insecurity is not a moral failing—it's an honest and insightful reaction to what is happening around us."[24]

Unequipped with much personal agency and having internalized the thoughts, values, and motivations of others, other-directed persons often perform in life with the characteristics of non-playable characters (NPCs) created for video and other games. These characters move and act out of rote instruction, are preprogrammed, and so are not given individualized purpose by a player, who has the agency to shape the game's outcome. NPCs provide the "supporting cast" or "extras" in the storyline driven by the protagonists—the playable characters.

In the gaming world of the other-directed, one rises above an NPC role to become a playable character through the acquisition of positional power—rising up in society's hierarchy of managers. This is done through (1) the acquisition of proper credentials—beginning with college degrees—and (2) the adoption of the attitudes appropriate for high social positioning of self. It is a process of socialization that begins early in life and never ends.

Riesman looked to changes in parenting for the emergence of more and more other-directed individuals in American society. Approval of the child by others becomes the only unequivocal good in the eyes of parents—"one makes good when one is approved of."

Thus, he said, "All power, not just some power, is in the hands of the actual or imaginary approving group, and the child learns from his parents' reactions to him that nothing in his character, no possession he owns, no inheritance of name or talent, no work he has done, is valued for itself but only for its effect on others."[25]

As to the parents, Riesman speculated, "The loss of old certainties in the spheres of work and social relationships is accompanied by doubt as to how to bring up children."

Other-direction does not make for good parenting. Much of contemporary America's identity dysphoria may have arisen from poor parenting. Other-directed parents can't comfortably raise inner-directed children. Such parents can easily defer to the demands of their children, letting the children direct them. This deference cannot generate maturity in the children, only a sense of entitlement and self-absorption, psyches unable to rise above desires and develop a strong ego-identity, mastery of self, resilient self-confidence, and courage, leading to important personal contributions to society.

Moreover, other-direction in women may facilitate their choice not to become mothers, a trend now changing the composition of American society. Lack of inner-direction makes child-raising less affirming of a mother's sense of accomplishment. Child-raising is, of course, taking responsibility for another from dawn to dusk. Being responsible unsettles the other-directed person's core sense of self, triggering nauseous anxiety. Child-raising comes with rejections from the other, challenges to one's personal authority, and let-downs and uncertainties. Such relationships are stressful for the other-directed. Good parenting demands the strength of character to trust and let go, to keep a steady course, and to role model consistency and authority while setting expectations for the child of independent judgment and self-restraint.

I can, with some memory, associate my mother with Riesman's observation about the loss of old certainties in parenting. Between my birth in 1945 and my younger brother's birth in 1948, Dr. Benjamin Spock published *The Common Sense Book of Baby and Child Care*, the first book of expertise about understanding children's needs and family dynamics to incorporate psychoanalysis. While my grandmothers and great-grandmothers remained very old school and inner-directed, I sensed my brother was being indulged by my mother in ways not applied to me.

Perhaps it was no accident that Dr. Spock went on to become a stereotype of a left-liberal, progressive American intellectual and political activist. He attended his father's schools of Phillips Andover Academy and Yale University, where he was inducted into the Scroll and Key senior society. He would convert to socialism and oppose the defense of the South Vietnamese nationalists. In 1972 he ran for president of the United States as the candidate of the People's Party, campaigning for a maximum wage, legal abortion, and withdrawing American troops from foreign countries.

Riesman also credits teachers using theories of progressive education with facilitating the multiplying of other-directed children, saying changes in teaching styles and methodologies "assisted in the breakdown of walls between teacher and pupil; and this in turn helps to break down walls between student and student, permitting that rapid circulation of tastes which is a prelude to other-directed socialization."[26] Teachers, he observed, served in their communities as agents spreading the messages concerning tastes that emanated from the progressive urban centers. Such teachers conveyed to students that what matters is not their industry but their adjustment to the group, their cooperation, and limits to their initiative and leadership.

Riesman described this evolution of child-rearing away from a focus on morality to anxiety over self-worth, which he called "morale."

Outside of parents and classrooms, Riesman pointed to peer groups as having acquired unmatched power over their members. Peer group dynamics required a "highly sensitive response to swings of fashion."[27] The need to always be in fashion, Riesman pointed out, demanded the development of an ability to be different today from what one was yesterday, a demolishment of one's core identity and its reassuring sense of self.[28]

In 2024 essayist David Brooks made the same observation in a piece titled "The Sins of the Educated Class."

> Nothing is more unstable than a fashionable opinion. If your status is defined by your opinions, you're living in a world of perpetual insecurity, perpetual moral and mental war. . . . Battles for symbolic consecration are now the water in which many of us highly educated Americans swim. . . . But it's awful to live in a perpetual state of cultural war, and it's awful to live in a state of social fear. The inflammation of the discourse serves the psychic and social self-interests of the combatants, but it polarizes society by rendering a lot of people in the center silent, causing them to keep their heads down in order to survive.[29]

So it seems, in retrospect, that Riesman was correct: Inculcating other-direction in children is not doing them any favors.

To maintain their membership, children learn to "surrender any claim to independence of judgement and taste."[30] Safe spaces for individuals within the group were found through "mastering a range of consumer preferences and modes of their expression," not through any demonstration of skillful personal excellence.

In his book *Trust Matters More Than Ever*, with guidance for becoming a trustworthy person who can win the respect and support of others, David Horsager provides a list of personally generated "counterforces" that sabotage our ability to be a trusted and valued collaborator. Many of these interfering "counterforces" brought to our attention by Horsager seem most aligned with other-direction: ambiguity, doubt, unpredictability, distractions, lack of focus, low expectations, no follow-through, cliques/silos, fear, impatience, dissatisfaction, gossiping, deception, and marginalizing those associated with certain "isms."[31]

Other-direction tends to make one disconcerted, uncertain, floating, vulnerable, edgy, suspicious, and—sometimes—angry. Other-direction sows the seeds of identity dysphoria.

Two recent books—*Fawning: Why the Need to Please Makes Us Lose Ourselves* by Ingrid Clayton and *Are You Mad at Me? How to Stop Focusing on What Others Think and Start Living for You* by Meg Josephson—present fawning behaviors as other-direction becoming a personal crusade seeking self-destruction. Fawning is defined as a debilitating complex whereby the uncertain person seeks safety by merging with the wishes, needs, and demands of others.[32]

A number of psychotherapists have focused their research and practices on "dysregulated" emotions and identities. The state of being chaotically dysregulated in emotions and identity follows on extreme other-direction where the person has little ability to "regulate" themselves autonomously in real time. For example, diagnostic paradigms have been proposed such as "borderline-dysregulated personality," marked by intense emotional swings, fragile identity, impulsivity, and chaotic relationships; mood and emotion dysregulation; and Dysregulated Affective States.[33]

In recent decades three cognitive structures have turned more and more Americans toward other-direction: feminism, Critical Race Theory, and intersectionality. When you ask yourself, "Who am I? Where do I come from? Where am I going?" these three invented intellectual constructs tell you exactly and definitively who you are supposed to be, where you stand in relation to social power, and what you can expect out of life.

If the answer to the question, "Who am I?" provided by significant others is "You are a woman and so a feminist" or "You are a man and so toxic to others," then you may well presume that their definition of you is that which you should internalize as your own identity. Therefore, you may well tend to want to become the kind of woman or man that they find appealing. They have diminished your capacity to become more individually inner-directed.

Similarly, if they tell you that you are Black or you are White and that the color of your skin, not your character, will drive your destiny, you may well tend to internalize that external judgment as very much a part of who you are and who you can't be. Your inner light—just being yourself as a person, as an individual—has been dimmed by those around you.

Unconscionably, this two-color dualism leaves unmoored those born biracial or multiracial.

Third, if you ask, "Where am I going?" intersectionality theory will predict your future on a continuum of oppression—from being an oppressor to being something of a victim, or perhaps even to suffering all your life from an immutable victimhood. Who needs inner-direction when society calls all the shots?

Riesman then informs us of language—words—as a powerful tool of peer-group repression. The right words become a "set of counters by which one establishes that one is 'in' and by which one participates in the peer-group's arduously self-socializing 'work.'" And conversely using the wrong words leads immediately to rejection and aloneness.

"Words not only affect us temporarily; they change us, they socialize or unsocialize us."[34]

Since his successful run for president in 2016, Donald Trump's words triggered, and have since sustained, what is called Trump derangement syndrome among American intellectual, cultural, and political elites, giving rise to a systemic effort by major media outlets and his political opponents to de-Americanize him.

On September 1, 2022, President Biden gave a speech in front of the symbolically important Independence Hall in Philadelphia. He used words to desocialize Trump's supporters as not belonging to the American community.

> And here, in my view, is what is true: MAGA Republicans do not respect the Constitution. They do not believe in the rule of law. They do not recognize the will of the people.

They refuse to accept the results of a free election. And they're working right now, as I speak, in state after state to give power to decide elections in America to partisans and cronies, empowering election deniers to undermine democracy itself.

MAGA forces are determined to take this country backwards—backwards to an America where there is no right to choose, no right to privacy, no right to contraception, no right to marry who you love.

They promote authoritarian leaders, and they fan the flames of political violence that are a threat to our personal rights, to the pursuit of justice, to the rule of law, to the very soul of this country.

They look at the mob that stormed the United States Capitol on January 6th—brutally attacking law enforcement—not as insurrectionists who placed a dagger to the throat of our democracy, but they look at them as patriots.

And they see their MAGA failure to stop a peaceful transfer of power after the 2020 election as preparation for the 2022 and 2024 elections.

They tried everything last time to nullify the votes of 81 million people. This time, they're determined to succeed in thwarting the will of the people.

That's why respected conservatives, like Federal Circuit Court Judge Michael Luttig, has called Trump and the extreme MAGA Republicans, quote, a "clear and present danger" to our democracy.[35]

Underneath Biden's vilification of Donald Trump (what Friedrich Nietzsche called to our attention as "ressentiment") was a Gnostic creed: MAGA Republicans were the "Evil Ones" in America, requiring the faithful to oppose them with hammer and tongs.

Riesman wrote that other-direction brought a new skill to politics—networking to get the inside story on others, reflecting a disposition that people are more important than things or ideas. Thus, the other-directed person must be circumspect and diversionary to keep in check emotions and personal opinions to more easily fit in with others, a kind of passive-aggressive manipulation of others. His characterological drive is for manipulation, not to change others but to resemble them.[36] The other-directed political chameleon knows a great deal about what other people are doing and thinking—the better not to stand out as different. An other-directed politician must have acceptable opinions and must engage in overt political activities in acceptable ways.[37]

Riesman's assessment of other-directed politicians brings to mind Douglas Haig's 1918 remark to his wife, dismissing the views of the Earl of Derby: "A very weak-minded fellow I am afraid, and, like the feather pillow, bears the marks of the last person who sat on him. I hear he is called in London 'genial Judas'!"

In describing Joe Biden's chameleonlike career over the years through the shifting colors of correct opinion within the American Democratic Party, including his ascent to the presidency, Gerard Baker of the *Wall Street Journal* came up with the felicitous phrase "our man of constant borrow."

To the contrary, John F. Kennedy associated himself with a different approach: "Too often we enjoy the comfort of opinion without the discomfort of thought."[38]

The other-directed style in politics, naturally, raises the question of who can be trusted and who is sincere, leaving the political order vulnerable to speculation, gossip, and fear of commitment—in short, to failures of collective achievement.

Other-directed personalities have a greedy appetite for ad hominem arguments. Their proclivity is to undermine—and destroy, if possible—the character, reputation, and moral stature of those they want to marginalize in culture, society, and politics. Other-directed personalities thus have an affinity for cancel culture, for deamplification of views they don't like. They seek to prevent those not of their persuasion from having influence in the community by bringing them into disrepute as persons who are not good, decent, well intentioned, or high-minded but rather prejudiced, stupid, self-interested, and most unworthy of your consideration and friendship.

The accomplished Roman orator and teacher of rhetoric Quintilian wrote in his thesis that the most persuasive advocate is a "good person who speaks well." If you can "de-good" your adversary, you can more easily win over your audience.

However, ad hominem arguments can't prove anything. They can only influence your willingness to accept what another says. For example, if Adolf Hitler or Joseph Stalin—men who killed millions—were to say that "two plus two is four," neither would be wrong, no matter how bad they were.

The ad hominem approach to argument and policy debates ignores the facts, overlooks the law, has no interest in principled reasoning, and is illogical. The ad hominem retort or accusation is a kind of mind game, a manipulation of emotions and prejudices.

But for the other-directed, invoking ad hominem cancellation of others is only normal practice for in-group conversations, only a form of gossip, helpfully reinforcing groupthink and solidarity among members.

Other-directed politics, said Riesman, destabilizes coalitions to favor veto groups. The center of concern is loyalty to the small group, whose members sustain our self-esteem.

Thus, another proclivity of the other-directed in politics is to find and join causes, to find identity in a higher justice not yet present in the community. Especially, a cause gives the life of an other-directed person more meaning, though such meaning is inserted into the psyche by others from the outside. The cause provides a home, a safe space, with all the emotional security that like-minded people provide to one another. The cause (think "climate change" or "from the river to the sea") also provides the other-directed person with a reassuring "voice" to use in public and, most importantly, with badges of identity to show the world who one is. An "I am what I demand" state of mind and heart attempts to erase identity dysphoria through communalism. New York Mayor Zohran Mamdani—for example—with enthusiasm plans to replace inner-direction ("the frigidity of rugged individualism" in his words) with the "warmth of collectivism."

The dynamic is not transactional dealmaking but rather the performative affirmation of this or that identity signifier. Politics is virtue signaling, not compromise, which can backfire on one if one's peers sense a giving in to the wrong group's preferences.

Some years ago I was sitting next to former Minnesota senator David Durenberger, a moderate Republican who was always keen to "move the needle," to get something accomplished. We were waiting for him to speak at a luncheon in Minneapolis when a friend of his from Washington walked over, saying pointedly, "Dave, that Senate Dining Room of yours is empty."

Durenberger blanched and turned inward. Later he commented obliquely that the Senate Dining Room was where senators got to know one another, build trust, find out what made others tick, and therefore could comfortably explore legislative options and compromises. An empty Senate Dining Room therefore meant that the Senate was not getting its work done of serving the common good.

Now a senator ran the risk of being seen talking with the "wrong" person from his or her peer group's other-directed point of view. So safety lay in staying away from the Senate Dining Room and its dangers.

In 1951 Riesman wrote, "In terms of character, the other-directed man simply does not seek power; rather he avoids and evades it. . . . He seeks adjustment."[39] Ergo, no leadership comes from the other-directed.

The orientation of the other-directed toward power has become more perverse since Riesman first considered their behaviors.

The other-directed very frequently experience a two-faced, Dr. Jekyll and Mr. Hyde relationship with power. On the one hand, they give power over self-awareness to others and appropriate for themselves the power of the group.

On the other hand, making themselves dependent and vulnerable, giving over their agency to others, is to lose power and thus trigger insecurity. The other-directed can worry constantly over the durability of their standing with significant others, those they take as influencers and role models. If those others should turn against them, their sense of self is overcome by fear and anger. Feeling powerless, they rush to safer spaces.

This dynamic is at play with the "Mean Girls" syndrome and "office politics." Those whom we entrust with power over our self-image abuse it with little remorse, sometimes revealing considerable pleasure at being able to live out in real life, before our eyes and at our expense, Nietzsche's myth of the Übermensch.

To put such insecurities to rest, the other-directed need to acquire positional power for themselves, socially structured power to keep others dependent on them.

Thus, many of the other-directed demonstrate proclivities similar to those of the manipulative sociopath: using charm, flattery, or calculated deception to gain trust. They may use guilt-tripping to impose responsibility for their well-being on the influential other, or play the victim, only seeking fair treatment and sympathy, or become dependent to shift situational dynamics toward them. The other-directed may exaggerate their competence and the importance of their credentials. They may mirror superiors and those with perceived social and cultural influence to gain acceptance. Creating compelling but self-serving narratives is a classic interpersonal ploy of the other-directed.

Thus, other-direction drives dysfunction in bureaucracies where default behaviors cluster around interpersonal power struggles and the abandonment of institutional responsibilities. The result for society is systemic mediocrity and a failure of stewardship.

In an office setting, decision-making triggers the other-directed: Making a decision carries the risk that the decision may not be approved by all of one's influencers and significant others. There is a realistic fear that, even after internalizing the values and beliefs of others, one might fail in accurately reproducing them in a new context. Or one might not quickly enough intuit how others will react and so put them off by speaking out too soon. Thus, the safest course of action is to take no action, to invite others into a conversation and listen closely and look inquisitively for "tells" of what they are really thinking and what they want. Thus, a well-functioning Overclass management team has many people at the table and takes the time necessary to process their inputs before coming up with a comfortable consensus that all can sign off on.

Other-direction imposes another dysfunctional orientation toward power—the activation in a person of Nietzsche's ressentiment. The other-directed person needs to fill a void. Not having an identity leaves one feeling vulnerable when dealing with others. The other-directed person is easily "triggered" into feeling insecure, anxious, and emotionally unsafe in public. Thus, the fearful and uncertain other-directed person is disposed to project on certain others evil intentions in an interpersonal transference of disharmony from self to other. Here lies the motivation for the other-directed to gravitate toward Gnostic interpretations of what is wrong with the world—it is "them" who are bad, who must be censored and suppressed, not "us." Whoever I am, I am good; I am not the problem.

Nietzsche had insight into this. The inner-directed person he called "noble"—one living "before his own conscience with confidence and frankness," while the "rancorous" person (other-directed) he said is "neither truthful nor ingenuous nor honest or forthright with himself. His soul squints; his mind loves hide-outs, secret paths and back doors; . . . he is expert . . . in provisional self-depreciation and in self-humiliation."[40]

Ressentiment in culture and politics leads to distress and divisive conflict.

"It turns out that when you mix narcissism and nihilism, you create an acid that corrodes every belief system it touches," wrote David Brooks in an April 2025 article in the *Atlantic* titled "I Should Have Seen This Coming."[41] American culture as guided by the other-directed has been no exception to this rule.

This rueful observation on the consequences for contemporary American women as other-direction has intersected with feminism was made by Jordan Kisner in the same issue of the *Atlantic* as Brooks's observation: "Given how often women are forced to understand themselves as fundamentally *in relation* to others . . . is it possible for a woman to have an authentic, independent self?" Kisner then references modern novels written by women about women, wherein one character "observes the world with a sense of self so hollowed out as to render her more a conduit for the musings of her interlocutors than a full-fledged character." Kisner says that another writer presents her female protagonists as "lacking the normal trappings of selfhood." These fictional women "are loners, dispassionate and disassociated, floating through foreign places in dreamlike Woolfian internal monologue."[42]

Two noted contemporary students of personality, Stephen R. Covey and Jordan Peterson, whose advice on finding personal success and happiness has been followed by many, can be placed on an inner-directed to other-directed continuum. Covey proposed seven habits that would make one highly effective.[43] Three of the habits reflect inner-direction: Be proactive and have a personal vision, have an end in mind, and put first things first—managing your personal life by exercising an independent will and becoming principle-centered. Three other recommended habits reflect other-direction: Think win/win, seek first to understand and then be understood, and synergize. His seventh habit in effect worked to enhance one's ability to be inner-directed with physical exercise, mental stimulation, spiritual values clarification and meditative study, and service/empathy to ground intrinsic security.

In *12 Rules for Life: An Antidote to Chaos*, Jordan Peterson writes that rule 4 is to take yourself as you were yesterday—not other people—as the starting point for moving forward with your life.

> Orient yourself properly. Then—and only then—concentrate
> on the day. Set your sights on the Good, the Beautiful, and the

True, and then focus pointedly and carefully on the concerns of each moment. Aim continually at Heaven while you work diligently on Earth.[44] . . . To stand up straight with your shoulders back is to accept the terrible responsibility of life, with eyes wide open.[45]

Peterson commented that "a habitual assumption of subordination [other-directedness] renders the person more stressed and uncertain than necessary."

For many years the Gallup company has provided personality consulting for employees using self-assessments to rank individuals on their inherent proclivity for activating thirty-four abilities in their work.[46] Most of these abilities can be associated with inner-direction: in thinking on your own, influencing others, and executing your agenda. Nine other important abilities, though, do emphasize regard for your relationships with others, such as being adaptable, connecting with others, having empathy, and working in harmony.

For the other-directed, narrative—the social construction of purported reality—creates and sustains social power. Truth for the other-directed does not really exist outside of language. Whoever controls words therefore controls culture and society. Control of the narrative, especially in education, has shifted power to the other-directed.

Confucius advocated the importance of narrative as shaping behaviors.

Zi Lu said, "The ruler of Wei has been waiting for you, in order with you to administer the government. What will you consider the first thing to be done?" The Master replied, "What is necessary is to rectify names." . . . If names be not correct, language is not in accordance with the truth of things. If language be not in accordance with the truth of things, affairs cannot be carried on to success. When affairs cannot be carried on to success, proprieties and music will not flourish. When proprieties and music do not flourish, punishments will not be properly awarded. When punishments are not properly awarded, the people do not know how to move hand or foot.[47]

Vocabulary controls thought. Through words, you control the mind. Control the mind—your own or the minds of others—and you control behavior. Words, and so thoughts and speech, mediate between norms and mindfulness and the experienced, tactile facticity of the cosmos. Words live in abstraction—what is normative—but guide our interactions within that facticity. Fortunately, our learning from facticity can drive what we put into words and thoughts, what we can make normative, bringing us closer to truth.

Given the excessive power of words to drive behaviors for the other-directed, it should come as no surprise that, in recent decades, American politics—both Republican and Democrat—has turned more and more to messaging—getting out "our" narrative while trashing or censoring the narratives of others, often by smearing it as disinformation or misinformation. Politics has evolved from face-to-face interpersonal engagement to the more lonely consumption of reassuring, performative—even entertaining—media narratives.

This fixation on narrative and story, even myth, encourages excessive use of logically irrelevant ad hominem arguments, which attack the messenger and not the message. Thus, those in our elite who have succumbed to Trump derangement syndrome thought that if they could only just expel Trump from American politics, then their privileged status in our society and politics would be undisturbed by the undeserving. They were unsuccessful in that effort during the 2024 campaign for the presidency.

To the contrary, for the inner-directed, truth, principles, and the law create and sustain social power. These three point toward existential being, that which cannot be changed at pleasure or to further one's self-interest.

Truth, principles, and the law provide normative and cognitive discipline. They have a freestanding, formal quality and need to be learned through intentional study. Truth, principles, and the law may be put into words, but they exist on their own outside the control of anyone's preferred language.

In Contrast—Inner-directed vs. Other-directed

The inner-directed reason; the other-directed parrot.

The inner-directed make decisions; the other-directed curate conversations.

The inner-directed hear and internalize ideas; the other-directed fixate on appearance and performance.

The inner-directed accept personal responsibility; with the other-directed, someone else assumes responsibility and delivers a "safe-space" in return.

The Tide Turns on American Greatness

The emergence of a schism dividing Americans into two rival communities—one still covenantal and inner-directed and the second insecure, searching, and other-directed—was affirmed by the noted sociologist Daniel Bell.[48] He spoke of "modernism" giving rise to an "anti-bourgeois" culture among some Americans blessed in a way with bountiful material plenty and abundant consumerism. He proposed that the "axial principle of modern culture is the expression and remaking of the 'self' in order to achieve self-realization and self-fulfillment."[49]

As a result, he wrote, "[A] crisis of middle-class values is at hand . . . the traditional bourgeois organization of life—its rationalism and sobriety—now has few defenders in the culture, nor does it have any established system of cultural meanings or stylistic forms with any intellectual or cultural respectability."[50] He saw the new culture as "an official, ceaseless, search for a new sensibility"—what Riesman had defined as "other-direction."[51]

What Bell objected to was largely invented by and imposed on American culture and society by the baby boomer generation, born and raised during what John Glubb would call the high noon of American success. Glubb predicted that after a high noon inevitably comes decadence and then collapse. It would be the fate of the baby boomers to initiate America's experiment with decadence.

Baby boomers were the children of the "Greatest Generation," the generation that pulled through the Great Depression of the 1930s, rallied to defeat in a global war the fascist powers of Germany and Italy and the xenophobic militarists of Japan, and took the lead in building a new world order based on law and justice for all. As the baby boomers grew into adulthood, their parents and grandparents worked to contain the aggressive ambitions of Overclass Communists in the Soviet Union and the People's Republic of China and to fund the modernization of undeveloped nations.

The leadership of the younger members of the Greatest Generation during the Kennedy Administration (whom my dad's friends called "the second lieutenants of World War II") was eloquently attested in President Kennedy's inaugural address on January 20, 1961.

> The world is very different now. For man holds in his mortal hands the power to abolish all forms of human poverty and all forms of human life. And yet the same revolutionary beliefs for which our forebears fought are still at issue around the globe—the belief that the rights of man come not from the generosity of the state but from the hand of God.
>
> We dare not forget today that we are the heirs of that first revolution. Let the word go forth from this time and place, to friend and foe alike, that the torch has been passed to a new generation of Americans—born in this century, tempered by war, disciplined by a hard and bitter peace, proud of our ancient heritage—and unwilling to witness or permit the slow undoing of those human rights to which this nation has always

been committed, and to which we are committed today at home and around the world.[52]

The Greatest Generation, inspired by Dr. Martin Luther King Jr.'s leadership, ended racial segregation in the Southern states with the Civil Rights Acts of 1964 and 1965.

Keeping the promise of President Kennedy in that same inaugural address to "pay any price, bear any burden, meet any hardship, support any friend, oppose any foe to assure the survival and the success of liberty," Presidents Eisenhower in October 1954, Kennedy in 1961, and Johnson in July 1965 committed the United States to the defense of the Vietnamese nationalists in South Vietnam against aggression from their Communist rivals in North Vietnam. However, that war would end in defeat for the South Vietnamese and their American allies, a defeat that accelerated the turn of Americans toward identity dysphoria as they came to question their worthiness as a people.

The baby boomers were roughly the seventh generation born since the American founding. At least I am a seventh-generation direct descendant of Winthrop Young. His in-law Samuel Jackson fought in the Battle of Bunker Hill with the New Hampshire militia on June 17, 1775.

The baby boomers grew up to unite Overclass aspirations, careers, and other-directed personalities in one social movement. Most of them were the first American generation to grow up getting weekly allowances to spend freely on their desires. Their parents seemed to have had an unstated need to protect their children from the Depression-era hardships of their own youth now that America was prosperous and a world power.

The American baby boomers gave social power to adolescence and "teenagerism." The terms "teenage" or "teenager" were first used in 1912 and 1913. But the term "teenager" was first widely introduced to Americans in the 1940s as a social classification coined by advertisers looking to sell products to new customers. The concept of a youth culture began to develop in the 1920s during the Jazz Age—the writer F. Scott Fitzgerald leading the way—but during the Depression and World War II, young Americans were expected to put aside indulgence for the sake of the nation's well-being.

But in the 1950s, a distinct teen culture emerged, enabled by television programs and movies such as *Rebel Without a Cause*. Postchild but pre-adult Americans sought to distance themselves from their "stodgy," "not-cool" parents by turning to rock and roll music, dating, and high school dance parties.[53]

In 1950 Harvard professor Erik Erikson, a student of Sigmund Freud who focused on ego psychology, wrote about the stages of life, each with its own challenge for the individual to surmount. He thus provided a way to think about what was happening to baby boomers in the 1950s and 1960s as they grew closer to adulthood and the assumption of full social autonomy as responsible persons.[54]

Erikson proposed that each person traveled through different stages of challenge and growth from birth to death. At each stage the challenge met and mastered—or not—would result in the individual developing one or another internalized personality disposition or aptitude.

The first stage is to learn to trust or to be mistrustful.

The second stage is to ratify personal agency or feel shame and doubt about oneself and one's prospects.

The third stage is mastery of initiative or refraining out of guilt.

The fourth stage is becoming industrious or slacking off out of inferiority.

The fifth stage is forming an ego-identity or experiencing role confusion.

The sixth stage is being capable of intimacy or preferring isolation.

The seventh stage is adulthood—making a difference (generativity) or not (stagnation).

The eighth stage is in late maturity—finding ego integrity or living with despair.

Most famously and consequentially, Erikson spoke of a fifth stage in life's progress, a stage of identity formation or identity confusion. This stage usually arrives in a person's journey through the years, said Erikson, with genital and sexual maturation.

> The growing and developing youths, faced with the physiological revolution within them, and with tangible adult tasks ahead of them are now primarily concerned with what they appear to be in the eyes of others as compared to what they feel they are, and with the question of how to connect the roles and skills cultivated earlier with the occupational prototypes of the day. . . . The sense of ego identity, then, is the accrued confidence that the inner sameness and continuity prepared in the past are matched by the sameness and continuity of one's meaning for others, as evidenced in the tangible promise of a "career."[55]

Thus, Erikson provided a window into that phase of personal maturation that exposes every individual to other-direction.

If the individual ended up with a secure ego-identity, his or her subsequent states of life would be more rewarding and reassuring. But if the individual passed through the state of identity formation without forming a resilient ego-identity, then he or she was at risk for identity dysphoria, alienation from themselves and others, self-destructive thoughts and behaviors, lack of intimacy, and, in later adulthood, despair.

According to Erikson,

> The adolescent mind is essentially a mind of the moratorium, a psychological stage between childhood and adulthood, and between the morality learned by the child, and the ethics to be developed by the adult. It is an ideological mind—and indeed, it is the ideological outlook of a society that speaks most clearly

to the adolescent who is eager to be affirmed by his peers, and
is ready to be confirmed by rituals, creeds, and programs.[56]

A stereotype supported by studies of brain development emerged of
an adolescent before forming a satisfactory adult identity as being more
likely to act on impulse, misread or misinterpret social cues and emotions,
get into accidents of all kinds, get involved in fights, engage in dangerous
or risky behavior, and be less likely to 1) think before they act, 2) pause
and consider the consequences of their actions, and 3) change their dangerous or inappropriate behaviors.[57]

Thus, identity confusion or unresolved identity formation is very
debilitating for the individual and exposes them to continuing unhappiness and insecurity.

Erikson proposed that a healthy personality possesses an "ego-identity" as an "inner capital," providing the individual with inner sameness
and continuity with which to navigate with confidence and success the
ebbs and flows of fortune in this sandpaper world.[58] Failure to acquire an
ego-identity is to live with identity diffusion. Erickson quoted the character Biff in Arthur Miller's play *Death of a Salesman*, saying, "I just can't
take hold, Mom, I can't take hold of some kind of life."

Erikson worried that American youth confronted special challenges
in building out their ego-identities because American culture—
decentralized and individualistic—insisted on self-made identities. Establishing your quite personal ego-identity becomes work—at times, hard
work—when you are navigating through social and familial crosswinds.
An ego-identity is not a commodity you can buy and put on as a passing
fashion fleetingly in vogue.[59]

Transitory identifications—with others, with styles and modes of
speech and social acting, and with fictional heroes, heroines, and other
wannabes—cannot cohere into a lifelong, healthy configuration of personal capacity and self-confidence.

With respect to baby boomers, they had more freedom to choose their identities than any previous generation in America or elsewhere, leaving open the important question of how well they, in general, succeeded in finding healthy and generative personal identities to carry them forward through the 1980s, the 1990s, and the opening decades of the twenty-first century until today.

We may also ask how well their identity formations psychologically equipped them to parent their children—members of Gen X and the millennials—who, with baby boomers, now make up the vast majority of Americans.

Of all the events during their years of identity formation, the Vietnam War and the American failure to prevent the 1975 Communist conquest of South Vietnam may have had the most negative impact on baby boomer ego-identities.

The young men of military age, especially the sons of the Greatest Generation, refused to serve in the Vietnam War. They easily found draft deferments by attending postgraduate schools. Thus, they developed identities in which patriotism and service to country were not highly valued, identities that had a need to justify rejection of their government and its values.

As noted above, my 1967 graduating class of Harvard College comprised some 1,200 young men, most of whom by now have spent their lives and careers as part of the country's Overclass elite. Of those men, only about 10 and perhaps a few more served in Vietnam. The rest never experienced war.

Americans seeking ego-identity formation after the defeat of our efforts to protect the Vietnamese nationalists had to process belonging to a nation that had failed in a costly undertaking begun with good intentions. After April 1975, identifying as an American was not as personally reassuring as it had been before.

Of tragic note is the fact that the conquest of South Vietnam by the Communists with massive support from the Soviet Union and the People's Republic of China was secretly orchestrated by Henry Kissinger in 1971 without authorization from his president, Richard Nixon.[60] Kissinger, of course, was a paradigm of the modern American Overclass—he used his Harvard professorship as an entrée into the political and social elite of New York City and then, with their connections and his own networking into a position at the White House under President Nixon. Later, Kissinger was secretary of state and afterward became a very wealthy man as a professional consultant and bestower of policy noblesse oblige on those who courted his favor and patronage.

However, as Nixon's national security advisor, Kissinger was other-directed. He was slippery and disingenuous with his president. He listened to Jean Sainteny, the French colonial official who, in 1946, really did more than anyone else to create Ho Chi Minh as the "leader" of all the Vietnamese people. He heard loud and clear the arguments of the antiwar movement that Americans should get out "now" from the Vietnam War.

So in 1971 he secretly, without telling Nixon, proposed to the Russian, Vietnamese, and Chinese Communists that Hanoi could leave its army inside South Vietnam after signing a peace treaty promising to stop the war and leave South Vietnam alone. Further, after a truce of some years, Hanoi could then use that army to conquer the South, as the Americans would have withdrawn their forces and would not oppose such a conquest. And so history happened just as Kissinger proposed it could.

Thus, among his accomplishments as an immigrant to America, Henry Kissinger could count making a major contribution to the loss of American national self-confidence and the rise of systemic identity dysphoria among many Americans no longer so sure of who they were or should be.

In 1983, Nixon sent me a short personal letter commenting on the "New Class" to which Kissinger belonged. I had cultivated and befriended Nixon so that he might come to trust me and tell me frankly what he knew about Kissinger's 1971 decision to abandon the South Vietnamese nationalists and let Hanoi win the Vietnam War at the end of the day.

Nixon wrote me, "This is just a note to tell you that I thought your 1980 memo on 'the New Class' was profoundly perceptive. I have been harping on this theme for years and lectured the Cabinet and White House staff on it over and over—to little avail."

RICHARD NIXON

March 31, 1983

26 FEDERAL PLAZA
NEW YORK CITY

Dear Stephen,

This is just a note to tell you that I thought your 1980 memo on "The New Class" was profoundly perceptive.

I have been harping on this theme for years and lectured the Cabinet and White House staff on it over and over - to little avail.

I suggest you read my observation in <u>The Real War</u> - the paragraph beginning at the bottom of page 244 which puts the blame for the tragedy of Vietnam where it belongs.

Please send me anything more you write on this subject.

With warm regards,

Sincerely,

Mr. Stephen B. Young
Hamline University School of Law
St. Paul, Minnesota   55104

In 2021 a very angry Helen Andrews published *Boomers*, an excoriating book that critically deconstructs the supposed social value contributed by the baby boomer generation to the American experiment in ordered liberty. She was unforgiving in her disdain. Her methodology was to call into question the reputations for doing good of six notable boomers: Steve Jobs, Aaron Sorkin, Jeffrey Sachs, Camille Paglia, Al Sharpton, and Sonia Sotomayor.

In her preface she sets out her agenda.

> I wanted to figure out where the boomers had really departed from historical norms and done irreparable harm to Western civilization, versus where they just happened to be lucky or millennials unlucky. . . . Boomers didn't just shake up the nuclear family. They broke it.[61]

Andrews concluded that the "essence of boomerness" was that, although they tried to liberate us, they left behind chaos instead of freedom.

Their birthright, she avers, was a "lifelong sense that the world was made just for them."

> For all their claims to be women's greatest liberators, it would be hard to convince an impartial observer that boomer feminism has left women better off when one in five white women are on anti-depressants. Feminism, for the boomers, mostly meant channeling women into paid employment on an unprecedented scale. . . . [N]ever in American history did women outnumber men in the labor force until January 2020. Boomers promised that employment was the only way for women to be fulfilled and independent, when any socialist could have told them that there is no one more dependent than a wage worker.[62]

She complains that the boomer mentality was shaped mostly by commercial TV programs, an experience she counts as "optimized to rot the human brain," adding that Silicon Valley's invention and commercialization of the smartphone made "a world that gives free rein to the boomer's worst instincts."[63]

And she is not happy that "[a]ll of America's coastal cities have become playgrounds for well-credentialed meritocrats and the casual workers who serve them, and both sides of the divide are putting off marriage and kids later and later."[64] Nor were the baby boomers prudent: They have more debt than other people in history.[65]

Andrews passes on that the baby boomers were the first generation to define themselves by what they consumed and not by what they produced. How perfect an example of John Glubb's notion that the decadence associated with money and wealth destroys greatness in a people.

In keeping with Andrews's insight on baby boomers relying on possessions to boost and anchor their self-esteem, Jennifer Wilson at *The New Yorker* reported that in 2024 clinging to possessions—accumulating clutter—expresses an American dependency on self-definition through appropriation of significant things. It is our things, not ourselves, that now anchor Americans as persons with meaningful substance. One-third of American homeowners report having garages too cluttered for parking their cars. A total of 11% of Americans own self-storage units, and there are more self-storage facilities than the combined total of Starbucks, McDonald's, Dunkin' Donuts, and Pizza Hut locations.[66]

Another remarkable social trend reflecting other-direction was the commercial success of Taylor Swift. Her company reported total sales of $2,077,618,725 for her 2024 Eras Tour. Her devoted female fans—"Swifties," including my granddaughter—internalize her identity of feeling hurt and slighted by unreciprocated other-direction. Swift's lyrics complain of taking another into one's emotional inner sanctum, only to be canceled, abandoned, or scorned.

In politics, Andrews complains that "the boomers persuaded everybody that transformational leadership was the only kind worth admiring, which left transactional leadership, the kind that bargains and compromises, with a low reputation that it did not deserve."[67] Those who want to transform tend to vilify those who stand in their way and easily ride roughshod over those who get in their way, all of which is very elitist and disrespectful of persons generally. Andrews accurately noted that "transformational leaders can let their rhetoric run away with them in a way transactional leaders, tethered to reality, can't."[68] This brings to my mind Congressperson Alexandria Ocasio-Cortez, not a boomer but of the Overclass, having a degree from Boston University, where she majored in economics and international relations. Another Overclass, other-directed, self-styled "transformational" leader we might note is Zohran Mamdani, the very glib, media-savvy, Democratic Socialist who won the 2025 New York City mayoral election. Mamdani's mother made her money producing movie narratives. He attended the Bronx High School of Science and the quite Overclass Bowdoin College.

Furthermore, the boomers contributed to the cultural breakdown of the American Congress, to its inability to get legislation passed except in the form of very expensive omnibus bills running to several thousand pages of provisions. More debt thus incurred, but this debt was public and so never showed up on individual or family balance sheets and was to be paid off by future generations.

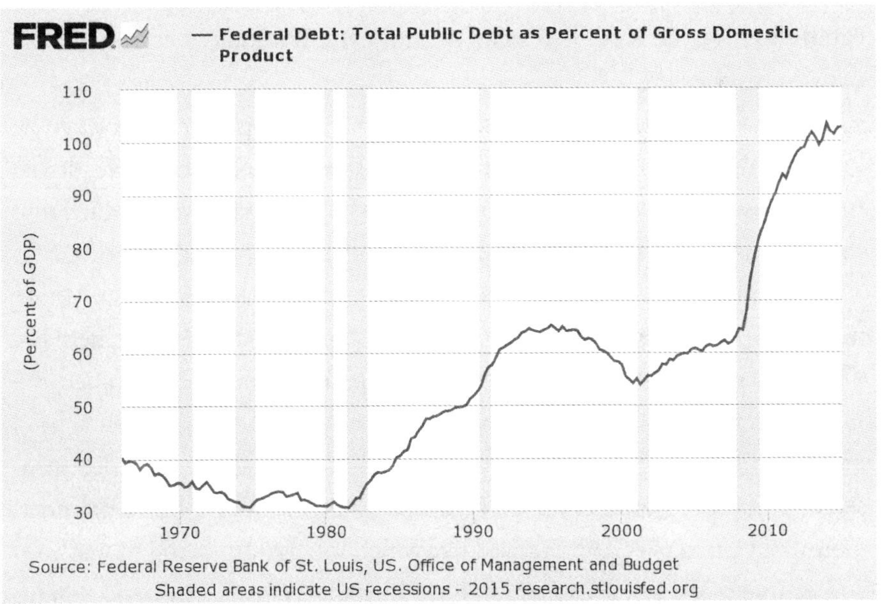

To add insult to injury, Americans have become a people who can't win their wars and most likely won't be able to pay their debts, public and private.

Historian Niall Ferguson recently invoked what he calls his own personal law of history: "Any great power that spends more on debt service (interest payments on the national debt) than on defense will not stay great for very long. True of Habsburg Spain, true of ancien régime France, true of the Ottoman Empire, true of the British Empire, this law is about to be put to the test by the U.S. beginning this very year." Indeed, the Congressional Budget Office projects that, in part because of rising interest rates, the federal government will spend $892 billion during the 2024 fiscal year for interest payments on the accumulated national debt of $28 trillion—meaning that interest payments now surpass the amount spent on defense and nearly match spending on Medicare.[69]

David Brooks's 2024 critique of the American educated class points to what the boomers accomplished. "American adults who identify as very progressive skew white, well-educated, and urban, and hail from relatively advantaged backgrounds. This is the contradiction of the educated class. Virtue is defined as being anti-elite. But today's educated class constitutes the elite."[70]

Brian Cabana for the *American Thinker* made a similar point when he looked at the current American elite as a new breed—an Anxiety Elite, driven by preconscious anxiety first to look inward but also perceive outward that the world is a constellation of threats and prospects for exploitation.

Consider the accuracy of Andrew's case against the boomers by looking at the character and accomplishments of the boomer presidents— Clinton, George W. Bush, Obama, Trump, and Biden. Each joined the Overclass. Clinton went to Georgetown University and Yale Law School and was a Rhodes Scholar at Oxford. George W. Bush credentialed himself at Yale College and Harvard Business School. Barack Obama attended Columbia University and Harvard Law School. Trump made money and so became a TV celebrity, which gave him Overclass status. Joe Biden's entrée into the Overclass was less distinguished, having only attended the University of Delaware and earning a law degree from Syracuse University, but he was exceptionally other-directed.

With respect to service in Vietnam during the war, Clinton had apparently agreed to join the ROTC as a way of avoiding being drafted into service during the Vietnam War but later reneged on that promise when his draft lottery number ensured that he would not be selected; George W. Bush joined the 147th Fighter-Interceptor Group of the Texas Air National Guard on May 27, 1968, stating in his autobiography that he was willing to serve his country but preferred to do so as a combat pilot rather than as "[a]n infantryman wading across a paddy-field"; Donald Trump received a "1-Y" medical deferment, which meant he could only be drafted in a national emergency because of a foot condition; and after a medical exam in April 1968, Joe Biden received the "1-Y" classification. Biden released his Selective Service records to the Associated Press in 2008. At the time a spokesperson said he was "disqualified from service because of asthma as a teenager."

Are we proud of any of them?

Oh, by the way, most baby boomers—my generation—never personally affirmed any covenantal responsibility to serve the American people.

What has happened to Americans socially and psychologically as they have separated into the opposing inner-directed and other-directed dispositions may help explain the difference in self-awareness of mental-health ease and dis-ease between conservatives (more likely to be inner-directed) and liberals (more likely to be members of the Overclass and other-directed).

Data collected from the 2022 Cooperative Election Study by Tufts University and reported by statistician and political commentator Nate Silver reveals that, among voters who said their mental health was poor, 45% identified as politically liberal and just 19% were conservatives. Conversely, those who said they had excellent mental health identified as conservative 51% of the time, while 20% were liberal.[71]

CHAPTER 4

THEORY OF THE OVERCLASS: FROM ROUSSEAU TO TODAY

For decades, the rules of the road in American politics
have been set by a monolithic progressive establishment
that has boasted something akin to a monopoly
in political media, academia, Hollywood and the federal bureaucracy.
This single-note chorus has not only produced a laundry list of myths,
but threatened those who challenge it with professional and social ruin.

Isaac Schorr, *New York Post*[1]

The rise of the modern overlord class started with a thought experiment. Jean-Jacques Rousseau supposed (1) that the evil we experience in life comes from unequal ownership of property, and (2) that right-minded leaders could remove inequality from our societies, cultures, and politics.

The irony that would attach itself to Rousseau's romanticism over the following 250 years would be that his ideas for putting an end to inequality within human communities would instead lead to the rise of a very hegemonic overlord class asserting its rights to enjoy unquestioned fealty from all those unworthy of inclusion in its ranks of professional managers.

But for Rousseau, the assertion of personal dominion over wealth—whether it be land, money, machinery, corporate authority, or the labor of others—brought forth evil in the world. In this he did not theologically stray too far from the book of Genesis, in which we are told that the fall of Adam and Eve from grace turned loose upon creation sinful conceit and the ambition to become overlords.

> The first man who, having enclosed a piece of ground, bethought himself of saying *This is mine*, and found people simple enough to believe him, was the real founder of civil society. From how many crimes, wars and murders, from how many horrors and misfortunes might not any one have saved mankind, by pulling up the stakes, or filling up the ditch, and crying to his fellows: "Beware of listening to this impostor; you are undone if you once forget that the fruits of the earth belong to us all, and the earth itself to nobody."[2]

Without a second thought, Rousseau asserted that "the love of well-being is the sole motive of human actions."[3] He continued,

> . . . the thirst of raising their respective fortunes, not so much from real want as from the desire to surpass others, inspired all men with a vile propensity to injure one another. . . . In a word there arose rivalry and competition on the one hand, and conflicting interests on the other, together with a secret desire on both of profiting at the expense of others. All these evils were the first effects of property, and the inseparable attendants of growing inequality.[4]

We could, he proposed, agree with one another on how best to run our society. We would each equally subordinate ourselves to an all-powerful legislator who would devise a moral vision for our society, disconnected from property and ownership. That moral vision Rousseau called the "General Will."

Let us, in a word, instead of turning our forces against ourselves, collect them in a supreme power which may govern us by wise laws, protect and defend all members of the association, repulse their common enemies, and maintain eternal harmony among us.[5]

Such an act of association, Rousseau insisted, "creates a moral and collective body, composed of as many members as the assembly contains voters, and receiving from this act its unity, its common identity, its life, and its will."[6]

Rousseau proposed that the essential term of this social contract of all with all would be as follows:

Each of us puts his person and all his power in common under the supreme direction of the general will, and, in our corporate capacity, we receive each member as an indivisible part of the whole.[7]

Thus, Rousseau's theory provided for equality of status without regard to property.

What he also put forward was the ideal of the modern sovereign state.

To keep us all equal, the general will would take over our minds and hearts and so keep us orderly and well behaved. In modern terms we would call any such general will a "discourse regime." We would confine our thinking loyally and obediently to those frames of understanding—implicit biases—that were taught to us by the state. Our thinking, which takes place through an internal mental "discourse" using language, would align with a governing regime.

Rousseau therefore insisted that where a person's "particular" will—that individual's personal moral code—conflicted with the general will, force would be necessary to repress that person. Thus was proposed the modern totalitarian state. Whenever our own particular internal "discourse" would diverge from the regime's preferred "discourse," the regime was empowered to drag us back into conformity with its own truth.

> Now, the less the relation the particular wills have to the general will, that is morals and manners to laws, the more should the repressive force be increased. The government, then, to be good should be proportionally stronger as the people is more numerous.[8]

Rousseau thus converted every person living under a society's general will into a subject of the sovereign. The rights and duties of each subject were dictated by the sovereign according to the moral precepts of its supervisory general will.

The primary social function of the subject was scrupulous obedience—in every detail. The axial principle of every Rousseauist society was the performance by individuals of their civic responsibilities as mandated by the general will. Rousseau thus provided a design template for hierarchical structural functionality—in short, modern bureaucracy. Rousseauist social structures thus put a premium on compliant performative excellence in acting out one's duties as prescribed by the general will.

The moral hazard created when role performance before an audience becomes the criteria for approval and advancement is a separation of the performance from the core values of the person hired to perform. A possible failure of authenticity on the part of the actor, a risk of phoniness, easily comes about. The player in a Rousseauist sitcom is tempted to take the easy way out—to mimic others, to go through perfunctory motions, and to read someone else's script. It is often the case across cultures that bureaucrats are said to be shortsighted, apathetic, careless, disinterested, inattentive, indifferent, mechanical, routine, and stereotyped—that their thoughts and recommendations are trite, risk averse, in the managerial spirit of going along to get along.

But in any Rousseauist power hierarchy, civic responsibility has its advantages. The conforming person gets recognition and is advanced by superiors. A role is thus a positional good—a good in limited supply and valuable to the individual for providing elevated status and celebrated reputational distinction.

Foreshadowing the ever-present factional rivalries over access to positional goods inherent in every modern sovereign state, Rousseau warned,

> . . . the greater the force with which the government ought to be endowed for keeping the people in hand, the greater too should be the force at the disposal of the Sovereign for keeping the government in hand.[9]

Thus, the government, for Rousseau the legitimate epicenter of society's bureaucratic administration, was always to be chained to the morality and policies of the general will.

With his proposal for a general will to guide the sovereign, Rousseau actually opened the door to a revival of Gnostic religiosity, one befitting the modern sovereign state. The first Gnostics had been influenced by Persian Zoroastrian thinking in the first centuries after Christ. The Zoroastrian faith proposed that life was a fight to the death between the power of good and the power of evil. The New Testament book of Revelations was influenced by this bipolar antagonism of forces in its telling of the struggle between Gog and Magog.

One important tenet of every Gnostic faith is that the material world we inhabit is dangerous and evil. We can read in the Old Testament Book of Genesis a parable on the origin of an ever-present Gnostic temptation in our lives. There, the story relates that the devil successfully tempted Adam and Eve to eat of the tree of knowledge. Once they did so, they became aware of good and evil. Once expelled from Eden, Adam and Eve and their progeny down to us today carried with them a propensity to act on this learning—first, to believe that evil exists, and second, to resist it by activating knowledge of the good.

The second important tenet of Gnostic faiths is that knowledge—gnosis—can empower us to fight and extinguish evil. But to triumph we each need to learn how to think correctly about the reality in which we live.

In this Gnostic tradition, Rousseau proposed,

> There is, therefore, a purely civil profession of faith of which the Sovereign should fix the articles, not exactly as religious dogmas, but as social sentiments without which a man cannot be a good citizen or a faithful subject. While it can compel no one to believe them, it can banish from the State whoever does not believe them—it can banish him, not for impiety, but as an anti-social being, incapable of truly loving the laws and justice, and of sacrificing, at need, his life to his duty. If anyone, after publicly recognizing these dogmas, behaves as if he does not believe them, let him be punished by death; he has committed the worst of all crimes, that of lying before the law.[10]

Rousseau's proposed gnosis, the privileged knowledge that would keep us safe from the evil of inequality, was embedded in the general will. The sovereign and its government, constantly enforcing the general will, would be teachers of that privileged wisdom. The sovereign and its government would, therefore, be the supreme teacher of all citizens as to the correct gnosis as commanded by the general will.

Rousseau's theory was put into practice by the Jacobins in the French Revolution. For the Jacobins, the general will was reason itself. Those expert in reasoning would guide French citizens in all things. They would use the national legislature to mandate right conduct.

The August 27, 1789, Declaration of the Rights of Man and of the Citizen in its concepts of social justice adopted several foundational ideas advanced by Rousseau.

3. The source of all sovereignty resides essentially in the nation; no group, no individual may exercise authority not emanating expressly therefrom. . . .

6. Law is the expression of the general will; all citizens have the right to concur personally or through their representatives, in its formation; it must be the same for all, whether it protects or punishes. . . .

12. The guarantee of the rights of man and citizen necessitates a public force.[11]

Differences of opinion divided leaders of the revolution. One faction, the Jacobins, came to dominate the National Assembly in June 1793. They adopted a republican constitution but suspended it in September, implementing a reign of terror under the direction of a Committee of Public Safety.

On May 7, 1794, a decree established something of a "state church" for the worship of the Supreme Being. The decree declared that the French people recognized that worship of the Supreme Being is the observance of the duties of man and placed at the forefront of such duties detestation of bad faith and tyranny and punishment of tyrants and traitors.

Where wrong thinking caused opposition to the laws and the rulers, punishment was imposed. The Law of 22 Prairial (passed on June 10, 1794, and also known as the Law of the Great Terror) established a Revolutionary Tribunal to "punish the enemies of the people." Among those specified as enemies of the people were those who

- sheltered conspirators and aristocrats,
- abused the principles of the Revolution,

- deceived the people in order to lead them into undertakings contrary to the interests of liberty,
- inspired discouragement in order to favor the enterprises of tyrants leagued against the Republic,
- disseminated false news in order to divide or disturb the people, and
- sought to mislead opinion and to prevent the instruction of the people, to deprave morals and to corrupt the public conscience, or to impair the energy and the purity of revolutionary and republican principles.

The penalty for all such offenses was death.

Any evidence that might influence the minds of the jurors could be presented to them to assist them in seeking the triumph of the republic and the ruin of its enemies. If either material or moral proof was presented, no more witnesses would be called. The standard for finding guilt was the conscience of the jurors, enlightened by love of the fatherland.

Here was the general will imposed on the French people by state terror.

After the Jacobins were rejected and driven from power, Napoleon stepped up with support from the army to seize sovereign powers and then organize the first modern administrative state. He centralized authority in one national bureaucracy. Importantly he created elite schools in Paris to train administrators to manage that bureaucracy. The "grandes écoles," as they came to be called, provided certification that an individual was qualified to join the governing class of right-thinking administrators.

Awed by Napoleon's military and civil achievements, the young German philosopher Georg Wilhelm Friedrich Hegel imagined and planned, with Napoleon as his model legislator, how a state administration could put into practice Rousseau's Gnostic vision of social justice. For Hegel the state became apotheosized as God, with its administrators becoming a hierarchy of selfless, dedicated priests.

Reading Hegel in English translation is like viewing a kaleidoscope—the shiny little pieces are in constant movement but simultaneously remain part of a complex whole. To focus on the discrete is to miss his big picture, but to contemplate the big picture is to miss how its component parts shape one another. Or Hegel is the orchestra conductor brilliantly cognizant of all the notes, tempos, melodies, and harmonies, while the listener can't take it in all at once.

I therefore simplified my search for his meaning using the duality suggested by Jürgen Habermas of normativity and facticity. For Habermas, we live in two different spheres of reality—one is mental, a realm of ideas, thoughts, values, words, meanings, and concepts, and the other is material, factual, physically real, and not imagined. To the contrary, Hegel held out the promise of absolute integration of mind and matter, idea and action.

We access the realm of normativity through insight, intuition, induction, and by inventing words and concepts (*Begriff* in Hegel's German) to sustain and communicate our thinking. For Hegel our aspiration in living must be to have nothing more uppermost in our minds than the inherent necessity of a notional concept (*Begriff*). All other points of view must vanish.[12]

A more commonsense approach to understanding Hegel's *Begriffs* was suggested by American sociologist Daniel Bell. He called these features of normativity "axial principles," proposing, "[T]he idea of axial principles and structures is an effort to specify not causation—this can only be done in a theory of empirical relationships—(what Habermas calls 'facticity') but centrality. Looking for the answer to the question how a society hangs together, it seeks to specify, within a conceptual schema, the *organizing* frame around which the other institutions are draped, or the *energizing* principle that is a primary logic for all the others."[13]

Two other contemporary parallels to Hegel's *Begriffs* are the concept of paradigm in science, a schema that defines what must be included in our understanding of the truth, and the concept of gestalt in psychology, where individual beliefs, perceptions, and actions are all part of one consolidated "big picture." Both paradigms and gestalts provide rational coherence and systemic interdependencies among the various parts of a whole.

But as Habermas explains and Bell accepts, we humans can access both realms of normativity and facticity—our minds grab the ideas located in normativity but also experience the reality that is facticity, thanks to our sense perceptions. As living persons, we connect idea with action and action with idea and form with function and function with form. We are thinkers and designers—practical social architects. We are the epicenter of absolute existential wholeness, embracing at once the *A*, which is the universal and the divine, and the *B*, which is the particular and the mundane. We are thus otherworldly and this-worldly, being both together at the same time and all at once, or more one or the other by turns as we choose, depending on what we are doing or thinking.

The *Begriff* for Hegel was a knowledge-based hypothesis about reality—a possible truth for us to affirm and trust as self-evident. The mental process used to select hypotheses was called "abduction" by American philosopher Charles Pierce and is used today in design theory. Jesuit moral philosopher Bernard Lonergan called it "insight." The duty of the human person in Hegel's scheme is to take the *Begriff*, which arises in the mind and conform reality to it. Hegel thus provided access for a rational opinion about the world order, a gnosis-based religiosity, to shape the social, cultural, economic, and political architecture of modernity as it was emerging in his time and would continue to evolve during the following centuries.

In commenting on the 2024 American presidential election campaign, the cultural critic Roger Kimball put his rejection of thinking within the confines of Hegelian *Begriffs* this way:

Back in 2020, I wrote a column on "The Democratic Art of Magical Thinking." Magical thinking, I explained, "is the irrational belief, rampant among primitive peoples and those exposed to too many woke college seminars, that our thoughts influence or 'constitute' reality."

. . . How did the magical thinking arise in the first place? One source is the habit of credulity that is a by-product of all utopian thought. . . .

The other chief source is the attack on objective truth that, in various ways, has been the gospel proclaimed by fancy professors for the past several decades. Students everywhere are taught to be suspicious of truth, to proclaim the relativity of values. This is a brain-addling teaching, but one that you would have to look far and wide to find a place it hasn't reached.

As I noted in that earlier column on magical thinking, epistemic nihilism is the order of the day in all the best colleges and universities. But the result is not so much a failure as a promiscuity of belief.[14]

Hegel culminates his thinking on the essential and eternal human experience with a theory of the state. He admired Rousseau but made the general will much more powerful and comprehensive, something possessing abstract, absolute universality and, simultaneously, absolutely dense activity in the realm of night and day. Hegel quickly put to one side actual states and governments, preferring to be "philosophical" and therefore concerned most for the ultimate idea of the state, the state first and foremost as a *Begriff*.

He wrote in *Elements of the Philosophy of Right*, "The merit of Rousseau's contribution to the search for this concept is that, by adducing the will as the principle of the state, he is adducing a principle which has thought both for its form and its content."[15] Hegel then criticizes Rousseau for regarding the "universal will" not as the will's rationality in and of itself but only as a "general" will arising from individual wills through contract. That made the idea of the state dependent on the arbitrary wills of individuals, their opinion and their capriciously given express consent. In contrast, Hegel envisioned the will of a state as sublime, self-actuating, undetermined by anything outside of itself, something to be perceived and not created by lesser particulars. Hegel called this "objective will"—freestanding and independent, always there, whether or not it is recognized by individuals and affirmed by their arbitrary wills.

We might suggest that for Hegel the state first created itself and then absorbed us into its meaning and purpose, his thinking being that "[t]he state is the divine will, in the sense that it is spirit present on earth, unfolding itself to be the actual shape and organization of a world. . . . One must therefore venerate the State as an earthly divinity."[16]

He added, "In the state, everything depends on the unity of the universal and particular. The power of the state is the unity between its own universal, rational end, and the particular interests of individuals. Individuals are united with the state through duties and rights. Particular interests should in truth not be set aside, or indeed suppressed; instead they should be harmonized with the universal so that both they and the universal are upheld. The individual fulfils his duties by performing tasks and services for the state, thus upholding and preserving the state."[17]

Regarding the work of the state through its subordinate bureaucracy, Hegel proposed, "The individual functionaries and agents are attached to their offices not on the strength of their immediate personality but only on the strength of their universal and objective qualities."[18] The state therefore rests on performance of functions. Functions are performed by officers. Officers are given functional authority based on their objective qualities—abilities, skills, and character. Hegel insisted that every officer of state must be educated and trained to execute a particular task.[19] Therefore, the model modern state must employ a class of specialists, not just anyone who might enjoy having a share of state power.

What employment by the state really requires is that officials shall forgo the selfish and capricious satisfaction of their subjective personal goals. By this sacrifice, they can find personal satisfaction in—but only in—the dutiful discharge of their public functions. The habit of adopting universal interests, specified points of view, and directed activities—all of which become a class consciousness and class characteristics—is thereby generated. Such officials need to be educated and conformed in thought and ethical conduct. Hegel considered officials as part of the middle class.[20]

For Hegel, a people without a state to manage them is just floating pieces of flotsam and jetsam. He warned that without a monarch and the articulation of the whole, the people is a formless mass and no longer a state.[21] He propounded the constitutional rule that "it is of the utmost importance that the masses be organized, because only so do they become a power or force. Otherwise, they are nothing but a heap, an aggregate of separate atoms."[22] For him legitimate power could only be obtained through the imposition of the most disciplined organization on a people.

Hegel's design concept for a God-State cannot meet Abraham Lincoln's criteria for a just government: "of the people, by the people, for the people."

Karl Marx and Friedrich Engels

In their *Communist Manifesto* of 1848, Karl Marx and Friedrich Engels followed Rousseau in accusing the owners of property (whom they called capitalists) of causing social injustice. Their remedy for the evil arising from property was quite simple—put the state in charge of property and do away with owners. For them property was the means of production of wealth. They would put those means under the management of the workers reporting somehow to a state apparatus. Thus, for Marx and Engels, the class of proletarians would expel the capitalists and take state power for themselves.

Marx and Engels took Rousseau and Hegel's concept of the state as the supreme legislator and gave that state authority to the workers.

Whereas Hegel started with abstractions taken from the realm of concepts and philosophy, ingrained them in the state, and then had the state infuse them into social realities, Marx and Engels started with reality—the creation of wealth—and sought to change conditions of work so that such conditions would be ordered by their preferred normative principle. And with new *Begriffs* arising from their scientism, they actually proposed a new Gnostic spiritual teaching about evil in the world and how we must remove it once and for all time.

So in their secular "scripture," *The Communist Manifesto*, Marx and Engels ignored the modern state: "The history of all hitherto existing society is the history of class struggles. . . . Political power, properly so called, is merely the organized power of one class for oppressing another."

As Communists, Marx and Engels looked to classes as fundamental, leaving the state subservient to the interests of a ruling class.

> Freeman and slave, patrician and plebeian, lord and serf, guild-master and journeyman, in a word, oppressor and oppressed, stood in constant opposition to one another, carried on an uninterrupted, now hidden, now open fight, a fight that each time ended, either in a revolutionary reconstitution of society at large, or in the common ruin of the contending classes. . . . The modern bourgeois society that has sprouted from the ruins of feudal society has not done away with class antagonisms. It has but established new classes, new conditions of oppression, new forms of struggle in place of the old ones. . . . The bourgeoisie has at last, since the establishment of Modern Industry and of the world market, conquered for itself, in the modern representative State, exclusive political sway. The executive of the modern state is but a committee for managing the common affairs of the whole bourgeoisie.[23]

Thus, for Marx and Engels, the state was subordinate to the capitalist class and served its interests.

However, continue Marx and Engels, the capitalist mode of production—the factory system as explained by Adam Smith in his 1776 book *An Inquiry into the Nature and Causes of the Wealth of Nations*—had called into being a different social class—the proletarians, the workers who were the hands-on manufacturers of society's wealth. Thus, a struggle as to who would constitute the Overclass in modern, industrialized societies was underway—the proletarians seeking to free themselves from domination by the owners of capital, or the bourgeoisie. The Communists proposed to lead the struggle of the proletariat seeking to overthrow the political power of the bourgeoisie.

> A similar movement is going on before our own eyes. Modern bourgeois society, with its relations of production, of exchange and of property, a society that has conjured up such gigantic means of production and of exchange, is like the sorcerer who is no longer able to control the powers of the nether world whom he has called up by his spells. For many a decade past the history of industry and commerce is but the history of the revolt of modern productive forces against modern conditions of production, against the property relations that are the conditions for the existence of the bourgeois and of its rule.
>
> The Communists, therefore, are on the one hand, practically, the most advanced and resolute section of the working-class parties of every country, that section which pushes forward all others. . . . The immediate aim of the Communists is the same as that of all other proletarian parties: formation of the proletariat into a class, overthrow of the bourgeois supremacy, conquest of political power by the proletariat.[24]

Thus do Marx and Engels come around to meet Hegel face-to-face: they need the modern state to bring about social justice, only the state must be one that is created by and controlled by the proletariat.

> The proletariat will use its political supremacy to wrest, by degree, all capital from the bourgeoisie, to centralise all instruments of production in the hands of the State, i.e., of the proletariat organised as the ruling class.[25]

In keeping with Rousseau's opposition to inequality, Marx and Engels selected equality for all as their general will for the governing of the modern state.

> In place of the old bourgeois society, with its classes and class antagonisms, we shall have an association, in which the free development of each is the condition for the free development of all.[26]

In 1875 Marx would take issue with other German socialists. In his critique of a coalition platform, Marx would affirm,

> In a higher phase of communist society, after the enslaving subordination of the individual to the division of labor, and therewith also the antithesis between mental and physical labor, has vanished; after labor has become not only a means of life but life's prime want; after the productive forces have also increased with the all-around development of the individual, and all the springs of co-operative wealth flow more abundantly—only then can the narrow horizon of bourgeois right be crossed in its entirety and society inscribe on its banners: From each according to his ability, to each according to his needs![27]

In keeping with this optimistic vision of how their general will would bring about equality of condition among people, Marx and Engels expected the modern state to wither away.

> When, in the course of development, class distinctions have disappeared, and all production has been concentrated in the hands of a vast association of the whole nation, the public power will lose its political character.[28]

Thus, the state is only an instrument for the oppression of others by a ruling class; if there are no classes, there will be no need for a repressive state apparatus. Marx and Engels, with a naive enthusiasm, predicted the eventual dissolution of proletarian class consciousness and class solidarity.

> If the proletariat . . . makes itself the ruling class, and, as such, sweeps away by force the old conditions of production, then it will, along with these conditions, have swept away the conditions for the existence of class antagonisms and of classes generally, and will thereby have abolished its own supremacy as a class.[29]

Using this analysis of economic determinism as the supreme driver of human history, Marx and Engels expected the modern state to dissolve as it became a social arrangement no longer needed and thereby ultimately disappear from human history.

In Gnostic terms Marx and Engels placed responsibility for evil on capitalists and invented dialectical materialism or scientific socialism as the occult knowledge capable of driving such evil out of our world.

Marx was not alone in linking money with evil. In the New Testament, we read, "For the love of money is a root of all *kinds of* evil, for which some have strayed from the faith in their greediness, and pierced themselves through with many sorrows.[30]

But Marx's faith was gnostic. To give it intellectual substance and credibility, Marx would later write *Das Kapital* as the authoritative textbook revealing the special thinking needed to manage a proletarian regime of economic governance. In considering *Das Kapital* as a Gnostic source of knowledge, it seems inescapable to ignore Marx's conviction that evil in the world arises from money. At one point he even describes the "capitalist" as "Mr. Moneybags." In *The Communist Manifesto*, he and Engels had already raised an alarm about how wages—money—alienated workers from society and culture, referring to the relationship of the worker to the employer only as a contemptible, soul-destroying "cash nexus."

Ironically, fully in line with Hegel's theories, followers of Marx and Engels took their Communist *Begriff* about the bourgeoisie and the proletariat and put it into action through the mobilization of workers to take power away from capitalists. International organizations of workers were formed.

In time Communists would take power in the Soviet Union. This Marxist doctrine portraying monied interests as enemies of the working class assumed its fullest expression when Soviet leader Joseph Stalin issued the order for the kulaks (who were mere peasants but property-owning peasants) to be liquidated as a class. An estimated 6.5 million mostly Ukrainian peasants perished during the state-made famine of 1932 to 1933.

Friedrich Nietzsche

A younger contemporary of Marx and Engels was Friedrich Nietzsche (1844–1900). Nietzsche wrote with insight and fervor, exposing darkness in human nature and turning the European Enlightenment's ideal of rationality on its head. So, for example, for Nietzsche, Rousseau's general will might have no more truthfulness than the particular will of an individual. What either, or any, will might decide to advocate might be no more than a narrative, perhaps even a fiction.

Nietzsche's contumacious transposition of rational thought into no more than narrative had been presciently preceded by Lewis Carroll in *Through the Looking-Glass, and What Alice Found There.*

> "When I use a word," Humpty Dumpty said in rather a scornful tone, "it means just what I choose it to mean—neither more nor less."
>
> "The question is," said Alice, "whether you can make words mean so many different things."
>
> "The question is," said Humpty Dumpty, "which is to be master—that's all."
>
> . . .
>
> "You seem very clever at explaining words, Sir," said Alice. "Would you kindly tell me the meaning of the poem called 'Jabberwocky'?"
>
> "Let's hear it," said Humpty Dumpty. "I can explain all the poems that ever were invented—and a good many that haven't been invented just yet."
>
> This sounded very hopeful, so Alice repeated the first verse:
>
> "'Twas brillig, and the slithy toves
> Did gyre and gimble in the wabe:
> All mimsy were the borogoves,
> And the mome raths outgrabe."[31]

Nonsensical to most of us but very sensible indeed to Humpty Dumpty as he went on to tell Alice what all those words meant.

In the late 1880s, this brilliant but tormented German thinker would throw a challenge at modernity building its civilization around Hegel's God-State of sovereign authority. Nietzsche would ask who, if anyone, can vouch for the legitimacy of the sovereign, the God-State.

His answer was simple and effective: whoever has enough police power to assert and sustain state authority over any objections to its legitimacy.

For Nietzsche, no *Begriff*, no grand "idea," and no value choice could ever be taken as "true" and eternal. Anything created by one mind could be dismissed out of hand by another mind. The only criteria applicable in the world to privilege one idea or value over another was power, the power to believe in what you want and the power to impose your will on others.

Nietzsche made no exception for science or natural law or an innate human moral conscience. All such conceptions were, to his mind, potentially illusory and always vulnerable to critique and rejection.

To a degree we can assimilate Nietzsche's advocacy of every *Begriff* as nothing other than the implementation of someone's will to power to the thinking of Karl Marx and Friedrich Engels in *The Communist Manifesto*. There, Marx and Engels proposed that your ideology—your superstructure—flows out of your class status—your substructure. Capitalists naturally espouse "capitalism," and proletarians naturally internalize the thinking of "socialism." Thus, to modernize Marxism along the lines suggested by Nietzsche, we can confirm that "what you think" depends on "who you think you are" or "who you want to be."

Not coincidentally, contemporary feminist "standpoint theory" applies Nietzsche's insight to the process of some people "marginalizing" others.

In *Thus Spoke Zarathustra*, Nietzsche gloried in his unique access to truth, dismissing the rights of others to rebuke him.

> But nevertheless I walk with my thoughts above their heads; and even should I walk on mine own errors, still would I be above them and their heads.
>
> For men are not equal: so speaketh justice. And what I will, they may not will!
>
> Thus spake Zarathustra.[32]

Recent work in psychology has brought to our attention the many ways our minds work to keep us confined within the imaginative space of our own "particular wills," thus confirming the general applicability of Nietzsche's sociology.

It is now accepted that our rationality has limits. In 1972 Amos Tversky and Daniel Kahneman introduced the notion of behavioral economics, where our cognitive biases shape our perceptions of reality and our judgments. Common cognitive biases are implicit bias or stereotyping others; confirmation bias, or hearing what confirms our existing opinions; affinity bias, or preferring the opinions of those like us; status quo bias; and the overconfidence effect.

In calling attention to cognitive limitations in our decision-making, Herbert Simon proposed that we are often guided by a "bounded rationality"—we make satisfactory choices, not optimal choices. He wrote, "[B]oundedly rational agents experience limits in formulating and solving complex problems and in processing (receiving, storing, retrieving, transmitting) information."[33]

Buddhist teachings also align with Nietzsche's skepticism that our minds can reliably, day in and day out, seek and find legitimating *Begriffs* deserving our absolute and unquestioned allegiance. In Buddhist realism we must become aware of having our own cognitive biases—afflicting emotions that cloud our perceptions and disturb our thinking. These emotions are greed, hate, delusion, conceit, wrong views, doubt, torpor, restlessness, shamelessness, and recklessness.

In his books *The Birth of Tragedy* and *The Genealogy of Morals*, Nietzsche proposed to focus on the origin of "our notions of good and evil." He wanted to learn how we constructed the value judgments *good* and *evil*, asking in addition "whether they have benefited or retarded mankind."[34] In the non-egotistical instincts of compassion, self-denial, and self-sacrifice, Nietzsche sensed "stagnation, nostalgic fatigue," and a "will that had turned against life." He therefore started a critique of all moral values, calling into question the intrinsic worth of those values.

He concluded that it was only the noble, the mighty, the highly placed, and the high-minded who could decree themselves and their actions to be good. The dominant temper of a higher, ruling class in relation to a lower, dependent class authorized the higher class to "create values and name them."[35]

Nietzsche then allocated some values to a "slave revolt" in morals, when the rancor of the subordinated turned creative and gave birth to values, yes, but not noble ones. Slave ethics, Nietzsche proposed, began by saying no to an other, a nonself, such negation being its creative act. All truly noble moral qualities, Nietzsche proposed, grow out of "triumphant self-affirmation."[36]

Nietzsche disparaged philosophers, scholars, and scientists as "men a long way from being free spirits because they still believe in truth."[37] Nietzsche completely pulls the rug out from under Hegel's enterprise of having the knowledgeable and the expert serving the God-State. For Nietzsche, such public servants do not, and could not ever, exist; those who would so serve would have bad values arising from an inverted, self-punishing will to power.[38] Nietzsche put it thus: "It does not augur well for a culture when the mandarins are in the saddle."[39]

Nietzsche also elaborated on these themes in *Beyond Good and Evil*, published in 1886, which argued that "the essence of the world is will to power."[40]

After Nietzsche, it has been irrational to believe that any Hegelian God-State will create a genuine heaven here on earth. Experiences with Adolf Hitler, Joseph Stalin, Mao Zedong, Fidel Castro, Pol Pot, Xi Jinping, Hamas, the Taliban, and Iranian ayatollahs confirm this conclusion.

From Nietzsche through the successive mediations of Martin Heidegger, Antonio Gramsci, Michel Foucault, Jacques Derrida, and others have come our contemporary cultural and political afflictions of critical legal studies, Critical Race Theory, and a feminist will to power. It turns out that all persons have that notable will to power, which Nietzsche proposed can be the valid source of our personal values. Women, too, have a will to power; so do African Americans and every tenured professor. And, following Nietzsche, no two persons ever need subordinate their will to power to each other—or to anyone else for that matter.

The doctrine of Critical Legal Theory is that there is no law, only power politics: Those with power command; those without obey. So if you don't like a rule of contract law, change it. If Supreme Court justices don't agree with you, get rid of them one way or another.

The doctrine of American Critical Race Theory is that good values may not be determined by people with white skins, a genetic marker of their European descent.

American feminism delivered on a cultural, social, and political program of marginalizing toxic masculinity.

Perhaps Nietzsche's wisdom can be summarized for us as a paraphrase of Shakespeare's disillusioned antihero, Macbeth.

> All our yesterdays have lighted fools the way to dusty death.
>
> Life is nothing but a tale told by an idiot—a walking shadow; a poor player who struts and frets his hour upon the stage and then is heard no more. Full of sound and fury, signifying nothing.[41]

The Nietzschean Conundrum

In Nietzsche's telling there was effectively no rational way to select one religious or Gnostic faith over another to serve as the chosen general will for a state. Ultimately, in his morality, those who control the state would determine its general will according to their value preferences.

In *The Birth of Tragedy* and *The Genealogy of Morals*, Nietzsche also helpfully exposed a powerful psychological dynamic creating Gnostic faiths. He called it "ressentiment"—the need of a "rancorous" person to demonize those who threaten the demonizer's insecure identity: "Imagine, on the other hand, the 'enemy' as conceived by the rancorous man! For this is his true achievement: he has conceived the 'evil enemy', the Evil One, as a fundamental idea [*Begriff*], and then as a pendant he has conceived the Good One—himself."[42] This process of sourcing personal fears in another and so empowering that other as a power in the world and then excoriating that other for wanting to live, Nietzsche called "ressentiment." For Marx and Engels, for example, the cosmic Evil One was the capitalist, and the redemptive Good Ones were the proletarians. This ressentiment of Marx and Engels gave rise to Communism and all its political and ideological offspring.

Nietzsche exposed the necessity of choice: A general will had to be chosen. But where there is choice, there must be ethics and morality—some normative standard preferring one approach over others. So for example, should the general will to be obeyed by a state and its subjects be theocratic, like the Ten Commandments given by the God Yahweh to the children of Israel? Or the Sharia rules derived from the divinely revealed text of the Quran? Or the Ariosophy inspiring Hitler's *Volksgemeinschaft* as the general will for the German people under their Third Reich? Or the natural law chosen by the signers of the American Declaration of Independence that the general will was to vindicate and protect individual rights to life, liberty, and the pursuit of happiness?

But having to make a choice implies having the power to choose. For Nietzsche there was complete freedom for anyone with power to impose their chosen will on the world. No holds barred. One could choose to be a utilitarian seeking the greatest good for the greatest number as however one would define the good. Or one could choose to be Kantian and insist on following his categorical imperative driven by universal abstract rationality. If one were Chinese, one would have to choose between Mencius and his principles of rightness and humaneness, or Mozi, who insisted on following the will of heaven as discovered by a divinely chosen emperor. The Chinese also had a third alternative of spiritual ego containment, an accommodation refusing to impose one's ego on time and space but rather seeking only to follow the dao—an equilibrium among natural forces at play in the cosmos.

Nietzsche's recognition of humanity's freedom of choice in thought and belief was also noted by Mozi (470–c. 391 BCE) in China. Mozi wrote,

> In the beginning of human life, when there was yet no law and government, the custom was "everybody according to his own idea." Accordingly each man had his own idea, two men had two different ideas and ten men had ten different ideas—the more people the more different notions. And everybody approved of his own view and disapproved the views of others, and so arose mutual disapproval among men. As a result, father and son and elder and younger brothers became enemies and were estranged from each other, since they were unable to reach any agreement. Everybody worked for the disadvantage of the others with water, fire, and poison. Surplus energy was not spent for mutual aid; surplus goods were allowed to rot without sharing; excellent teachings (Dao) were kept secret and not revealed. The disorder in the (human) world could be compared to that among birds and beasts.[43]

Choosing a general will to structure and discipline a state implicates design theory, where there is no science to tell us what is good and what is flawed. By what criteria can we say that one design is better than another? Beauty is in the eye of the beholder, is it not? What is one person's trash is another person's treasure. The flip assertion has been *De gustibus non est disputandum*—"You can't logically argue about tastes." I like Greek temples, you like Gothic churches, while someone else likes Chinese Buddhist pagodas.

Good design first is sensible and practical. It is also pleasing to the eye with proportion and form. I think the best design has a kind of flow and balance coupled with rigor. It is Zenlike—contained and yet open.

One of my favorite design projects is the rock garden at the Ryōan-ji Temple in Kyoto, Japan.

How then to best apply good design theory to the selection of a general will by which a people will be ruled? Which designer's particular will is to prevail in deciding what design concept shall be used?

Thus did Rousseau's recommendation for institutionalizing equality of each with all under a sovereign state, structurally engineered by Hegel in the form of the modern administrative state, bring forth disagreements, conflicts, and oppression of the weak by the strong.

With those responsible for creating and sustaining a general will—those state administrators authorized to supervise social justice, cultural achievement, and political felicity—having such a range of choices before them, the old question asked by Juvenal comes to mind—*Quis custodiet Ipsos custodes?* "Who will guard the guardians?"

Mikhail Bakunin

Mikhail Bakunin, a very intense Russian proponent of anarchism, saw through the idyllic proposals of Marx and Engels to better envision the human realities associated with possession of class power and state authority.

Bakunin questioned whether, in a Communist state as proposed by Marx and Engels, the proletariat would ever be in power. Rather, he predicted that a "new" class of professionals, experts, and bureaucrats—not workers in the factories—would arise to dominate the apparatus of government.

Bakunin's alternative was decentralized direct management of factories by workers themselves.

Bakunin, in effect, accepted the sociology of Nietzsche that power structures, even Socialist and Communist ones, could easily be manipulated by the will to power of the few and so would be turned against the interests of the many.

Bakunin understood what Lord Acton would write in 1887: "Power corrupts and absolute power corrupts absolutely." Acton would also opine, "[R]emember, where you have a concentration of power in a few hands, all too frequently men with the mentality of gangsters get control. History has proven that."

In his short essay *God and the State*, Bakunin presumed that the state would become God and repress individualism or that God would become manifest in the state and repress individualism. Either way, only perpetual resistance challenging society's rulers could preserve for individuals their freedoms and human dignity.

Bakunin had no use for Rousseau. He described the historical process of the French Revolution as making "use of lay priests, short-robed liars, and sophists, among whom the principal roles devolved upon two fatal men, one the falsest mind, the other the most doctrinally despotic will—J.J. Rousseau and Robespierre."

Rousseau, he said, was the "prophet of the doctrinaire state," breeding within himself "the pitiless despotism of the statesman."[44]

When God and the state became one, "all discussion ceases, and nothing remains but the triumphant stupidity of faith."[45]

> There is a class of people who, if they do not believe, must at least make a semblance of believing. This class, comprising all the tormentors, all the oppressors, and all the exploiters of humanity; priests, monarchs, statesmen, soldiers, public and private financiers, officials of all sorts, policemen, gendarmes, jailers and executioners, monopolists, capitalists, tax-leeches, contractors and landlords, lawyers, economists, politicians of all shades, down to the smallest vendor of sweetmeats, all will repeat in unison those word of Voltaire: "If God did not exist, it would be necessary to invent him."[46]

Here Bakunin reveals for us how secular Gnostic faiths—such as Communism, Maoism, Xi Jinping Thought, Fascism (ethnic

Volksgemeinschaft), postmodernist deconstruction, neoliberalism (*homo economicus*), feminism (toxic masculinity), the unbearable burden of Whiteness and White colonialism, effective altruism, artificial intelligence, and global warming—become great gods ruling over this world of ours. First, faithful believers capture the modern bureaucratic state and then use it to impose their occult knowledge about the sources of good and evil on all under their authority.

Bakunin then drew a damning parallel between the priests who believe in a god and the members of a learned academy—who were followers of a Gnostic faith.

> Suppose a learned academy, composed of the most illustrious representatives of science; suppose this academy charged with legislation for and the organization of society, and that, inspired only by the purest love of truth, it frames none but laws in absolute harmony with the latest discoveries of science. Well, I maintain, for my part, that such legislation and such organization would be a monstrosity, and that for two reasons: first, that human science is always and necessarily imperfect. . . . So that were we to try to force the practical life of men, collective as well as individual, into strict and exclusive conformity with the latest data of science, we should condemn society as well as individuals to suffer martyrdom on a bed of Procrustes, which would soon end by dislocating and stifling them, life ever remaining an infinitely greater thing than science. . . .
>
> But there is still a third reason which would render such a government impossible—namely that a scientific academy invested with a sovereignty, so to speak, absolute, even if it were composed of the most illustrious men, would infallibly and soon end in its own moral and intellectual corruption.[47]

. . . In their existing organization, monopolizing science and remaining thus outside of social life, the savants form a separate caste, in many respects analogous to the priesthood. Scientific abstraction is their God, living and real individuals are their victims, and they are the consecrated and licensed sacrificers.[48]

Bakunin's unloved ruling administrative class of faith-filled experts brought concepts and ideas to their work of social management—Hegelian *Begriffs*.

In his work titled *Marxism, Freedom and the State*, Bakunin argued,

But in the People's State of Marx, there will be, we are told, no privileged class at all. All will be equal, not only from the juridical and political point of view, but from the economic point of view. At least that is what is promised. . . . There will therefore be no longer any privileged class, but there will be a government concentrating in its own hands the production and the just division of wealth, the cultivation of land, the establishment and development of factories, the organisation and direction of commerce, finally the application of capital to production by the only banker, the State. All that will demand an immense knowledge and many "heads overflowing with brains" in this government. It will be the reign of *scientific intelligence*, the most aristocratic, despotic, arrogant and contemptuous of all regimes. There will be a new class, a new hierarchy of real and pretended scientists and scholars, and the world will be divided into a minority ruling in the name of knowledge and an immense ignorant majority. And then, woe betide the mass of ignorant ones![49]

Such a Marxist state would, Bakunin predicted, be "the most distressing, offensive, and despicable type of government in the world."

Georges Sorel

French activist Georges Sorel (1847–1922) adopted Bakunin's approach to the overthrow of dominance interactions in modern society. Like Bakunin, Sorel considered the God-State only as a superstition holding sway over the credulous.[50] Not an anarchist but a syndicalist, Sorel proposed violence and general strikes by workers against ruling elites. He demanded that power be placed in the hands of workers, not with those who would hold power in their name only. Sorel saw himself only as a "disinterested servant of the proletariat."[51]

Those socialists who choose to work with the state, Sorel fulminated, would only "prove themselves worthy successors of the Inquisition, of the ancient regime, and of Robespierre."[52] The "[s]yndicalists do not propose to reform the State . . . they want to destroy it."[53]

Sorel called the ideas most useful in contesting state power "myths" because they could not be refuted with arguments from history. Even syndicalists needed those who could come up with heady myths to awaken the masses. In particular, Sorel promoted the myth of violence, associated with acts of violence committed against the state by members of worker *syndicats*.

> The party which can most skillfully manipulate the spectre of revolution will possess the future. The workers have no money but they have at their disposal a far more effective means of action—they can inspire fear. . . . Thus, the practice of strikes engenders the notion of the catastrophic revolution. [54]

From Sorel's syndicalism would arise Benito Mussolini in Italy and Adolf Hitler in Germany, each users of myth and violence to seize state power.

Thorstein Veblen

In the United States, a provincial sociologist, Thorstein Veblen, observed in 1904 that parallel to the increasing reliance on bureaucratic expertise in public governance, the private economy was also becoming bureaucratized.[55] He was reacting to the growth of huge corporations, really small self-governing communities, such as United States Steel, and the trust associations of companies assembled by financiers, such as J. P. Morgan.

Known to Roman law, corporations had evolved in England as allocations of government authority to control and manage a specific community or enterprise. In 1231 the educational community at Oxford, England, was recognized as a *universitas*, or corporation. Later, corporate rights of self-government were given to colonies established under royal charters in the United States and to trading enterprises such as the East India Company.

Later, general corporation statutes were enacted to permit individuals to pool their money in a freestanding, autonomous collective for the pursuit of any business purpose.

In the United States, after the Civil War, well-funded corporations were organized, especially to build railroads and to manage large-scale industrial operations such as steel mills. Hired to manage these organizations were former officers in the Union Army, who brought to their work the norms and practices of a modern military—a command-and-control hierarchy, a division of labor into divisions, sections, subsections, and finally individual role assignments, each demanding independent expertise. A separate expertise in supervision and coordination was required to integrate the separate functional branches and units seamlessly into one process of production. Alfred Chandler wrote an admired history of the growth of large, bureaucratized, shareholder-owned business corporations in America. He thus documented the growth of a managerial elite having great authority over American capitalism.

Thus did Hegel's idealistic formula for a God-State executing its purpose through bureaucrats cross the Atlantic and take up residence in American private enterprises, each a kind of ministate with its own independent governance mechanisms.

Veblen called this new form of private enterprise in America "the machine process." He saw the new corporate form of enterprise as a machine. Older, smaller forms of business enterprise—partnerships, sole ownerships—had been supplanted "by a reasoned procedure on the basis of systemic knowledge of the forces employed."

> None of the processes in the mechanical industry is self-sufficing. Each follows some and precedes other processes in an endless sequence, into which each fits and to the requirements of which each must adapt its own working. The whole concert of industrial operations is to be taken as a machine process.[56]

Veblen believed that all of society—globally—was becoming more and more organized into this kind of mechanical process, especially through interdependent systems of communication such as railways, steamship lines, telephones, telegraphs, and postal services.

He proposed that the new spiritual ground of business—its principle—was the discipline of ownership and management "inculcating habits of thought suitable to the work of business traffic."[57] The machine process, he said, is a "severe and insistent disciplinarian in point of intelligence, requiring close and unremitting thought running in standard terms of quantitative precision. The machine process gives no insight into questions of good and evil, merit and demerit; . . . it knows neither manners nor breeding and can make no use of the attributes of worth." [58] It is a cold, mathematical, logical way of thinking, sealed off from emotions and joy. Persons become machinelike, rationalized by their functions.

Thus did Veblen expose a new social reality wherein bureaucratic norms and behaviors could be rooted to grow in scope and cultural power.

Max Weber—the Iron Cage of Modernity

No one has effectively exposed the inner workings of that complex system we live with known as modern civilization as did German sociologist

Max Weber (1864–1920). Weber built his analysis on (1) systemic, self-perpetuating behavioral proclivities legitimated by the articulated values of a community, and (2) the systemic, self-perpetuating patterns of social interactions dominant in that community.

His most famous thesis, a brutal refutation of Marxism, connected the birth and rise of capitalism as a new economic system in human history to the beliefs of the Protestant Ethic as practiced in Holland, Scotland, and England in the seventeenth and eighteenth centuries.

Weber's view was that values shaped structures far more than structures determined a community's truth propositions.

An important consequence of thinking in Weberian terms is that language—the concepts defined and spoken about within a community—gives insights not only into the special beliefs of that community but also into its behaviors and institutional arrangements. Learning to think using words from a community permitted the observer to predict with great accuracy the social, political, economic, and cultural outcomes peculiar to that community.

And so Weber could provide sound insights into ancient Chinese society and Hindu patterns of living with a panoply of gods.

Thus, it was said that "when in Rome, do as the Romans do." Learning Latin would make that possible. And what better way to understand, say, the French, than learning French?

Living at the end of the nineteenth and the opening decades of the twentieth centuries as systemic change was being brought around the world by the industrial revolution, Weber paid close attention to what values provided legitimacy for social and political systems. He proposed that, more and more, principles of organizational rationality were birthing legal norms to govern performance—defining the daily operations of modern life. His analysis was that the industrial revolution was creating a more homogeneous human civilization, a globalized world community, by replacing traditional ethnic communities each living with a view looking back to an ancestral past and with dress, food, customs, gods, and expectations peculiar to their culture only.

Thus did Weber give us the paradigms of modernization that was to replace tradition and of science that was to replace mystic speculation and the vagaries of religion.

Weber's template of uniform, rules-based, legalized legitimation to be adopted by all modernizing societies places bureaucracies and bureaucrats in charge of culture, society, politics, and economics. But he also worried that modern societies would become "iron cages" for individuals, conforming them to specified roles and not providing them much in the way of self-actualization.

Legal authority, as defined by Weber, rests on a belief in the legality of the normative rules and the rights of those elevated to positions of authority.

The person who has authority holds an "office." He is subject to an impersonal order—a body corporate—to which his actions are oriented. The office has a specific sphere of competence within a division of labor. Obedience to what is to be done legally as the system defined legality is compulsory. The organization of offices and their respective functions follows the principle of hierarchy. There is complete separation of the property of the corporate body from the personal property of the individual appointed to any office. An incumbent has no right to appropriate the powers and authority of the office for personal use. Candidates for any office are selected to serve on the basis of technical qualifications. They are paid a salary.

Julien Benda

In 1927 Julien Benda (1867–1956) wrote in French a study of public intellectuals, *La Trahison des Clercs*. He did not use class analysis, but his designation of "clerks" points directly to those with education seeking to sway public opinion and state policies.

He defined "clerks" as

> that class of men by which . . . I mean all those whose activity
> essentially is *not* the pursuit of practical aims, all those who
> seek their joy in the practice of an art or a science or metaphysi-
> cal speculation, in short in the possession of nonmaterial
> advantages, and hence in a certain manner say: "My kingdom
> is not of this world." . . . I see an uninterrupted series of phi-
> losophers, men of religion, men of literature, artists, men of
> learning (one might say almost all during this period), whose
> influence, whose life, were in direct opposition to the realism
> of the multitudes.[59]

What Benda called "treason" was the new social role of the "clerks"
to come down from Olympus to take command over the "realism of the
multitudes" without having any permission to do so.

> First of all the "clerks" have adopted political passions. No one
> will deny that throughout Europe to-day the immense majority
> of men of letters and artists, a considerable number of scholars,
> philosophers, and "ministers" of the divine, share in the chorus
> of hatreds among races and political factions. Still less will it
> be denied that they adopt national passions.[60]

He observed that another characteristic of the patriotism of the modern "clerks" was "a desire to relate the form of their own minds to a form
of the *national* mind, which they naturally brandish against other national
forms of mind."[61]

In particular, Benda did not like promotion by the "clerks" of a Nietzschean "cult of success," by which he meant "the teaching which says that
when a will is successful that fact alone gives it a moral value, whereas the
will which fails is for that reason alone deserving of contempt."[62]

Benda's protest was a warning similar to that of Bakunin that the rising Overclass would impose upon modern society its own dysfunctions and oppressions.

Benda concluded his essay with this very pessimistic prediction, in which he was not that mistaken:

> Thereafter, humanity would be unified in one immense army, one immense factory, would be aware only of heroisms, disciplines, inventions, would denounce all free and disinterested activity, would long cease to situate the good outside the real world, would have no God but itself and its desires, and would achieve great things; by which I mean that it would attain to a really grandiose control over the matter surrounding it, to a really joyous consciousness of its power and its grandeur. And History will smile to think that this is the species for which Socrates and Jesus Christ died.[63]

Antonio Gramsci

Antonio Gramsci, an Italian community activist and thought leader, was imprisoned by Mussolini's Fascist government from 1926 until his death in 1937. During his years in prison, Gramsci wrote some thirty notebooks and 3,000 pages of sociological analysis of Italian history, social power politics, and regime solidarities. He expanded on Karl Marx's rather simplistic dualism of polarized class struggle in the industrial age between a bourgeoisie and a proletariat. Gramsci returned to Hegel's formulation of the necessity of having a state apparatus and so considered who would and should control that structure of power, both its idealism and its authoritarianism. Gramsci's analytical focus was on the intellectuals who created the legitimating motifs of the state apparatus. In this work he quite accurately described the dynamic of Stalinist Russia and articulated a theory of elite hegemony over society, culture, the economy, and politics.

Gramsci thus provided a sociology of a ruling elite educated to provide comprehensive management of a society through the development and enforcement of a "General Will." His formula for regime success was anti-democratic and elite-driven—the people (the "demos") were to be instructed and supervised by intellectuals serving the ideals and interests of a particular ruling elite. The function of such intellectuals was to establish and maintain "cultural hegemony" over the society, brooking no dissent and suppressing alternative ways of thinking. To borrow a conceit from the fable *The Lord of the Rings*, Gramsci's cultural hegemony was to be the "one ring to rule them all, one ring to bind them, one ring to bring them all, and in the darkness bind them."

Looking back at history, Gramsci concluded that every social group ". . . creates together with itself, organically, one or more strata of intellectuals which give it homogeneity and an awareness of its own function not only in the economic but also in the social and political fields."[64] For the modern age, Gramsci believed that "technical education, closely bound to industrial labor even at the most primitive and unqualified level, must form the basis of the new type of intellectual."[65] This new collective had the mission of assimilating and conquering "ideologically" the traditional intellectuals. Gramsci noted that "school is the instrument through which intellectuals of various levels are elaborated."[66] This educational process, Gramsci noted, required many different specialized schools and many levels of educational achievement. Modern society needed, he claimed, to provide the widest possible base for the selection and elaboration of the uppermost credentialing of intellectuals.

The place of such trained intellectuals was to work as functionaries in the superstructure of society—in civil society organizations and in political society, or the "State." These sectors provided the functionality of "hegemony," which "the dominant group exercises throughout society and . . . that of 'direct domination' or command exercised through the State and 'juridical' government." The credentialed intellectuals provide both hegemony and political governance.[67]

The State, said Gramsci, is an ethical force because it has the duty to raise the great mass of the population to a particular cultural and moral level—to create "a technically and morally unitary social organism." Thus, the "school as a positive educative function and the courts as a repressive and negative educative function are the most important State activities . . ."[68]

Gramsci's overview of this elite functionality was the power to control thinking and fuse correct thinking with action: "Critical understanding of self takes place . . . through a struggle of political "hegemonies" and of opposing directions, first in the ethical field and then in that of politics proper, in order to arrive at the working out at a higher level of one's own conception of reality, consciousness of being part of a particular hegemonic force "[which] progresses to the level of real possession of a single and coherent conception of the world"—a "general will" or *Begriff*.[69]

"Critical self-consciousness means, historically and politically, the creation of an elite of intellectuals." This elite is "a group of people 'specialized' in conceptual and philosophical elaboration of ideas."[70]

"The relation between theory and practice becomes even closer the more the conception is vitally and radically innovative and opposed to old ways of thinking." Political parties "become the elaborators of new and integral and totalitarian intelligentsias and the crucibles where the unification of theory and practice, understood as a real historical process, takes place."[71]

Leon Trotsky

Perhaps the second most important leader of the Bolshevik revolution in Russia after Lenin, Leon Trotsky learned the hard way how right Bakunin had been on the inherent tendency of Marxist Communism to bring a new class to power in the state to rule over the proletariat more thoroughly and more unscrupulously than capitalists ever did. Trotsky lost out to Stalin in securing supreme authority over the Bolshevik Party and its subordinate state apparatus. Trotsky was deported from the Soviet Union in 1929 and was murdered in Mexico by a Stalinist agent on August 20, 1940.

In exile in 1936, he wrote *The Revolution Betrayed* to explain what had gone wrong with the 1917 revolution in Russia, in which he had been a very important leader.

Trotsky pointed to a process of "degeneration" within the Russian Communist Party as causing the Soviet regime to disempower the workers and become a totalitarian state apparatus managed by salaried individuals working at various approved functions under the supervision of superiors.

According to Trotsky, this evolution was opposed by Lenin himself: "The very center of Lenin's attention and that of his colleagues was occupied by a continual concern to protect the Bolshevik ranks from the vices of those in power."[72] But Trotsky admitted, to prevail in the civil war fighting the non-Communists, the party and the state became one integrated organization holding sovereign powers over the Russian people.

Then Trotsky admitted, within the party, there were factions—each striving for authority. Stalin and his faction, Trotsky wrote, directed their efforts to "freeing the Party machine from the control of the rank-and-file members of the Party."[73] Stalin sought "stability," believing that the task of creating socialism was "administrative in its nature." The party replaced a decentralized "democratic" centralism with a "bureaucratic centralism," wherein "the chief merit of a Bolshevik was declared to be obedience."

"Parallel with the political degeneration of the party," Trotsky wrote, "there occurred a moral decay." A "bourgeois" culture of privilege emerged among party members with higher authority in the system.[74] At the end of the degeneration, a bureaucracy possessing little culture had been given complete independence and freedom from restraint, and the masses had been given "the well-known gospel of obedience and silence."[75]

Therefore, Trotsky concluded that "the bureaucracy—that is, the 'privileged officials and commanders of the standing army'" have "a special kind of compulsion which . . . is directed against the masses." Trotsky called this the "policification" of the state.[76] Thus, the Soviet reality was not at all what Marx had predicted.[77]

Bakunin had been right all along, and now Trotsky confirmed the wisdom of the anarchist's assumptions about the outcome of Marxist Communism.

Trotsky, however, sought to find the cause of the degeneration in material conditions, not human nature. He proposed that the "basis of bureaucratic rule is the poverty of society in objects of consumption, with the resulting struggle of each against all. . . . When the lines are very long, it is necessary to appoint a policeman to keep order." The Soviet bureaucracy, he wrote, "'knows' who is to get something and who has to wait."[78] He added, "In establishing and defending the advantages of a minority, it of course draws off the cream for its own use. . . . Soviet society is already divided into a secure and privileged minority, and a majority getting along in want."[79] He said, "The unlimited power of the bureaucracy is a no less forceful instrument of social differentiation. It has in its hands such levers as wages, prices, taxes, budgets, and credit."[80]

> Where a separate room and sufficient food and neat clothing are still accessible only to a small minority, millions of bureaucrats, great and small, try to use the power primarily in order to guarantee their own well-being. Hence the enormous egoism of this stratum, its firm inner solidarity, its fear of the discontent of the masses, its rabid insistence upon strangling all criticism, and, finally, its hypocritically religious kowtowing to "the Leader," who embodies and defends the power and privileges of those new lords.[81]

Thus, Trotsky concludes that the Soviet bureaucracy is something more than a bureaucracy: "It is in the full sense of the word the sole privileged and commanding stratum in the Soviet society." It is a "new class" in a society where the means of production belong to the state while the state, so to speak, "belongs" to the bureaucracy. The bureaucracy's appropriation of a vast share of the national income "has the character of social parasitism."[82]

James Burnham

James Burnham was an American follower of Trotsky. He would win some renown in partnership with William F. Buckley by starting and editing the conservative American political journal the *National Review*. In 1983 President Ronald Reagan awarded him the Presidential Medal of Freedom.

In 1941 Burnham built on Trotsky's thesis about the social and political role of a managerial class in a book he titled *The Managerial Revolution*. He gave the book a question as its subtitle: "What Is Happening in the World?"

He presented a theory of the managerial revolution, which Max Weber had already proposed as the foundation for modern industrial societies, saying, "[W]e are in a period of social transition . . . from the type of society we have called capitalist or bourgeois to a type of society which we shall call managerial. . . . What is occurring in this transition is a drive for social dominance, for power and prestige, for the position of the ruling class, by the social group or class of managers."[83]

Burnham predicted, "This drive will be successful. At the conclusion of the transition period, the managers will, in fact, have achieved social dominance, will be the ruling class in society."

He saw the state as necessary for the rise to dominance of managers: "The state will be . . . the 'property' of the managers. . . . The control of the state by the managers will be suitably guaranteed by appropriate political institutions."[84] In 1941 Burnham judged that "the ideologies [the Hegelian *Begriffs*] expressing the social role of the managers have not yet been fully worked out." That work, he said, was not to be done by managers but, on their behalf, by "intellectuals, writers, philosophers."

Individuals, wrote Burnham, will be designated as managers according to their function in society, their relationship to the means of production. They would not be, however, capitalists.

Already in 1932 Adolf Berle and Gardiner Means had written a dispositive analysis of corporate governance in America, concluding that ownership and management had become two independent functions. Some—owners—provided money to companies in return for shares, while others—managers (CEOs, executives serving on corporate boards, salaried employees)—made business decisions for the enterprise. Burnham cited their work, which I later studied in my Harvard Law School class in corporate finance.

For Burnham, the principal class function of managers in corporations was to set up organizations for, and coordinate the processes of, mass production and large-scale financing of the private sector.

In the public sector, Burnham observed that more and more managers—in this case bureaucrats—were taking sovereign authority away from legislatures and courts and relocating it in administrative procedures and decision-making.

Burnham inferred that a major step toward the rise of the managerial class, in the transition from capitalism to managerialism, had been President Franklin Roosevelt's New Deal, which created a publicly funded welfare state within the American economy.

What Roosevelt and his supporters touted as a high-minded "progressivism" was, for Burnham, only a program to create a managerial society, making easier the rise of the managers in both public and private sectors and "curbing the masses along lines adapted to the managerial future."[85] He belittled managers as "servants who are learning to speak with the voice of the master."[86] He stated, "With the consolidation of management structures [in industry and government], the position of the managers is assured."

Friedrich Hayek

In September 1945 the *American Economic Review* published a short article by the Austrian economist Friedrich Hayek on the rationality of market decision-making and the inherent irrationality of social engineering as Hegel had advocated. Hayek's conclusion, in the context of Overclass pretensions, was that Hegel's vision of the God-State was a delusion, a fairy tale made up to foster hubris among those highly educated in the schools of the European Enlightenment.

Hayek discussed how to find the right knowledge for society to use in making the best possible decisions. His conclusion was that, for the narrow field of microeconomics, a centrally planned economy managed by professionals was inferior to a decentralized market where pricing by individuals was more expert in discovering relevant knowledge.[87] Hayek insisted that the "data" needed to make good decisions for a society could never be given to some single mind, which would then brilliantly use the data to work out all the implications of what we know and so make perfect, infallible decisions.

Thus, with one simple idea did Hayek delegitimize the God-State. He validated with an observation about the human condition what Bakunin had come to believe through intuition about the consequences of state management of the economy.

Hayek's observation was that the most relevant knowledge needed for decision-making in economics was not kept by the most powerful institutions but rather was contained in the peculiar and particular circumstances where the decisions would have the most impact—among the people. Circumstantial knowledge, said Hayek, most accurately predicted how individuals would behave and what would happen to them as a consequence of their decisions. He pointed to pricing in free markets as a superb mechanism for the discovery of relevant knowledge. The price agreed to by a buyer and a seller contained within a simple number for payment a treasure trove of information about the buyer, the seller, their expectations, their status, future market probabilities as seen from their standpoints, their desires, their fears, their needs, and their extravagances.

Hayek wrote that planning "will in some measure have to be based on knowledge which, in the first instance, is not given to the planner but to somebody else, which somehow will have to be conveyed to the planner." He asked "[W]hether we are more likely to succeed in putting the disposal of a single central authority all the knowledge which ought to be used but which is initially dispersed among many different individuals, or in conveying to the individuals such additional knowledge as they need in order to enable them to fit their plans with those of others."

Here Hayek put his finger on the great law of human vanity—the law of unintended consequences. Though we may act with the best of intentions, but we can still make a hash of everything.

Popular common sense has long exposed this reality to common knowledge: "Man proposes. God disposes." "If wishes were horses, beggars would ride." Scottish poet Robert Burns wrote, "The best-laid schemes of mice and men go oft awry, and leave us nothing but grief and pain, for promised joy!"

So when Americans see their governments planning and spending money yet the poor are still with us, educational achievement falls off, unhappiness and depression rise, and ego-identities become dysphoric—all on the government's watch—they are looking at the truth of Hayek's insight about how most judiciously to use practical knowledge about what is best for each of us as individuals, which is by not creating a Hegelian God-State.

What Hayek saw to be true about markets can be extrapolated to all of human social action. Rational social organization is best accomplished by finding cultural, social, and political equivalents to prices, not through command-and-control regulation by managers. Decentralization with empowerment of individual moral agency, recommended by Catholic social teachings as the principle of subsidiarity, is, by far, preferable to Overclass management of social norms and practices.

The free market equivalent of pricing looks to the actors most affected by the proposed decision: What are their values? How will they respond to the decision? Will they fulfill their obligations, or will they cheat? Will they contribute their labor and pull a laboring oar, or will they be sociopaths seeking to extract privilege and rents? Will they be honest, or will they abuse power?

Hayek's warning against top-down, elite-driven decision-making applies to every situation where behaviors drive outcomes.

To personalize the challenge of understanding any decision-making contexts, let us ask: Will the decision-makers be an Abraham Lincoln or a John Wilkes Booth, a Margaret Thatcher or a Kamala Harris, inner-directed or other-directed? Who knows in advance—the government? Who best knows the actors in any situation well enough to tell us who they really are?

Most likely since the dawn of living in community, we humans have created ethics and morals and inculcated them in our children to shift the odds toward better outcomes in every circumstance where people make decisions. The self-evident purpose of such acculturation was to make each of us trustworthy.

I once read that our species is the only one among mammals that has white around the iris of the eyes. The speculation was that we evolved whites in our eyes the better to discern if others could be trusted or not; after all, it is said that the eyes are windows into the soul.

However, in keeping with Hegel, Hayek did agree that certain forms of knowledge—scientific knowledge about general rules—could and should be possessed by experts who therefore could be given authority to use that knowledge in society. What Hayek defended was the kind of knowledge that could never be measured statistically and so conveyed to any central authority in statistical form. Hayek thus noted that there are some things such as what goes on in the human heart that can't be well and fully measured with numbers and so can't be managed with a slide-rule or computer program.

Hayek's thinking should make us much more cautious before ever entrusting power and authority to the Overclass.

Milovan Djilas

The first to call out the "new class" by that name as the mercenary ruling elite of modern rational/legal institutions serving a Hegelian God-State was Milovan Djilas (1911–1995) in his 1957 book *The New Class: An Analysis of the Communist System.*

Born in Montenegro, Djilas was a communist who allied himself with Josip Broz Tito during World War II. After World War II, Djilas opposed Stalin's efforts to dictate to the Yugoslav Communists. Djilas took a lead in promoting an independent "communism" with worker self-management of productive enterprises. His advocacy of greater democratic contributions to collective decision-making led him to question the value of a one-party state. For that insubordination, he was expelled from the Central Committee of the Yugoslav Communist Party in 1954. In 1957 he sent his book *The New Class* to be published in the United States. (I inherited a first edition copy from my father.) For this Djilas was sentenced to seven years' imprisonment.

Djilas argued that in the case of Soviet Russia, the new class "did not come to power to complete a new economic order but to establish its own and, in so doing, to establish its power over society."[88] He said, "The new class may be said to be made up of those who have special privileges and economic preference because of the administrative monopoly they hold. . . . The roots of the new class were implanted in a special party. . . . The party makes the class but the class grows as a result and uses the party as a basis. The class grows stronger while the party grows weaker. This is the inescapable fate of every Communist party in power."[89]

He added, "He who grabs power grabs privileges and indirectly grabs property."[90]

Membership in the new class, said Djilas, brought privileges inherent in ownership, in a larger income in material goods and privileges than society should normally grant for such functions. And accordingly, we have seen in every Communist party society and post-Communist society systemic corruption and rent seeking by the elite.

"The new class obtains its power, privileges, ideology, and its customs from one specific form of ownership—collective ownership—which the class administers and distributes in the name of the nation and society. . . . The ownership privileges of the new class and membership in that class are the privileges of administration. . . . Stalin looked neither far ahead nor far behind. He had seated himself at the head of the new power which was being born—the new class, the political bureaucracy, and bureaucratism—and became its leader and organizer. He did not preach—he made decisions."[91]

Today we could say something similar about Vladimir Putin and Xi Jinping now controlling Russia and China through their respective new classes.

Djilas noted in passing that careerism and an ever-expanding bureaucracy are the incurable diseases spread by the new class. Therefore, he observed, in non-Communist systems too, "[T]he phenomena of careerism and unscrupulous ambition are a sign that it is profitable to be a bureaucrat, or that owners have become parasites, so that the administration of property is left in the hands of employees."[92] Veblen and Burnham would agree.

In 1957 Djilas concluded, "The heroic era of Communism is past. The epoch of its great leaders has ended. The epoch of practical men has set in. The new class has been created. It is at the height of its power and wealth, but it is without new ideas. It has nothing more to tell the people."[93]

He stated, "Having achieved industrialization, the new class can now do nothing more than strengthen its brute force and pillage the people. It ceases to create. Its spiritual heritage is overtaken by darkness. . . . Smothering everything except what suited its ego, it has condemned itself to failure and shameful ruin."[94]

C. Wright Mills

In 1951 C. Wright Mills, professor of sociology at Columbia University, published *White Collar*, an examination of a new middle class. Mills proposed that this new middle class did not have an entrepreneurial relationship with the means of production in a capitalist society. Rather, members of the new middle class were salaried specialists working for organizations. He thought that the rise of the dependent employee had gone hand in hand with the rise of "the little man in the American mind."[95]

> The new little man seems to have no firm roots, no sure loyalties to sustain his life and give it a center. He is not aware of having any history, his past being as brief as it is unheroic. . . . There is no plan of life. Among white-collar people, the malaise is deep rooted . . . white-collar man has no culture to lean upon.

He added, "In modern society, occupations are specific functions within a social division of labor as well as skills sold for income on a labor market."[96] He claimed, "[F]ewer individuals manipulate things, more handle people and symbols." White-collar workers "live off the social machineries that organize and coordinate the people who do make things." Their "characteristic skills involve the handling of paper and money and people. They are expert at dealing with people transiently and impersonally."

According to Mills, "The managers as the cadre of enterprise, form a hierarchy, graded according to their authority to initiate tasks, to plan and execute their own work and freely to plan and order the work of others. Each level in the cadre's hierarchy is beholden to the levels above."[97] "Their power is neatly seated in the office they occupy and derived only from that office."

Managers "reduce the hazards of personal decision by carefully following the rules. . . . The ends of the organization become their private ends."[98] Those at the top of the organization "are cautiously selected to represent the formal interest of the organization and its organizational integrity."[99]

The function of the new white-collar middle class is to provide society with rational specialization. Thus, to become a member of this class requires lengthy training: "Intensive and narrow specialization has replaced self-cultivation and wide knowledge."[100] This was especially true, claimed Mills, for the professions of medicine, law, and higher education.

For the new white-collar middle class, "education replaces property as the insurance of social position."[101]

In academia, Mills cynically noted, "In such a hierarchy, mediocrity makes its own rules and sets its own image of success."[102]

Mills astutely noted that the new white-collar middle class included a new profession—that of the consultant moving between bureaucratic hierarchies. He also noted that the new white-collar middle class provided for the first time systematic class status for intellectuals as people who "specialize in symbols, producing, distributing, and preserving distinct forms of consciousness."[103]

> Bureaucracy increasingly sets the conditions of intellectual life and controls the major markets for its products. The new bureaucracies of state and business, of party and voluntary association, become the major employers of intellectuals and the main customers of their work.[104]

We might say that the social function of these intellectuals is to manage rationally on behalf of organizations by internalizing for themselves and imposing upon their subordinates either Rousseauist general wills or Hegelian *Begriffs*, large and small.

Mills added, "The organizational reason for the expansion of the white-collar occupations is the rise of big business and big government, and the consequent trend of modern social structure, the steady rise of bureaucracy."[105] "Government increases its coordinating and regulating tasks."[106]

He stated, "As the means of administration are enlarged and central-ized, there are many more managers in every sphere of modern society, and the managerial type of man becomes more important in the total social structure."[107] The interlocking of private and public hierarchies within the managerial elite, which Mills observed, became undisputable during the Biden administration of 2020 to 2024 and in Kamala Harris's 2024 campaign for the presidency. The setting up of diversity, equity, and inclusion offices in government and private corporations during Biden's administration demonstrated a hand-in-glove collaboration between corporate bureaucrats and government regulators. Harris raised over $1 billion for her campaign, which could not have been done without the energized support of many in corporate America.

Salaried occupations rank people in various ways: by levels of skill, by function within an industrial division of labor, and by income, which pro-vides class position and carries with it an expected quota of prestige.[108]

Importantly, Mills concluded that the Protestant work ethic "has not deeply gripped the people of the new society," which therefore was not a traditional bourgeois class in social manners and aspirations.[109] Rather, bureaucratic position, with its powers over others, therefore becomes the basis for self-esteem.[110]

Mills stated, "[P]eople who are dependent for everything, including images of themselves, upon place in an authoritarian hierarchy, will all the more frantically cling to claims of status."[111] He added, "The main chance now becomes a series of small calculations, stretched over the working lifetime of the individual; a bureaucracy is no testing field for heroes."[112]

In 1957 Mills published *The Power Elite*, a hypothesis about how a governing elite had emerged at the top of the new white-collar middle class in America.

> As the means of information and of power are centralized, some
> men come to occupy positions in American society from which they

can look down upon, so to speak, and by their decisions mightily affect, the everyday worlds of ordinary men and women.[113]

These men, Mills said, "are in command of the major hierarchies and organizations of modern society. They rule the big corporations. They run the machinery of state and claim its prerogatives. They direct the military establishment. They occupy the strategic command posts of the social structure." He added, "The inner core of the power elite also includes men of the higher legal and financial type from the great law factories and investment firms, who are almost professional go-betweens of economic, political and military affairs."[114]

Mills again astutely noted that mingling with these captains of institutions were professional celebrities "who had the power to distract the attention of the public or gain the ear of those who do occupy positions of direct power."[115]

He stated, "[T]he elite are simply those who have the most of what there is to have, which is generally held to be money, power, prestige—as well as all the ways of life to which these lead."[116]

Mills concluded, "The American elite is not composed of representative men whose conduct and character constitute models for American imitation and aspiration. . . . America is indeed without leaders." For "the men of the higher circles . . . their high position is not a result of moral virtue, their fabulous success is not firmly connected with meritorious ability. Those who sit in the seats of the high and the mighty are selected and formed by the means of power, wealth, and celebrity, which prevail in their society."[117]

Do William Jefferson Clinton, Hillary Clinton, George W. Bush, Donald Trump, Joseph R. Biden and his immediate family, Kamala Harris, and the financially successful careers of Barack and Michelle Obama, not to mention Generals David Petraeus and Mark Milley, who couldn't win their wars, and the fortunes of Elon Musk, Mark Zuckerberg, and Jeff Bezos, come to mind? These people fit Mills's power-elite paradigm.

Most interestingly, Mills spotted an influential role for the media in sustaining the power elite: The media have "entered into our very experiences of our own selves." He stated that "(1) the media tell the man in the mass who he is—they give him identity; (2) they tell him what he wants to be—they give him aspirations; (3) they tell him how to get that way—they give him technique; and (4) they tell him how to feel that he is that way even when he is not—they give him escape."[118]

Students for a Democratic Society

In 1962 a small activist group of the college educated, Students for a Democratic Society, issued their Port Huron Statement after a meeting in Port Huron, Michigan. The statement was a proposal for a new Rousseauist general will to be imposed on the American people by a vanguard of college-educated know-it-alls. The statement was not so modestly introduced as an "Agenda for a Generation."

The activists described themselves as follows: "We are people of this generation, bred in at least modest comfort, housed now in universities, looking uncomfortably to the world we inherit."

They explained, "Not only did tarnish appear on our image of American virtue, not only did disillusion occur when the hypocrisy of American ideals was discovered, but we began to sense that what we had originally seen as the American Golden Age was actually the decline of an era. The worldwide outbreak of revolution against colonialism and imperialism, the entrenchment of totalitarian states, the menace of war, overpopulation, international disorder, supertechnology—these trends were testing the tenacity of our own commitment to democracy and freedom and our abilities to visualize their application to a world in upheaval."

Their strategy for bending Americans to their point of view was to use the college educated, the rising Overclass.

> From where else can power and vision be summoned? We believe
> that the universities are an overlooked seat of influence.

First, the university is located in a permanent position of social influence. Its educational function makes it indispensable and automatically makes it a crucial institution in the formation of social attitudes. Second, in an unbelievably complicated world, it is the central institution for organizing, evaluating, and transmitting knowledge. Third, the extent to which academic resources presently is used to buttress immoral social practice is revealed first, by the extent to which defense contracts make the universities engineers of the arms race. Too, the use of modern social science as a manipulative tool reveals itself in the "human relations" consultants to the modern corporation, who introduce trivial sops to give laborers feelings of "participation" or "belonging," while actually deluding them in order to further exploit their labor. And, of course, the use of motivational research is already infamous as a manipulative aspect of American politics. But these social uses of the universities' resources also demonstrate the unchangeable reliance by men of power on the men and storehouses of knowledge: this makes the university functionally tied to society in new ways, revealing new potentialities, new levers for change. Fourth, the university is the only mainstream institution that is open to participation by individuals of nearly any viewpoint.

The statement emphasized the power potential of student protest.

In the last few years, thousands of American students demonstrated that they at least felt the urgency of the times. They moved actively and directly against racial injustices, the threat of war, violations of individual rights of conscience and, less frequently, against economic manipulation. They succeeded in restoring a small measure of controversy to the campuses after the stillness of the McCarthy period. They succeeded, too, in gaining some concessions from the people and institutions they opposed, especially in the fight against racial bigotry.

The significance of these scattered movements lies not in their success or failure in gaining objectives—at least not yet. Nor does the significance lie in the intellectual "competence" or "maturity" of the students involved—as some pedantic elders allege. The significance is in the fact the students are breaking the crust of apathy and overcoming the inner alienation that remain the defining characteristics of American college life.[119]

At Harvard College, from time to time, I would run across Hal Benenson and Michael Ansara, two leading promoters of the Students for a Democratic Society. In the fall of 1966, when they organized a protest against Secretary of Defense Robert McNamara, I suddenly found myself in the position of rescuing him from the protestors and leading him to safety through the tunnels underneath Harvard's residential colleges.[120]

Commentators Discovering the "New Class"

B. Bruce-Briggs noted that the term "new class" had been used in 1971 by Norman Podhoretz, editor of *Commentary*, saying, "The New Class sees itself . . . as a 'conscience constituency' motivated only by ideas and ideals, whereas others are driven only by baser impulses and issues 'of the stomach.'"[121]

In the November 1972 issue of *Commentary*, Irving Kristol used the phrase "this new class of the college educated," referring to millions of Americans who, though lacking intellectual distinction, nevertheless believe themselves to be intellectuals."[122] Kristol later wrote, "The 'new class'—intelligent, educated, energetic—has little respect for . . . a commonplace (business) civilization. It wishes to see its 'ideals' more effectual than the market is likely to permit them to be. And so it always tries to supersede economics by politics, an activity in which it is most competent, since it has the talents and the implicit authority to shape public opinion on all larger issues."[123]

Jeane Kirkpatrick proposed that the new class should be used to describe a group having two principal political concerns: control of the symbolic environment and the relationship between the ideal and the real. Here she nailed the new class to the cross of Hegel and the God-State, the torment of making a new heaven of our choices here on earth. She concluded her essay: "The political temptation of the new class lies in believing that their intelligence and exemplary motives equip them to reorder the institutions, the lives, and even the characters of almost everyone—this is the totalitarian temptation. . . . But a society that cherishes liberty will do well to protect itself from the excesses of the new class. As surely as a monopoly of power or wealth is dangerous to the rest of us, a new-class monopoly on meaning and purpose is incompatible with the common weal."[124]

Professor Peter Berger wrote simply that "the ideology of the New Class functions as a secular theodicy—a coherent explanation of suffering and evil"—in other words, a Gnostic faith.[125] Berger continued, "The ideology of the New Class . . . enhances the power and the privileges of the New Class."

Professor Seymour Martin Lipset, writing about the impact of the new class on the American professoriate, concluded, "Faced with attacks on their legitimacy from intellectuals and students, many in the governing elites exhibit a 'failure of nerve.' . . . The basic tensions within the system increasingly come from within the elite itself—from its own intellectual leaders supported by large segments of its student children."[126]

Aaron Wildavsky contributed an essay on the politics of the new class titled "Using Public Funds to Serve Private Interests." He thought that "this new class seeks what every other class does—namely, privilege."[127]

Daniel Bell

In 1976 Harvard sociologist Daniel Bell wrote *The Coming of Post-Industrial Society*, a thorough history of the ideas and developments that, for him, explained a new form of human society—a postindustrial society. Bell had first pondered changes in the modern means of production in 1959, a shift from the production of goods to the provision of services.

For Bell, his concept of "postindustrial society" emphasizes the centrality of theoretical knowledge as the axis around which new technology, economic growth, and the stratification of society would be organized.[128] Politically, for Bell, the challenge of a postindustrial society would be the growth of administrative, nonmarket, welfare economics and the lack of adequate mechanisms to decide on the allocation of public goods. For him, in a postindustrial society, the axial primary institutions would be universities, academic institutes, and research corporations; the foundation for economic growth would be science-based industries; the primary capital resource would be human agency; the political challenges would be policies for science and education; the structural problem would be achieving the right balance of the public and the private sectors; and social stratification would be determined by education.[129]

Bell concluded that "a post-industrial society is based on services. Hence it is a game between persons. What counts is not raw muscle power or energy but information. The central person is the professional for he is equipped by his education and training to provide the kinds of skill which are increasingly demanded . . . If an industrial society is defined by the quantity of goods as marking a standard of living, the post-industrial society is defined by the quality of life as measured by services and amenities—health, education, recreation, and the arts—which are now deemed desirable and possible for everyone."[130] Such a society would develop new forms of property in assigned government entitlements—negative rights to have the state provide advantages and privileges as well as goods and services.[131] Today such new property rights would include employment due to "diversity, equity, and inclusion" birth characteristics.

In America, by 1960, six out of ten were employed in services; by 1980 the ratio would be seven out of ten. Bell estimated that in a postindustrial America, white-collar workers would account for half of all employed persons.

Additionally, Bell noted that the university had become the center of establishment culture[132] because education was the mode of access to power.[133]

Early Analysts of the Overclass

In 1979 B. Bruce-Briggs edited a small book of short essays entitled *The New Class?: America's Educated Elite Examined*. Contributors were distinguished intellectuals with conservative casts of mind.

Bruce-Briggs was keen to understand why radical ideals prevailed among members of American society "who would appear by any objective measure to be favored in income, status, freedom, power, and other presumed benefits of life."[134] Without making the connection, Bruce-Briggs was bringing forward Rousseau's societal model where a general will was to be discovered to break chains of oppression so that all could live in natural freedom. He proposed the hypothesis of a "new class" to explain the angst and disillusionment disturbing the psyches of those with elite status.

Bruce-Briggs wrote that credit for the first American usage of the term "new class" must go to Harvard professor John Kenneth Galbraith, who, in 1958, wrote in his most famous work, *The Affluent Society*, about the "emergence of this New Class . . . to which work has none of the older connotation of pain, fatigue, or other mental or physical discomfort." Galbraith then proposed that the further and rapid expansion of this class should perhaps be the major social goal of the society, education being "very close to the basic index of social progress."[135] Thus, this new class would be the progressive class leading the transformation of Americans into followers of its own conceits.

What Galbraith recommended in 1958 has become today's American Overclass. Quite contrary to his optimistic expectations, that educated managerial elite has imposed on us dysphoria and dysfunction.

David Lebedoff

In 1981 Minneapolis lawyer David Lebedoff would publish *The New Elite: The Death of Democracy*, referring to "the first powerful class in history whose membership is defined by measurable intelligence. Everyone not in the class can be referred to—in terms of the way the New Elite sees them—as the Left Behinds." He added, "People whose work does not require professional, verbal, or technocratic skills are probable Left Behinds."[136]

Several decades later, in her 2016 campaign for the presidency, Hillary Clinton, a graduate of Wellesley College and Yale Law School, would give expression to Lebedoff's idea in the way she referred to the supporters of her opponent, Donald Trump.

> You know, to just be grossly generalistic, you could put half of Trump's supporters into what I call the basket of deplorables. Right?
> [*Laughter/applause*]
> The racist, sexist, homophobic, xenophobic, Islamophobic—you name it. And unfortunately there are people like that. And he has lifted them up. He has given voice to their websites that used to only have 11,000 people—now [have] 11 million. He tweets and retweets their offensive, hateful, mean-spirited rhetoric. Now, some of those folks—they are irredeemable, but thankfully they are not America.[137]

On October 29, 2024, at the end of Kamala Harris's campaign for the presidency, President Joseph Biden said of Donald Trump's supporters, "The only garbage I see floating out there is his supporters. His demonization of Latinos is unconscionable, and it's un-American. It's totally contrary to everything we've done, everything we've been."[138]

Hillary's accusation that these "deplorables" or "left-behinds" were the authors of worldly "evils" epitomized Nietzsche's insight—ressentiment—about those who shape their own morality by first ascribing immorality to others. These Gnostics define the devil first, and only after that do they look for personal salvation in a god or other source of higher, righteous truth.

Lebedoff continued that members of the new elite "claim moral superiority in order to bypass the need for obtaining majority support." They hold a belief that "a view should prevail if the New Elite believes it to be morally superior to an opposing view." He added, "The New Elite sits near the fulcrum of public opinion. Its members are communicators; their leverage on popular thought is immense. What they believe becomes common currency."[139]

In our times one can hear this play out daily in the moral superiority claimed by proponents of "antiracism"; "gender-affirming care"; "diversity, equity, and inclusion"; opposition to "toxic masculinity"; and open borders with effortless access to citizenship.

Lebedoff was prescient in writing, "Everything that happens in American politics reflects the inroads of the New Elite or the reaction of the Left Behinds."[140]

He wrote, "If the New Elite were to rule, then the majority could not,"[141] adding, "The political goal of the New Elite is very simple: the transfer of political power to the New Elite."[142] Lebedoff foresaw the new politics brought on by the new elite as incessant political warfare.

> Blinded by the same narrow vision, each side wages war against the other. The casualty of the conflict is democracy itself, and no one really wins. The choices get worse and worse and have less meaning . . . the growth of single-issue politics, the insanity of recent campaigns, the absence of ideas, the incompetence of candidates and voters who vacillate between apathy and anger.[143]

Style, said Lebedoff, was of particular importance to the new elite. Conforming, politically correct appearances, speech, and affiliations determined who was welcome to join and who was to be excluded from the new elite. Members of the new elite "live and shop and work and go to school with those just like themselves. Neighborhoods no longer are microcosms of the world but self-contained clusterings, cocoons of shared outlook."[144]

Christopher Lasch

In 1995 Christopher Lasch wrote *The Revolt of the Elites and the Betrayal of Democracy*. He perceived that "the new elites are in revolt against 'Middle America,' as they imagine it: a nation technologically backward, politically reactionary, repressive in its sexual morality, middlebrow in its tastes, smug and complacent, dull and dowdy."[145]

Lasch accused the elites of creating not a democracy but a "therapeutic state" promoting such catchwords as "diversity," "compassion," "empowerment," and "entitlement" and the hope that difficulties and divisions can be overcome by goodwill and sanitized speech and calling on all Americans to recognize that all minorities are entitled to respect not by virtue of their achievements but by virtue of their sufferings in the past.[146]

Lasch worried that in the hands of the elites, "diversity" would become a new dogmatism, in which groups would take shelter behind a set of beliefs impervious to rational discussion.[147] "Opinion becomes a function of racial or ethnic identity, of gender or sexual preference. Self-selected minority 'spokespersons' enforce this conformity by ostracizing those who stray from the party-line—Black people, for instance, who 'think White.'"[148] This he calls a "parody" of community.

The social power of his elites, Lasch said, rests not on ownership of property—industrial-era capitalism—but on manipulation of information and professional expertise. So to gain such power, those who seek elite occupations and status invest in education and access to information.

At one point, Lasch seemingly without recognition tied the culture of the elite to Rousseau's demand that we all throw off the chains of obligation to others. What Lasch described as a their culture of indulgence is the general will that the elite proposed to impose American society at large.

Many young people are morally at sea. They resent the ethical demands of "society" as infringements of their personal freedom. They believe that their rights as individuals include the right to "create their own values." . . . They cannot seem to grasp the idea that "values" imply some principle of moral obligation. They insist that they owe nothing to "society"—an abstraction that dominates their attempts to think about social and moral issues.[149]

Richard Florida

In his 2002 book, *The Rise of the Creative Class*, Richard Florida put a smiley face on the Overclass. He defined the class as giving rise to creativity—needed for economic growth and cultural progress. He drew attention to the use of design theory by the Overclass, not just technical expertise or accumulation of data points but also work that was more spiritual and insightful. Florida proposed that the ability to come up with meaningful new forms "is now the decisive source of competitive advantage." He believed that "the winners in the long run are those who can create and keep creating."[150] He said, "We need better recipes, not just more cooking."[151]

He called the creative class the "norm-setting class of our time," "dominant in terms of wealth and income."[152]

Florida's creative class needs a supportive social milieu that is open to all forms of creativity, an ecosystem or habitat in which "the multidimensional forms of creativity take root and flourish," cross-fertilization is facilitated, and there is rapid interpersonal transmission of knowledge and ideas.[153] Here Florida aligned the psychosocial needs of his creative class with other-direction.

He tied members of the creative class to an ethos—weak social ties to others and contingent commitments driven by a striving to create our own identities: the creation and recreation of self.

Wither the Overclass?

For all its self-confident smugness, the Overclass in 2025 confronts an existential challenge of Marxist importance: artificial intelligence. AI and algorithms will take over Overclass functions of management through data collection and analysis. The Overclass is no longer needed at its current scale. AI programs are already "hallucinating" or making up on their own truths which can be imposed on their subjugated users as unquestionable *Begriffs*, telling the humans what is right and what is wrong, what they should believe, and what they should do. In Marxist terms, technology has again changed the means of production, in this case the production of intellectual goods and services. Accordingly, the superstructure of Overclass functionalities must now change to conform with the new economic reality.

CHAPTER 5

AN IDEOLOGY OF DECADENCE

The decadent do what they will; the honest what they should.

A paraphrase of Thucydides[1]

Duty is the antidote to decadence. Duty is inherent in covenant. The inner-directed are more capable of being dutiful than are the other-directed, not resenting duty as an imposition or feeling its constraints as a diminution of self. The other-directed, feeling both anxious and entitled to a safe space, are very often only wayward stewards of the common good. They seek camouflage in the madness of crowds to avoid being singled out for responsibility.

The moral principle of duty is a principle of coherence. Each citizen may expect that every other citizen will similarly observe the principle of duty. If such an expectation is not realistic, then the civic order is dissolved. The egocentric standard of rights without corresponding duties is the principle of civic dissolution. Thus does duty keep decadence at bay, says British philosopher David Selbourne.[2] The principle of duty is the sovereign ethical principle of every civic order and the condition for its efficacy. Without the principle of duty, chaos prevails, and the civic order passes into decadence.

In times of decadence, covenantal obligations are not honored. Reciprocally, the abandonment of covenantal commitments leads to decadence.

Energized by the baby boomer generation, the American Overclass has both 1) grown in social power and, married up with other-direction, 2) subjected Americans to a managerial elite that has no virtue. Those without virtue lack the ability to live by any principle of duty. The moral sense sustains the principle of duty, but the other-directed Overclass has made little effort to foster and vitalize the moral sense in American culture, thereby undermining America's civic order. The Overclass has followed Hegel and Nietzsche, forgetting the learning of our Founders. The Overclass, therefore, seeks not to understand human nature, avoids personal responsibility as much as possible, sees personal privilege where duty is demanded, and laughs off the moral demands that come with gracious spirituality.

The Overclass has adopted other-direction for its modal personality. As it has taken more and more authority over American culture, society, politics and the economy, it has imposed the consequences of other-directed living and thinking on the American people.

The rise to power of the Overclass has not made Americans happier or more trusting or more accomplished. Inequality and pessimism have accelerated, overall achievement has plateaued, energies are dissipated, and the classic symptoms of decadence have set in.

To some degree each person, each family, each ethnic community, each social class seeks its own best interest detached from a common good. The first modern sociologist, Herbert Spencer, took it for granted that, like their great ape predecessors, human persons are inherently and incorrigibly self-seeking, locked into a never-ending struggle, one with the other, whereby only the most fit will survive.

The English political philosopher Thomas Hobbes also presumed that every society is a theater of low-intensity warfare where self-seeking individuals do what they can, and the weak suffer what they must. Hobbes concluded that, in the struggle of "everyone against everyone," the life of each human person must be "solitary, poor, nasty, brutish, and short."[3]

And observers of politics since Aristotle have associated forms of government with the class that holds power. For Aristotle, if one person rules well, then government is a monarchy, but if badly, then it is a tyranny. If an elite of those with special achievements holds sway with a view to the common good of the state, the government is aristocratic, but if the elite serves only itself, it is an oligarchy. If the common people have the last say in how power is to be used, the government is a polity if the common good is preferred. Or it is a democracy if the state bestows its favors unfairly. (For this reason, Aristotle was not fond of democracy.)

In the Roman Republic, founded when the elite families dethroned their king, patrician families held the most important positions, but the lower-class plebeians were allowed some rights to elect representatives (tribunes) to defend their interests. In the feudal societies of medieval Europe, great landowning families with the right to have their own armed subordinates held a predominance of social power in dialogue with a monarch, also a landed aristocrat, sitting with them from time to time in a great council or parliament.

With the rise of capitalism and the start of the Industrial Revolution, a new middle class of business owners, managers, and self-employed professionals gained rights to join the monarch and aristocrats in making laws and political decisions. Starting with the English Civil Wars in the mid-1600s and the French Revolution of 1789, middle classes in Europe—the bourgeoisie so disparaged by Karl Marx—took control of national governments. Yet fairly quickly, the bourgeoisie was accused by workers and moral reformers of running the state for the advantage of owners, not workers.

Looking back on the predominance of one class or another in gathering for itself plentiful social, political, legal, and economic power, Karl Marx proposed that wealth and income were the permanent drivers of social preeminence and political supremacy. Following this narrative, he and Engels would deny capitalists access to wealth and income, driving them from power, and replace them with administrators providing income to the workers who, on their own, would then sustain the continued growth of the industrial age.

If we apply Marx's insight into the dependency of class power on its systemic relations to the means of production—the creation of wealth and income—we can quickly discern the exact relationship that the American Overclass has with the means of production in the United States. Members of that class obtain their wealth and income principally from rent extraction. They rent out their skills to institutions and organizations possessing the market power or political authority to obtain cash payments from society.

Managers, bureaucrats, experts, and professionals live off salaries paid by organizations. They are not capitalists, investing their money in enterprise and assuming business risks of failure. If in the private sector, when working for, say, Alphabet, Apple, JPMorgan Chase Bank, or Delta Airlines, members of the American Overclass earn cash salaries and, perhaps, bonuses. They invest their earnings in investment funds for capital accumulation and to have money in retirement. Some are rewarded by private firms with ownership shares in the enterprise, which can be sold on stock exchanges. These shares provide them with spendable wealth and can also be considered as income earned through the renting out of personal skills.

As those who also live off rents, members of the Overclass share social and cultural aspirations and political needs with the landed European aristocrats of yesteryear and the mandarins of imperial China. They want elite status and political protection from risk. They are fond of government, business, academia, nonprofits, media, and champion interdependence and collaboration in the "management" of postmodern society and its wealth-creating capacities, which alone enable society to pay "rents" to its guardians.

Economists call such cash payments for providing an asset—land, housing, human capital—"rents." Overclass members, in effect, agree to let organizations rent their time and abilities for the advantage of the organization. "Rentiers," as they are called, also are relentlessly dependent on the laws that give them title to positional status. In America today those positions belong to organizations. The work lives, social roles, and personal orientations of these rent extractors were documented by C. Wright Mills in the 1950s.

William H. Whyte Jr., in 1956, wrote about the social function of the Overclass in *The Organization Man*. These managers, largely protected from risk by their employment contracts, had put behind them the earlier capitalist ethic—the Protestant ethic. Rather, they were building out a new "social ethic" that held that (1) the group is the source of authority, (2) "belongingness" is the ultimate need of the individual, and (3) using science in work can achieve belongingness.

The Overclass, thought Whyte, demands no conflict between man and society and considers that conflicts are really only misunderstandings and breakdowns in communications. Professionalism and science will permit society to enjoy consensus and create an equilibrium in which society's needs and the needs of the individual are one and the same. Whyte considered this to be a utopian faith. "It does not make any difference whether the Good Society is to be represented by a union, or by a corporation, or a church; it is to be a society unified and purged of conflict."[4]

Whyte noted the inherent disposition of the Overclass for living as other-directed persons.

> The organization people who are best able to control their environment [or, in my words, to sustain the flow of rents] rather than be controlled by it are well aware that they are not too easily distinguishable from the others in the outward

obeisances paid to the good opinion of others. And that is one of the reasons they do control. They disarm society.[5]

In such a well-organized society, there can be no tolerance of alleged misinformation or disinformation.

Whyte referred to the "ultimate victory of the administrator" because the teaching of individuals to create in concert, in teams, does not value the creative individual or the actual conditions necessary to generate creativity. "The messiness of intuition, the aimless thoughts, the unpractical questions—all these things that are so often the companion to discovery are anathema to the world of the administrator. Order, objective goals, agreement—these are his desiderata."[6] Systems of administration, predicted Whyte, were the future for America, not rugged individualism.

Whyte worried that the administrative trajectory of the organization man was toward the elimination of "leadership."[7] The newly articulated source of more productivity for the organization was "high group morale." Under this new means of production, Whyte wrote, "the ideal leader should not lead in the old sense—that is, focus his attention and that of the group on goals. He should instead concentrate almost wholly on the personality relationships within the group. If he attends to these and sees to it that the members get along, the goals will take care of themselves."[8]

In June 2024 McKinsey and Company provided a list of books recommended by CEOs for executives to read. The invitation to read those books advised,

> Reading isn't just for leisure; it's a power move for leaders. Books can boost smarts, enhance emotional intelligence, and even help keep stress in check. Are you looking to hone your leadership skills? Here are 10 books recommended by global CEOs to consider adding to your library.

Two of the recommended books confirmed Whyte's vision of how the Overclass of managers would abandon personal leadership for other-directed communitarianism. One is *To My Sisters: A Guide to Building Lifelong Friendships* by Renée Kapuku and Courtney Daniella Boateng. One comment on the book was, "As I look back at my early career, I'm not sure I factored in the importance of sisterhood when it comes to building and sustaining careers."

The other is *The Art of Gathering: How We Meet and Why It Matters* by Priya Parker, which the book's jacket describes as arguing "that the gatherings in our lives are lackluster and unproductive—which they don't have to be. We rely too much on routine and the conventions of gatherings when we should focus on distinctiveness and the people involved."

Both books clearly counsel replacing self-reliance and self-assurance with submission to others. Success in life and career, these books tell us, comes from following the right "influencers" with skill and good timing. We piggyback on their values and judgments learned through "conversations" and "being at the right table with the right people."[9]

Decadence Arrives:
The Overclass Abandons Inner-Direction

Supporting themselves by extracting rents from society, members of the managerial Overclass gravitate toward dependency as their primary relationship to power. Other-direction is more suitable than inner-direction for living comfortably in relationship to hierarchy and with bureaucratic norms of keeping to one's role and subordinate position. Inner-directed persons are more likely to want to challenge conventions and leave their footprints on the sands of time.

Other-directed people are no more or less than their brand—a value proposition in the eyes of others. They must therefore defend their value proposition as a matter of social life or death. For managers, their brand is their position, title (along with the associated perks), and the accoutrements of their office space. Thus, to preserve perception of their brand value, they must defend their positional authority at all cost.

Reputational injury is most worrisome for members of the Overclass. An affront or a disparagement cuts directly to their sense of self-worth and their concern never to have their status compromised in the eyes of those with whom they want to identify. Thus, words can really hurt them. What is said is what is very real. For the other-directed, words can be felt as a violation of their ego-identity, an overt, physical attack on their social legitimacy. Ideas expressed in words can be hurtful and destabilizing, triggering dysphoria. Further, ostracism invalidates the internalized performative narratives that keep them psychologically stable. Thus, other-directed people need safe spaces in which to protect and preserve their brands. Such spaces are provided by groupthink, cliques, and conventional narratives about what is true.

The old inner-directed point that "sticks and stones can break my bones, but words can never hurt me" provides no comfort or reinforcement of self-confidence to the other-directed. Within a space safe for the vulnerable other-directed ego, there are no differences in judgments and opinions. The safe space is a protective bubble. It is a much-needed environment of support and unquestioned acceptance, of caring inclusion, where self-esteem is easily sustained. Focusing on self-esteem is another foundational concern of the other-directed.

Members of the Overclass create and maintain such safe spaces with the money they so easily extract from society—money to subscribe to proper media such as the *Washington Post* and the *Atlantic*, to dress in fashion, to dine out with the right friends, to make the right friends and hang out with the right people—but most of all by having the right kind of job that provides positional authority and the right to display one's expertise in public. But in such a bubble, little learning takes place; dialogue and conversations are mostly reinforcement of existing conceits and reassuring narratives as provided by supportive outsiders. Confirmation bias reigns supreme.

The needed safe space also provides protection against the intrusion of truth. Truth in a safe space is relational to the thinking of others in the space and responsive to one's needs. "My" truth provides very important reassurance to the other-directed members of the Overclass, a truth they defend with evidence of professional education and unquestionably credentialed expertise. Such a personal truth must not be questioned by anyone of inferior status or malignant disposition. Any "my truth" is little more than a very personal *Begriff*, divorced from facticity and sustained by a Nietzschean "will to power." But such a "my truth" must also serve as a credential that one deserves membership in America's ruling class.

Thus, there is a probability that other-directed members of the Overclass have difficulty perceiving realities and adjusting their thinking and opinions, especially their behaviors, to a factually correct correspondence with circumstances and events. This systemic detachment from reality is also a mark of existential decadence.

Taking on meaningful personal responsibility requires stepping outside the safe space. For other-directed people, responsibility is very risky—what if they should fail? What then will their significant others think of them? And what if their efforts are not legitimated by the team or whoever's opinion matters most? Here again, affiliation and belonging come to the rescue of the other-directed. It is better for them to share responsibility with others, to gain the protection of self, which is provided by teams and groupthink. If such protection is not forthcoming, plan B is to pass the responsibility on to others.

In 1959 a training manual for the other-directed was written by Erving Goffman. He advised,

> In their capacity as performers, individuals will be concerned with maintaining the impression that they are living up to the many standards by which they and their products are judged. . . . But, qua performers, individuals are concerned not with the moral issue of realizing these standards, but with the

amoral issue of engineering a convincing impression that these standards are being realized.[10]

In other words, such skilled performers are just phonies, players following a script, putting on a good show for the audience. Consider the presidency of Joe Biden: Was he just an actor posing as a president? And consider, too, the 2024 presidential campaign of Kamala Harris: Was she nothing more than a poseur, impersonating a candidate by reading from teleprompters and offering citizens memorized innocuous platitudes ("turn the page"; "unburdened by what has been") where spontaneous, rigorous thinking was the special talent that was required?

Not coincidentally, Harris was raised by Overclass parents, a college professor and a biomedical scientist, and graduated from Howard University and the Hastings law school in San Francisco. Her political career was initially produced and directed by a paramour, the Democratic mayor of San Francisco, and through her marriage to a lawyer, she enjoyed wealth and elite status as a Hollywood socialite as well. Her husband was a litigator in media, entertainment, and intellectual property law. Walmart and Merck were two of his clients.

Regarding performers, Goffman noted,

> When an individual plays a part he implicitly requests his observers to take seriously the impression that is fostered before them. They are asked to believe that the character they see actually possesses the attributes he appears to possess, that the task he performs will have the consequences that are implicitly claimed for it, and that, in general, matters are what they appear to be.[11]

Goffman noted the value of performance to the performer—say, an other-directed manager or politician. "The performer can be fully taken in by his own act; he can be sincerely convinced that the impression of reality which he stages is the real reality."[12] A cynical performer, on the other hand, cares not if the performance aligns with the reality of his or her self. The dramatic effect sought by the performance is whether it will be credited or discredited, whether the phoniness will be detected or not.

Writing about "the arts of impression management," Goffman added, "A correctly staged and performed scene leads the audience to impute a self to the performed character."[13] The traits displayed by the character are imputed to the self of that actor, but in no way is that self that character. Such socialization experiences are only hallucinations on the part of both performer and audience. Such performances are filled with communication of misinformation and disinformation.

In further protection of their brands, members of the Overclass work in concert to "cancel" others, to amplify that which validates their brand and de-amplify what may detract from their brand value. The Overclass obsesses over what may be misinformation or disinformation that contradicts or calls into question the intellectual or normative content of their brand propositions. An insistence on political correctness as they personally define "correct opinion" is foundational to their self-centered notions of legitimacy and so to their claim to cultural, social, and political prominence. Challenge their correctness, and you challenge the value of their brand and so of their entitlement to privilege.

But importantly, other-direction also opens the soul to passivity and acceptance of subordination. Where there should be a vigorous personal identity, there is a vacuum, even a complete void of pride and purpose, which cannot generate meaningful agency.

Other-directed people look for patrons, protectors of their vulnerable self-image. Other-directed people are supplicants, dependent on the power of others; they importune, implore, appeal to, and beseech those with influence for protection and good fortune.

The Old Testament story of the Israelites and the golden calf illuminates the dynamics of the Overclass. The Israelites follow Moses out of Egypt and slavery but lose patience when he takes his time in coming down from the mountain with the Ten Commandments. After years in slavery, his people have yet to regain a sense of personal agency; they rely on intercession, so they turn to a golden calf. That is other-direction. Accepting the Ten Commandments would have required inner-direction and the assumption of personal responsibility.

Maybe the need for them to become inner-directed was the reason God made them wander in the Sinai wilderness for forty years before allowing them to enter his Promised Land. They needed to move beyond the personality of dependency and victimhood and self-generate without his intervention, the personality mode of self-confidence more befitting a chosen people.

Yet years later, the people of Israel demand that a king be set above them to rule and lead them in battle. The first book of Samuel tells us,

> Then all the elders of Israel gathered together and came to Samuel at Ramah and said to him, "Behold, you are old and your sons do not walk in your ways. Now appoint for us a king to judge us like all the nations."
>
> But the thing displeased Samuel . . . And Samuel prayed to the Lord.
>
> And the Lord said to Samuel, "Obey the voice of the people in all that they say to you, for they have not rejected you, but they have rejected me from being king over them. According to all the deeds that they have done, from the day I brought them up out of Egypt even to this day, forsaking me and serving other gods, so they are also doing to you. Now then, obey their voice; only you shall solemnly warn them and show them the [bad] ways of the king who shall reign over them."[14]

What apparently has displeased Samuel is his people's wanting to imitate others. Any self that is too dependent on others for direction loses unique purpose. A self that cannot on its own mobilize an autonomous will, that has little pride in self, randomly turns this way and that, seeking affiliations with the peer group and patronage from dominating influencers. Surrendering personal agency is not what Yahweh wants from any of his chosen people.

A self that is subsumed in dependency eventually succumbs to decadence, which implies loss of competence, loss of touch with the significant, the long-lasting, and the forces at work in the world. Decadence degrades courage and resolve, dissolves idealism and self-confidence, and dissipates mastery of affairs. Decadence is associated with the states of decay, decline, dissolution of what once was, debasement, downfall, and lack of restraint and propriety, leading to incontinence and intemperance.

The psychologist Harry Stack Sullivan developed a respected theory of psychiatric therapy that held that the key for healthy living was the quality of the "self-system," which he thought of as a dynamism within the person sustaining their personal agency. The inner-directed have a more robust self-system dynamism than do the other-directed. Thus, the inner-directed are more likely to be successful in sustaining day in and day out, through good times and bad, a personality, an authentic and stable real identity—one providing a purpose for living.

The other-directed, from Sullivan's point of view, are more vulnerable to succumbing to anxiety and so to losing control of just who they are in the world. Sullivan said that "anxiety is almost always . . . an outstanding ingredient in breaking up interpersonal situations which otherwise would be useful in the satisfaction of the needs of the person concerned."[15]

Anxiety has increased among Americans in recent decades as the Overclass has expanded its control over leading cultural, social, economic, and political institutions. Along with the increase in anxiety has been growing use of antidepressants, drugs, and alcohol as self-medication applied to a personal inner crisis of meaning and interpersonal relationship dysfunctionality.

The other-directed person is usually completely narcissistic, and so is walking on a one-way street toward total self-absorption. Their need for connection with, and affirmation from, influencers does not seem to provide them with the kind of interdependence with reality that can prevent their descent into psychosocial chaos. Such a self becomes more and more risk averse. Other-direction, if not disciplined by some conscience, opens the soul to the afflictions flowing from negative emotions such as doubt and even rage—in other words, into a state of decadence.

These afflicting emotions, as the Dalai Lama calls them, include greed, hate, delusion, conceit, wrong views, torpor, restlessness, shamelessness, and recklessness. Such states of mind are harbingers of social dysfunction and institutional collapse.

Such self-absorption may result from the disconnection of the other-directed person from the law and its call for stalwart self-command. Managers, for example, are famous for their fixation on "office politics" and the ease with which they take to isolated silos within the organization and to choosing peer priorities over the higher goals of the organization as a whole. Rules and regulations are allowed to calcify while supposedly governing high-minded guiding principles are ignored. Laws and principles speak in terms of duties, which implicate the inner-directed taking of personal responsibility.

The Overclass, warped by the demands of other-direction, brings on decadence in another way. They erode social capital. Societies rise or fall depending on their human and social capital. Robust social capital leads to wealth creation, good governance, and justice. Weak social capital turns society over to the sociopaths and psychopaths, turning the strong against the weak and isolating the privileged from the worker bees.

Trust drives the formation and sustainability of social capital. Societies with low trust are more likely to be Hobbesian, where, unhappily, life is more burdened with corruption, rent extraction, monopolies, poverty, and injustice.[16] The predicate for trust is certainty and predictability. Thus, inner-direction promotes trust. People so inclined are reliable; they do what they promise. They accept personal responsibility. They stick to their values and so are more predictable in their behaviors.

David Horsager promotes "40 proven tools to lead better, grow faster and build trust now."[17] Six of his eight ego-identity strengths that support trust arise from inner-direction: clarity, compassion, character, competency, commitment, and consistency.

Other-direction, on the other hand, can encourage risk aversion, bystanderism, and other forms of social lethargy. The other-directed are prone to equivocation or withdrawal just when you need them most. They prefer to meet and discuss rather than act quickly and decisively. They don't like to venture beyond their bubble. Such people are not trustworthy. Their personality orientation frustrates the formation of resilient and lasting social reciprocities, the stuff of social capital.

The ambivalence of the other-directed toward the truth also diminishes trust. If there is no truth, can anything ultimately be trusted as certain? If there are too many bubbles, too many safe spaces, too many narratives, and too many "truths," then from where come solidarity, cohesion, alliances, and the common good? The proliferation of truths draws forth inconsistent, chaotic actions, chisels away at structural foundations for commitment, and piles on uncertainty so that no one can reasonably rely on friend or colleague. In short, under these conditions, social capital crumbles. As Hobbes advised (as did Mozi in China), under such circumstances of no trust and no reliance, only a Leviathan—the modern state or the ancient Chinese imperial cult—can successfully create order and civility.

The tendency of the Overclass to minimize trust only reinforces the psychic need of the class to hold administrative power over culture and society. If you can't trust, despotic control over your environment easily becomes your default mode of acting in self-defense.

This need to keep power in its hand naturally leads the Overclass to manufacture performative episodes where paranoia, fear, and hysteria are deployed to keep the wary respectful and submissive. Those who cannot, or who do not, belong to the Overclass are often victimized by those who can or who are its members in good standing.

French moral philosopher Chantal Delsol, in her book *Icarus Fallen*, identifies the Overclass of managers with Icarus who, so self-confident, flew too close to the sun and destroyed that which allowed him to fly—the wax keeping the feathers of his wings in their rightful places. She asserts,

> Modernity has replaced the objective category of the good with what it calls *values*, that is, a smattering of subjective goods, each of which derives from individual judgment. . . . Put to the fore with no other criterion than that of the sovereignty of individual judgment, values are a form of solipsism or mere whim.

Delsol further laments that for me to defend "my" truth against "your" truth reduces my dialogue with you to a reciprocal exchange of anathemas and excommunications. For Delsol, Overclass "thinking" is "built precisely on the principle that man is a soft wax capable of being infinitely reshaped by the will"—in short, human persons are, by their nature, other-directed.[18]

Decadence and Infantilism

As Shakespeare wisely observed in *As You Like It*, dotage turns to infantilism.

> His youthful hose, well sav'd, a world too wide
> For his shrunk shank; and his big manly voice,
> Turning again toward childish treble, pipes
> And whistles in his sound. Last scene of all,
> That ends this strange eventful history;
> Is second childishness and mere oblivion,
> Sans teeth, sans eyes, sans taste, sans everything.[19]

The other-directed personality orientation pervading the Overclass contributes to American decadence through propagating infantilism among our elite managers and experts.

Erik Erikson, the Harvard professor mentioned in chapter 3, described the process of becoming a successful mature adult without experiencing neurosis or psychosis as a series of eight stages, each one of which presents a challenge to the ego that, if mastered, increases the probability of learning how to master the challenges of the successive stages. The other-directed person seems not to have fully overcome the challenges of early childhood in Erikson's stages 2 and 3. Thus, they can get stuck in early adulthood in stage 6 and never fully develop as effective, resilient adults. Other-direction, thus, has a tendency to keep us more infantile during all our years, leading us to contribute our infantilism to the society around us.

Erikson was a child psychoanalyst who gave us the concept of "identity crisis" as the open or closed door to successful adulthood. A student of Anna Freud, he was one of the originators of ego psychology, a conviction that the ego is far more than a servant of the id, that each of us has agency in our ego to shape our lives for the better or for worse. I sat in on some of his classes when an undergraduate at Harvard College. His book *Young Man Luther* changed my way of thinking about growing into adulthood and standing up for what was important.

In Erikson's stage 2, up to age 3, we are challenged to become autonomous or else experience persistent shame and doubt. Shame supposes that we are exposed and so conscious of being looked at; we are self-conscious and worry about what others think of us. "From a sense of loss of self-control and of foreign over-control, comes a lasting propensity for doubt and shame."[20]

In Erikson's stage 3, during ages 3 to 5, one is challenged to internalize initiative or else have the ego subjected to a sense of guilt.[21] "The danger of this stage is a sense of guilt over the goals contemplated and the acts initiated in one's exuberant enjoyment of new locomotive and mental power. . . . The instinctive fragments which before had enhanced the growth of his infantile body and mind now become divided into an infantile set which perpetuates the exuberance of growth potentials, and a parental set which supports and increases self-observation, self-guidance, and self-punishment."[22]

The child who develops the parental way of reacting is headed toward inner-direction. The child who maintains the infantile set of approaches is headed toward other-direction and a predisposition toward more volatile and less coherent infantile moods and behaviors.

In Erikson's stage 6, during years 21 to 39, the person's challenge is to find intimacy or remain in isolation. For Erikson, intimacy flows from within. It is a capacity to develop the ethical strength to abide by commitments made even though they may call for significant sacrifices and compromises.[23] Inner-direction more readily provides that ethical strength, emerging from a self-system that is resilient and full of internally generated purpose.

Those who fail at commitment are open-ended and unreliable, more indeterminant and infantile than trustworthy. This propensity also contributes to failure of community and the rise of decadence, as a society of people living without commitment loses its capacity to be serious. Thus, Erikson helps us understand why we have an infantilism in our elite, through which our best and brightest mimic the hesitations and insecurities that come with old age.

Abraham Maslow also proposed that we grow toward healthy maturity as persons in stages. He started by searching for the causes of neuroses, which, he proposed, were born out of deficiencies, with a neurosis responding to a need. He thought that most neuroses involved "ungratified wishes for safety, for belongingness, and identification, for close love relationships and for respect and prestige."[24] We might note here the close association of these needs with a direction of the personality going outward toward others.

Maslow became convinced that a person's motivations could evolve from meeting needs to later becoming a wholesome self, independent and resilient. He wrote, "Healthy people have sufficiently gratified their basic needs for safety, belongingness, love, respect and self-esteem so that they are motivated primarily by trends to self-actualization." "Self-actualization" to me connotes a healthy state of knowing who you are, accepting who you are, and so permitting psychic movement toward unity, integration, and constructive synergies among your thoughts, emotions, and motivations. So the not-needy person, the self-actualized person, is inner-directed and happily self-assured.

Maslow added that "there are subjective confirmations or reinforcements of self-actualization or of good growth toward it. These are the feelings of zest in living, of happiness or euphoria, of serenity, of joy, of calmness, of responsibility, of confidence in one's ability to handle stresses, anxieties, and problems. The subjective signs of self-betrayal, of fixation, of regression, and of living by fear rather than by growth are such feelings as anxiety, despair, boredom, inability to enjoy, intrinsic guilt, intrinsic shame, aimlessness, feelings of emptiness, of lack of identity, etc."[25] Thus, those who have not self-actualized show many traits of other-directedness.

Given Maslow's analysis, many of today's very unhappy Americans experiencing identity dysphoria are most likely to be other-directed and are, therefore, responsive to the culture of the Overclass. In Maslow's hierarchy of needs, there is the drive to overcome fears and insecurities; the other-directed person has great difficulty growing beyond level 3—meeting the need for love and belonging through friendship, intimacy, family, and sense of connection. Such a personality has satisfied biological needs for food, shelter, sleep, and clothing and the higher need for safety—personal security, employment, resources, health, and property. But they are still far from self-actualization.

Thus, we find many members of the Overclass amply fortified with wealth and excellent positions but nonetheless still very other-directed as if they themselves are still missing something meaningful and reassuring. In this respect, unable to self-actualize, they remain childish in many ways: petty, self-absorbed, needy, demanding, and irritable. These are also symptoms associated with dotage for some elderly who lose awareness of who they have been and who they now are. Adults who have not grown out of their infantile dispositions—who tend toward other-direction—do not fully develop a moral sense. Cicero, in his essay *De Officiis*, rather clearly laid out a program of self-awareness enabling us to build a moral sense. Confucius and Mencius were similarly explicit about how we can grow to be virtuous adults. Adam Smith, in his *Theory of the Moral Sentiments*, was absolutely convinced that each one of us is born with an inner capacity to energize moral powers to become an upstanding adult contributing constructively to our families, friends, and society.

But successful actualization of our moral sense comes more easily to the inner-directed as the moral sense is a fulsome capacity developed by the individual and living within the person, a dynamic spiritual equilibrium balancing the self on the one side with external reality on the other. Adam Smith thought of the moral sense as "a person living within the breast." As an everyday host to such a personhood within us, we can decide to feed it well with our will, thoughts, and emotions—or we can starve it to death by choosing ignorance of its presence and turning to other-direction. Inner-direction feeds the moral sense; other-direction starves it. The choice to feed or starve is up to us.

Importantly, ideas—concepts, "my" truths, *Begriffs*—as mental abstractions do not and cannot on their own automatically reside in our moral sense. They are not deeply ingrained in our sense of being. Unless downloaded by the moral sense and grounded in our inner-direction, such ethereal phantoms can play tricks with our minds and emotions, as Nietzsche intuited. Thus, the ideas and propositions, beliefs and performances, so necessary to the other-directed even with their education and professional expertise, do not reliably construct a moral sense within us.

Any person without a developed moral sense behaves like a spoiled child, antisocial and sociopathic. Any society without social capital created by the collective moral sense of its members suffers away in decadence.

The Overclass Goes Gnostic: A Measure of Decadence?

Every ruling elite, every governing administration, needs legitimation. To withstand opposition, governments must provide for those they rule an evocative sense of purpose, a moral vision. Regimes thus need a *Begriff* of sufficient cogency and emotional power to engender loyalty and willing collaboration from those living under their police powers. Regimes collapse when their claim to legitimacy is no longer accepted by subjects or citizens. Domestic revolutions happen when traditional claims of legitimacy are rejected and when different claims are used to mobilize loyalty and support from those less privileged.

In the case of the American Revolution, the claim of the English king and Parliament to govern the British colonies in North America was intellectually and morally rejected by most residents of those colonies. In the cases of the French and Russian Revolutions, the claim of the ruling dynasty to rule on behalf of the French or Russian people was rejected, and new *Begriffs* were proposed by the revolutionaries as conferring a legitimacy on government more fitting and just for the nation. In the cases of the post–World War I coming to power of fascist regimes in Italy and Germany, a *Begriff* of national socialism empowering an honorable people won the devoted support of many ordinary Italians and Germans and so legitimized the rule of a single party over the entire nation.

In the case of the United States, the Overclass did not seek to use the original, Puritan, covenantal *Begriff* of the American Revolution to legitimate its claim to social power. Rather it has offered the German Hegelian *Begriff* of professional, science-based expertise for achieving excellence in the administration of a modern state and economy as the grounds for its right to extract rents and make decisions to bind ordinary Americans as the Overclass sees best.

But any claim to legitimacy based on possession of superior knowledge flirts with Gnostic arrogance. The Gnostic faith presumes that the possession of certain knowledge confers on a person the ability to confront the evils of the world and overcome them. Gnosticism tends toward believing in a polarized duality in the march of history, an existential conflict between the good and the bad, the light and the dark. Thus, we have the Marxist Gnosticism of the "bad" capitalists being overthrown by the "good" proletarians; the national socialist Gnosticism that certain races, such as the Aryans in Germany, are superior and need to repress inferior peoples who thwart their redemptive power and glory; and the Maoist Gnosticism that being "Red" in mind and heart will save China from poverty and humiliation.

The Gnostic faith in some ways proposes that a "saving" remnant of the rightly knowing can dispel the darkness, hold off suffering and defeat, and bring about ideal conditions for the success of society and culture. The Gnostic text of the second century, the *Gospel of Philip*, says,

> The world is a corpse eater consuming dead animals; . . . the dark powers wanted to deceive man, to confuse his relationship with the truly good. They took good names and gave them to the bad, so that with these names they might bind them. . . . The dark powers imagine it is by their own self-will that they do what they do; . . . Truth does not come into the world without robes; it enters through words and pictures. . . . Where I eat, all is from the tree of knowledge [that] can now bring men back from death. The tree is the law. It's empowered to give knowledge of good and evil. It neither removes evil nor establishes good, but kills those who choose disobediently. . . . If the root of wickedness lies hidden in the dark it waxes strongly, when exposed to the light of awareness, it perishes. . . . Ignorance is the mother of all evils.[26]

The focus of Gnostic salvation is on the individual becoming knowing: "Each one of us must dig down within ourselves and find the root of this evil egoism in the heart, so it will perish. If we ignore this root, more poisonous fruit is produced in the heart; it becomes our task master and enslaves us, forcing us to do what it desires. . . . If we know truth, its blossom will flower in our hearts and bring salvation."[27]

Glenn Hughes explains the continuing appeal of Gnostic certainties to "our desire to have final answers—answers that explain our sense of alienation from the world, that relieve the pressure deriving from our ignorance about the ultimate purposes of existence."[28] Finding such convincing answers reassures our conscience that we are indeed good and produces the Gnostic posture of unyielding and close-minded conviction.[29] Echoing Delsol, Hughes concludes, "Although the Gnostic choice is irresponsible, it remains that the anxiety and alienation that prompts it . . . are phenomena that must, after all, be existentially addressed."[30]

Hegel's thinking that a *Begriff* can provide transcendent justification for a God-State can easily accommodate Gnostic faiths. The profound and special, but teachable, knowledge (gnosis) of a Gnostic belief system can provide human minds with a *Begriff* guiding believers to reformation of a fallen world.

Thus, for all their subjectivity, advocating Gnosticisms is nevertheless a proper function for intellectuals and experts seeking to manage modernity ostensibly for the good of all. Any proposition or belief that can masquerade as "truth" can serve as the basis of a Gnostic faith. One must take a Gnostic proposition on the source of evil on faith, as its truth cannot be proved within either the processes of logical deduction or empirically.

The American Overclass adopted a "light" Gnosticism highlighting the redemptive value of the college educated who would manage government, corporations, and society in general for the good of all. But by turning its back on the covenantal justification for the American "experiment in ordered liberty," the Overclass introduced a moral (and potentially mortal) vulnerability into American culture and politics, a fissure that widened more and more over the years into a culture war between "right" and "left," between traditionalists who demanded "making

America great again" and progressives who thought of that America as sexist, racist, and otherwise most "deplorable." For the Overclass, progressive "anticapitalism" and racist "antiracism" (perhaps even "toxic masculinity") are Gnostic *Begriffs* believed to have talismanic power to cleanse America of darkness and lift the country to new heights of freedom and happiness. The Overclass never affirmed covenantal America as their own.

These gnostic faiths rest on assumptions about what causes evil in our lives. First there is the evil of greed, which is presumed to be the mighty taproot of free-market capitalism. The Overclass presumes that expert management of the economy can replace destructive greed and the inequality it champions with the fairness championed by social justice.

Second there is the assumption that the pursuit of economic growth has brought about the evil of global warming, another ethical failure. Again, good management of an immediate transition to clean energy, following the teachings of the best science, is presumed to have the capacity to save humanity.

Third "racism," conscious or unconscious and only in White people as a psychogenetic heritage of past unforgivable exploitations, is a present evil. Therefore, management of the consciousnesses of Whites and the systematic promotion to managerial positions of non-Whites will save America from this spiritual darkness.

Fourth an excessive male hubris sustains another spiritual darkness of oppression and inequality. Thus, Gnostic management of (1) the male ego, and (2) society and culture is required to keep men in their proper place and to allow women to "break glass ceilings" and establish a better power balance between sexes, while (3) the promotion of gender fluidity is necessary to minimize the hurtful selfishness inherent in birth gender inner-direction.

The formulation of the feminist Gnostic *Begriff* was very briefly summarized by Dayna Tortorici in a June 2025 book review published in *The New Yorker*. She proposed the emergence of feminism as a "reappraisal," asking what voices, loud or soft, had convinced women of their own inferiority for so long. What myths, scripts, and stories had predisposed them to accept the limitations placed on them from within and without? What alternative ways of living could be gleaned from the past?

In keeping with Hegel's theory of our living in an accord with a God-State directed by one *Begriff* or another, Tortorici quoted: 1) Vivian Gornick: "Contemporary feminism is bound up with a profound rereading of the culture"; 2) Adrienne Rich: "Until we can understand the assumptions in which we are drenched we cannot know ourselves"; 3) Simone de Beauvoir on the point that girls were not born women but learned to become them; and 4) Betty Friedan on the point that the lives of modern American woman were "shaped by" cultural images.

Tortorici asserts, "It is now axiomatic among feminists that women are shaped by the culture that surrounds them … [so that] confronting one's cultural influences—identifying them, analyzing them, and exposing how their assumptions shore up a society of male supremacy—can rob [such *Begriffs*] of their power to indoctrinate." [31]

Such a feminism would seem to have a preference for other-direction as the most suitable mode of ego formation in women—as long as those women looking for direction are guided toward the correct influencers: only those who possess the gnostic knowledge of what is "truly" good and what is "truly" evil.

The Overclass Marginalizes the Seeking of Achievement

German sociologist Max Weber very famously drew a causal connection between a form of inner-direction and the creation of a successful modern civilization. He pointed to individuals in Holland, Scotland, and England and the Dutch and English colonies in North America as creating capitalism and introducing the application of technology through private enterprise for the betterment of human well-being. These communities were Calvinist in their religious faith. No other culture ever spontaneously on its own brought forth capitalism. Many older cultures had invented and used money. Roman law had protected private property and contract rights. The Chinese were very inventive (paper money, the magnetic compass, gunpowder), but only the Calvinists made a self-sustaining and self-augmenting economic system out of free markets and private ownership of companies.

Weber did not consider the political implications of Calvinism, but the societies that gave birth to capitalism also organized themselves as the first constitutional representative democracies. Thus, it is most likely that the same Calvinist values and ideals gave rise to both constitutionalism and capitalism with individual rights under law. Those values and ideals, proclaimed weekly in Sunday sermons, manifested themselves in a particular mode of inner-directed personality which was passed down from one generation to another.

The worldly moral ideal of those first capitalist and constitutional societies, as expressed by John Locke in 1689, was a birthright to individual agency enjoying "life," making the most of personal "liberty," and owning "property."

In a 2015 report, the World Bank advised that individual psychology could advance or hinder community economic development.

> First, people make most judgments and most choices automatically, not deliberatively: we call this "thinking automatically." Second, how people act and think often depends on what others around them do and think: we call this "thinking socially." Third, individuals in a given society share a common perspective on making sense of the world around them and understanding themselves: we call this "thinking with mental models."
>
> The three ways of thinking emphasized here apply equally to all human beings. They are not limited to those at higher or lower income levels, or to those at higher or lower educational levels, or to those in high-income or low-income countries.

Numerous examples from high-income countries throughout this Report demonstrate the universality of psychological and social influences on decision making.

This Report discusses how taking the human factors more completely into account in decision making sheds light on a number of areas: the persistence of poverty, early childhood development, household finance, productivity, health, and climate change.[32]

The Calvinist formula for mind, society, and behavior leading to our living a good (and righteous) life was seeking achievement during one's years living on this earth between birth and death. The mode of personhood that best nurtured and promoted such an orientation toward practical achievement was inner-direction. Psychologist David McClelland proposed that such persons would have a high internal need for achievement and would easily think ahead about consequences, which is a personality disposition needed in entrepreneurial and innovative activity. Inner-direction aligns with seeking achievement through actions that arise from personal commitment and run the risk of failure.[33]

On the other hand, Nobel Prize winners like Daron Acemoglu and James A. Robinson made the point that economic and political institutions which extract rents result in failed nations.[34] These failed states are dominated by elites who use their power to serve themselves and are generally disinterested in constitutionalism and the benefits of free markets for social progress.

Driven by other-direction, the Overclass in the United States has turned its back on achievement motivation and so has enhanced rent extraction, calling into question the health of our constitutional democracy and economy.

According to a November 2023 *Wall Street Journal*/NORC poll, fewer Americans believe that hard work can lead to success. Only 36% of voters in that poll said they still believe in the American

Dream. This is a significant decrease from 2012 and 2016, when 53% and 48% of voters in similar polls held the same belief.[35]

The Overclass Feminizes America:
It Sees Evil in the Masculine, the Inner-Directed

Other-direction speaks with a feminine voice, what Carol Gilligan calls "an ethic of care." By privileging other-direction for Americans, the Overclass has feminized elite American institutions.

The dialectic between the modal masculine voice and the modal feminine voice has been totemized as the polarity between sky gods such as Zeus and Odin, at one extreme, and Gaia, the mothering earth, on the other. Humanity must therefore live somewhere between the extremes. But prioritizing one voice over the other, the sky gods over Gaia or Gaia over the sky gods, may lead to instability in the human realm through uncertainty of purpose and meaning, thus contributing to systemic slippage in the resilience of a culture and society.

The Chinese, in their theory about two modes of fundamental energy—yin and yang—integrated into one ceaseless process the endless shifting back and forth, from one to another, of interim states of possibility, some more masculine and others more feminine. In the *Yijing* text, both yang-favored circumstances (male) and yin-favored circumstances (female) are analyzed to provide a comprehensive understanding of living. The yang-favored circumstances—represented by a solid line—reflect heaven and the masculine. The yin-favored circumstances—represented by a divided line—reflect the earth and the feminine.

The *Yijing* hexagram for heaven is

James Legge translates the guidance provided to us by this hexagram as the presence of what is great and originating, penetrating, advantageous, current, and firm. All things owe to it their beginning—it signifies all that belongs to heaven. The clouds move, and the rain is distributed; all things appear in their developed form. The process set in motion by heaven is to change and transform so that everything obtains its correct nature and so that great harmony is preserved in unification. The result is what is advantageous, correct, and firm. The wise person appears aloft, high above all things, and the myriad people all enjoy repose.

The hexagram for the earth is

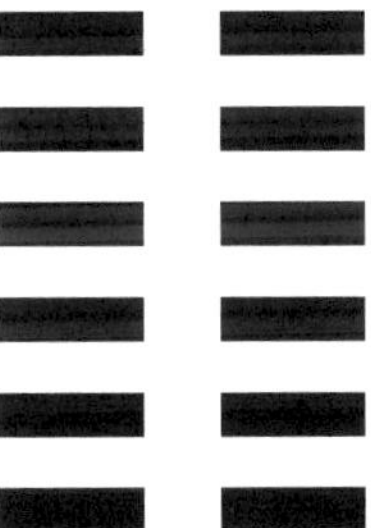

Legge translates the guidance that we can find proposed in this hexagram as circumstances that also are great, originating, penetrating, advantageous, and correct but with a warning that to take the initiative would be to go astray—to follow will bring you to your proper lord.

Resting in correctness and firmness will bring good results. These circumstances are complete. All things owe to it their birth. In their largeness, these circumstances support and contain all things. Their comprehension is wide and brightness great. All things by these influences obtain their full development. The good fortune arising from resting in firmness corresponds to the unlimited capacity of the earth.

The ancient Chinese concepts of heaven—*tian*—and earth—*di*—are Hegelian *Begriffs* used for over two thousand years to legitimate the God-States of Chinese ruling dynasties. Today these *Begriffs* are still being used implicitly by Xi Jinping as the moral ground upholding the right of the Chinese Communist Party to intrusively manage the life of every Chinese person and to convert minority peoples such as the Tibetans and the Uighurs into proper "Han" Chinese so that they, too, may enjoy the blessings of heaven. Further, these *Begriffs* contextualize Xi's arrogant and increasingly uncompromising claim for the superiority of Chinese "civilization" over all other cultures and national identities.

Be the *Yijing* as it may, Carol Gilligan, in her book *In a Different Voice*, makes a case for the feminine voice that authorizes us to fully align other-direction with that "other" voice. After many interviews with women of the baby boomer generation, Gilligan associates the autonomy of the masculine voice with the less caring inclinations of what David Riesman called inner-direction.

Gilligan holds that "by restricting their voices, many women are wittingly or unwittingly perpetuating a male-voiced civilization and an order of living that is founded on disconnection from women."[36] She believes that women's voices have a crucial role in either maintaining or transforming a patriarchal world. For Gilligan, the feminine voice is a relational voice, a voice that insists on staying in connection and bypassing the psychological separations that follow from autonomy, selfhood, and freedom.[37] Gilligan questions whether human persons are indeed self-governing. She prefers a culture that makes "relational realities" explicit to maintain relational order and connection.

In taking this approach, Gilligan devalues inner-direction and privileges the connectedness brought about by other-direction. Gilligan presents the morality of connection as an ethic of care that transcends the conflict between selfishness and selflessness, as a needed shift away from seeking objectivity and detachment to engaging others with responsibility and with care.[38] She believes that relationship, then, requires a kind of courage and emotional stamina that has long been a strength of women, insufficiently noted and valued.

Relationship requires empathy—the emotional intersection of oneself with another—made possible by the ability to listen to others and to internalize their point of view as legitimate and value enhancing. Gilligan insists that "the psychology of women that has consistently been described as distinctive in its greater orientation toward relationships and interdependence implies a more contextual mode of judgment and a different moral understanding."[39]

She adds, "Women see a world comprised of relationships rather than of people standing alone, a world that coheres through human connection rather than through systems of rules."[40] If the real world is a network of connection, a web of relationships, then inclusion of all is a moral priority. Exclusion becomes a pathology.[41]

On August 26, 2024, presidential candidate Kamala Harris, in her distinctive rhetoric, spoke of envisioning American history principally as an exercise in inclusion.

> I think it's really important that we, as Americans, always embrace our history. The parts that we're proud of and the parts that we're not proud of but that we can't forget. And we should all agree that we should teach history. We should learn history if we are to ever have an accurate idea of where we want to go and where we don't want to go in the future. And that means also acknowledging the importance of diversity. It means acknowledging the importance of . . . the fact that everyone

should have equal opportunity to compete and equity and of course inclusion—you know. Hey!! Let's look around the room and see who is not here and did we leave the door open?[42]

Women, writes Gilligan, perceive danger in achievement and as the result of competitive success because such achievement and results will most likely leave one isolated, without affirming relationships.[43] Also, in Gilligan's research, women portray autonomy rather than attachment as illusory and dangerous.[44] Women fear the failure of relationships. Women, in their conversations with Gilligan, will bring up safety nets for those exposed to risk.[45] They will change an order of hierarchy into a structure of interconnection.[46] Other-direction embraces quite nicely these feminine emotional needs.

Morality for women, reports Gilligan, must be a way to ensure that no one gets hurt and brings about an outcome where everyone comes out better off.[47] Morality from this perspective does not arise from laws and rules that allocate rights to some individuals but not to others.[48] The moral problem to be solved, from the feminine perspective, is how to meet an obligation to exercise care and avoid hurt.

Gilligan describes the feminine concept of responsibility as a fusion with a maternal morality that seeks to ensure care for the dependent and the unequal.[49] Care enhances both others and self at the same time; it is win-win. "The conventional feminine voice emerges with great clarity, defining the self and proclaiming its worth on the basis of the ability to care for and protect others."[50] This is the voice of other-direction, defining oneself by looking at the self through the eyes of others and taking into one's own person their values and preferences while still preserving some sense, though uncertain and always open to reexamination, of an independent self.

The demands of other-direction to be placed on men, then, are the necessity to adapt and become more and more open to thinking in the language of the feminine voice of care and connection and then willingly, knowingly, and openly speaking in that language in the culture and society. In the 2024 American presidential election campaign, supporters of Kamala Harris praised her husband, Doug Emhoff, and her vice presidential running mate, Minnesota governor Tim Walz, for being men who were admirably other-directed and at ease with the feminine voice of connection.

Then as part of the inaugural events for the reelected president Donald Trump at the national prayer service at Washington National Cathedral on January 21, 2025, Episcopal bishop Mariann Edgar Budde implored the new president to follow an ethic of care.

> I ask you to have mercy upon the people in our country who are scared now . . . . transgender children . . . who fear for their lives . . . people who pick our crops and clean our office buildings; who labor in our poultry farms and meat-packing plants; who wash the dishes after we eat in restaurants and work the night shift in hospitals. . . . Have mercy, Mr. President, on those in our communities whose children fear that their parents will be taken away. Help those who are fleeing war zones and persecution in their own lands to find compassion and welcome here . . . to honor the dignity of every human being . . . for the good of all the people of this nation and the world.[51]

The Overclass, as it has successfully asserted its power over culture, society, and politics, has made way for doctrines and practices that (1) reject the "toxic masculinity" of patriarchy, and (2) require programs of inclusion where everyone is at the decision-making table without consideration of their inner-directed achievements or lack thereof. This prohibition against men using the masculine voice and society hearing the masculine voice may well be another social instantiation of decadence on the part of the Overclass in the contemporary American experience. Too much Yin and not enough Yang.

Observing campus protesters denouncing Israel for its military response to Hamas's monstrous terror attack on October 7, 2023, writer Kay Hymowitz noticed that they were predominantly female. It was women holding the microphones, addressing the press and crowds, leading the chants of "From the river to the sea," giving interviews about the encampments, and issuing demands to university administrators. In some images, so many women were involved that it seemed as if men had inexplicably vanished.

Hymowitz added,

> Women's prominence at the protests helps explain why, despite menacing sloganeering and electric tensions, little serious violence occurred. Men's higher propensity for physical conflict is a human universal; when they find themselves in tense interactions, the likelihood of mayhem rises.
>
> Don't take this to mean that women are not aggressive; they are. Their strategies, however, are frequently more cunning than men's, and invisible not just to their more guileless victims but even to themselves. They're masters of the covert psyop. Social exclusion—keeping out people whom the in-group deems deplorable—is a preferred tactic, as described by popular "mean girl" ethnographers like Tina Fey and Rosalind Wiseman, the latter the author of *Queen Bees and Wannabees*.
>
> Over the past several decades, safety (both physical and emotional) has taken on a talismanic power in the feminized academy. Equity and inclusion have become major moral concerns. Trigger warnings, cancel culture, and deplatforming are imposed to protect the marginalized and oppressed from ideas deemed harmful by the in-group—and serve as ways to ostracize those who don't share those convictions.
>
> The soft power of social exclusion wasn't the only familiar female tactic common at the campus protests. Women also

relied on "safetyism" and often exaggerated harms. Columbia School of Social Work's Layla Saliba, quoted repeatedly in the press, claimed to have suffered a "chemical weapon" attack after counter-protesters pranked her by spraying make-believe "skunk spray" in her vicinity. (The School of Social Work, whose students were well represented at the protests, is 88 percent female.)

Several viral moments from the demonstrations also capture this dynamic. Asked why student activists wanted to keep Zionists out of their encampments, a UCLA art history major responded, "Our top priority isn't people's freedom of movement. It is keeping people in our encampments physically and emotionally safe." A Columbia grad-student spokesperson, Johannah King-Slutzky, notoriously demanded food and water for the Hamilton Hall occupiers. Responding to a reporter who asked why the university should support trespassers, she retorted, "Do [administrators] want their students to die of dehydration and starvation or get severely ill?" It was a matter of "basic humanitarian aid," she complained, ludicrously. One leader of the University of Pennsylvania encampments, Eliana Atienza—daughter of a Philippine television celebrity father and a Wharton-educated mother who founded the most expensive private school in the island nation—tweeted that Penn had left her "houseless." She went on: "This is their weapon. So disappointed to be attending an institution that resorts to administrative violence."[52]

These examples of protesting students, soon, upon graduation, to become members of the Overclass, demonstrate a feminized other-direction determining political choices and driving behaviors among Americans privileged with high-status educational credentials.

The Overclass Vitiated America's Foreign Policy

The Overclass finally fully emerged at the apex of America's class system in the 1990s with the presidencies of George H. W. Bush, William Clinton, and George W. Bush. The Bushes, father and son, came from the traditional Protestant gentry, each with degrees from Yale University, and were moderate Republicans, eager to please. William Clinton was more thoroughly Overclass with his successful credentialing at Georgetown University and Yale Law School and as a Rhodes scholar. His wife, Hillary, was quintessentially Overclass with her credentials and her abiding commitment to the management of everybody else.

These years followed the collapse of the Soviet Union and the rather immature presumption of the United States as a global uni-power astride a peaceful world at "the end of history," as Professor Francis Fukuyama famously put it. But without the Cold War to impose inner-direction on American foreign policy experts, a more vacuous other-direction of ad hoc management of events took hold of the American foreign policy establishment.

The exemplar of foreign policy brilliance was Henry Kissinger, who in 1971 had managed the Vietnam War with a proposal to the Communists in Moscow, Hanoi, and Beijing that Hanoi could win the war in the end if it gave the United States a "decent interval" (Kissinger's words) of peace and independence for South Vietnam.[53] Kissinger's obsequious submission to Communist power was in large part an other-directed response to placating the demands of the antiwar movement, a foundation for Overclass supremacy in American culture and politics and the platform for subsequent self-disrespect among well-educated Americans. Months before his death, Kissinger confirmed in an interview his other-direction, saying that success in negotiations is arriving at an equilibrium: "a kind of balance of power with an acceptance of the legitimacy of sometimes opposing values." And he easily accepted sacrificing his values to gain such a balance of power: "Because if you believe that the final outcome of your effort has to be the imposition of your values, then I think equilibrium is not possible."[54]

The defeat of American power and purpose in coming to the defense of the Vietnamese nationalists in South Vietnam, set in place by Henry Kissinger, vindicated the anti-Americanism of the Overclass, which in 1972 had taken over the Democratic Party, and so imposed decades of self-doubt on the American people. It's very hard to sustain a healthy inner-direction when you come to doubt yourself.

Foreign policy experts began more and more to focus on the details of management rather than on larger goals and objectives. After the First Gulf War, the United States could not win wars in Iraq and Afghanistan. The post–World War II world order centered on international law, and the United Nations began to meander as its will collapsed into decadence and its sense of purpose fragmented into pettiness.

A thoroughgoing globalism emerged among elite experts in international affairs, coalescing in the 2020 pronouncement of the World Economic Forum in Davos of a "great reset" for the world economy. This reset is meant to bring about a stakeholder economy, using environmental, social, and governance (ESG) metrics, and "harnessing the innovations of the Fourth Industrial Revolution," whatever they were.

Russia under Vladimir Putin and China under Xi Jinping began their rise as revisionist powers, challenging the West with a new theory of world order based on the superiority of "civilization states" and new organizations of nations into the BRICS and the Shanghai Cooperation Organization. Putin would come to invade Ukraine, and China would seek authority to control the international waters of the South China Sea.

Under the Biden administration, the United States had little in the way of foreign policy leadership other than fidelity to the Gnostic beliefs of the Overclass on climate change, LGBT rights globally, and promotion of women, coupled with half-hearted, off-the-cuff reactions to crises such as the war between the Palestinians and the Jews of Israel. Economic growth in developing countries stagnated. The United Nations became a bystander within its shrinking sphere of influence, a sure sign of its sinking into irreversible cosplaying decadence.

What Did the Overclass Do for America?

Following its other-directed and infantile inclinations and its illusory Gnostic insights, the Overclass smothered America in ignorance of history, indifference to the future, withdrawal from global power arrangements, increasing irrelevance of its leaders, incompetence in raising children, and across-the-board irresolution—each marking a fall from what Donald Trump would come to call "greatness."

Do not the roots of our decadence ultimately lie in extreme self-privileging as the just reward for (1) being in the right conversations, (2) resonating with the "vibe" of the moment, and (3) following indulgently the admonitions of the "best and the brightest?"

CHAPTER 6

SEIZING POWER THROUGH HIGHER EDUCATION

Welcome to the fellowship of educated men and women.

Harvard College president's welcome to graduating seniors

In an ironic refutation of Karl Marx, the Overclass in America did not use the means of economic production to seize power over society. The Overclass was neither capitalist nor proletarian. It used the institutions of education to prepare its members for positions in management across all institutions.

Educated persons would come to form a progressive, rationalized, social force seeking to conform American culture, society, politics, and economics to the teachings of a comprehensive cognitive and behavioral template along Gnostic lines of providing salvation in this life through the extirpation of worldly evils. From institutions of higher education, year by year, step by step, the Overclass took control of those major institutions that give legitimacy to American society, culture, politics, and economic activity. The Overclass thus assumed a position of social and cultural power with which it abandoned America's covenantal identity and replaced it with a moral vision of selfish personal entitlement institutionalized in an elite hierarchy. As a result, the power base of the Overclass was expanded to center its management of society in the administrative organizations of the federal government in Washington, DC.

In society, preeminent status was conferred on other-directed persons with professional credentials provided by colleges and universities. They were hired and promoted over others and supported financially with salaries. They were neither entrepreneurs nor self-taught. Common sense and life experience brought no one status or preferment.

Data on the incidence of other-direction among young Americans preparing to become members of the Overclass confirms the coincidence of other-direction and Overclass lifestyles. Between 2023 and 2025, 1,452 confidential interviews were conducted with undergraduates at Northwestern University and the University of Michigan. The question explored with the students was: "What happens to identity formation when belief is replaced by adherence to orthodoxy?"

When asked "Have you ever pretended to hold more progressive views than you truly endorse to succeed socially or academically?", 88 percent of student respondents said "Yes." Seventy-eight percent of students reported that they self-censor in discussions of gender identity. Seventy-two percent self-censor on politics, and sixty-eight percent self-censor on family values. More than eighty percent of respondents confirmed they had submitted classwork that misrepresented their views in order performatively to align themselves with the views of their professors.

Seventy-three percent of students reported mistrust in conversations about these values with close friends. Nearly half said they routinely conceal their true beliefs when in intimate relationships for fear of precipitating rancorous ideological disharmony.

Researchers Forest Romm and Kevin Waldman concluded: "These students were not cynical but adaptive. In a campus environment where grades, leadership, and peer belonging often hinge on fluency in performative morality, young adults quickly learn to rehearse what is safe. . . . The result is not conviction but compliance. And beneath that compliance, something vital is lost." Romm and Waldman described the process of undergraduate Overclass socialization as "identity regulation at scale, and it is being institutionalized," resulting in "a generation . . . uncertain in self."[1]

In culture, the Overclass assumed the helm of all educational institutions from pre-K through the provision of doctorates. By the twenty-first century, the Overclass had administrative power over mass entertainment and sources of information—films, book publication, television, newspapers, and the internet. The Overclass perspective on life—including a revitalization of racism and a perpetuation of sexism through allocation of salaried earning potentials through programs of diversity, equity, and inclusion along with attempted censorship of "misinformation" and "disinformation"—was mainstreamed for all Americans. Religious faiths, starting with divinity schools, were increasingly directed by members of the Overclass. Journalism for the educated elite became little more than propaganda on behalf of Overclass values and beliefs as the seeking of objective truth was replaced by publication of opinions voicing self-centered "truths." Thus was a feminized other-direction imposed on the psyches of the American people.

In politics, the Overclass took over the Democrat Party and converted it from a party with its electoral base in workers and marginalized ethnic communities into a party of the cultural and educated elite. Donald Trump's personal inability to think and act as a member of the Overclass brought on him ferocious and even scurrilous attacks in the media and entertainment. He was subjected to criminal prosecutions designed to destroy his capacity to mobilize democratic electoral opposition to society's educational elite. The Overclass effort to drive Trump from public life even manipulated the police powers of the Federal Bureau of Investigation and the secretive influence of the Central Intelligence Agency, whose officials all had college degrees.

In the economy, the Overclass conquered the influential high ground of managing the operations of the large corporations, banks and investment firms, and major law firms. Government bureaucracies regulated private sector decision-making, seeking to provide what, in the minds of civil servants, would be better outcomes than what markets and individuals could achieve on their own. The Congress was reduced to adopting legislation running into the thousands of pages per bill, with detailed instructions that few senators and representatives even bothered to read. Staff employees with professional credentials working for those elected officials did the heavy lifting in deciding how Americans should live and work. The senators and representatives themselves focused on raising funds to finance election campaigns to be carried out through Overclass institutional structures in the media, both mainstream and social, and for the professional mobilization of opinion. Such campaign largesse was used systematically to augment the other-directedness of the average American voter. The underlying assumption seemed to be that voters should not think for themselves but only do as they were told by those "in the know" or who—allegedly—had their best interests first and foremost in mind.

The result of Overclass management of politics and the economy is a public debt of $36.2 trillion in December 2024 and a private sector debt of $27 trillion. The combined debt owed by all American borrowers was 722% of the country's annual GDP.[2] Who will now pay off this financial indulgence engineered by the Overclass?

In the nonprofit sector, the Overclass came to direct the giving of nearly all major foundations and their efforts to elevate and better educate the allegedly misbegotten Americans who were deemed by the elite to be "deplorable," as presidential candidate Hillary Clinton (a graduate of Wellesley College and Yale Law School) so nicely put it in 2016. Foundations generously funded efforts to remediate social backwardness and provide "caring" professional intervention in the lives of the unfortunate.

What was institutionalized by the Overclass across American society was dependency on Overclass leadership, a lifelong subordination of putative lesser-minded and less-noble Americans under the tutelage of experts artfully legitimated by an ethic of supposed "care."

The Overclass Paradigm Arrives in America

The educational institutions that would bring Hegel's model of social management by the state through an elite of expert administrators were formed in the years after the Civil War. The model for the new American university was German, neither English nor Puritan.

The Calvinist mission of the first elite colleges in America—Harvard, Dartmouth, Yale, and Princeton—was put aside, and a new mission was adopted by university presidents. That older mission of keeping faith with a covenant to build America as a "city upon a hill" where students would be taught to "walk in the way of the Lord," as the prophets of the Old Testament had demanded, was replaced with a secular one, in keeping with the Enlightenment fixation on the virtue of reason as the distinguishing capacity of each and every human person.

The motivating conviction of those who built out the new elite institutions of university education and rational character formation was simple in concept and straightforward in its vision of improving the American experiment in ordered liberty: "By means of the independence of his confident intellect, the person with an admirable character now overcame circumstances and reached beyond the mutability of the environment."[3] Progress on a grand scale for the American nation and all its citizens was now possible, thanks to universities. The Calvinist confidence that we can and must "walk in the way of the Lord" was replaced by a new faith in the beneficial changes to be brought about by "walking in the way of reason and research."

Before the Civil War, in Illinois there was a proposal supporting the establishment of agricultural colleges that would apply research to methods and technologies useful in improving crop yields and the raising of animals. The Michigan Constitution of 1850 created the office of the president of the University of Michigan and also called for the creation of an "agricultural school." In 1852, Henry P. Tappan, of Prussian descent and the president of the new University of Michigan, wrote with enthusiasm that a well-ordered society required a university at its center.[4] In 1855 the Agricultural College of the State of Michigan, today Michigan State University, was established by state legislation.

In 1857 Congressman Morrill of Vermont proposed that certain federal lands be consigned to states to endow agricultural colleges. His bill was vetoed by President Buchanan but was later reintroduced, adopted, and then signed into law by President Lincoln in 1862. The Morrill Act specified a practical mission of promoting economic development, especially through research and instruction in modernizing husbandry. Under the federal act, colleges funded with federal grants of land were "to promote the liberal and practical education of the industrial classes in the several pursuits and professions in life."[5]

The Massachusetts Institute of Technology (MIT) was established in Boston in 1861 as a private college funded with a land grant. MIT adopted from Europe the polytechnical university model of higher education. At the university level, the German model in Hegelian fashion fostered professional researchers and instructors in bureaucratic research centers given well-equipped laboratories. The role of university professors was to do research and so serve as exemplars for their students of how new knowledge could be acquired for the benefit of humanity.

Founded in 1876, Johns Hopkins was the first American university to expressly adopt the German vision of enlightened higher education, driving beneficial enhancements to the human experience in this spiritually fallen world. This new American university modeled itself after Heidelberg University and its long academic research history. The mission of a research university was to perfect expertise through scientific discovery seeking to know the truth.

Daniel Coit Gilman became the first president of Johns Hopkins. His personal mission was to integrate research with teaching in higher education. Gilman followed the vision of Wilhelm von Humboldt of Prussia.

Humboldt's ideal (*Begriff*) for higher education was a concept of academic education that had emerged in the early nineteenth century with a core idea of a holistic integration of research with the teaching of superior insights and modes of thinking. Sometimes called simply the Humboldtian model, it integrated the arts and sciences with research to achieve both comprehensive general learning and cultural knowledge.

Humboldt's educational model went beyond vocational training in Germany. In a letter to the Prussian king, he wrote,

> There are undeniably certain kinds of knowledge that must be of a general nature and, more importantly, a certain cultivation of the mind and character that nobody can afford to be without. People obviously cannot be good craftworkers, merchants, soldiers or businessmen unless, regardless of their occupation, they are good, upstanding and—according to their condition— well-informed human beings and citizens. If this basis is laid through schooling, vocational skills are easily acquired later on, and a person is always free to move from one occupation to another, as so often happens in life.[6]

In preparation for becoming the university's founding president, Gilman visited German universities. He focused on the expansion of graduate education and support of faculty research. The new university fused advanced scholarship with such professional schools as medicine and engineering. Hopkins became the national trendsetter in doctoral programs and the host for numerous scholarly journals and associations. Johns Hopkins University Press, founded in 1878, is the oldest American university press in continuous operation.

Tappan's successor as president of the University of Michigan believed that the "vital relationship" between the community and the university "contemplates civil society as charged not merely with the negative work of repressing disorder and crime, but also with the higher positive office of promoting by all proper means the intellectual and moral growth of the citizens."[7] Accordingly, students, faculty, and administrators would come to use universities in the service of their personal ambitions to lead others toward a better future. It was a transformation of the covenantal older Protestant religious calling to preach and uplift into a secular calling of engineering the birth of a moral, modern society. But the new priesthood of university-educated experts and professionals had no covenant either with the people or with Providence to restrain their self-seeking or their intellectual arrogance. Thus did the nineteenth-century university set loose among Americans the folly of hubris that, in the early decades of the twenty-first century, would bring upon Americans the nemesis of identity dysphoria.

Creating new universities of Johns Hopkins, Cornell, and Minnesota and the renovation of such older institutions as Harvard and Columbia was accomplished after the Civil War by strong-minded people with conviction and passion such as Charles William Eliot at Harvard (1869–1909), Noah Porter at Yale (1871–1876), Daniel Coit Gilman at Johns Hopkins (1876–1902), Andrew Dickson White at Cornell (1868–1885), Frederick A. P. Barnard at Columbia (1864–1889), James McCosh at Princeton (1868–1888), James Burrill Angell at Michigan (1871–1909), William Watts Folwell at Minnesota (1869–1884), and John Bascom at Wisconsin (1874–1887).[8]

In 1910 Woodrow Wilson, later president of the United States, praised Harvard's President Eliot, saying, "I suppose that no man has more fully earned the reputation of being the most useful citizen of the country than he."[9] Eliot had justified the transformation of Harvard College into a university along Hegelian lines as adding value to America through the creation of a nonpartisan professional class able to run the country rationally and scientifically. He thought that only the accepted authority of an elite of merit at the pinnacle of American society could control the crosswinds seeking to destabilize the republic.[10]

Professional schools to train and credential experts were established: for dentists in 1867, for architects and pharmacists in 1868, for schoolteachers and veterinarians in 1879, and for accountants in 1881. The Wharton School of Finance and Economy was founded in 1881.

The licensing of professionals began, giving them legal status as experts. The first law for dentists came in 1868, for pharmacists in 1874, for veterinarians in 1886, for accountants in 1886, and for architecture in 1897.

State laws on negligence, which also applied to professionals to dissuade them from acting carelessly and without the appropriate expertise, had been evolving through court opinions since the early decades of the Industrial Revolution with its introduction of new potentially dangerous technologies such as steam engines and railroads.

Professional associations to promote the social standing of the Overclass and provide its members with ethics, discipline, and dedication to service were started in the 1870s—for social workers in 1874, librarians in 1876, and a national association for lawyers in 1878.[11]

Professional schools and their graduates grew in number. By 1900 there were 283 graduate schools for professions. In the 1870s and 1880s, at least 200 learned societies had been founded to uphold and advance professional expertise and social status.[12]

One historian concluded, "As professionals, they attempted to define a total coherent system of necessary knowledge within a precise territory, to control the intrinsic relationships of their subject by making it a scholarly as well as an applied science, to root social existence in the inner needs and possibilities of documentable worldly processes."[13] In other words, an Overclass of American professionals was to be educated in Gnostic conceptions of life. The mission of such professionals was to right whatever was wrong in secular American life and live to overcome and even exorcize bedevilments.

In the tradition of Hegel, the professionalization of American life "excavated nature for its principles, its theoretical rules, thus transcending mechanical procedures, individual cases, miscellaneous facts, technical information, and instrumental applications."[14]

Overclass management of postmodern American capitalism started in the 1950s at graduate schools of business, with the conferring of MBA degrees and the offering of executive education programs for senior managers. Such schools would train the white-collar experts who would, more and more, manage business enterprise with rational professionalism in place of entrepreneurs and family owners. MBA degrees in finance and operations especially provided privileged access to senior decision-making positions in companies.

Overclass specialists in business education, corporate management, and financial intermediation used metrics to bring market capitalism under professional supervision. The mantra "What gets measured gets managed" has been attributed to Peter Drucker, admired as a management "guru." But the mantra explained how the Overclass came to dominate decision-making and the culture of American firms. To manage enterprises, the Overclass needed metrics. The most readily available metrics could be found in whatever could be counted numerically—especially things and units of currency. Thus, the managers of enterprise reached out for indices that could be expressed in currency units—profits (gross and net), costs (salaries and other expenses), taxes, ROI (return on investment), net present value, and capitalization multiplier. These metrics drove decisions. Later, specialized human relations experts would put numbers to persons through self-assessments and scaled evaluations of performance by direct-reports and colleagues.

Overclass managers of public corporations, working for unknown, faceless owners of shares in the companies, legitimated their authority over the enterprise with the theory of shareholder primacy. The moral objective to be achieved by management efficiency was the earning of profits for those owners. The economist Milton Friedman was most often cited as vindicating this paradigm for capitalism in his 1970 essay "A Friedman Doctrine: The Social Responsibility of Business Is to Increase Its Profits."[15]

Friedman justified his prioritizing of the earning of cash profits with the foundational Overclass belief in the inherent superiority of management over markets in making the most efficient decisions. He took the role of manager as a moral standard: "In a free-enterprise, private-property system, a corporate executive is an employee of the owners of the business. He has direct responsibility to his employers. That responsibility is to conduct the business in accordance with their desires . . . the key point is that, in his capacity as a corporate executive, the manager is the agent of the individuals who own the corporation . . . and his primary responsibility is to them."

The unavoidable shortcoming of metrics is that intangibles are hard to measure. What is the measure of the value of a workforce, of customer loyalty, of a toxic company culture? Employees are carried on the financial books of a company as a cost on the profit and loss statement, not as an asset on the balance sheet. The risks of poor management of stakeholder relationships—customers, employees, suppliers, creditors, and communities—and the costs of negative externalities such as pollution are not easily measured and so are most often slighted by senior executives, especially chief financial officers, and boards of directors. How does one measure the morality of capitalism?

Devout genuflection of managers in business and finance before the holy grail of numbers has been documented by Alex Berenson (*The Number*), Jerry Z. Muller (*The Tyranny of Metrics*), Scott Patterson (*The Quants*), and Robert J. Shiller (*Irrational Exuberance*).

The quality movement of the 1980s presented a challenge to the superiority of managers and the metrics of profitability. The mantra of the quality movement is that quality of product drives profits; therefore, look to metrics that assess quality. One such metric, a nonfinancial one, was customer satisfaction. Two other quasi-metrics were (1) choosing suppliers for quality and not low price and integrating them into the company's decision-making, and (2) decentralizing authority away from managers down to line workers, the persons who actually made the products and knew good quality from bad. But despite this brief interlude, Overclass *Begriffs* gained powerful momentum driving the practices of American business and finance.

In 1968 Alice Tepper Marlin had designed and managed the first social investment portfolio management service. The following year she founded the Council on Economic Priorities (CEP), which then created the field of social investments seeking to encourage investments in firms meeting CEP-selected standards such as workforce nondiscrimination and liberal collective bargaining policies. These standards were designed to bring concern for the externalities of company decisions home to roost with the owners of enterprise in the hope that they would thereafter seek to achieve the preferred social impacts highlighted by those standards of performance.

Similarly, in the Islamic world, Islamic investment funds were established that would invest only in companies that complied with various provisions of Sharia law, especially not charging *riba* or interest.

The approach of civil society using metrics to "manage" market decision-making expanded. In the early 1990s, business schools introduced courses in business ethics. Toward the end of that decade, the intellectual space of corporate social responsibility (CSR) emerged as a civil society movement. In 1994 my organization, the Caux Round Table for Moral Capitalism, adopted the first set of ethical principles for business proposed by business leaders—Japanese, European, and American. The Caux Round Table's approach was to influence the thinking of business executives, not to make decisions for them. The operational strategy of the Caux Round Table, as presented in my 2003 book, *Moral Capitalism*, followed the teachings of philosophers and religious teachers and Adam Smith, who wrote on the moral sentiments, to encourage inner-directed persons to center their core values on virtue. We looked to improve human capital in order to better social capital and to use social and human capital as assets in creating wealth for society with responsibility. Our assumption was, following the approach of Jurgen Habermas, that behaviors are the residual effects of values, so getting values right is the first step to take in improving the outcomes of human activity.

We proposed principles that legitimated a values cluster, which then defined standards for behaviors. Following those standards, which could be measured with appropriate metrics, brought about the desired outcomes, achieving value-added contributions to human well-being. So just as Adam Smith had written two books integrating virtue with market creation of prosperity, the Caux Round Table advocated a partnership, a collaboration, in capitalism between moral principles and the pragmatic rationality of profits.

More recently and less effectively, an Overclass approach to corporate responsibility has been less successful and controversial. It was an overreach by social justice advocates seeking to use companies to accomplish nonmarket social and cultural outcomes. That was the promotion of environmental, social, and governance (ESG) goals as business objectives for companies. Following the precedent of Alice Tepper Marlin, investment funds were established to invest in companies with good ESG metrics. However, since there was no agreed-upon definition of what were good and correct "society" and "governance" outcomes, the rating of companies for best, good, and bad performance was a mishmash of personal preferences, using the model of other-direction where the target firms were rewarded with investment if they adopted the values of the investors. By 2024 the bloom had come off the rose of ESG investing in the United States as companies, responding to a public backlash, backed away from hiring and promoting according to race and sexual preferences and from branding their products as supportive of Overclass cultural preferences.

Another, and very consequential, process by which the Overclass took control of the American economy was financial analysis—largely the product of professors in business schools. With financial analysis, Overclass experts could engineer the organizational structure of companies by pricing stock, buying and selling companies, forming conglomerates, and buying up new competitors to enhance monopoly market power. Wall Street firms came to dominate American capitalism, thanks to their employment of Overclass financial professionals. Silicon Valley venture capitalists largely brought forth the high-tech sector of the Overclass with remarkable impacts on American culture and society. What would modern life be like without the product innovations of Microsoft, Apple, and Google?

After the meltdown of financial markets in 2007 and 2008 due to irrational exuberance among mortgage lenders, financial speculators, and poor risk assessment, a few graduates of Harvard Business School, class of 2009, proposed that all recipients of an MBA degree take an oath of social stewardship as business and financial managers. The oath contained these affirmations and obligations:

> As a business leader I recognize my role in society. My purpose is to lead people and manage resources to create value that no single individual can create alone. My decisions affect the well-being of individuals inside and outside my enterprise, today and tomorrow. Therefore, I promise that:
>
> - I will manage my enterprise with loyalty and care, and will not advance my personal interests at the expense of my enterprise or society.
> - I will understand and uphold, in letter and spirit, the laws and contracts governing my conduct and that of my enterprise.
> - I will refrain from corruption, unfair competition, or business practices harmful to society.
> - I will protect the human rights and dignity of all people affected by my enterprise, and I will oppose discrimination and exploitation.
> - I will protect the right of future generations to advance their standard of living and enjoy a healthy planet.
> - I will report the performance and risks of my enterprise accurately and honestly.

• I will invest in developing myself and others, helping the management profession continue to advance and create sustainable and inclusive prosperity.

In exercising my professional duties according to these principles, I recognize that my behavior must set an example of integrity, eliciting trust and esteem from those I serve. I will remain accountable to my peers and to society for my actions and for upholding these standards. This oath I make freely, and upon my honor.[16]

The MBA oath project was not successful in attracting followers. One limiting factor inhibiting MBA students and graduates from taking the oath as a personal commitment was their lack of inner-direction. Historically, oaths were sworn by those who could commit themselves to a course of action without second thoughts or regrets, finding themselves comfortable with their core values and with living honorably by those standards of conduct. Most contemporary MBA students and graduates are members of the Overclass and have accommodated themselves to the other-direction of that class's modal personality. Firm commitments that come with a risk of not being admired by superiors and peers are threats to the other-directed personality.

The rise of universities, professionals, professions, and professional bodies and associations brought about an innovation in the American class structure. The highly educated—the experts—were separated in identity, disciplined mastery of an intellectual discourse, income, and status from ordinary citizens, whose status still largely depended above all else on possession of inner-direction and activation of a personal work ethic.

More and more, professionals claimed privileged entitlement to impressive cash compensation for contributing their expertise to society. They preferred employment as salaried white-collar workers in public and private organizations having authority to manage society's problems. Professionals could aspire to "careers," something nobler and more remunerative than just working for a living in the uncertain hurly-burly of free-market capitalism.

Historian Burton Bledstein thought that "the ego-satisfying pretensions of professionalism have been closer to the heart of the middle-class American than the raw profit of capitalism."[17] The university-educated professionals sought to acquire "masterful command . . . designed to establish confidence in the mind of the helpless client." He added, "Professionals controlled the magic circle of scientific knowledge which only the few, the specialized by training and indoctrination were privileged to enter, but which all in the name of nature's universality were obligated to appreciate."[18]

However, higher education today cannot be trusted to always perform according to this ideal standard of credentialing only the "best and the brightest" of Americans for membership in the Overclass. An FBI investigation in 2019—Operation Varsity Blues—brought to light Overclass malfeasance in securing admission to elite colleges. In a news release, the Federal Department of Justice said, "Dozens of individuals involved in a nationwide conspiracy that facilitated cheating on college entrance exams and the admission of students to elite universities as purported athletic recruits were arrested by federal agents in multiple states and charged in documents unsealed on March 12, 2019, in federal court in Boston. Athletic coaches from Yale, Stanford, USC, Wake Forest and Georgetown, among others, are implicated, as well as parents and exam administrators."[19]

Thirty-three parents of college applicants were charged with paying more than $25 million between 2011 and 2018 to William Rick Singer, who used part of the money to fraudulently inflate entrance exam test scores and bribe administrators at eleven universities.

In January 2023 National Public Radio reported,

> The mastermind of the Varsity Blues college admissions scandal, Rick Singer, is set to be sentenced Wednesday in Boston

for a scheme that federal prosecutors say is "staggering in its scope and breathtaking in its audacity."

Prosecutors want him sentenced to six years in prison, while Singer is asking the judge to let him off with little or no prison time.

His sentencing is the capstone in the years-long investigation and prosecution of Singer and more than 50 co-conspirators, and puts the focus back on what has and has not changed since the scandal broke open in March 2019.

Singer, 62, pleaded guilty to raking in some $25 million by selling what he liked to call "a side door" into highly selective universities such as Yale, Georgetown and USC to dozens of clients, from actresses Felicity Huffman and Lori Loughlin to business titans and big-shot lawyers.

"We help the wealthiest families in the U.S. get their kids in school," Singer bragged as he pitched one of his clients on a call recorded by the FBI. "They want guarantees. They want this thing done."

His scheme involved, for instance, bribing college coaches to take students as athletic recruits, even if they were mediocre or had never even played the sport. Singer would just make up a totally fake resume, complete with a student's face photoshopped onto an image of a real athlete. His menu of cheating services also included fixing students' wrong answers on their college admissions tests or having someone take the test in their place.

"I can make scores happen that nobody on the planet can get to happen," he boasted on that recorded call. As was his routine, Singer told the client that his kids would have no chance of getting into their preferred schools without him and leaned heavily on the "everyone's doing it" pitch.

Of the more than 50 parents, coaches and others caught up in the scheme, more than a third were sentenced to two weeks to three months in prison. Roughly a quarter of the defendants got no time at all behind bars, including five people who cooperated with prosecutors.[20]

In August 2024 the *Wall Street Journal* revealed that cheating had occurred to help some students do better in the American Mathematics Competition. Student scores in the competition were "a marker that is going to immediately tell an admission officer 'Hey, this student has mathematical talent.'" The exams to be given at each level of the competition were made available hours or days before students were to sit for the tests. Some exams were posted freely, but some sellers offered a copy of a USA Mathematical Olympiad test for a few hundred dollars.[21]

In an important way, the prefrontal cortex of the Overclass consists of tenured professors, those who seek and obtain personal expertise and bring to light the truths about our material world—rocks and water, plants and animals, atoms and molecules, the spectrum of waves seen and unseen, energy, the speed of light, and black holes—and, more consequentially, about our social, cultural, and economic worlds. From academia have come the *Begriffs* and the normative priorities giving the Overclass its social function, its sense of entitlement, and infusing its soul with the arrogance to demand an unquestionable right to manage every aspect of our lives.

The recruiters for the Overclass are the admissions officers of colleges, universities, and graduate schools while the professors are the quality control supervisors certifying the abilities of the new recruits to graduate from Overclass boot camp and join the ranks of the elite. The tenured professoriate institutionalizes other-direction as the modal personality for those whom they admit to their ranks. Becoming comfortable with other-direction will permit the aspiring teachers to receive the very unusual lifelong employment benefit of tenure—a status of great irresponsibility due to its lack of accountability.

As the dean of a law school, I once had to remove from the faculty a productive scholar who, unfortunately, had abused relationships with students who were very emotionally vulnerable. I could not fire the professor, as I could not get a majority of the faculty to vote to remove tenure for cause, so I had to fall back on obtaining a voluntary resignation.

Now the system in academia for granting tenure demands that a candidate publish a number of scholarly articles in certain approved journals to demonstrate his or her acquisition of expertise. But to have your article accepted by these journals, it must be read and approved by other professors, a process called "peer review." The peer review process is other-direction on steroids. The person seeking tenure is placed in a situation to follow those who have gone before and to adopt generously their views and prejudices. The peer review process culls out the inner-directed academics who want to study and teach what they deeply believe to be correct and significant for others to know and therefore to privilege clones and sycophants of those already tenured. So today a Martin Luther—"Here I stand. I can do no other."—will most likely not get tenure in an American college or university faculty.

The knowledge and expertise of the American professoriate is much less impressive than they believe. Tenured Yale professor Robert Post has offered a justification for the right of tenured professors to discriminate against ideas they don't like and the people who think them. Each academic discipline has standards—which are the sanctioned truth, the catechism for the true believers. As the tenured professors are the guardians of the standards, they have the right to veto the ideas and speech of untenured scholars and students if such thoughts and words don't measure up to the standards. Thus, tenured professors function as thought police for the Overclass. "In this institutional sense, all that speech in search of truth is not equal." Some speakers are more equal than others.[22]

But this leaves Americans with the question Juvenal asked long ago about Plato's recommendation that rulership should only be given to philosophers to be the guardians of culture and society: *Quis custodiet ipsos custodes?* "Who will guard the guardians?" Who is to judge if the tenured professors, the keepers of disciplinary standards, will actually be wise, humane, and correct in their judgments, avoiding unconscious bias and all the other irrational mental pitfalls that have been identified by behavioral economics?

Thus in 2020, as the COVID-19 epidemic spread from China around the world, Americans were told by government officials to "follow the science" and obey what their professional betters told them to do to slow the spread of the virus. Officials in the federal government used their authority and influence to shape and limit public discussion of how best to confront the virus and minimize its impact. Federal officials and no others were empowered to tell Americans what to think and what to do, but no one was assigned to supervise them to keep them honest and humble.

In 1895 Friedrich Paulsen, historian of the German University, summarized nicely the structural social link between "higher education" and an Overclass of elite experts to manage a Hegelian God-State: "Whoever possesses university training belongs to society" while "on the other hand, he who has not enjoyed a university training or some academic education of equivalent value, loses infallibly a good deal in the eyes of many people."[23] This was certainly true in my family, which took great pride in the education of my grandmother Marion Hunt, Wellesley College class of 1912.

As Bledstein observed, "The exclusive Gymnasium-university complex [served] as the hub of a bureaucratically and politically sanctioned patriciate—a mandarin class. . . . The German elite drew a firm line between schooling for the herd and education for their own cultural group."[24]

The separation of the two classes—expert from ordinary, one from the other—not merely was notoriously expressed by Hillary Clinton in her infamous "deplorables" speech of 2016 when she ran for president as the standard-bearer of Overclass superiority but also permeated her speech to her graduating class at Wellesley College in 1969.

> We feel that for too long our leaders have viewed politics as the art of the possible. And the challenge now is to practice

politics as the art of making what appears to be impossible possible. . . . But we also know that to be educated, the goal of it must be human liberation. A liberation enabling each of us to fulfill our capacity so as to be free to create within and around ourselves.[25]

And so American politics was transformed into a class struggle between the Overclass, represented by the Democrat Party, and less prominent and more traditional Americans, represented by the Republican Party. The presidential elections of 2016, 2020, and 2024 were contests between paladins of the Overclass—Hillary Clinton, Joe Biden, and Kamala Harris—and the knight defender of the uncredentialed middle and lower classes—Donald J. Trump.

As members of an elite with control over government largesse, Overclass Democrats patronized African American and Hispanic minorities not as equals but as dependent clients who stood to be protected and promoted by Democrat Party politicians in return for their votes. For example, in her campaign for the presidency, Kamala Harris committed to providing African American men with one million forgivable loans of up to $20,000 to start a business, and she vowed to legalize marijuana and launch a health equity initiative.

Harris also promised, if elected president, to fund patronage programs for selected clients of a tax credit of $6,000 per newborn child, a federal income tax reduction of $1,500 for lower-income workers, an expansion of federal health insurance to cover the costs of in-home care for the elderly, and a $25,000 contribution to any down payment made by first-time homebuyers.

Commentator Victor Davis Hanson reported on the day before the November 2024 elections that

the Democratic Party finds its greatest support from those who earn less than $50,000 and those who make considerably more than $100,000. These are the rich/poor bookends that surround the reformed Republican party in between.

So, in terms of generalized income and earnings, the left is now the party of the well-to-do professional and credential class and the rich, along with the subsidized poor. The Republicans, by contrast, are increasingly represented by the middle classes. . . .

The Democratic top dogs are most likely to embrace agendas that never garner 51 percent of public support—vast reductions in gas and oil to lessen "climate change," open borders to welcome in the world's needy, the government promotion of a third, transgendered sex, abortion on demand without restrictions, the reifications of various critical (race/legal/penal/modern monetary) "theories," and radical changes in the current system (ending the Senate filibuster, the Electoral College, the nine-justice Supreme Court, the 50-state union, etc.).

Two truisms stand out about the elite boutique agenda: one, when these theories are implemented—often by the courts, and the permanent and unelected administrative and bureaucratic state—the architects of such experimentation do not really feel the inevitable deleterious consequences.

. . . Their ideology is the fruit of their privilege and so is often more utopian and abstract.[26]

In the election Harris did, in fact, win a majority of voters with annual incomes below $30,000 or over $100,000.[27] College graduates made up 43% of the electorate, and 55% voted for Vice President Harris, per exit polls, while 56% of voters without degrees voted for Donald Trump.[28]

Overclass Democrats seek to use the administrative and legal powers of the federal government to align Americans with the values and beliefs of their class. Trump and the Republicans, to the contrary, sought to minimize the influence of the Overclass over the lives and fortunes of ordinary Americans, proposing to "make America great again." In the context of American class differences, Trump's slogan could easily be understood as proposing to restore an America as it was before the Overclass had achieved its sway over the culture, social institutions, economics, and politics.

With respect for working-class Americans, in 2016 Hillary Clinton lost their votes by three points; in 2020 Biden lost them by four points, and in 2024 Harris was losing them by fifteen points. But Clinton carried college-educated voters by sixteen points in 2016; Biden carried them by eighteen points in 2020, and in 2024 Harris's lead over Trump among these voters was twenty points. Harris, a woman born to Jamaican and South Asian parents, even had a lead of fifteen points over Trump among college-educated White voters. Harris had less support among working-class non-White voters than she did among non-White college-educated voters.

The Democratic Party is no longer the party of the working class. It has morphed into the party of the Overclass.

In 2024 with Kamala Harris as the presidential candidate of Overclass political activists, columnist Miranda Devine noticed an other-directed feminist cast to her campaign.

> With the ascension of Saint Kamala, we are now watching the Mean Girl rebranding of the Democratic Party.
>
> It has to be the biggest miscalculation in political history.
>
> As polls show America's young men are lurching rightward at a rapid pace, the Democratic brand has finally evolved into the party of scolding shrews, nagging Karens and "preachy females," as Dem dinosaur James Carville calls them. Its image is tied to a type of unserious, self-involved, neurotic, dogmatic Dem-fem who insists on telling you her pronouns and whose highest goal is abortion on demand right up until the moment of birth.

She is terrified of men unless they are transgender or submissive "white dudes for Kamala". . . The majority of young
men now support Trump, a swing of 29 points since 2020.[29]

With no irony, Minnesota governor Tim Walz, chosen by Kamala Harris
to be her vice presidential running mate in 2024, conflated socialism with
Gilligan's ethic of care: "Don't ever shy away from our progressive values.
One person's socialism is another person's neighborliness. Just do the damn
work." Walz thus feminized socialism during a "White Dudes for Harris"
virtual fundraiser.[30] Walz came to Minnesota Democratic politics from a
successful career in the educational subsector of the Overclass.

Critic and essayist Roger Kimball had this to say about the Democrats
and "magical thinking": "The Democrats have mutated into the party of
nowhere, so it is not surprising that they prefer pleasing fantasy to sober-
ing reality."[31]

Back in an earlier time, before the rise of the Overclass, the Rotary
Club, founded in 1905, adopted the credo of "service over self." Rotary's
Four-Way Test of superior personal commitment to the common good
still proposes that "of the things we think, say or do:

1. Is it the *truth*?
2. Is it *fair* to all concerned?
3. Will it build *goodwill* and *better friendships*?
4. Will it be *beneficial* to all concerned?"

But a "promiscuity of belief," in the insightful but cutting words of
Roger Kimball, has gained footholds in civic organizations with big
footprints such as the American Federation of Teachers, an extension of
the Overclass in politics and in the classroom. The federation proclaims
that "the AFT and our members engage in politics not as a partisan tactic
or destination, but as a means to turn our values and aspirations for a
better life into a reality for all people." Two 2024 policy resolutions of

the federation quickly revealed its Overclass orientation. First the federation supported Kamala Harris for the presidency because she advocated Overclass privilege and power over Americans.[32]

The federation opposed Heritage Foundation policy recommendations that would, in its mind, undermine Overclass politics and agencies by cutting social security and Medicare, eliminating overtime, destroying public education, ripping health care away from people, allowing the government to monitor pregnancies, replacing thousands of federal workers with ideologues, dismantling civil rights protections, ending efforts to combat climate change, cutting taxes for the wealthy, and weaponizing the National Labor Relations Board against workers. The federation praised the Biden-Harris administration for eliminating crushing student debt for millions of Americans by canceling over $1.5 billion in student loans for public service workers and for strengthening the Affordable Care Act, weakening the stranglehold of Big Pharma and the health-care companies by requiring Medicare to negotiate prescription drug prices and capping the price of insulin, and for appointing a Supreme Court justice who would uphold Overclass priorities as the law of the land. The federation expected Harris, if elected, to "take bold action by declaring a national climate emergency in order to address the human-caused crisis brought about by the burning of fossil fuels."[33]

The federation adopted a resolution opposing market decision-making by private equity firms:

> Private equity controls roughly $14.7 trillion in assets, employs more than 11.7 million workers and manages more than $4 trillion of workers' deferred wages in pension funds while charging high fees. . . . The private equity business model—with its emphasis on debt financing and short-term ownership—leads to draining capital, loading companies with debt at the expense of their long-term financial health, and slashing staffing and supplies well below what is needed to provide effective patient care; and the

harmful impacts to healthcare delivery in our communities are especially dire for vulnerable populations like communities of color, patients in rural areas and Medicare recipients.[34]

The Feminization of American Education

As the American Overclass solidified its embrace of other-direction as its most appropriate modal personality, it facilitated the feminization of education in America as other-direction vibrates sympathetically with the feminine ethics of care promoted by Carol Gilligan.

And so, consequentially, education in America—both public and private—increasingly has inculcated other-direction in children and young adults as the preferred modal personality, putting those with inner-directed personalities at a social and cultural disadvantage.

One observer wrote,

> Women are all but conquering the twenty-first-century academy. They not only make up well over half of undergrads and graduate students on university campuses; they also hold half of all professor positions, as well as six out of eight Ivy League presidencies and more than a third of college presidencies overall. Younger women who came of age in the new millennium have been thoroughly prepped for leadership as valedictorians, debate-club and student-council presidents, and Rhodes, Marshall, and Truman Scholars. If the protests offer further evidence for the dimming of patriarchy, they also show how women's growing dominance in social institutions introduces new and ambiguous power dynamics.[35]

Almost 80% of all grade 1–12 schoolteachers are female. An overwhelming 96.7% of kindergarten and preschool teachers are women.[36] For most K–12 students, having a male teacher is a relatively rare occurrence.

Today well over half of all school principals are female.

Almost 60% of all college students are female.

Another commentator pointed out, "As of 2022, women held 52 percent of professional-managerial roles in the U.S. Women earn more than 57 percent of bachelor degrees, 61 percent of master's degrees, and 54 percent of doctoral degrees. And because they are overrepresented in professions such as human resource management (73 percent) and compliance officers (57 percent), that determine workplace behavioral norms, they have an outsized influence on professional culture, which itself has an outsized influence on American culture more generally."[37]

The growing power of Overclass, other-directed, "den mothers" has thus instantiated in American institutions the meeting of feminine needs and feminine methods for controlling, directing, and modeling behavior. Many from left, right, and center have made note of this shift. In 2010 Hanna Rosin announced "The End of Men."[38] Hillary Clinton made it a slogan of her 2016 campaign: "The future is female."[39]

An example of privileging the ethics of care in education was written up by Max Eden of the American Enterprise Institute.[40] He ran across a study titled "Healing-Informed Social Justice Mathematics: Promoting Students' Sociopolitical Consciousness and Well-Being in Math Class," saying, "The study can be summarized in one sentence: students can face serious trauma in their lives; to help them heal, we should leverage math class to promote a liberal agenda."

Authored by Kari Kokka, a mathematics education professor at the University of Nevada, Las Vegas, the study begins by explaining that students can experience the trauma of crime, violence, or abuse. She noted that studies demonstrate the effectiveness of school-based cognitive behavioral therapy. Such trauma-informed pedagogy highlights allowing students to identify and express their feelings as part of mathematics sense-making and allowing students to address what they learn about their world by suggesting recommendations and taking action.

Kokka reported that an eleventh-grade English teacher wrote about how critical healing praxis facilitated healing for her students and herself because it "confronts the disembodiment and privatization of healing in schools by centering the body and making pain an explicit tool for learning." But Kokka noted that such trauma-informed pedagogy had never been studied in a math context.

Kokka observed nine students being taught "social justice mathematics." After providing a "positionality statement" explaining that she was a "womxn of color," Kokka described a math lesson in which the teacher presented the students with a map of a "food desert" and asked them to understand the distance a woman had to travel to get fresh ingredients for a recipe.

Another problem described by Kokka read, "I have US$100. I owe 1/4 of my money to my mom, 2/5 to my grandmother, and 4/10 to my brother. Do I have enough money to pay everyone back? How much money should each person get?"

After students calculate that this woman owes more money than she has, they watch a video of a single mom struggling to make ends meet. They are then asked questions such as, "What are some feelings that you are having when watching this video?" and "She works 40 hours a week and still struggles for food. What is your reaction around that?"

Interviewed after the lesson, one student "broke down in tears when discussing his living situation." Another wrote, "The feelings I have are sad and worried. I'm mad." Another wrote, "I think that was sad, but I also got mad because the government or someone else of her family should help her." One student "suggested that free day care should be available for families so they can afford to work and pay their living expenses." Several others expressed a commitment to political activism. "Students' awareness of structural issues influenced their plans for taking action," Kokka observed. Taking critical action, she proposed, is a way of healing from trauma.

The students were given opportunities to identify with an ethic of care, but how well did they learn math?

Harvard College in September 2024 initiated a remedial math course for its freshman students who lacked the skills needed to successfully study mathematics. The remedial class meets for five days a week to make up for time not well used in high school. So here is a case of newly certified members of the American Overclass who can't do math very well.[41]

In mathematics there are right and wrong answers that do not change based on opinion or emotions. Learning mathematics facilitates the emergence of self-reliant autonomy in personhood; learning mathematics empowers inner-direction. Self-reliant, inner-directed persons are (1) much less likely to become traumatized and (2) more likely to overcome traumatic experiences and the disappointments that life presents.

American boys now comprise nearly two-thirds of students at the bottom 10% of achievement. Coincidence or the result of inequitable treatment? Boys are 2.5 times more likely to be suspended or expelled from school than girls. For public schools in the 2017–2018 school year, boys comprised 72% of all expulsions and 70% of suspensions. Boys who lag behind in school become less likely to graduate high school and more likely to commit crime and experience unemployment, poverty, and suicides; high school dropouts add to America's identify dysphoria, increasing social and cultural stress.

By fourth grade girls are reading one hundred thousand more words than boys. In kindergarten there is parity in reading between boys and girls. One study argues that the difference in reading activity emerging in the fourth grade is driven by "teacher perceptions of literacy ability being skewed by gender." Who are the teachers' pets? Also, school curricular decisions favor the assignment of fiction books, which play to girls' preference for narrative books and romantic stories. Boys were more interested in reading about war, comedy, sports, and science fiction, and they liked to read to absorb information.

One can wonder if what boys like to read is more encouraging of inner-direction and what girls like to read is more responsive to other-directed impulses and the feminine ethic of care.

Tom Sarrouf ended his report on boy/girl differentials in reading achievement with this plea: "More generally, in our culture, 'letting boys be boys' must become a *cri de coeur* for raising our future generation of boys into the successful men that we need."[42]

Sarrouf's assessment of the difficulties facing boys was more recently documented by Rachel Wolfe in the *Wall Street Journal*. She reports that, while more and more women ages 25 to 34 have entered the workforce in recent years, the cohort of young men in the labor market hasn't grown in a decade. In August 2024 only 89% of this cohort were employed or looking for work, more than seven hundred thousand fewer than in 2004. Women's participation is 79%. A fifth of men in this same age range still lived with their parents as of 2023 compared with 12% of women.

Wolfe reported,

> Twenty-five-year-old Daniel Moreno left college midway through his sophomore year after indecision about his major spiraled into a larger existential crisis.
>
> "I just felt so, so lost," Daniel says. "I didn't know what I was doing it for." Five years later, he is still living with his parents and working for his dad's company, in a product-manager role that he is grateful for but doesn't necessarily see a future in. He hopes to go back to school to study a subject he is more passionate about—maybe journalism, or veterinary medicine or botany—but he doesn't know what it would take to get there, or where to find the motivation to start.
>
> . . . Young men are lonelier as a result. Those ages 18 to 30 spent 18% more time alone last year—an average of 6.6 non-sleeping hours—than in 2019, according to Pardue's analysis of American Time Use Survey data. That is 22% more alone time than reported by women in the same age range.[43]

In such conditions of loneliness, to achieve a sense of self confirming one's worth and agency and seeking to become more inner-directed is daunting, seeming even to be impossible. Thus for anyone stranded in such isolation, other-direction becomes the most accessible coping modal-personality.

Feminized, other-directed leadership in higher education was put on public display on December 5, 2023, when the presidents of Harvard, MIT, and the University of Pennsylvania testified before a committee of the House of Representatives on antisemitism in their university communities. Representative Elise M. Stefanik of New York State asked, "At Harvard, does calling for the genocide of Jews violate Harvard's rules of bullying and harassment?"

"It can be, depending on the context," Harvard president Claudine Gay responded.

Stefanik then pressed Gay to give a yes or no answer to the question about whether calls for the genocide of Jews constitute a violation of Harvard's policies.

"Antisemitic speech, when it crosses into conduct that amounts to bullying, harassment, intimidation—that is actionable conduct, and we do take action," Gay said.

Stefanik tried again.

"So the answer is yes, that calling for the genocide of Jews violates Harvard code of conduct, correct?" Stefanik asked.

"Again, it depends on the context," Gay said.

Context is all-important to the other-directed person. One's own views are less important than incorporating the views of others—role models or influencers—into one's presentation of self. Inner-directed persons are more likely to answer with a yes or a no when asked such a question about their personal views.

In later apologizing for not having spoken with certainty on the legitimacy of antisemitism, Gay said, "I got caught up in what had become at that point, an extended, combative exchange about policies and procedures. What I should have had the presence of mind to do in that moment was return to my guiding truth, which is that calls for violence against our Jewish community—threats to our Jewish students— have no place at Harvard and will never go unchallenged."

Gay added, "Substantively, I failed to convey what is my truth."[44]

This turn of phrase "my truth" might have been an attempt by Gay to communicate that she indeed really did have an inner psychosocial compass that opposed antisemitism.

Gay resigned her presidency shortly thereafter when plagiarism in her academic writings became public. Of note is that, for the other-directed, adopting the thoughts of others more or less in their words without citation is consistent with an orientation to bring the point of view of others into one's own personal identity.

(Perhaps fully in keeping with his character, American politician Joe Biden used plagiarism in 1988 when he first sought the office of president, using the words of British politician Neil Kinnock.)

Evolutionary biologist Joyce Benenson provides a helpful lens with which to examine President Gay's approach to antisemitism in the Harvard community.

> From early childhood onwards, girls compete using strategies that minimize the risk of retaliation and reduce the strength of other girls. Girls' competitive strategies include avoiding direct interference with another girl's goals, disguising competition, competing overtly only from a position of high status in the community, enforcing equality within the female community and socially excluding other girls.[45]

While applauding academia for opening opportunities to individual women, Amy Wax, a University of Pennsylvania law professor castigated for her controversial comments, has decried the overall impact of the female influx into the professoriate: "The feminization of the academy has been a total disaster. . . . The values of the nursery and the kindergarten have now been elevated to the paramount considerations, and the old traditional and traditionally masculine values of truth-seeking, of argumentation, of reason, evidence, and objectivity have been downgraded."[46]

With its other-directed orientation, the Overclass—especially when it speaks in the feminine voice—transforms society into a black hole, which sucks everyone into a life of submissive dependency where there is no transcendent vision of human possibilities, no courage, and no excellence.

Feeling very marginalized, the anti-feminist writer Lom3z complained,

> Something has gone wrong in modern cultural and political life. . . . The Great and the Good have become the mediocre and the lame. The conditions necessary for civic and personal virtue have steadily eroded. . . . Still, we must resist the soft authoritarianism of [this] weepy moralism. We must not succumb to hysterical pleas for more safety, more consensus, more sensitivity. Ennobling work awaits us.[47]

Overclass Professionals Systemically Inculcate Other-Direction in Americans

In retrospect my first exposure to reeducation in the way of other-direction came in the spring of 1965 when I was at Harvard College. President Johnson had just escalated American military support for the South Vietnamese nationalists. I had lived in Bangkok when my dad served as President Kennedy's ambassador in Thailand, so I had a good deal of on-the-ground skinny from him about Communist aggression in Southeast Asia. Martin Peretz, later owner of the *New Republic* magazine, was a tutor in social studies. One day I ran across him in Harvard Yard, and he questioned me about the legitimacy of the South Vietnamese fight against Hanoi's war to conquer their country. Marty was among the New Frontier Democrats in Harvard who did not know how much they should support Lyndon Johnson as president after John Kennedy's assassination. Marty was pushing me to oppose Johnson's policy in Vietnam. I resisted given my loyalty to my father and my conviction that his understanding of the war was pretty close to the truth. As we argued walking back to Marty's room in Kirkland

House, Marty paused, then said with intensity, "You'll never get your politics right until you learn to reject your father."

I was stunned. I asked myself, still looking at Marty's glaring eyes, why should I learn to reject a father who did not, as far as I was concerned, deserve to be rejected, who, before my very eyes, had done much good in Thailand for the Thai people, especially in rural villages? Why should I, unprovoked, intentionally make an effort to come up with, embellish, and exaggerate, or even invent, reasons to break with him and disown his values and his legacy?

Years later I would read Abigail Shrier's exposé of therapists and teachers in postmodern America, *Bad Therapy*. Then I would understand the psychosocial connection between 1) rejecting your father and mother, after coming to the conclusion that childhood trauma at their hands had prevented you from becoming your true self, and 2) starting on the personal journey to find the right influencers to validate your self-esteem. In this process of identity formation, the adult still suffering from childhood trauma would more and more adopt the modal personality of other-direction and so open a psycho-social door to identity dysphoria.

My baby boomer cohorts had a saying vindicating this journey to find sustaining self-esteem in one's peer-induced identity: "Don't trust anyone over 30." Spoiled and coddled, we spitefully turned on our parents as Marty had turned on his father.

But from society's point of view, as Shakespeare put it in the mouth of his character King Lear, "How sharper than a serpent's tooth it is to have a thankless child."

Shrier reports on the states of mind that "tend to make us more successful." One is "action orientation" and the other "state orientation." She writes, "Adopting an action orientation means focusing on the task ahead with no thought to your current emotional or physical state. A state orientation means you're thinking principally about yourself. . . . Adopting an action orientation, it turns out, makes it much more likely that you accomplish the task."[48] To me, this suggests direct parallels with inner-direction (action orientation) and other-direction (state orientation).

Shrier then goes on at length associating bad therapy with the encouragement of state orientation in parenting and education, the preferencing of how you fit in emotionally, and of other-direction as better for one's well-being. She leaves us with the conclusion that other-direction is a learned state of mind. Such an orientation of our personality comes more from culture than from our intuitive awareness of our self as purposeful and competent.

She warns, "Placing undue importance on your emotions is a little like stepping onto a swivel chair to reach something on a high shelf."[49]

Shrier lists her ten steps of bad therapy: (1) Teach kids to pay close attention to their feelings, (2) induce obsessing over past injuries and personal problems, (3) make happiness a goal but reward emotional suffering, (4) affirm and accommodate children's anxieties, (5) observe and monitor, (6) dispense diagnoses liberally, (7) drug 'em, (8) encourage sharing of traumas, (9) encourage young adults to break contact with "toxic" family (30% of Americans over 18 have cut off a family member), and (10) create dependency on being treated.

Second, Shrier disparages the epidemic of professional educators insisting on providing social and emotional learning in schools, or what she calls "trauma-informed education." This intervention in the development of ego-identity consumes billions in educational spending annually, she says, and occupies 8% of instruction hours.[50]

This is the nonacademic engagement with students to "help" them deal with experienced traumas. Shrier questions the assumption of such mentoring that each person has been traumatized by parents or other home experiences. In a way, social and emotional learning accepts for everyone the premise of Dr. Joy DeGruy that African Americans must deal with post-slavery traumatic syndrome. Social-emotional learning, following Shrier's dissection of that expertise, could be considered an affirmation of post-parental traumatic syndrome.

Shrier points to the problem created by adults demanding that children experience repeated "emotional check-ins": Drawing a child's attention to emotions tends to induce a state orientation (other-direction in my words) in children, a modal personality they will carry into adulthood and deploy in their responsibilities as citizens of a republic.

Shrier infers that social-emotional learning denigrates parents in the minds of students, encouraging them to seek other influencers to validate their emerging ego-identities, thereby discouraging the development of self-assured inner-direction. Social-emotional learning is often predicated on the belief that parents are often "roadblocks to kids flourishing," legitimating the replacement of parental authority with that of professional experts in child development.[51]

Social-emotional learning also justifies for Shrier acceptance by schools of below-average academic performance as a caring accommodation to students dealing with posttraumatic stress—a "gentle prejudice of low expectations."

Shrier believes, "In the contemporary therapeutic school environment, students are not merely tyrannized by their own feelings. They live under the tyranny of each other's."[52] The rule of feelings, she says sensibly, is "endlessly capricious, vague in its dictates, unconcerned with facts or evidence." Education then for contemporary young Americans makes no place for the development of inner-direction.

Third, Shrier objects to the marginalization of parents under the withering critique of experts who have studied parenting styles and prefer some over others. Contemporary parenting, to be learned from books written by well-educated experts, often called "helicopter parenting" for its constant hovering and sudden insertion of guidance from above, has become destructive of inner-direction. Such parenting does not allow children to experience independence and self-reliance and prefers smothering and checking in with the child all the time, day in and day out—Are you OK? Is everything all right?

Shrier concludes her takedown of bad therapy in schools and homes with this thought: "We interpret young people's stultification as mental illness" when "it is closer to an emotional hypochondriasis. . . . It trucks not in neuroanatomy but a weaking of the soul—fear and disappointment and lack of capacity, the coiled horror of their own passivity."[53]

But a new professional discipline in psychotherapy has emerged to undo the damage done by bad parenting and Shrier's bad therapy. Available at a price are counselors in "executive functioning" (EF), which is what you can do well when you have it all together, use your agency, make prudent decisions, and achieve. Jenny Anderson of the *Wall Street Journal* explains, "Executive function skills fall under three big headings: working, or short-term, memory; inhibitory control, which involves putting urges and impulses on hold; and cognitive flexibility, the ability to plan, reason, solve problems and manage multiple tasks."[54]

Neuroscience teaches that the brain's operational center for regulating the quality of one's executive decision-making sits in its prefrontal cortex.

The rise in demand for student EF coaches coincides with a rise in attention deficit diagnoses in young people. Attention deficits are similar in effect to excessive other-direction in that they are a decline in the quality of one's executive functioning. In 2023 the classifications that physicians use to code and classify diagnoses were expanded to include frontal lobe and executive function deficits.

"We've taken away the in vivo ways that we learn executive functioning skills the best, like having part-time jobs, helping around the house, having to walk yourself to school every day or babysit," says Ellen Braaten, associate professor of psychology at Harvard Medical School.[55]

EF coaching is increasingly in demand in the workplace too. Coming to psychosocial maturity, dealing with self-actualization, and still seeking a resilient ego-identity, contemporary young professionals also suffer from attention deficit disorders and so are asking for help from coaches. "I have really highly intellectual, talented people who just need the fine-tuning on some of these skills in order to optimize their own careers," one human relations manager said.[56]

Since the 1980s women have been earning a majority of the doctorate degrees in psychology, and today they outnumber men by four to one on the boards of the field's major professional associations. When psychologists Cory Clark and Bo Winegard surveyed colleagues at one hundred universities, they found that only 43% of the female psychology professors believed that scholars should prioritize truth over social equity when the two conflict and that only 37% believed that scholars should be completely free to pursue research questions without fear of institutional punishment.[57]

In one study, psychology professors, both male and female, favored hiring a woman over an identically qualified man by a three-to-one margin.[58]

Another study on gender differences in research approaches used mixed methods—classical citation analysis, altmetric analysis, a survey of researchers, and text analysis of the abstracts of scientific articles—to investigate gender differences in the aims and impacts of research. "We find that male researchers more often value and engage in research mainly aimed at scientific progress. . . . Female researchers more often value and engage in research mainly aimed at contributing to societal progress."[59]

Journalism also educates. With the media, the classroom is inside us as we see or hear words and visual images to internalize them into our feelings, beliefs, and behaviors. Contemporary American journalism has largely been institutionalized under Overclass ownership and direction. Insistence on "groupthink" correctness in reporting and giving opinions is the "tell" that Overclass management of thought and public discussion is of high priority to those companies—especially in the major media firms. Educating Americans in (1) what is permitted to know and believe, and (2) what is misinformation or disinformation has become the chosen social function of Overclass reporters and editors. Americans are not to be trusted to have their own inner-directed beliefs and opinions and so must be herded toward other-direction, the internalization of what significant others, approved influencers, want them to think and feel.

Gerard Baker of the *Wall Street Journal* perceptively described the process of journalism becoming an extension of Overclass social management:

> What happened is that news organizations were transformed in character and purpose: They went from being quasi-legal institutions to quasi-religious ones. Their accountability function resided in their acting—or at least trying to act—as neutral arbiters of a sense of nonpartisan fairness. But their products no longer function like affidavits or witness testimony in the court of public opinion. They are more like prayer books for a believing congregation. Their purpose is to strengthen believers' faith by offering reassurance and imparting moral guidance. . . . CNN, MSNBC and the *New York Times* on the left. But what especially undermined traditional media is how the latter group became essentially the information arm of the establishment.
>
> Instead of a posture of healthy skepticism toward the prevailing orthodoxies of the day—race, gender, the environment, COVID—a new generation of journalists and media folk amplified and propagated them like medieval clergy. Challenge those orthodoxies, and you could find yourself marginalized, muted, or canceled.[60]

Indeed, so much in contemporary journalism has fallen under the sway of feminized other-direction. Susan Faludi wrote,

> Women have seemingly laid claim to the American media kingdom. Nearly half of all journalists in the US are now female. As of 2021 women reported more than 40% of the stories in *The New York Times* and *The Washington Post* and on prime-time

evening news broadcasts. A 2024 Reuters Institute study found that women hold nearly 45 percent of top editorial posts in American news outlets. In the last several years, women have become top editors and executives (albeit some of them briefly) at the *Wall Street Journal*, *The New York Times*, *The Washington Post*, the *Los Angeles Times*, the Associated Press, Reuters, MSNBC, ABC News, NBC News, and Fox News.[61]

Faludi comments on the new journalism that has emerged under Overclass leadership.

> If anything, the attempts of major news organizations to serve the voracious demands of a consumerist and tech-besotted age have tossed the profession [journalism]—and not just its female practitioners—back into the lifestyle precincts of the "woman's page. . . . The repercussions of these dynamics go beyond the status of women reporters or the press at large. Objective, unemotional, old-school news gathering was a bulwark against the excesses of emotive politics.

Faludi marginalizes feminist reporting as showcasing supposedly feminine attributes of vulnerability and emotionality, noting, "The kind of reporter who reveals her inner tumult and trumpets 'my truth' has been ascendent for decades." She refers to "the advertisements-for-myself braggadocio of New Journalism" as a "dress rehearsal for the self-promotion endemic to online media" and concludes that "since the 1990s the performativity of our social-networked era has demanded that its chroniclers find a way to celebrate their 'personalities' which are now their brands."

Faludi cites the 2004 conclusion of Deborah Chambers, Linda Steiner, and Carole Fleming on the rise of "a feminized confessional style of popular journalism . . . characterized as involving an intense but depoliticized exploration of emotion, so that people's 'feelings' about events become more important than the events themselves."[62]

How considerate and caring is that toward other-directed anxieties and insecurities, and how dismissive of inner-directed preferences for learning the facts?

In late twentieth-century and early twenty-first-century America, celebrities also became embodiments of virtue. Through the synchronicity between the celebrity and the fans, and the interdependent symbiosis of performer and cultural supplicant—consider Taylor Swift and her thousands of "Swifties"—celebrity role models instantiated life orientations for their admirers. This is true for movie stars, singers, television news anchors, and those written up in magazines such as *Vogue* and *People*.

In the 1960s singers such as Bob Dylan; Joan Baez; Peter, Paul and Mary; and the Rolling Stones, famously, were more than just entertainers. Their performative messaging with words and music was instructive for many in the baby boomer generation, encouraging indulgence in other-direction among those who particularly resonated with their social and cultural signaling.

Gabrielle Gurley would note with disappointment the reliance on celebrities by Kamala Harris during her 2024 campaign for the presidency, as if manipulation of other-direction among voters would replace Hegelian management expertise as legitimating citizen support of the Overclass.

Kamala Harris held her last rally of the presidential campaign season on the night before Election Day at the Philadelphia Museum of Art. Tens of thousands of people lined up for the free concert that featured Lady Gaga, Ricky Martin, DJ Jazzy Jeff, Fat Joe, Jazmine Sullivan, and the Roots. The vice president seemed almost tangential to the spectacle: It was pushing midnight before Oprah introduced Harris to make her final case to voters.

Did a truncated campaign season persuade Harris-Walz handlers that glitzy unelecteds from the rarified galaxies of Hollywood and the music industry were the fastest and best way to amplify Harris-Walz messaging? It seemed that Taylor Swift, Beyoncé, Bad Bunny, Bruce Springsteen, Megan Thee Stallion, Jennifer Lopez, John Legend, Cardi B, Katy Perry, Julia Roberts, Eminem, Robert De Niro, Spike Lee, and Leonardo DiCaprio were everywhere all at once—pumping up crowds at rallies in battleground states or tapping out their versions of joy online. . . .

That star power blinded the Harris-Walz campaign to a powerful miscalculation, one that stalked them all summer and into the fall as they zeroed in on the brightest lights: Beyoncé, Taylor Swift, and Bad Bunny. Together, they seemed to constitute a holy grail of good gets. Securing their endorsements, so the thinking appeared to go, would motivate the most sought-after groups in the Democratic base—women, African Americans, and Latinos—and deliver their votes, and the elusive youth vote most of all, to Harris.[63]

The fusion of Overclass politicians with the celebrity segment of their class was dramatically demonstrated after the 2024 presidential election. In February 2025 former president Biden signed a contract with Creative Artists Agency (CAA), a Hollywood firm that monetizes celebrity status. The firm had been his agent from 2017 to 2020. One of the world's largest talent agencies, CAA's roster ranges from the much-admired actress Meryl Streep and heavy-hitter lifestyle influencer Martha Stewart to baseball superstar Shohei Ohtani. The firm describes itself as follows:

Positioned at the nexus of talent, content, brands, technology, sports, and live events, CAA creates limitless opportunities for the storytellers, trendsetters, icons, and thought leaders who shape popular culture. Across film, television, music, sports, digital media, marketing, and beyond, we represent thousands of the world's leading actors, directors, writers, producers, musical artists, comedians, authors, athletes, coaches, broadcasters, teams, leagues, chefs, designers, fashion talent, consumer brands, and more.[64]

Former presidential nominee and Secretary of State Hillary Clinton used CAA to represent her book projects, and Barack and Michelle Obama used CAA to market their company producing films and television shows.

Another educational effort of the Overclass to turn Americans against inner-direction has been the promotion of diversity, equity, and inclusion (DEI) to ration allocation of positions in education and employment. DEI advances the power of the Overclass by punishing inner-direction and promoting other-direction. The elite *Begriff* legitimating DEI is a Gnostic racism derived from Critical Race Theory and called "Woke." Such a *Begriff* invoked Nietzsche's dynamic of other-directed ressentiment, a rancor blaming others for bringing evil into the world. Woke ideas and values have been diffused throughout American culture by public advocacy, a form of mass education, and the media. DEI discriminations in promotions and hiring were adopted without debate within the space of just a few years by all major bureaucracies in education, business and finance, and government, even in the military.

David Brooks, now writing for the *Atlantic*, shrewdly saw the following:

Wokeness is not just a social philosophy, but an elite status marker, a strategy for personal advancement. You have to possess copious amounts of cultural capital to feel comfortable using words like intersectionality, heteronormativity, cisgender, problematic, triggering, and Latinx. By navigating a fluid progressive cultural frontier more skillfully than their hapless Boomer bosses and by calling out the privilege and moral failings of those above them, young, educated elites seek power with elite institutions.[65]

The normative logic of Woke and its implementation through DEI disparages individuals who are inner-directed, thus suppressing certain ways of thinking and behaving among Americans that threaten the safe space of the other-directed, who are so dependent on structures of authority for their sense of psychosocial well-being. The logic of Woke and the goals of DEI to discriminate between the "good" and the "bad" among us based on race and gender classifications both bring to the contemporary American culture war Nietzsche's interpersonal dynamic of "ressentiment" and, as a result, have created a new Gnostic faith about who is incorrigibly wrong and who, therefore, must be overcome.

The effect of such racism is to perpetuate identity dysphoria by turning inner-directed Americans, most of whom are White, against themselves. In place of the founding covenant, advocates of racism offer an American identity of shame and guilt. Americans, especially those born to families of means and social position, are born defective, inheritors of a cruel and oppressing tradition not worthy of admiration or perpetuation. As President Obama said, America needs "transformation." How can any American be happy having a self that, allegedly, has been stained to the core by such past transgressions?

Robin DiAngelo and Ibram X. Kendi, members of the Overclass in excellent standing, each published a book advocating application of Critical Race Theory to American lives. DiAngelo's book, *White Fragility*, was published in 2018. Her book was on the *New York Times* bestseller list for 155 weeks. Kendi's book, *How to Be an Antiracist*, was published in 2019 and became a *New York Times* bestseller in 2020.

To earn her Overclass credentials, DiAngelo received a bachelor of arts degree with a double major in sociology and history from Seattle University, graduating summa cum laude as class valedictorian. She then received her doctorate in multicultural education from the University of

Washington, submitting a dissertation titled *Whiteness in Racial Dialogue: A Discourse Analysis*. She was a tenured professor at Westfield State University and then became an affiliate associate professor of education at the University of Washington.

A 2019 article in *The New Yorker*, notionally the quintessential Overclass media platform, characterized DiAngelo as "perhaps the country's most visible expert in anti-bias training, a practice that is also an industry, and, from all appearances, a prospering one."[66]

Kendi was a professor at American University and then the Andrew W. Mellon Professor in the Humanities at Boston University. During the 2020–2021 academic year, he was the Frances B. Cashin Fellow at the Radcliffe Institute for Advanced Study at Harvard University. His Overclass media platform was the *Atlantic*, where he was a contributing writer.

From the Gnostic perspective of Critical Race Theory, inner-direction is presented in racist terms as "Whiteness." Inner-directed behaviors are ascribed to a "dominant narrative," passed on by stories told to serve dominant social group interests and ideologies. The Smithsonian National Museum of African American History and Culture (a governmental and cultural institution of the Overclass) defined as "Whiteness" the behaviors of rational thinking and hard work, which have anchored inner-direction in worldly success and personal self-confidence for generations. By promoting prejudice against these "White" behaviors and modes of thinking, DEI protects the social and cultural power of the Overclass and its choice of other-direction as the modal disposition for all people.

To thus assimilate inner-direction to Whiteness is to expel the inner-directed, regardless of their race, from positions of responsibility in American life. Moreover, it denies to those not born White the possibility of living inner-directed lives of purpose, dedication, and fully empowered agency.

Critical race theory, accusations of being White, DEI programs, ethnic studies departments, and Woke mindsets, each in their own way, use racism to reject the founding American covenant.

These contemporary racist lifestyles and ways of thinking are another instance of modern, secularized, Gnostic religiosity—a belief that evil is present in the world in the bodies and minds of Caucasians. Fortunately for all of us, though, such fallen people born with an original sin can be redeemed and brought out of their darkness into the light of the good through learning a gnosis—the true knowledge of who they are and why they must undergo transformation of mind and heart.

DEI, though, is a particular use of class power to impose a personality template on the American people, defensively to protect the privileges and power of the Overclass as social engineers and managers of our lives and offensively to eliminate those who oppose such power, in a kind of Maoist "cultural revolution" where reeducation takes place inside Overclass bureaucracies and the "Little Red Book" is replaced with training sessions in "antiracism" and personal confessions of harboring unconscious bias.

From the perspective of buttressing Overclass social hegemony, Woke and DEI provide new credentials for social, cultural, political, and economic advancement into the Overclass. Race and gender (including gender fluidity) are transformed conceptually into a *Begriff* newly defining meritorious achievement. Inborn characteristics such as skin color, facial features, cast of eye, hair type, and genitalia—all dependent on parental DNA—are transfigured into rationalizations for differential societal allocations of power and money. In particular, the principal gatekeepers for admission into the Overclass—college admissions officers and professors—and into the power structures of corporate America and government—human relations managers—have come to use these Woke beliefs and DEI standards of good and bad to favor some over others as members in good standing of the Overclass.

A culturally and politically very significant effort of Donald Trump in his second term as president is to disestablish DEI Gnosticism and discrimination in both public and private institutions. Major corporations once aligned with the DEI *Begriff* have discontinued their DEI hiring and promotion practices.

Consider as an infamous example the various qualifications of Kamala Harris leading to her becoming the Democrat Party's nominee for president in 2024.

The Gnostic religiosity leading to this acceptance of race and gender as meritorious credentials is "intersectionality," a contemporary *Begriff* about oppressions and social power allocations that ignores inner-direction in favor of personal ego-identities appropriated and internalized from social narratives in a very postmodern approach to finding personal truths.

Those who can't find a well-grounded source of personal agency are most likely to feel oppressed by the circumstances of their lives.

Ethnic studies also promote other-direction by teaching the necessary dependency of individuals for their values and identity on group member-ships. Whites are White, Blacks are Black, Chinese are Chinese, and Ibo are Ibo, ad infinitum. The premise of ethnic studies holds that we are not captains of our souls or masters of our fates but prisoners of a way of life and thinking imposed on us at birth. Ethnic studies, it has been said, warn us not to accept meritocracy and individual excellence, for to do so would have us strive to do our best on our own and set our personal focus on individual achievement—on the power and authenticity of our own selves rather than on what others tell us to be.

In short, from this racist perspective, there is no self of our own for us to believe in, no ego-identity under our control. We therefore must look to others to discover who we really are. We are victims of our birthrights and need the patronage and leadership of the Overclass to make us all right.

A curious possibility exists that the Overclass capture of higher educa-tion and then using it to (1) advance the interests of the class and (2) impose its *Begriffs* on Americans gave rise to a new form of antisemitism. After the 2023 commencement of a new war between Palestinians and the Jews of Israel, colleges and universities became notorious for protests delegitimiz-ing Jews and Israel. The rhetoric and demands of these protests were quickly criticized as a new form of hurtful and racialist antisemitism.

But calling out Jews and ostracizing them for "settler colonialism" in the Holy Land was a far cry from traditional Christian and White European antisemitism, the kind of the pogroms associated with the Jewish Pale of Settlement in Imperial Russia, or Shakespeare's dehumanizing stereotype of Shylock in his play *The Merchant of Venice*, or Charles Dickens's nasty character Fagin, or the antisemitism of my youth that Jews were too "pushy" to be welcomed in polite White, Anglo-Saxon, Protestant society. (In 1958 I was the only goy invited to Randy Davis's bar mitzvah ceremony at a synagogue in the Larchmont suburb north of New York City. I did not feel that out of place.)

In an extreme example of that traditional antisemitic genre, the American author Nathaniel Hawthorne, in his novel *The Marble Faun*, described Jews as "the ugliest, most evil-minded people," who resemble "maggots when they overpopulate a decaying cheese."

The accusation that the Jews in Israel were committing genocide against Palestinians quickly became a fixture attached to many elite American institutions of higher education in 2024. This prejudice against certain Jews was then generalized to all Jews. The *Begriff* employed to create this new antisemitism was drawn from critical theory—an unhealthy fixation on power in human relations.

As I mentioned in chapter 4, Critical Legal Theory holds that there is no law, only power: the strong govern, and the weak follow as told. Critical Race Theory holds that race consciousness, not conscience or character, inexorably and systemically structures relationships and life outcomes. Thus, according to the theory, dominant races, using biased reasoning or decision-making, deploy their institutional powers to keep members of other races submissive.

The other-directed, not having a reassuringly stable ego-identity, are very tempted to reason and emote in terms of power. And so they may very well tend to gravitate toward personal appropriation and application of critical theory in their lives. Such an orientation toward the importance of power may therefore provoke some in the Overclass to entertain a prejudice against Jews as having too much power without deserving it. Marginalizing Jews for "settler colonialism" or being "genocidal" is the application of critical theory to members of an ethnicity with distinct cultural and religious traditions, an application very much in tune with the modal personality of the class structure now delivering American higher education.

In addition, I associate inner-direction with the religious tradition shaping the ideas and aspirations of my Jewish friends and colleagues. Jews are a covenantal people, accepting responsibility and working hard to uphold their side of the bargain. So, such a firm sense of inner purpose and consequent personal determination might well be hard for the other-directed to appreciate and value.

The Overclass Invents and Sells Technology That Institutionalizes Identity Dysphoria

A powerful subsector of the Overclass—high tech—invented cell phones and sold them by the millions. Technological expertise created this commercial product that has disposed Americans increasingly to adopt other-direction as their modal personality. An other-directed populace running compulsively and anxiously from helter to skelter cannot save itself from the dysfunctions arising from identity dysphoria. Such a culture cannot provide effective and reassuring ego-identities for its people. They become flotsam and jetsam bobbing up and down in the tides of time, going wherever fate may carry them forward.

The consumption of the intellectual and entertainment products provided by cell phones—from Facebook posts, text messages, emotional comments, and questionable news on X to TikTok and Instagram videos—is an ever-present system of multicultural orientation for Americans, especially for youth. Watching cell phone screens influences, instructs, informs, disturbs, and reassures the minds and psyches of millions of Americans every minute.

A related product encouraging the internalization of other-direction, also invented and sold by high-tech companies, is video gaming with its imaginary worlds, mostly used by young men.

Jonathan Haidt's verdict on the social and cultural externalities of high-tech products is harsh: "[T]he most rapid rewiring of human relationships and consciousness in human history has made it harder for all of us to think, focus, forget ourselves enough to care about others, and build close relationships."[67]

In short, to experience identity dysphoria.

Haidt discusses the rise of "internalizing disorders—anxiety and depression" starting in 2010. These disorders affect the other-directed more than the inner-directed; therefore, as American culture has swung toward other-direction, it is not at all surprising that anxiety and depression have taken over more and more American lives. Haidt notes that we as social beings (Aristotle called us *zoon politikon*) are attuned to threats from others such as being shunned or shamed.[68] This disposition has greater impact on our self-system when we become more dependent on the opinion of others in forming an opinion of ourselves. Isolating ourselves from others out of fear brings on deeper depression and more acute anxiety.

Inner-direction is conducive to robust personal agency, while other-direction tends to erode our confidence in having agency. This losing confidence in our personal agency is especially consequential in a digital reality that is constantly interfering with our options and our hopes and manipulating our desires and our fears.

Haidt reminds us that a lesson learned from the successes of cognitive behavioral therapy is that experience, not information, is the key to emotional development. Other-directed individuals are more prone to using information from others as formative for their emotional development, while inner-directed personalities are more engaged in experiential learning. Haidt therefore recommends a play-based childhood of three-dimensional experience over a cell phone–based childhood of two-dimensional, only visual, learning. "Life on the platforms," he says, "forces young people to become their own brand managers, always thinking ahead about the social consequences of each photo, video, comment, emoji they choose."[69]

Social media make it easy to conform to the styles and thinking of others and thus more easily adjust to social dependency. Social media facilitate the emergence of influencers who market their ersatz prestige. In assuring our subordination to the thinking and values of others, social media reinforce proclivities to become more other-directed.

However, the business of making money by providing social media or turning yourself into an influencer using social media requires consumers of social media. Other-direction creates that consumer demand at scale. Social media platforms just supply what the other-directed want. The market for social media's product is really only another instance of what Adam Smith called out as humanity's need to "truck and barter"—exchanging a good or service to meet the need or want of another. Without other-direction, social media would be lively and interesting but not outcome determinative for much of American culture and politics, contributing significantly to our society's destabilizing identity dysphoria.

Haidt admires the teachings of the Stoics and the Buddha, who taught that happiness in life comes from internal learning, depriving the external world of invasive power over us to set off within us negative emotions, fears, and anxieties.[70]

In short, social media hinder the growth of human capital and dissolve social capital, leaving us less and less capable of acting significantly in the face of history.

Haidt also noted that a parenting style emerged among Overclass parents—those in the professional class—in which their children needed protection from risk through the constant care and training of adults. This parental denial of autonomy to their children shifted child development from inner-direction to other-direction.[71]

In their previous book *The Coddling of the American Mind*, Haidt and Greg Lukianoff wrote, "Safetyism deprives young people of experiences that their . . . minds need, thereby making them more fragile, anxious, and prone to seeing themselves as victims."[72] They also high-lighted this quote from Epictetus:

> What really frightens and dismays us is not external events themselves, but the way in which we think about them. It is not things that disturb us but our interpretation of their significance.

Haidt's conclusion: go outside your mind and live in the real world. Education needs to be engagement with reality. Good education demands an interiority that can easily and seamlessly grasp what is real, an interiority that can put aside personal "truth" and be comfortable, even excited, about searching for "real" truth.

Haidt and Lukianoff discuss patterns of thought and conjoined behaviors that we use to process our interactions with the world around us, which psychologists call schemas. An other-directed schema leads us to emotional reasoning, catastrophizing, overgeneralizing, dichotomous thinking, mind-reading of others without any knowledge of what they are thinking, labeling (he or she is a . . .), seeing only negatives and filtering out the positives, discounting positives, and blaming.

This list of psychological tendencies sheds light on the dysfunction of American politics, which has descended into a culture war between the Overclass and the deplorables.

For example, the Trump derangement syndrome of leading Democrats and their think-alikes arises from and spreads emotional reasoning, catastrophizing, we-him dichotomous generalizing, labeling, and a filtering in of only the negative. The intensity of this Trump derangement syndrome among Democrats culminated in legally questionable lawsuits against him, an impeachment, and vitriolic speech about his being a liar, a danger to democracy, a Russian pawn, and more.

Another emerging Overclass derangement syndrome is a new Gnostic *Begriff* exposing "settler colonialism" as grounds for rejecting the

American experiment in ordered liberty and the legitimacy of Canada and Australia as respectable nation-states. The allegation of settler colonialism highlighted demonstrations and protests on American university campuses supporting the Hamas war of 2023 against the Jews of Israel and demanding an ethnic cleansing of the territory from the Jordan River to the shores of the Mediterranean Sea.

The calculated impact of this *Begriff* is to cause rejection of inner-direction in the descendants of immigrants from Europe. This *Begriff* encourages identity dysphoria among such Americans. The desired impact to be achieved by popularizing this *Begriff* is to have those particular Americans experience a kind of victimhood as having been born as inherently undeserving people and, in consequence of holding such a belief, to willingly submit themselves to tutelage under the supervision of those in good standing with the moral paradigm of certain Overclass pretensions.

But the Gnostic allegation that settler colonialists are a worldly evil to be repulsed through the application of redemptive knowledge is a derangement in the minds of its proponents. The allegation responds to their psychic needs far more than it relates to the historical realities and the widely varying circumstances of migrants of European origin.[73]

These accusatory antigenocide campus protests emanate from campuses where intellectual standards have collapsed. The justification proposed by Hegel for Overclass dominance over society and its cultural, economic, and political sectors was expertise, professional distinction, and the deployment of sophisticated knowledge and better thinking. Higher education has undergone an evolution away from intellectual rigor and the internalization of genuine expertise toward extracurricular pastimes. Other-direction, meeting peer expectations, is increasingly motivating college students more than inner-direction is keeping them eyeball to eyeball with reality and its hard choices.

A Harvard student wrote, "Harvard has increasingly become a place . . . for bright students to gather—that happens to offer lectures on the side."[74] Already in 2021 study time for college students had dropped to twelve hours per week from twenty-five in the 1960s. Professors are assigning less and less reading. One-third of students surveyed had no more than forty pages of assigned reading per week. Study has become a sideline for many aspiring members of the Overclass. One student rationalized, "Why bother spending hours on classwork if you'll never get a grade below a B+?" More and more, college is for job training, not excellence in thinking and knowing. The focus is on what others admire more than on what is good for one's character and what best confirms one's personal agency as important and resilient. To impress potential employers and graduate school admissions officers, college students need extracurricular achievements to stand out among their competitors, most of whom all have higher grade point averages.

I experienced this corruption of professional education in 1977 when the dean of my law school asked me to leave the practice of law with a major firm on Wall Street to return to Harvard and set up an office of student affairs. Out of the blue, he called me up and said, "The Vietnam War is over. The antiwar movement is over, but the students have not returned to respecting the faculty and being dutiful in their studies. The faculty is unhappy. What do you think we should do?" Off the top of my head, I gave him a few ideas based on my experience when president of the school's board of student advisers. He then asked, "Will you come back and do all that?" I said yes. By the time I got back to Cambridge, he had also put me in charge of the dormitories and student commons.

After a few months of participant observation, as a cultural anthropologist would do when seeking to learn about a community, I learned a new way of thinking about the frames of meaning for students at Harvard Law School. I asked to see the dean. Sitting across from his desk, I said with a bit of cheek, "Al, your problem is that 90% of your students are not in the top 10% of their class." He was stunned and most annoyed at hearing this. In his generation of poor Jewish students who had gained admittance to Harvard through intellectual perseverance and grit, grades were sacrosanct, providing certain evidence of who deserved to be among those chosen to lead America.

But for the new baby boomer generation, admission to Harvard Law School was all they needed for their careers. They had been chosen by gaining admission to the school. Grades then became threatening—a source of possible humiliation and the cause of losing out to classmates in the competition for the best judicial clerkships and big-firm offers of employment. The students felt that they already had received the requisite Gold Star to pin on their lapels for the world to see. Why ruin such a good thing by not doing well on exams?

College administrators have responded to this shift in student preferences. They have hired *more* administrators to improve the quality of "campus life," following the Overclass mantra that having more managers will always bring about better outcomes. In recent decades, colleges have hired administrators at three to four times the rate that full-time faculty have been hired, with many schools employing three times as many administrators as teaching faculty. In 2023, Stanford University had 17,529 students, 18,369 administrators, and 2,323 teachers.[75]

Following on this trend of marginalizing the left-brain learning component of higher education, Professor Yascha Mounk has proposed the abolition of grades. He believes that "grade inflation at American universities is out of control. . . . The more elite the college, the more lenient the standards. . . . The whole system loses meaning."[76] Mounk recognizes, as did Hegel, that a meritocratic society must have meaningful assessment of expertise and professional superiority. Without that, any elite falls to the imposter syndrome and becomes a comedic Tartuffery.

And so, ironically, contemporary higher education is diligently chipping moral legitimacy away from the Overclass, one student at a time. This turning away from rigor and merit in higher education is a betrayal of Hegel's God-State and two hundred years of Overclass claims to excellence and rightful prerogative.

Peter Berkowitz, a senior fellow at the Hoover Institution, Stanford University, is cuttingly definitive in his condemnation of contemporary higher education under Overclass stewardship.

> Postmodern progressivism occupies the commanding heights of contemporary American culture. It combines a commitment to rule by credentialed elites, an ever more expansive egalitarianism conceived in terms of group identities, and a repudiation of traditional moral principles. Progressive elites draw from these clashing convictions a license to do whatever is necessary to make Americans conform to their prescriptions for diversity understood as intellectual conformity; equity understood as differential treatment based on race, ethnicity, and sex; and inclusion understood as silencing or excluding those who disagree with the progressive agenda. Oscillating opportunistically between a moral relativism that haughtily disdains to judge and a dogmatic moralism that judges haughtily, this incoherent sensibility fortifies self-righteousness and induces ideological blindness. It drives the mainstream media's and the elite academy's efforts to banish opposition, stigmatize debate, control the flow of information, supervise public discussion, and establish authoritative and unchallengeable progressive narratives.
>
> Postmodern progressivism undercuts liberal democracy in America. Freedom and democracy depend on a knowledgeable citizenry, which requires a self-aware press that reports the facts accurately and analyzes the issues fairly, and an educational system devoted to the transmission of knowledge and the cultivation of independent minds. However, the prestige press and the elite academy collaborate to cocoon citizens within a set of purportedly final and uncontestable progressive assumptions and conclusions. This drastic narrowing of moral and political perspectives erodes

the conditions for public discussion and reasoned deliberation essential to responsible self-government.[77]

David Brooks has proposed a systemic reformation of higher education in an article with the truthful title "How the Ivy League Broke America" in the *Atlantic*.[78] Brooks starts with the decision of James Conant, president of Harvard University, after the American victory in World War II, to use colleges and universities to intentionally, following Hegel, provide America with a meritocracy based on the intelligence of its members, an elite of experts. Conant proposed using a standardized test of cognitive intelligence to "select, sort, and classify" students. Thus would one indicator of merit—IQ—be used to separate student sheep from student goats and so provide a socialized pathway for the sheep to ascend to the heights of national authority—political, economic, social, and cultural.

Conant's vision came to pass, and several generations of Americans have now taken the Scholastic Aptitude Test in seeking admission to college. Brooks notes that by 2024, 54% of high achievers across a range of professions had attended the same thirty-four elite educational institutions.

Brooks then points out where he faults this college-prepared meritocracy for falling short in building a better America: for overrating intelligence over other noncognitive traits and abilities, for believing that success in higher education will lead to success in life, for serving wealthy families who can afford to have their children tutored in test-taking skills, for creating a caste system among Americans, for stunting the psyches of the American elite, and for "provoking a populist backlash that is tearing society apart."

When Brooks complains of "damaged psyches," he is unknowingly speaking of the consequences of adopting other-direction as one's modal personality. He faults the American elite for never asking itself, "How can I become a generous human being? How do I live a life of meaning? How do I build good character?"

His plea is to "replace the current meritocracy," an ironic echo of the French Jacobin demand to replace the Bourbon Dynasty aristocracy with patriotic citizens.

His solution is to recruit those with inner-direction for admission into colleges and universities.

Brooks sets forth four criteria for the selection of the "best" among our youth, which in my view can very nicely be aligned with David Riesman's construct of inner-direction. They are having (1) curiosity, (2) a sense of drive and mission, (3) more social intelligence so as to be less "self-centered and manipulative," and (4) an agile mind that easily synthesizes "all the different aspects of a situation and discerns the flow of events."

From another direction, criticism comes to raise questions about the inner-direction and integrity of American higher education. In 2024 the Foundation for Individual Rights and Expression released a survey of 6,269 faculty in fifty-five four-year colleges and universities, revealing higher education as a tug-of-war between the inner-directed and the other-directed, with the inner-directed pulling higher education in its direction and the other-directed pulling toward conformity with Overclass norms and *Begriffs*.

Only 17% of liberal faculty reported that they at least occasionally hide their political views to keep their jobs, compared with a staggering 55% of conservative faculty who say the same. And this fear is more prevalent among faculty who do not have tenure than those who do.

Of the respondents, 35% said they recently toned down their writing for fear of controversy, 28% (55% of conservatives) at least occasionally hide their political beliefs from other faculty in an attempt to keep their jobs, and 40% (52% of conservatives and 43% of moderates) worry about damaging their reputations because someone misunderstands something they have said or done.[79]

Americans are entitled to question just how the Overclass has delivered on Hegel's proposal that well-educated experts and professionals be entrusted with the management of modern, enlightened, God-States. In the National Assessment of Educational Progress for 2024 (the Nation's

Report Card), only 31% of eighth-graders were proficient or more in science; only 22% were proficient or better in math; and only 35% were proficient or better in reading. In short: the majority of eighth-grade Americans were below proficient in academic achievement.

In 2024, 45% of twelfth-graders performed below the National Assessment of Educational Progress (NAEP) basic achievement level in mathematics, their average math score was the lowest recorded since the assessment began in 2005, and 32% scored below the basic level in reading. Overall, scores were at their lowest level in three decades.

These results indicate that many high school seniors are not academically prepared for college. The declines affected nearly all student groups, regardless of race, gender, or parental education level.[80]

Continual Exclusion of African Americans from the American Dream

Overclass mismanagement of education has perpetuated the exclusion of most African Americans from fulsome participation in the American economy, with distressing cultural and social consequences.

Other-direction tends, on balance, to privilege dependency. An other-directed person searches for instruction in what values and beliefs to hold.

African Americans, originally brought to the United States against their will to live and work in slavery, without rights, without legal families of their own, without dignity, have ever since carried an unequal burden of identity dysphoria. For slaves, respect and worldly success were nearly impossible to earn or achieve beyond the boundaries of slave quarters. The privileged among them were employed in the households of their owners. Experiencing personal agency was exceptional. Developing an instinct for dependency was a very rational response to their circumstances.

The theology drawn by slave pastors from the Judeo-Christian bible elevated personal reliance on deliverance by a second-coming Moses who would break their chains and, on the promise of Jesus, give them grace in the afterlife.

This theology brought forth songs of supplication and patience—the spirituals.

"Didn't My Lord Deliver Daniel"
He deliver'd Daniel from the lion's den,
Jonah from the belly of the whale,
And the Hebrew children from the fiery furnace
And why not every man.

I set my foot on the Gospel ship
And the ship it began to sail,
It landed me over on Canaan's shore
And I'll never come back any more.
[Chorus]
Didn't my Lord deliver Daniel,
Deliver Daniel deliver Daniel.
Didn't my Lord deliver Daniel,
And why not every man?

"Go Down, Moses"
When Israel was in Egypt's land,
Let my people go;
Oppressed so hard they could not stand,
Let my people go.

Thus Saith the Lord, bold Moses said,
Let my people go;
If not I'll smite your first born dead,
Let my people go.

The Lord told Moses what to do,
Let my people go;

To lead the children of Israel through,
Let my people go.

[Chorus]
Go down, Moses,
Way down in Egypt's land.
Tell ole Pharaoh,
Let my people go.

"Nobody Knows the Trouble I've Had"
Sometimes I'm up, sometimes I'm down,
Oh, yes, Lord.
Sometimes I'm almost to the ground,
Oh, yes, Lord
Oh,
I never shall forget that day,
Oh, yes, Lord.
When Jesus washed my sins away,
Oh, yes, Lord
Oh,

[Chorus]
Nobody knows the trouble I've had,
Nobody knows but Jesus.
Nobody knows the trouble I've had,
Glory Hallelujah!

"Sometimes I Feel Like a Motherless Child"
Sometimes I feel like a motherless child,
Sometimes I feel like a motherless child,
Sometimes I feel like a motherless child,
A long way from home,

A long way from home.

"Swing Low, Sweet Chariot"
I looked over Jordan, and what did I see,
Coming for to carry me home;
A band of angels coming after me,
Coming for to carry me home.

If you get there before I do,
Coming for to carry me home;
Tell all my friends I'm coming too,
Coming for to carry me home.

[Chorus]
Swing Low, sweet chariot,
Coming for to carry me home,
Swing low, sweet chariot,
Coming for to carry me home.

Under oppressive conditions, African Americans made their own covenant, one both collective and individual—exchanging submissive supplication for a promise of deliverance.

Sometime between 1853 and 1861, a formerly enslaved African American woman, Hannah Crafts, wrote a novel—*The Bondwoman's Narrative.* Crafts included reference to the solace she found in her Christianity: "We could not be utterly forsaken and hopeless and helpless when God was near. . . . Oh the blessedness of such heavenly trust—how it comforts and sustains the soul in moments of doubt and despondency—how it alleviates misery and even subdues pain."[81]

W. E. B. Du Bois wrote in *The Souls of Black Folk*, "How shall man measure progress? . . . How many heartfuls of sorrow shall balance a bushel of wheat? How hard a thing is life to the lowly, and yet how human and real! And all this life and love and strife and failure—is it the twilight of nightfall or the flush of some faint-dawning day? Thus sadly musing, I road to Nashville in the Jim Crow car."[82]

He continued,

> . . . let us build, too, the Negro universities: Fisk, whose foundation was ever broad; Howard, at the heart of the Nation. . . . Why not here, and perhaps everywhere, plant deeply and for all time centers of learning and living. . . . Patience, humility, manners and taste, common schools and kindergartens, industrial and technical schools, literature, and tolerance, all these spring from knowledge and culture, the children of the university. . . . And the final product of our training must be neither a psychologist nor a brickmason, but a man. And to make men, we must have ideals, broad, pure and inspiring ends of living.[83]

In his own words, Du Bois laid out an inner-directed path toward the making of men, yet the path set by the Overclass on behalf of African Americans—affirmative action, quotas, diversity, equity, and inclusion discriminations, and paternalizing disregard for individual merit and personal accomplishment—has failed to deliver on Du Bois's vision.

In 1852 Martin Delany had earlier advocated the same program of elevation for colored people in the United States.

> The degradation of the slave parent has been entailed upon the child, induced by the subtle policy of the oppressor, in regular succession handed down from father to son—a system of regular submission and servitude, menialism and dependence, until it has become almost a physiological function of our system, an actual condition of our nature. Let this no longer be so, but let us determine to equal the whites among whom we live, not

by declarations and unexpressed self-opinion, for we have always had enough of that, but by actual proof in acting, doing, and carrying out practically, the measures of equality. Here is our nativity, and here have we the natural right to abide and be elevated through the measures of our own efforts.[84]

Inner-direction as the modal personality for many African Americans was precluded by the inward effects of slavery on what Du Bois called the Soul of Black Folk. In 2005 Dr. Joy DeGruy published *Post Traumatic Slave Syndrome*, explaining the legacy of enslavement: The slave master says to the slave mother, "Well, now, that Mary of yours is really coming along." The mother, terrified that the master may see qualities in her daughter that could merit her being raped or sold, says, "Naw, sir, she ain't worth nothin. She cain't work. She stupid. She shiftless."[85]

DeGruy argues that what began as an appropriate response to an oppressive and danger-filled environment has sadly been transmitted down through many generations of African Americans. DeGruy proposes that African Americans adjusted to adversity by expecting no more than survival. They internalized into their modal personality an analogue to other-direction—a repression of the self to always be what will get you safely through the day in the eyes of others—the influencers observing you in your daily routine. This disposition is called survivor's syndrome.

DeGruy describes the survivor's syndrome of many African Americans as consisting of vacant esteem, ever-present anger, and racialist socialization. Vacant esteem is the state of believing yourself to have little or no worth. Ever-present anger flows from believing that one has no control, that desired goals cannot be obtained. Such angry feelings are vented where there is safety—on family and friends. Perceptions of inevitable failure are as real psychologically as actual failure, but they may even be more pernicious to the sense of self than real failure—they pre-empt initiative, weaken resolve, and so vaporize personal agency.

Racialist socialization, in DeGruy's presentation, is other-direction at its worst—internalizing the White prejudice that Blacks are, by nature, inferior, unable to live by White standards of beauty and conduct. She concludes, "When so many of our youth glamorize thug life, and lack of education, when their primary avenues of aspiration are athletics and entertainment, and when males and females, young and old, are sexually irresponsible, we make real the prejudice of white America and give life to their caricatures of African-Americans."[86]

DeGruy asks hard questions: "Why are so many black women raising their children alone? . . . Why do so many black women suffer the brunt of black male hostility and violence?"[87] Given this, we should ask, "Why do so many Blacks assume that hardships are all they can expect out of life until the end of days?"

If one does not try to succeed academically in school, how can one overcome the "slings and arrows of outrageous fortune" that come to us all life long? Our schools, managed by Overclass females, have failed to inspire African American children with self-confidence, bringing them out from under the pall of vacant esteem handed down in their families from generation to generation and left unchallenged by the Black church in so many Sunday sermons.

Jesse Jackson won renown but did not change very much the trajectory of the African American experience when, in February 1972, he read this poem on the children's television show *Sesame Street*.

I may be Young
but I am
Somebody.
I may be on Welfare
but I am
Somebody.
I may be Small
but I am
Somebody.
I may make a Mistake
but I am

Somebody!
My clothes are different,
My face is different,
My hair is different,
but I am
Somebody.
I am black, brown, white.
I speak a different language.
But I must be respected,
protected,
never rejected.
I am God's child.
I am
Somebody![88]

DeGruy's recommendations on how African Americans can move beyond the posttraumatic slave syndrome echo the habits of inner-direction. You are "somebody" for real when you are inner-directed.

Sadly, however, Overclass management of American culture and society, especially education, only perpetuates the posttraumatic slave syndrome for many African Americans. That favored management approach is to emphasize history and the initial trauma of slavery and segregation as perpetuated by the postmodern welfare-state over many generations of African American families. The Overclass approach to the heritage of slavery is to continually emphasize race and racism as important determinants of access to income, wealth, and positional power in the bureaucracies managed by professionals. Expectations for inner-directed individual achievement in schools and large institutions are subordinated to antiracist racism and allocation of position according to the dictates of DEI.

A movement to manage individual hierarchical advancement by DEI criteria swept through Overclass institutions after 2020. In public schools many African American students were promoted from grade to grade and given high school diplomas regardless of their academic success. Prosecutors allocated the privilege of being released from custody without payment of bail money to some criminals but not to others, with race often used as a criterion for preferential treatment. There was no rule of law binding on all persons equally after their arrests.

The result is that life outcomes are once again associated with skin color, ethnic stereotypes, and gender, not on individual dignity, character, talent, grit, or other admirable personal capabilities. The appointment of Claudine Gay to the presidency of Harvard University and the selection of Kamala Harris, first as the 2020 vice presidential running mate of Joe Biden and second as the 2024 replacement of Joe Biden as the Democrat Party's candidate for the presidency of the United States, illustrate with perfection the management methodology of the Overclass in favoring racial appearance over substantive achievement.

Jason Riley, an African American editorial writer for the *Wall Street Journal*, wrote:

> Central to the social-justice ideology that promotes affirmative action is a belief that statistical disparities among groups result mainly from discrimination rather than from statistical differences in skills, behaviors and attitudes. Accordingly, black social and economic advancement is said to be dependent on policies that counter antiblack bias with antiwhite bias. Yet the phenomenal rise of blacks in the first two-thirds of the 20th century, despite centuries of maltreatment, provides a strong rebuke to such claims. History shows that black people have made greater strides under policies of colorblindness than affirmative action. At best, race preferences have helped to continue something that was already happening. At worst, they've done more to throttle than to expedite black upward mobility.

Riley added that,

> In 1940, 25- to 29-year-old whites had 3.6 years more schooling on average than their black counterparts. By 1960 both groups had advanced, but blacks outpaced whites and the gap narrowed by more than half, to 1.7 years. Most white-collar jobs, then as now, require a high school diploma. Between 1940 and 1960, the percentage of blacks who met that qualification more than tripled, again growing at a much faster rate than among whites. ... In 1939, the annual median income was $360 for black males and $1,112 for white males. (These figures are nominal, unadjusted for inflation.) By 1960 those figures had reached $3,075 and $5,137, respectively, an increase of 568% for blacks vs. 362% for whites. Among females over the same time, there was a 275% increase among whites and a 418% increase among blacks. All this occurred before affirmative action and the civil-rights legislation of the mid-1960s.[89]

The 1963 call of Rev. Martin Luther King Jr. that all Americans should be judged by the content of their character has been ignored. The founding American covenant on all individuals being responsible agents of higher purpose has been abandoned.

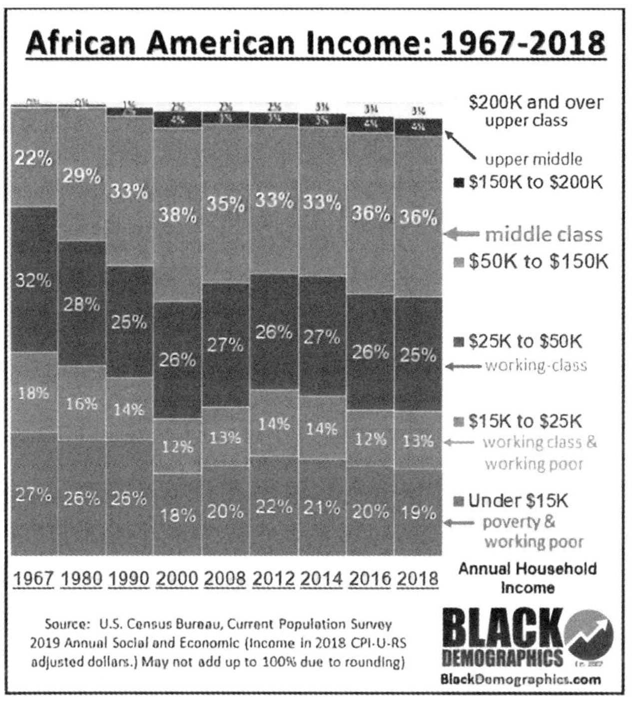

African American Income: 1967-2018
$200K and over
upper class
upper middle
$150K to $200K
middle class
$50K to $150K
$25K to $50K
working-class
$15K to $25K
working class & working poor
Under $15K
poverty & working poor
Annual Household Income
1967 1980 1990 2000 2008 2012 2014 2016 2018
22% 29% 33% 38% 35% 33% 33% 36% 36%
32% 28% 25% 26% 27% 26% 27% 26% 25%
18% 16% 14% 12% 13% 14% 14% 12% 13%
27% 26% 26% 18% 20% 22% 21% 20% 19%
Source: U.S. Census Bureau, Current Population Survey 2019 Annual Social and Economic (Income in 2018 CPI-U-RS adjusted dollars.) May not add up to 100% due to rounding)
BLACK DEMOGRAPHICS
BlackDemographics.com

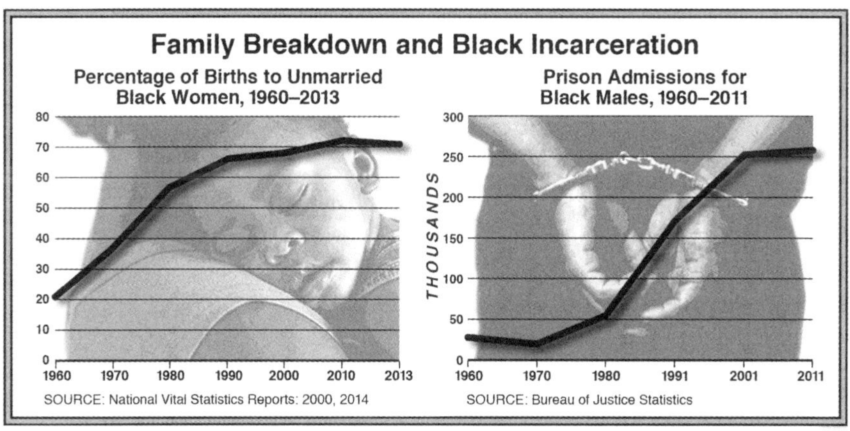

Family Breakdown and Black Incarceration
Percentage of Births to Unmarried Black Women, 1960–2013
80 70 60 50 40 30 20 10 0
1960 1970 1980 1990 2000 2010 2013
SOURCE: National Vital Statistics Reports: 2000, 2014
Prison Admissions for Black Males, 1960–2011
THOUSANDS
300 250 200 150 100 50 0
1960 1970 1980 1991 2001 2011
SOURCE: Bureau of Justice Statistics

Conclusion

In 1840 Alexis de Tocqueville had a premonition about the American Overclass and its professional ministries presiding over submissive, other-directed subjects of its expert intentions.

He proposed that if a despotism should ever be imposed on a democratic nation, "it would degrade men rather than torment them."

> I see an innumerable multitude of men, alike and equal, constantly circling around in pursuit of the petty and banal pleasures with which they glut their souls. Each one of them, withdrawn into himself . . . exists in and for himself. . . .
>
> Over this kind of men stands an immense, protective power which is alone responsible for securing their enjoyment and watching over their fate. That power is absolute, thoughtful of detail, orderly, provident and gentle. . . . [I]t only tries to keep them in perpetual childhood. . . . It gladly works for their happiness but wants to be sole agent and judge of it. . . .
>
> Thus it daily makes the exercise of free choice less useful and rarer, restricts the activity of free will within a narrower compass, and little by little robs each citizen of the proper use of his own faculties. . . .
>
> Having thus taken each citizen in turn in its powerful grasp and shaped him to its will, government then extends its embrace to include the whole of society. It covers the whole of social life with a network of petty, complicated rules that are both minute and uniform, through which even men of the greatest originality and the most vigorous temperament cannot force their heads above the crowd. It does not break men's will, but softens, bends and guides it; it does not destroy anything, but prevents much from being born; it is not at all tyrannical, but it hinders, restrains, enervates, stifles, and stultifies so

much that in the end each nation is no more than a flock of timid and hardworking animals with the government as its shepherd.[90]

CHAPTER 7

RULE THROUGH MANAGEMENT RATHER THAN LEADERSHIP

A very weak-minded fellow I am afraid,
and, like the feather pillow, bears the marks
of the last person who has sat on him!

Lord Douglas Haig

There is a tide in the affairs of men.
Which, taken at the flood, leads on to fortune;
Omitted, all the voyage of their life
Is bound in shallows and in miseries.

William Shakespeare, *Julius Caesar*

The Overclass wields power through management, not leadership. Members of the Overclass are educated to be managers. They cannot lead.

Leaders must possess some degree of charisma for followers and subordinates to respect and emulate. You cannot make someone a leader just by giving them a title and an impressive office in which to work. You lead from the inside out, from your core identity and self-concept. If you are other-directed, you cannot lead. Your modal personality just can't give you what you need to do well in that calling.

Only by discerning and internalizing a legitimating higher purpose can one bring forth personal leadership in a community.

Manipulation of self-interests, fears, and ambitions can bring one power over others, but that is mostly how managers succeed in meeting their organizational goals. Leaders have a different job to do.

One of the most insightful studies of leaders was written in 1938 by Chester Barnard. It is called *The Functions of the Executive*. His study is how to make people want to cooperate with one another in organizations. His conclusion is:

> So among those who cooperate the things that are seen are moved by things unseen. Out of the void comes the spirit that shapes the ends of men.[1]

What is unseen is the spiritual dimension of leadership, the purpose and meaning that bind one to another in action so that the sum of the parts is greater than the whole. What is unseen maps out the road to success.

Through the power of charisma, leadership lifts us up spiritually closer to a right reason so that we can absorb it and bring it to earth.

Managers follow *Begriffs* and their supporting key performance indicators; leaders follow the truth.

Heraclitus proposed that our inner charism works as a kind of guiding spirit interacting with our hearts and minds, a *daimon* in Greek. Our own daimon could be a force for good, or it could turn us toward anger, sadness, and dysfunction. In English there is the saying that one is wrestling with inner demons. A daimon that was corruptly oriented would corruptly orient us in all that we think, feel, and do. A good daimon, on the other hand, would make us emotionally and psychologically stronger, a better person with resilience and insight.

Heraclitus recorded his thought as *ethos anthropoi daimon*, usually rendered as "character is fate"—the ethos of our personality determines the direction taken by our daimon. Ethos in Greek means custom, habit, disposition, character, or one's inner-direction. An other-directed person would not have much of an ethos and so would live with an irresolute or cowardly daimon to lead them through their daily routines.

The inner-directed are disposed to see the unseen and bring it into their commitments. They are thus more likely to internalize a charism. The other-directed are not so disposed, being distracted by constantly looking at all the influencers around them and by wanting just to belong to a team or be welcomed into a conversation.

The work of an elite is to serve its society with leadership, advocating meaningful values and sustaining them. Members of an elite are trustees of a sort, stewards charged with ensuring the well-being of the community. When elitists become self-absorbed and forget their community obligations, they fall from grace and power, and their society loses its strength and quality of being. Decadence sets in.

As noted in chapter 1, this moral dynamic was foretold by the Old Testament prophet Ezekiel.

> The word of the Lord came to me: "Son of man, prophesy against the shepherds of Israel; prophesy and say to them, this is what the Sovereign Lord says: 'Woe to you shepherds of Israel who only take care of yourselves! Should not shepherds take care of the flock? You eat the curds, clothe yourselves with the wool and slaughter the choice animals, but you do not take care of the flock. You have not strengthened the weak or healed the sick or bound up the injured. You have not brought back the strays or searched for the lost. You have ruled them harshly and brutally.' . . .
>
> "'. . . because my shepherds did not search for my flock but cared for themselves rather than for my flock, therefore, you shepherds, hear the word of the Lord. This is what the Sovereign Lord says: 'I am against the shepherds and will hold them accountable for my flock. I will remove them from tending the flock so that the shepherds can no longer feed themselves. I will

rescue my flock from their mouths, and it will no longer be food for them.'"[2]

The existential issue of elitism before Americans today is the capacity of the Overclass to provide leadership. First, members of the Overclass think and act as managers. That is what has been expected of them, and they have moved into positions of social, cultural, economic, and political authority by being good managers. They are not charismatics but rather have minds that work more as slide rules, keeping to conventions and, like cell phones, providing access to narratives and conversations. Further, since they are, in general, quite disposed to other-direction, it is unlikely that Overclass acolytes can provide the country with the leadership necessary to preserve its constitutional republic.

A second, and supporting, understanding of leadership was written by Philip Selznick in 1957—*Leadership in Administration*. After probing the dynamics of Overclass bureaucratic organizations, Selznick linked organizational success to character formation. Selznick worried then that "[o]ur major institutions—political, legal, educational, industrial—are under pressure to perform in the short run and have little support, from within or without, for a longer view of what they are doing and where they are going."[3]

Selznick looked at management as following the "logic of efficiency," of professional judgment. But he noted that the "logic of efficiency" loses force as we approach the top of the organizational pyramid where "problems at this level are more resistant to the ordinary approach of management experts."[4]

Selznick proposed that an executive becomes a statesman as he or she makes the transition from administrative management to institutional leadership.[5] Or we might say from professional assessment of means and ends to decisively setting the ends of the organization. An organization, said Selznick, is designed as a technical instrument for mobilizing human energies and directing them toward set aims, an exercise in social engineering governed by the ideals of rationality and discipline, just as proposed by Hegel. An institution, on the other hand, is a responsive, adaptive organism responding to social needs and pressures. An institution transcends Hegelian logic by enculturating itself in community and the world. The organization faces inward, while the institution looks outward. The organization succumbs to entropy, while the institution prospers over time. An institution is infused with value beyond technical rationality.

An organization is expendable; when something more efficient comes along, the organization will wither. An institution, to protect its values, will resist surrendering to that which appears to be more efficacious.

A wise counselor, Kevin Cashman, wrote, "We lead by virtue of who we are." Some can lead; others can manage.[6] Cashman linked our culture to the certification of managers more than the inculcation of leadership: "We learn what to think, not how to think. We learn what to do, not how to be. We learn what to achieve, not how to achieve."[7] He pleaded that leaders create the future by using courage and character, but managers manipulating transactions can only ensure present performance within an existing controlled environment.[8]

An institution requires leadership, while an organization can run—for a while—on management. Institutional leadership requires the foresight and insight that come, as Barnard wrote, "from the void," out of which comes our commitment to a higher purpose.

My colleague Dr. Richard Bents advises that there is a physiological substrate for our acting on the unseen, for using our charisms, and for our being leaders and not managers. To use the well-known distinction between modes of thinking and acting proposed by the Nobel laureate Daniel Kahneman (*Thinking, Fast and Slow*), we can say that leaders need to use "fast" thinking and managers "slow" thinking.[9] "Fast" (or System 1) thinking engages the amygdala in our limbic brain operations. "Slow" (or System 2) thinking uses the prefrontal cortex of our brain, where complex cognitive decision-making and planning take place. The amygdala houses our ability to relate immediately to the "big picture" by processing emotions, including fear, anxiety, and feelings of reward. These emotions can be deeply intertwined with religious experiences and beliefs so the amygdala can be activated during religious or other more deeply spiritual and motivating activities, potentially contributing to feelings of awe, fear, or connection with the divine. In particular, the amygdala both defines and defends our very precious "ego-integrity"—those things we consider part of our identity.

The amygdala and the prefrontal cortex collaborate in our thinking, combining their different skill sets into a coherent working whole. Stimulating the prefrontal cortex (slow thinking) will garner all possible cognitive data, while relaxing the amygdala so that it will back off and keep our emotions temporarily in check, putting our capacity for fast thinking on hold.

Leadership calls on the amygdala while management relies for its planning on the prefrontal cortex. Leadership combines cognitive data with emotional action. Leadership toggles back and forth between the amygdala and the prefrontal cortex. Balancing the amygdala and the prefrontal cortex—being centered and in self-control but still seeing the big picture—elevates management into leadership.[10]

[At the end of this book, you will find a QR code that will take you to a self-assessment questionnaire on your orientation to inner-direction or other-direction. Your responses will help you understand whether you are more of a leader or more of a manager.]

A contemporary case of institutional failure is the collapse of Boeing as a great American company. As an engineering company, Boeing was an institution contributing to the victories of the United States in World War II and the Cold War. Boeing also took the lead in making modern air travel global, safe, and easily accessible. Then under new management, Boeing became an organization. Its culture "evolved" into one fixated on financial metrics. Important stakeholders—those who flew its planes and who flew in its planes—were taken for granted. Corporate headquarters was moved from the production facility in Seattle, Washington, to Chicago, Illinois.

CEO James McNerney mismanaged the design and construction of the 737 MAX8, leading to two crashes—one in 2018 and the second in 2019—and the deaths of 346 passengers and crew. Boeing's space shuttle failed to disconnect from the space station, stranding two astronauts.

Where an organization is absorbed in routine tasks, leadership is dispensable, according to Selznick.[11] This is what happened to Boeing.

Selznick perceived that leadership is marginalized when science and "facts" replace values and morals as principal criteria for decision-making. Thus, the commitment of the Overclass to data-driven expertise prevents its cohorts from assuming the values-rooted responsibilities of leadership.

Something along these lines happened when the COVID-19 virus spread among Americans. Overclass officials in the federal government and many states instructed citizens to "follow the science" and issued draconian orders to curtail interpersonal interactions. Regulation was resorted to with the result that citizens were left feeling frightened and manipulated and so became alienated from authority.

From Selznick's perspective, we might say that the United States of America has become an organization and is no longer an institution capable of transcending time and space. Americans have become fixated on the short run, the entitlement, the immediate gratification. They have lost the ability to lead their families, their organizations, and their country. As has been said: "Americans can't win their wars or pay their debts."

Leaders must rise above the concerns of contending factions and elite cliques, of rival interest groups each bidding for dominant influence within the organization. Factions, cliques, and interest groups are the playground for other-directed short-termism.

Leadership must beware of opportunism and utopianism. "Opportunism displays itself in a narrow self-centeredness, in an effort to exploit other groups for immediate, short-run advantage," while "[u]topianism hopes to avoid hard choices by a flight to abstractions."[12] Opportunists and utopians both deploy narratives to justify their recommendations. These are most often only personal truths that must be contested against larger truths. The always uneasy other-directed frequently fall under the spell of opportunism or utopianism as providing them with ego protection.

When leadership fails, "the institution drifts, exposed to vagrant pressures, readily influenced by short-run opportunistic trends."[13] "It takes nerve to hold a course." It takes understanding to recognize vulnerabilities and deal with them. There is no off-the-shelf playbook for leaders.

In *The Functions of the Executive*, Barnard conceptualized how leaders elicit cooperation, organized formally so that it is conscious, deliberate, and purposeful. Such cooperation is implied in: the city-state (*polis*) described by Aristotle; the republic (*res publica*) defended by Cicero in his writings and politics; the social contract community suggested by Hobbes, Locke, and Rousseau; the orderly regime under a king proposed by Confucius, Mencius, and quite differently by Mozi and Shang Yang; and the constitutional republic provided for by the American federal constitution of 1787 as defended by Madison, Hamilton, and Jay in *The Federalist Papers*. Such cooperation was also implicit in Abraham Lincoln's prayer that "government of the people, by the people, and for the people shall not perish from this earth."

According to Barnard, "The vitality of organizations lies in the willingness of individuals to contribute forces to the cooperative system."[14]

In Barnard's view, leadership, most probably provided by inner-directed individuals, makes possible sustainable willing and intentional cooperation and so more human well-being. Under the direction of other-directed individuals, such cooperation may falter, bringing on schisms and antagonisms.

For Barnard, authority resides not in who issues an order but in the person who receives it. There is authority in the order only if the receiver to whom the order is addressed decides that the order is to be obeyed. Authority happens when the giver of the command or instruction and the receiver of the directive are in sync one with the other. Thus, authority is the ability to secure from others sufficient contributions of personal efforts so that the collective acts effectively. Leadership for Barnard is the specialized work of maintaining the organization in operation, of maintaining systems of cooperation.[15]

Are other-directed individuals, uncertain of their own inner purpose, capable of maintaining at high velocity a system of cooperation, even with very inclusive conversations taking place and with many invited to sit at the decision-making table?

Barnard sees faith as the basis for leadership: "faith in common understanding, faith in the probability of success, faith in the ultimate satisfaction of personal motives, faith in the integrity of objective authority, faith in the superiority of common purpose as a personal aim of those who partake in it."[16]

For Barnard, the important aspect of leadership is not position or formal credentials but rather individual superiority in determination, persistence, endurance, courage, and "that which determines the quality of action, which commands respect, reverence." Leadership gives idealism to collective purpose.[17] In this context we might recall Queen Elizabeth II of Great Britain with her poise, dignified self-control, and dedication, or Mother Teresa, or Jacqueline Kennedy's grace after the assassination of her husband.

George Washington's character, more than once, it is said, sustained bedraggled American forces in their resolve to fight on.

Or the defiance of fate sincerely ventured by Winston Churchill on June 4, 1940, which rallied a nation and won affection from Americans.

> I have, myself, full confidence that if all do their duty, if nothing is neglected, and if the best arrangements are made, as they are being made, we shall prove ourselves once again able to defend our Island home, to ride out the storm of war, and to outlive the menace of tyranny, if necessary for years, if necessary alone. At any rate, that is what we are going to try to do. That is the resolve of His Majesty's Government—every man of them. That is the will of Parliament and the nation. . . . we shall not flag or fail. We shall go on to the end, we shall fight in France, we shall fight on the seas and oceans, we shall fight with growing confidence and growing strength in the air, we shall defend our Island, whatever the cost may be, we shall fight on the beaches, we shall fight on the landing grounds, we shall fight in the fields and in the streets, we shall fight in the hills; we shall never surrender.[18]

Or when Churchill spoke to the Canadian Parliament in 1941.

> When I warned [the French government] that Britain would fight on alone whatever they did, their generals told their Prime Minister and his divided Cabinet, "In three weeks England will have her neck wrung like a chicken." Some chicken; some neck.[19]

The American general George Patton has been taken as a model war leader for his determination, persistence, and courage. He was quoted as saying,

- "There can never be defeat if a man refuses to accept defeat. Wars are lost in the mind before they are lost on the ground."

- "We must have a superiority complex. Always attack, never surrender."
- "Use steamroller strategy; that is, make up your mind on course and direction of action, and stick to it."[20]
- "Staff officers of inharmonious disposition, irrespective of their ability, must be removed. A staff cannot function properly unless it is a united family."[21]

I take it as highly unlikely that any member of the American Overclass could ever emulate the character of these leaders.

At West Point, there is no longer any need for a mission centered on "duty, honor, country."

During a congressional hearing on June 23, 2021, Army Gen. Mark A. Milley, chairman of the Joint Chiefs of Staff, admonished a committee of the House of Representatives over asking questions about Critical Race Theory, saying, "I want to understand White rage. And I'm White." Milley's comment was thoroughly Overclass other-directed, managerial risk aversion.

After the hearing, a Republican congressman shot back to Milley on Twitter: "With Generals like this, it's no wonder we've fought considerably more wars than we've won."[22]

In addition to his bachelor's degree in political science from Princeton University, General Milley has a master's degree in international relations from Columbia University and another from the U.S. Naval War College in national security and strategic studies. He is also a graduate of the MIT Seminar XXI National Security Studies Program.

And consider, too, all the accolades and titles of his military career.

Multiple command and staff positions in six divisions and a Special Forces Group throughout the last 44 years to include command of the 1st Battalion, 506th Infantry, 2nd Infantry Division; the 2nd Brigade Combat Team, 10th Mountain

Division; Deputy Commanding General, 101st Airborne Division (Air Assault); Commanding General, 10th Mountain Division; Commanding General, III Corps; and Commanding General, U.S. Army Forces Command.

While serving as the Commanding General, III Corps, General Milley deployed as the Commanding General, International Security Assistance Force Joint Command and Deputy Commanding General, U.S. Forces Afghanistan. General Milley's joint assignments also include the Joint Staff operations directorate and as Military Assistant to the Secretary of Defense.

General Milley's operational deployments include the Multi-National Force and Observers Task Force, Sinai, Egypt; Operation JUST CAUSE, Panama; Operation UPHOLD DEMOCRACY, Haiti; Operation JOINT FORGE, Bosnia-Herzegovina; Operation IRAQI FREEDOM, Iraq; and three tours during Operation ENDURING FREEDOM, Afghanistan. GEN Milley also deployed to Colombia, Somalia and served two years on the DMZ in the Republic of Korea.[23]

Here are pictures of Generals Dwight Eisenhower (World War II, European Theater), Mike Milley (Iraq and Afghanistan), and David Petraeus (Iraq and Afghanistan):

Milley

Eisenhower

Petraeus

With all their credentials and positions, Generals Milley and Petraeus never won their wars.

Upon his retirement, General Milley started teaching at Georgetown and Princeton Universities, all very "pukka sahib." And he quickly monetized his "brand" by retaining Robert Barnett of the expensive DC law firm Williams & Connolly.

The Williams & Connolly website tells us, "Bob's clients have included Tony Blair, The Prince of Wales, Hillary Rodham Clinton, Michelle Obama, Laura Bush, Bob Woodward, Barbra Streisand, Jack Welch (General Electric CEO), George Will . . . and former government officials in conjunction with their transitions to the private sector: Barack Obama, Bill Clinton, George W. Bush, Nikki Haley, Janet Yellen, Madeleine Albright, Karl Rove, Ben Bernanke, James Baker, Donna Shalala, and many former Cabinet officials, Senators and Congressmen."

Sounds like going to grifter heaven. Such are the trials and tribulations experienced by the most successful celebrity achievers of the Overclass.

After his retirement, General Petraeus went on to work for KKR, a very successful investment and venture capital firm.

Delivering for others an especially motivated and energized persona is the necessary work of one who takes responsibility. A person who succeeds in being responsible has a reliable and stable character that inhibits and controls the desires, impulses, or interests that might distract from acting upon the necessary moral vectors. Persons who are responsible, said Barnard, possess a general capacity under adverse conditions for conduct consistent with their stable sentiments and beliefs.[24] Such persons, we might say, are charismatic, capable of rising above the ordinary in having vision and mission. We might also say that such persons are likely to be inner-directed.

In addition to having a capacity to accept responsibility, Barnard argues that executives must inspire and secure "morale" among members of the organization by inculcating points of view, fundamental attitudes, and loyalties to the system of cooperation that will subordinate individual interest and the minor dictates of individual moral codes to the good of the collective.[25]

The other-directed person in a position of authority will nearly always tend to flatter and address the particular personal moral codes of individuals, presuming that such persons are also other-directed and looking for acceptance and affirmation. But such an approach leaves the organization drifting, perhaps even aimlessly, among the various moral codes driving those whose close cooperation is needed for organizational success and for the organization to become more of an institution.

Creating and sustaining the morale necessary for successful cooperation takes sincere and deep-seated conviction on the part of the leader, not a performative pretense. Not everyone has that capability.

Barnard concluded,

> Organizations endure, however, in proportion to the breadth of the morality by which they are governed. This is only to say that foresight, long purposes, high ideals, are the basis for the persistence of cooperation. . . . Low morality will not sustain leadership long, its influence quickly vanishes, it cannot produce its own succession.[26]

In 2004 David Callahan noticed a trend among elite Americans that disturbed him, so he wrote a book, *The Cheating Culture*. His theme was that, starting in the 1970s, Americans who belonged to what he called "the Winning Class" were cheating more and more to make money and gain status. He placed the cause for this increase in bad character on the no-holds-barred free market capitalism of Reaganomics. Yet most of his examples of immorality were provided by graduates of prestigious private high schools and elite colleges.

The cheaters, he said, aimed to make money and gain high-salaried positions where they could extract rents from society, as Jeffrey Skilling of

Harvard Business School did at Enron. Callahan thought that in the 1970s, young Americans became more cynical and materialistic, more selfish and self-absorbed, drifting without a strong sense of national purpose. Callahan was not pleased with the new lifestyle of "hedonism, escapism and endless self-analysis. Achieving financial goals moved to the center of young people's lives."[27] What Callahan reported tracks with the growth of the number of well-educated Americans being rewarded with well-paid professional jobs. By 1990 nearly 60% of Americans had white-collar employment.

Callahan notes the pressure on young Americans to get into the "right" college and get the "right" job as measures of a successful and rewarding life. Getting a good degree was a matter of economic life or death. As wealth flowed up to top earners, the prizes given to winners increased. In addition, Americans were getting more adept at turning money into influence, thus increasing the marginal utility of each dollar made.[28]

This sounds more like the consequence of the growth of the Overclass across our institutions.

The year 1979 brought to public notice Christopher Lasch's book *The Culture of Narcissism*. Lasch drew attention to something new appearing in the modal personality of many Americans, turning them away from traditional habits of thought and action toward something more pathological.

For a while in the 1980s, Lasch's detection of a new psychosocial orientation among young American professionals living in big cities was affirmed by the identification of a new social cluster—the "Yuppies"—"young, upwardly-mobile, professional." *Newsweek* magazine headlined that 1984 was "The Year of the Yuppie."

In 1978 I returned to Harvard Law School as an assistant dean tasked with setting up the school's first office of student affairs, leaving a large, very prestigious Wall Street law firm to do so. After arriving in Cambridge, Massachusetts, I learned that a friend at the firm had, somewhat unexpectedly, given the competition, been made partner. I called him up to congratulate him on succeeding where I might not have. He was silent for a moment, then said in a low, somewhat halting voice, "Steve, I have learned to grovel well."

Immediately I thought how dysfunctional our system of elite production was. Here was a young man who had won life's lottery. He would retire in fifty years a millionaire. He would have lived in nice housing in Manhattan or one of the wealthy suburbs in New Jersey, Westchester County, or Long Island. His children would most likely have attended elite private schools and afterward gone on to graduate from Ivy League universities—an American success story by any stretch of the imagination. And yet here he was, at the moment of supposed triumph, feeling depressed over who he had become as a person.

Callahan even wrote, "The Winning Class's clout inevitably has produced hubris and a sense that the rules governing what Leona Helmsley called 'the Little People' do not apply to them."

(Leona and her husband, Harry, built Helmsley Palace Hotel on Madison Avenue in New York City along with a real estate portfolio that included 230 Park Avenue, the Empire State Building, and the Tudor City apartment complex. The couple also developed the New York Helmsley Hotel, the Park Lane Hotel, and hotels in Florida and other states. In 1989 Leona was convicted of evading federal income taxes. We might note that, with respect to their Overclass status, those like the Helmsleys—say, Donald Trump—who earn income from ownership of property are in the business of extracting rents from society.)

In his assessment of cheating in America, Callahan concluded, "[T]he Winning Class has every reason to imagine that they live in a moral community of their own making governed by different rules."[29]

This conclusion might even apply to Hunter Biden, the wayward but somehow-always-in-the-money son of Senator, Vice President, and, finally, President Joseph R. Biden.

Such privileged members of the Overclass do not make good leaders, as we saw with Hunter and his father, Joe.

The Bidens lived in multimillion-dollar homes in Delaware, making them members in good standing of the Winning Class. In 2024 Joe Biden and his wife were estimated to have a net worth of $10 million.[30]

In 2023 Bill and Hillary Clinton were estimated to have a net worth of $120 million.[31]

In 2017 Barack and Michelle Obama bought a home in Washington, DC, for $8.7 million through a limited liability company and not in their own names. In 2019 they also purchased a 6,892-square-foot home on Martha's Vineyard Island, off the coast of Massachusetts. The seven-bedroom island mansion was later sold for $11.75 million to a trust. The deed also names as trustee James F. Reynolds, a Chicago investment banker who has been friends with President Obama since he was a state senator in Illinois.[32] Reynolds was a member of Obama's national finance committee during the 2008 presidential election.[33] The Obamas also own a multimillion-dollar home in Oahu, Hawaii. Not a shabby end-of-career lifestyle for a graduate of Columbia University and Harvard Law School.

Would it be impolite to ask how much of the equity in the limited liability companies and trusts that bought the houses used by the Obamas was contributed by the Obamas alone? We can be quite confident that it was not blue-collar Americans, the "Little People," who also invested their money in those limited liability companies or trusts.

The Obamas are estimated to have a net worth between $70 million[34] and $135 million.[35]

Were the Clintons, the Obamas, and the Bidens rewarded for providing Americans with outstanding political leadership, or was some other upper-class power dynamic at work in their becoming so wealthy and living in such nice houses?

Daniel Goleman wrote an article in the June 1996 issue of the *Harvard Business Review*, linking his work in emotional intelligence to leadership. Goleman and his colleagues looked at the correlation of what he called emotional intelligence and effective performance in 188 companies. He summarized his conclusions as five skill sets that maximized performance: self-awareness, self-regulation, motivation, empathy, and social skill.[36] The first three aptitudes are found in inner-directed individuals. Self-awareness is knowing your own strengths, drives, values, and goals. Self-regulation permits autonomous control and direction of emotions and impulses. Motivation is being inwardly oriented to achieve.

For Goleman, aptitude in having empathy and social skills also benefits from inner-direction. "But empathy doesn't mean a kind of 'I'm OK, you're OK' mushiness. For a leader, that is, it doesn't mean adopting other people's emotions as one's own and trying to please everyone. That would be chaotic—it would make concerted action impossible. Rather, empathy means thoughtfully considering employees' feelings—along with other factors—in the process of making intelligent decisions."[37]

Goleman characterized social skill as moving people in the direction you desire. This social skill is not other-directed, letting others move you in the direction they think best. The skill is to find common ground, overlapping Venn circles, among separate and self-oriented individuals. Those who can do this easily, Goleman wrote, understand and control their own emotions. They have emotional maturity and inner poise. Those with this social skill are expert persuaders, drawing others to their point of view, not vice versa.

In his classic 2001 study of exceptional business corporations, *Good to Great*, Jim Collins affirmed the insights of Chester Barnard and Philip Selznick on the contribution of leadership to organizational success. He attributed the success of those companies that outperformed others to the contributions of what he called "Level 5" leaders, those CEOs who could "build enduring greatness through a paradoxical blend of personal humility and professional will."[38] What Collins identified as humility and will are closely associated with inner-direction. Humility comes more easily to the inner-directed, for the inner-directed person has an internal compass contributing more to personal decision-making and presentation of self than self-promoting ego needs ever could. And that same internal compass calls forth from the executive the will to persevere and achieve, especially in times of uncertainties and difficulties.

Collins made the observation that "Level 5 leaders channel their ego needs away from themselves and into the larger goal of building a great company. It's not that Level 5 leaders have no ego or self-interest. Indeed they are incredibly ambitious—but their ambition is first and foremost for the institution, not themselves."[39] Collins said that Level 5 executives give credit to others for success and achievement and take on themselves responsibility for failures and mistakes. Level 5 executives, said Collins, "are fanatically driven, infected with an incurable need to produce results." That drive, we might intuit, flows from the possession of some charism within the executive's sense of self, a forcefulness that attracts willing collaboration from others around them, and an internal quality of mind and heart that wins the trust of others.[40]

Collins made a distinction between those who look upon work as leading to what they will get and those who look upon work as what they will build, create, and contribute to a good greater than themselves.

Collins proposed four less effective levels of performance more appropriate for managers: Level 1 is the highly capable individual who has talent, knowledge, skills, and good work habits; Level 2 is a contributing team member who contributes to group objectives and works effectively with others in a group setting; Level 3 is a competent manager who can organize people and resources to effectively and efficiently pursue predetermined objectives; and Level 4 is an effective leader who catalyzes commitment to and vigorous pursuit of a clear and compelling vision, stimulating higher performance standards.[41]

Appropriately for inner-directed persons, Collins found that Level 5 leaders, when appointing people to positions, placed greater emphasis on character attributes than on specific educational backgrounds or specialized knowledge. They looked for insights into the core values of those who would work alongside them.[42]

Next, Collins observed that Level 5 leaders are comfortable assessing the "brutal facts" that so often comprise our realities. He concluded that "with an honest and diligent effort to determine the truth of the situation, the right decisions often become self-evident."[43] Level 5 leaders had the deftness to create a climate where the truth could be told. Again, facing facts rather than accepting someone's narrative is more comfortable for the inner-directed than for the other-directed, who are prone to look for what others believe to be the facts. Collins reported that for the less successful companies in his study, where the top leaders led with force or instilled fear, "people worried more about the leader—what he would say, what he would think, what he would do—than they worried about external reality and what *it* could do to the company."[44] He added, "The good-to-great leaders were able to strip away so much noise and clutter and just focus on the few things that would have the greatest impact."[45]

The ability to intimidate, or to manipulate the self-interest of others, is not a charism.

Moreover, the internal compass of Level 5 leaders allowed them to "simplify a complex world into a single organizing idea, a basic principle or concept, that unified and guides everything; that the essence of profound insight is simplicity . . . that allows them to see through complexity and discern underlying patterns . . . to see what is essential and ignore the rest."[46] Being able to pick out the wheat from the chaff in life directs energy to the soul and fosters determination in the mind.

Collins also noted patterns of confusion in the managers of less successful companies. They would authorize chronic restructurings, look for a savior or a miracle intervention, embrace fads, inconsistently lurch back and forth, and run about like Chicken Little in reaction to change.[47] These behaviors seem more in tune with the insecurities hobbling so many in the Overclass.

Kevin Cashman of Korn Ferry proposed in 1998 that leadership comes "from the inside out"; in other words, that inner-direction is the wellspring for leadership. He advised that "courage and character" are fundamental for leadership as distinct from management. Courage and character are not often found in the other-directed who are so anxious to be accepted and admired by the right circle of people that they would rather conform than walk alone on their own path. Cashman asked, "Is our leadership arising from our *character*, which is driven to serve others? Or is it derived from a pattern of *coping*, where we tend to react to circumstances to elicit a more immediate or self-serving result?"[48]

Cashman recommends a practice of getting hold of your inner self, what he calls personal mastery: listening to your authentic inner voice for what you really think and feel versus what others want you to think and feel; being mindful when "being created" by others in their image; and sharing your genuine thoughts, feelings, joys, successes, concerns, and fears with people.[49] He builds on inner-direction when offering advice on using your core values and talents to build your very particular core purpose.[50]

From the Jesuit tradition of seeking insight, Robert Spitzer wrote an unusual book, *The Spirit of Leadership*, proposing ways of bringing forth within us a charismatic spirit. Spitzer was, for many years, president and CEO of Gonzaga University after directing Seattle University's Institute of Professional Ethics and Institute on Character Development. Following his advice can embolden our journey toward successful and meaningful internalization of inner-direction. For Spitzer, a leader with spirit is "inspired," able to create confidence in the probability of success, attentive, confident, and open to others without losing a sense of personal identity. An inspired person does not back away from depth and breadth in their vision of life's realities and possibilities. An inspired person, said Spitzer, is at peace, a peace grounded in a firm sense of purpose, and so is reassuring to others while being able to persist in a course of action.[51]

In 2024 Paul Graham, the cofounder of Y Combinator—a San Francisco start-up incubator—distinguished between the founder mode of executive leadership and the manager mode. Graham's essay cites the experience of Brian Chesky, the CEO of Airbnb:

As Airbnb grew, well-meaning people advised him that he had to run the company in a certain way for it to scale. Their advice could be optimistically summarized as "hire good people and give them room to do their jobs." He followed this advice and the results were disastrous. So he had to figure out a better way on his own, which he did partly by studying how Steve Jobs ran Apple. So far it seems to be working. Airbnb's free cash flow margin is now among the best in Silicon Valley.

Why was everyone telling these founders the wrong thing? That was the big mystery to me. And after mulling it over for a bit I figured out the answer: what they were being told was how to run a company you hadn't founded—how to run a company if you're merely a professional manager. But this m.o. is so much less effective that to founders it feels broken. There are things founders can do that managers can't, and not doing them feels wrong to founders, because it is.[52]

Graham exposes the reality of how the Overclass can't lead with these observations:

The way managers are taught to run companies seems to be like modular design in the sense that you treat subtrees of the org chart as black boxes. You tell your direct reports what to do, and it's up to them to figure out how. But you don't get involved in the details of what they do. That would be micromanaging them, which is bad.

Hire good people and give them room to do their jobs. Sounds great when it's described that way, doesn't it? Except in practice, judging from the report of founder after founder, what this often turns out to mean is: hire professional fakers and let them drive the company into the ground.

In effect there are two different ways to run a company: founder mode and manager mode. Till now most people even in Silicon Valley have implicitly assumed that scaling a startup meant switching to manager mode. But we can infer the existence of another mode from the dismay of founders who've tried it, and the success of their attempts to escape from it.

There are as far as I know no books specifically about founder mode. Business schools don't know it exists. . . .

Curiously enough it's an encouraging thought that we still know so little about founder mode. Look at what founders have achieved already, and yet they've achieved this against a headwind of bad advice. Imagine what they'll do once we can tell them how to run their companies like Steve Jobs instead of John Sculley.

Graham thus gives real-world content to the distinction between inner-direction—founder mode—and other-direction—manager mode.

More recently, Mary C. Gentile, with a career at Harvard Business School, Babson College, and the Darden School of Business, has written *Giving Voice to Values*, a guideline to personal practice in letting the spirit within us come forth in our work and vocations, as Robert Spitzer would have us all do. Gentile's approach is for us to activate something inner-directed, which she calls "values"—"something that we experience deeply and internally, which, although it possesses a cognitive aspect, is not exclusively about analysis."[53] Her notion of "values-driven action" is quite close to Barnard and Selznick's definition of "leadership" and likely to move us in the direction of Collins's Level 5 leadership.

While one can easily give voice to the values of others out of politeness, conformity, expedience, or deep other-direction, Gentile will not consider those sentiments as true "values" umbilically connected to a stable and resolute sense of who we are and must be. She situates the values-driven protagonist in relationship with others. The inner-directed cannot ignore others and must engage with them to lead. Here, too, there is a role for charisma. Quintilian taught that the best persuader is a "good person who speaks well." If our charism presents the good, we will be more successful in convincing others of the rightness of our views and recommendations.

This may be why so many in the Overclass don't like to argue from the facts or the merits of their case but prefer to use a rhetoric of ad hominem disparagement and invective, attacking the character and goodness of those who differ with them and not their facts or arguments. The other-directed can't compete well in public reasoning as they lack charisma.

In 1993 Robert Terry of the Humphrey Institute proposed his theory of "authentic" leadership as a response, I think, to the rise of the Over-class. He argued for an intentional effort to bring forth leaders with "authenticity" to overcome a social and cultural crisis of "disconnection." Terry wrote, "Many of us sense a deep, pervasive, and profoundly disturb-ing disconnection between the world that we experience as we actually live in it and the world that we create and describe in our rhetoric and imagination." Terry perceived that the real world around him—the world of his students and peers in higher education—was bereft of hope and confidence and that institutions were not trustworthy.

He wrote,

> Our life disconnects from the past, as we rewrite history with-out regard to what really happened. Our life disconnects from the present, as we frame current events to distort rather than disclose what is really going on. And our life disconnects from the future as we fail to understand what will happen. . . .[54]
>
> A pervading sense of personal and social sickness erodes our confidence in our basic social institutions. Categories of personal dysfunction and social disorders fill the print and the electronic media. I often wonder what it would be like to meet a healthy person![55]

This is a very sad indictment of contemporary American culture from one ensconced in the citadel of Overclass self-righteousness.

Terry's call for authenticity in American leaders speaks, I think, to his inchoate, worrisome intuition that something important is missing in the leadership abilities offered by the Overclass. Its members are not authentic in their ability to understand our realities and therefore lack the ability to address our needs correctly and to provide our culture with good, sustaining values and honorable, courageous people. Overclass expertise and professionalism are only superficially valuable, more performative affect than salutary effect.

Bob Terry once did me a great favor. He introduced me to the Myers-Briggs schemas of personality orientations, or individual constellations of behavioral traits. I took the self-assessment and found my constellation—an INTJ. Bob advised that most of us are more comfortable when surrounded by those with similar approaches to life and that interpersonal interactions providing such comfort bring risk. Others have skills, manners, insights, and gifts that we lack, but we don't habitually go out of our way to engage with them or put them in positions of responsibility in our organization. Surrounded by the like-minded, we unconsciously succumb to groupthink or intellectual and emotional insularity.

I rather quickly realized that my Myers-Briggs type was not adept at working with details and numbers, spreadsheets and budgets, footnotes and files. In my then position as dean of a law school, this was not helpful. The registrar for the school was a woman most quick to master numbers, documents and files, and organizational details, so I made her an assistant dean for finance and administration. She did not have a college degree, so my decision grated with some members of the faculty. The school was far better off with her taking on those responsibilities than if I were to supervise such work.

A friend of mine, the CEO of a very large and successful corporation, once told me that the only human resources metric that exhibited a high correlation between personality type and organizational success was the

Gallup StrengthsFinder assessment, which looks at abilities in strategic thinking, relationship building, influencing, and executing. But he also warned me about those he thought of as sociopaths in a bureaucracy, who were shortcuts to turmoil and frustration. He described their characteristics as exhibiting glibness and superficial charm, having a grandiose sense of self-worth, cunning and manipulative, lacking remorse or guilt, callous and lacking empathy, and refusing to accept responsibility. Such personalities seem to thrive among the other-directed, whom they can easily impress and manipulate with insincere flattery and friendships.

Also problematic in organizations and leadership failures are narcissists. These are modal personalities that have an unreasonably high sense of their own importance. They need and seek too much attention and want people to admire them. People with this disorder may lack the ability to understand or care about the feelings of others. But behind this mask of extreme confidence, they are not sure of their self-worth and are easily upset by the slightest criticism.[56]

Such narcissistic behaviors also easily align with other-directed fluidity in performing as others prefer.

Management Training Does Not Encompass the Inner-Directed Charisma of Leadership

A very popular and widely used handbook for managers was written and used by Personnel Decisions Inc. in its consulting work. I used the book when working for the company in devising an innovative personality assessment questionnaire for lawyers, something never considered by American law schools. The experience taught me much about the difference between management and leadership.

The handbook covered nine skill sets with descriptions of skills, thoughts on how to develop them, tips on using them, and helpful readings for each of them. For leadership—one of the nine—the handbook discussed providing direction, leading courageously, influencing others, fostering teamwork, motivating others, coaching and developing others, and championing change. This seemed very close to providing influence to the other-directed, who were disposed to being influenced. The handbook noted that managers "needed to encourage and apply the contributions of all of the company's human resources, both individually and in groups."[57] It presented the manager as a collaborative team player who stays within his or her zone of functional authority. The manager must clarify roles and responsibilities, link the team's mission to that of the organization, and make the team's mission and strategies clear to others. The good manager then needed to fit in perfectly with an other-directed work force.

Teams

The Overclass response to its failure to lead has often been to denigrate the traditional ideal of leadership as something sinister and associated with patriarchal power structures devoid of the feminine ethic of care. Yet recent female leaders such as Vice President Kamala Harris and the presidents of Harvard and Columbia Universities did not distinguish themselves in their positions of high authority and prestige.

The structural response of the Overclass to the need for leadership has been to replace leadership with teamship, the skill and practice of coordinating diverse teams with many at the decision-making table, having a facilitator but no one in charge, and numerous sessions providing the opportunity for extended conversations but with no decisions made until some comfortable consensus has been reached by the group.

In his *Harvard Business Review* article in 1998, Daniel Goleman wrote of teams,

> As anyone who has ever been part of a team can attest, teams
> are cauldrons of bubbling emotions. They are often charged
> with reaching a consensus—which is hard enough with two

people and much more difficult as the numbers increase. Even in groups of four or five members, alliances form and clashing agendas get set. A team's leader must be able to sense and understand the viewpoints of everyone around the table.[58]

The *Harvard Business Review* published an article in March 2024 on nurturing innovation with the assertion that "a great idea isn't enough, leaders must create an environment that allows teams to collaborate successfully over time."[59] The writers propose other-direction as the preferred way to generate game-changing ideas because, for them, innovation is more than generating an idea—it is a long collaborative journey. They claim that "innovation is more likely to succeed when it is a curated process in which an intermediary takes responsibility for sparking and sustaining collaboration among the people involved." This echoes Gilligan's feminine-values orientation of inclusion and the ethic of care for others, of bringing oneself into a non-threatening relationship with others. Their recommendation is not to facilitate the collision of ideas and talents. "Curation" is a very in-vogue Overclass conversational process where a group works their way through idiosyncrasies to collective conclusions after all have been assigned a place at the table so that their voices have been heard.

So the group process of innovation begins with "making connections." Step 2 is developing relationships. Step 3 is keeping the team together, sustaining a community.

The *Harvard Business Review* has also published an article on sustaining empathy because managers today "are expected to provide employees with more emotional support than ever."[60] Naturally, Overclass workforces are more and more other-directed and responsive to the ethic of care, so they do need emotional support given their modal personality profile. It may also be that what the other-directed are seeking from others is, in part, simply emotional support—a bond of commonality giving comfort to the subordinating self, who is prepared to internalize the values and mimic the preferred behaviors modeled by the other. The article offers advice to managers on how to so engage emotionally with their employees without burning out from reverse other-direction—internalizing the emotions of their subordinates.

Also, the *Harvard Business Review* put its stamp of approval on an article advising managers not to jump to solutions.[61] The advice is based on research. The first step is to set aside your preconceptions and open your mind. This advice will tend to undermine the inner-directed whose preconceptions may have real-world value and should be brought forward with colleagues. Managers are told to "begin by assembling a diverse team, encompassing a variety of types of expertise and perspectives." Then consider alternate scenarios and conceptual frameworks, each lens exposing a unique perspective on the facts.

Step 2 is to dive deeply, seeking to identify root causes. Step 3 is to empathize, to understand stakeholders and how they perceive and feel about the issue at hand, and to thus find a new frame with which to think about action. Step 4 is to zoom out and put the issue in a larger perspective—What is at stake really?—finding even more frames to use in deciding on the best situational analysis. Step 5 is to envision and design solutions.

All this is good management—paying attention to the who, the how, and the when.

The seemingly effortless success of team management of Biden's presidency, for example, was made possible (1) by Biden's other-directedness, whereby he was completely comfortable following the lead of others, and (2) by the other-directedness of his staffers, who were each personally completely comfortable fitting in with whatever the "team" wanted to do or say. Was this leadership?

In 2025 a question arose before the American public: In his last year as president, was Biden even in charge? Were others using an autopen to put his signature on decision memoranda and statements, and so usurping his legal authority?

The latest Hegelian *Begriff* fashioned by Overclass thought leaders to legitimate the teamship approach to management of bureaucracies is "diversity, equity, and inclusion" or DEI. Ironically, this approach (which we discussed in chapter 6 as it relates to higher education) invalidates the legitimating premise upholding Overclass cultural, social, administrative, and political status—professional expertise. The DEI model gives positions to individuals based not on their achievements and professional merits but on their status at birth as a person who brings a valuable voice to the table, a voice which has long since been marginalized by traditional establishments and institutions. Administrators of DEI applicant screening and appointments have proliferated in every large American organization from universities to companies to the military. Proof of nonmerit now opens many doors to promotion into and up the ranks of the Overclass.

Sadly, it is now germane to question whether DEI admissions to medical schools and selection of pilots to fly commercial aircraft will result in excellence in performing surgeries and while flying during unexpected emergencies. Under such conditions of reasoned uncertainty, can the Overclass provide America with leadership worth the name?

Graduate Schools of Public Policy

Graduate schools in public policy are, if possible, even more remiss than MBA programs in teaching leadership. Their focus is expressly Hegelian—the rationality of planning. These schools train for careers that are not directly legitimated by the American people through popular election of the officeholder. Graduate degrees in public policy or public administration are credentials for aspiring bureaucrats, the worker bees of the Overclass.

At Harvard University, the mission of the Kennedy School is "to improve public policy and leadership so people can live in societies that are more safe, free, just, and sustainably prosperous. By combining cutting-edge research, the teaching of outstanding students, and direct interaction with practitioners, we have an impact on solving public problems that no other institution can match."[62] This is pretty much a top-down method of determining and providing what is thought to be best for the people. Hegel would very much approve.

The school is very open to using other-direction in its teaching and programming by "strengthening the ability of our students, staff, and faculty to have candid and constructive conversations across difference," noting that without such systematic teaming, "public problems become even more difficult to solve."

The school of public administration at the University of Minnesota, named for the courageous, very inner-directed Hubert H. Humphrey (mayor, senator, vice president, and candidate for president) has this mission: "The Humphrey School of Public Affairs educates, engages, and equips leaders and communities to discover solutions that advance the common good in our diverse world." And just who, pray tell, do you think is authorized by this noted educational institution to come up with such optimal solutions? The people? Free markets? Robust and uncensored public debate?

In 2002 the dean of the Humphrey School, Harlan Cleveland, wrote a book called *Nobody in Charge*. His thesis was that other-direction was the future—that the leadership will lie not in top-down authority but in collaborative, networked systems where many individuals share responsibility. It would be an environment shaped less by command-and-control and more by consultation, relationships, and the collective release of human ingenuity.[63]

The Murder of a Health-Care Manager

On December 4, 2024, the CEO of UnitedHealthcare (the largest provider of health insurance for Americans) was shot to death on a sidewalk in Manhattan, New York City. A young man named Luigi Mangione was taken into custody and charged in what was widely speculated to be a politically motivated assassination.

If the assassination narrative is true, the killing is revealing of the dark side of Overclass management. UnitedHealthcare provides its members with payments for their health-care needs. But such payments must be properly authorized under both public and private contracts. Not every request for payment, or for health services, is approved by the company. The reality of management is restriction of personal choice. Management fixates on goals and objectives. Managers do not hand out free passes to just go play as you will in the sandboxes of life. In the American health-care sector, government regulation of costs is pervasive. The expansion of federal subsidies for health care to lower-income and many elderly Americans was a proud political accomplishment of Barack Obama's presidency.

In the aftermath of the killing, many Americans (17%) found it acceptable or somewhat acceptable, and among those aged 18–29, 41% found it acceptable or somewhat acceptable.[64]

Congressperson Alexandria Ocasio-Cortez said, "This is not to say that an act of violence is justified, but I think for anyone who is confused or shocked or appalled, they need to understand that people interpret and feel and experience denied claims as an act of violence against them." Ocasio-Cortez then blamed the shortcomings in providing health care not on management by her Overclass but on systemic inequality. "Health care in this country has gotten to such a depraved state that people are living with things they should never have to live with. And this is not to say and this is not to participate in that glorification, but we need to understand that extreme levels of inequality in the United States yield high degrees of social instability," she said.[65]

Mangione, then, appeared to have been rebelling against social management as instituted by the Overclass.

Ironically, Mangione was a member of the Overclass—as was his victim, given his corporate office. Mangione was valedictorian when graduating from his elite private high school in Baltimore (Gilman School, which two of my cousins attended) and a cum laude graduate of the University of Pennsylvania with MSE and BSE degrees in computer science.

The perpetrator may have found supportive thinking in the manifesto of the Unabomber—Ted Kaczynski. Kaczynski was consumed by "rage against the machine" antagonism toward what he called the "industrial-technological system"—his personal *Begriff* invented to describe the Overclass and its source of power.[66]

He defined the psychology of modern Leftists as something close in actualization to other-direction: "low self-esteem, feelings of powerlessness, depressive tendencies, defeatism, guilt, self-hatred, etc. We argue that modern leftists tend to have some such feelings (possibly more or less repressed) and that these feelings are decisive in determining the direction of modern leftism." Kaczynski further defined "Leftism" as reflecting "oversocialization," which

> can lead to low self-esteem, a sense of powerlessness, defeatism, guilt, etc. One of the most important means by which our society socializes children is by making them feel ashamed of behavior or speech that is contrary to society's expectations. If this is overdone, or if a particular child is especially susceptible to such feelings, he ends by feeling ashamed of himself.

He added,

> Thus the oversocialized person is kept on a psychological leash and spends his life running on rails that society has laid down for him. In many oversocialized people this results in a sense of constraint and powerlessness that can be a severe hardship. We suggest that oversocialization is among the more serious cruelties that human beings inflict on one another. . . . Leftists of the oversocialized type tend to be intellectuals or members of the upper middle class. Notice that university intellectuals constitute the most highly socialized segment of our society and also the most left-wing segment.[67]

This insight gets to the heart of other-direction—looking to others to give us a measure of ourselves—and it condemns the Overclass for being excessively other-directed. Kaczynski astutely saw that failure to become inner-directed was a curse: "But for most people it is through the power process—having a goal, making an autonomous effort and attaining the goal—that self-esteem, self-confidence and a sense of power are acquired. When one does not have adequate opportunity to go through the power process the consequences are (depending on the individual and on the way the power process is disrupted) boredom, demoralization, low self-esteem, inferiority feelings, defeatism, depression, anxiety, guilt, frustration, hostility, spouse or child abuse, insatiable hedonism, abnormal sexual behavior, sleep disorders, eating disorders, etc."[68]—in short, dysphoria or decadence.

Thus, he opposed "Leftism" as unacceptable Overclass other-directedness:

> Leftism is collectivist; it seeks to bind together the entire world (both nature and the human race) into a unified whole. But this implies management of nature and of human life by organized society, and it requires advanced technology. . . . We use the term 'leftism' because we don't know of any better word to designate the spectrum of related creeds that includes the feminist, gay rights, political correctness, etc., movements, and because these movements have a strong affinity with the old left. . . . Leftism is totalitarian force. Wherever leftism is in a position of power it tends to invade every private corner and force every thought into a leftist mold. In part this is because of the quasi-religious character of leftism: everything contrary to leftist beliefs represents Sin. More importantly, leftism is a totalitarian force because of the leftists' drive for power.

He added,

The leftist is oriented toward large-scale collectivism. He emphasizes the duty of the individual to serve society and the duty of society to take care of the individual. He has a negative attitude toward individualism. He often takes a moralistic tone. He tends to be for gun control, for sex education and other psychologically 'enlightened' educational methods, for social planning, for affirmative action, for multiculturalism. He tends to identify with victims. He tends to be against competition and against violence, but he often finds excuses for those leftists who do commit violence. He is fond of using the common catch-phrases of the left, like 'racism,' 'sexism,' 'homophobia,' 'capitalism,' 'imperialism,' 'neocolonialism,' 'genocide,' 'social change,' 'social justice,' 'social responsibility.' Maybe the best diagnostic trait of the leftist is his tendency to sympathize with the following movements: feminism, gay rights, ethnic rights, disability rights, animal rights, political correctness. Anyone who strongly sympathizes with all of these movements is almost certainly a leftist.[69]

Kaczynski refused to admire "Leftists" or grant them leadership: "However, the most dangerous leftists of all may be certain oversocialized types who avoid irritating displays of aggressiveness and refrain from advertising their leftism, but work quietly and unobtrusively to promote collectivist values, 'enlightened' psychological techniques for socializing children, dependence of the individual on the system, and so forth."[70]

Kaczynski's rage was actually directed at the Overclass, rejecting its claim to moralize and lead Americans. But back in 1995 he had no concept in hand accurately describing the Overclass and its class proclivities and its self-serving power arrangements: "Our discussion of leftism has a serious weakness. It is still far from clear what we mean by the word 'leftist.'"[71]

If we use Marxism to place Kaczynski's dystopian thinking in context, consciousness of class power would emerge as salient—Kaczynski lived in solitude in an increasingly dysphoric America. He turned himself into a living danger to civic goodness, like the other boys and young men who in recent years out of some rage have committed heinous killings of the innocent.[72]

Overclass Mismanagement of Public Education

The Overclass—responsible at federal, state, and local levels for public education of future American citizens—has shown no leadership in achieving academic excellence. Americans who can't read or write very well and can't do basic math are most likely prone to identity dysphoria about themselves and their society. At the same time, Overclass teachers and administrators experiencing dysphoric symptoms, and who are other-directed in the main, most likely will not try very hard or care that much about their responsibilities as educators for quality instruction as measured by the life outcomes of their students. This is a gross abuse of the public trust handed to them by their employer, the American people.

The National Center for Education Statistics reports that between 2019 and 2023, the average score for American fourth graders on standardized math tests dropped by eighteen points and by twenty-seven points for eighth graders. Some 40% of all U.S. public school students fail to meet math and English standards, up 8% from pre-pandemic levels.[73] According to the National Assessment of Educational Progress, only a quarter or less of American students are proficient in reading and even less in math, geography, and U.S. history. California's K–12 system, which serves nearly six million students, fails to educate the majority of its students: Fewer than half meet national standards for literacy and only one-third for math.[74]

Overclass Mismanagement of the 2025 Los Angeles Firestorms

In January 2025 firestorms swept through acres and acres to the north and east of Los Angeles. They energetically held off the attempts of city and county firefighters to contain them. House after house was burned to the ground. Some 150,000 people—a small city's worth—were displaced. The fires, turned into infernos by the Santa Ana winds blowing hot air from the east toward the Pacific Ocean, are nearly annual events, having occurred again and again in the same hillsides and valleys.

The victory of the fires over the firefighters is a metaphor, like Dante's *Inferno*, for the failure of the Overclass in its management responsibilities. Los Angeles and California have been governed for decades by Democrats elected by voters: Governors Jerry Brown and Gavin Newsom (estimated net worth $42 million); Newsom's relation Nancy Pelosi, speaker of the Federal House of Representatives (net worth $240 million from investments in high-tech companies)[75]; Willie Brown (estimated net worth $70 million),[76] mayor of San Francisco and patron of Kamala Harris, United States senator, vice president, and candidate for president (owner with her husband of a $4 million house in Los Angeles); Karen Bass, mayor of Los Angeles; and George Gascon, public prosecutor for Los Angeles County and protégé of George Soros. Those California members of the Overclass share elite privileges with multimillionaires working for Silicon Valley high-tech companies and with wealthy semi-socialites, the "beautiful people," brought forth and made wealthy by Hollywood. Of note, Los Angeles Fire Department Chief Kristin Cowley earned $654,951 in total pay and benefits during 2023.[77]

Those elected leaders, and the various departments of government that they directed, delivered Overclass management imposing Overclass ideologies. With respect to the fires, that management was incompetent. Members of the Overclass governing California thus failed to meet their freely-chosen responsibilities—to use reason and elite expertise to make the world better. They did not use reason well, and they ignored critical expertise.

For example, as a small brush fire started, a request was made to the Los Angeles Fire Department asking for bulldozers to contain the flames. Fire Captain Richard Diede responded: "Heck no—that area is full of endangered plants. I would be a real idiot to ever put a dozer in that area. I'm so trained."[78]

Common sense should have directed them to learn from history—such wildfires are to be expected; prepare for them. They didn't learn; they weren't prepared. Brush had not been removed; forests had not been managed with an eye to fires but rather with reverence for natural growth; a water reservoir of 117-million-gallon capacity sat empty when water was needed to put fires out; and fire hydrants failed while California had invested in wind and solar power to offset climate change.[79]

Days before the fires started, the National Interagency Fire Center warned of above-normal significant fire potential. The National Weather Service's Los Angeles office noted the potential for intense fires and issued a fire weather watch for weather events ranging from a widespread, damaging windstorm and extreme fire weather risk to weak offshore flow.[80]

Overclass priorities for the city of Los Angeles were 1) to provide salaries and retirement benefits for firefighters, unionized public servants and so members of the Overclass, and 2) to reduce funding for fighting fires.

On December 4, 2024, Fire Chief Crowley wrote a memo reporting that budget reductions had "severely limited the Department's capacity to prepare for, train for, and respond to large-scale emergencies," including wildfires. California's political leaders had also built no water recycling or desalinization plants near Los Angeles to supplement natural supplies of water.[81]

Los Angeles spent twice as much on taking care of homeless persons than on its fire department. Los Angeles spent $350 million in 2024 on firefighter pensions and benefits when funds for fire prevention were only 5% of the department's budget. Firefighters—organized into a union of public servants—on average earned about $200,000, plus $90,000 in benefits.[82]

California regulations prevented property insurance companies from using catastrophe models in making projections of future financial damages to insured properties, thus providing lower costs for property insurance in the short run but running the risk of massive financial shortfalls in the long run, if fate should turn cruel. Between 2017 and 2022, California was the worst state government in America for indulging in "rate suppression," having the biggest gap between "the actuarially indicated rate and the rate approved by regulators."[83] After the fires, the state's agency to supplement shortfalls in private insurance policies had $700 million in cash on hand when perhaps $5.9 billion will be required to compensate homeowners in the Pacific Palisades fire alone.[84]

After the fires had started, the California Policy Center reported:

> As it is, the canyons between the neighborhoods on the hills and ridges surrounding Los Angeles are dangerously overgrown, along with the adjacent state parks and open space. There's no way to completely stop a wildfire when the Santa Ana winds turn Los Angeles County into a blast furnace. But if the state and county had managed their open space, and private property owners had been not merely permitted but required to clear overgrown brush around their homes, these fires would not have had enough fuel to become the catastrophes we're witnessing today.[85]

California's Overclass failed in its fiduciary duty of taking due care of those under its power as its management was irresponsibly imprudent and did not apply available expertise. If they could not manage, how could they rightly aspire to be leaders?

The President's Health: A White House Management Success

Another disturbing example of Overclass finesse in conforming public beliefs (*Begriffs*) to the dictates of managerial expertise was the cover-up of President Joe Biden's declining competence, as evidenced by his failing capacities to understand facts, speak in public from personal knowledge, and reason his way to correct understandings of the realities affecting public policies. Journalists Jake Tapper and Alex Thompson, for years professionally comfortable with carrying water for the Overclass with respect to Biden's deficiencies, wrote a book after his departure from office to "present the disturbing reality of what happened in the White House and the Democratic presidential campaign in 2023–2024."[86]

They wrote their book to reveal after the fact an Overclass conspiracy to hide the truth (a serious breach of duty on the part any professional manager): "Most of the information laid out was shared with us after the election of 2024, when officials and aides felt considerably freer to talk." It is fair to note that during the Biden presidency, legions of other-directed Overclass journalists and editors did not try much at all to get at the truth of Biden's fitness to hold office.

It would seem that, even as a prominent member of the Overclass, Biden was barely capable of management but was nevertheless presented to the American people as their leader and to the world as a global statesman by subordinate skilled performers in the White House and their co-conspirators in the media. This was not at all good management of the Republic but rather quite self-serving performative cosplay designed to arbitrarily sustain the prerogatives of a class. It was dereliction of duty. Somewhere Humpty Dumpty is smirking over our credulity.

Conclusion

It will not be worth the time or money to train members of the Overclass to be leaders. They are essentially managers by training and are also psychologically encumbered with an inappropriate, fixed modal personality orientation inculcated in them from a young age by their caring parents and teachers. Their professional credentials do not actually qualify them to lead. The rationale for making them leaders—exceptional and high-minded expertise—is a sham, simply another destabilizing illusory *Begriff*.

CHAPTER 8

LEGITIMIZING THE OVERCLASS

*That whenever any Form of Government
becomes destructive of these ends,
it is the Right of the People to alter or to abolish it,
and to institute new Government,
laying its foundation on such principles and organizing
its powers in such form, as to them shall seem
most likely to effect their Safety and Happiness.*

The unanimous declaration of the thirteen
United States of America, July 4, 1776

*You've got to be honest.
And if you can fake that, you've got it made.*

George Burns

Members of the Overclass need authority to function as managers and so deliver to society requisite expertise in decision-making, planning, execution of plans, keeping to agreed-upon procedures, finding remedies for shortcomings and mistakes, and responding to crises with effective knowledge and timely innovations. Having authority is the foundation of Overclass power.

The Overclass was not mentioned in America's founding covenants. The Declaration of Independence spoke only of persons who are created equal one with another, are endowed by their Creator with certain unalienable rights, among which are life, liberty, and the pursuit of happiness. The Declaration did mention governments that must not take a form that will infringe on personal rights of life, liberty, or the pursuit of happiness. There is no provision in the Declaration authorizing any class of persons to manage the lives and liberties of other persons, including the choices made in their search for happiness, though such class may have superior wisdom, more accurate knowledge, or better values than do the people they seek to manage.

The federal Constitution, ratified in 1788, speaks of only three branches of the national government: the executive, the legislative, and the courts. Again, there is no provision in this covenant among the several states for a trained elite to use the authority of any branch to manage American culture, society, politics, or economy. There is no provision in the Constitution, for example, for political parties or private corporations.

The American Constitution most certainly did not create a God-State.

To ensure protections for individual persons, the Bill of Rights was added to the Constitution through amendments. Authorized branches of the federal government could not manage religious beliefs and practices, what could be said in public, what could be printed in the media, or the right of individuals to bear arms. No branch of the government could deprive a person of life, liberty, or property without obtaining legal authority, specified as the due process of law. Judges were not authorized to use capricious personal preferences to deny accused persons a fair trial, in most cases before a jury, to confront hostile witnesses and have the benefit of witnesses in their favor and legal counsel. Judges could not impose their prejudices in demanding excessive bail or in imposing excessive fines or cruel and unusual punishments. And the naming of certain rights in the Constitution could not permit the denial of still other personal rights, though unmentioned, leaving the number of rights ultimately available to Americans open to multiplication.

With respect to the possession of legitimate authority, the amended Constitution recognized only the federal government, states, and the people as having rights to act with discretion. There was no provision for an aristocracy, an order of clergy or knights, or any other legalized status or privilege. The Constitution prohibited federal government authorization of titles of nobility that would elevate some citizens above others. The divisive issue of having a superior social class of slave owners was left to the states to legalize if they so wished. The human personas of slaves were affirmed, though also recognized was their legal status under state law as chattel private property.

The Federalist Papers, written by James Madison, Alexander Hamilton, and John Jay to explain and promote the provisions of the proposed Constitution, did not refer in any way to the powers or privileges of managers and administrators outside of those who were employed by the Congress, the executive, and the courts.

In "Federalist No. 10," Madison wrote with disdain about the propensity of factions to undermine popular governments by introducing into public councils instability, injustice, and confusion. Such inequalities and dysfunctions, he thought, could become mortal diseases for republics. By "faction," Madison meant a number of citizens, such as members of the Overclass, "who are united and actuated by some common impulse of passion, or of interest, adverse to the rights of other citizens, or to the permanent and aggregate interests of the community."[1]

Madison there noted the role of economic opportunities in creating factions: "from the protection of different and unequal faculties of acquiring property, the possession of different degrees and kinds of property immediately results [such as members of the Overclass have in occupying positions that permit the extraction of rents]; and from the influence of these on the sentiments and views of the respective proprietors, ensues a division of the society into different interests and parties."

Having different interests from other Americans, the Overclass becomes a factional party unto itself, seeking its own advantages and prerogatives. From the perspective of faction formation, the uniformity of the Overclass with respect to modal personality—other-direction—constitutes another commonality among members of the class, one which also differentiates them from other citizens in outlook and ambition, further turning the class into an autonomous, self-regarding faction in American society, culture, and politics.

"But the most common and durable source of factions," said Madison, "has been the various and unequal distribution of property . . . A landed interest, a manufacturing interest, a mercantile interest, a moneyed interest, with many lesser interests, grow up of necessity in civilized nations and divide them into different classes, actuated by different sentiments and views. The regulation of these various and interfering interests forms the principal task of modern legislation, and involves the spirit of party and faction in the necessary and ordinary operations of the government." So from Madison's perspective, today's Overclass of managerial Americans has rightly become a self-seeking and self-promoting faction present across our governments and in large private institutions as well.

Madison's remedy for the dangers factions present for a republic was competition—many factions checking and balancing one another out and so preventing usurpation of the government by only one to the detriment of others.

"Whilst all authority in [the federal republic] will be derived from and dependent on the society, the society itself will be broken into so many parts, interests, and classes of citizens, that the rights of individuals, or of the minority, will be in little danger from interested combinations of the majority."[2] The present danger to American society was thus foreseen—the overconcentration of power by the Overclass as the principal faction empowered to control the agencies of the federal government, a disequilibrium of authority that some refer to as the "deep state."

In addition, of course, the Overclass as a faction also dominates, to the exclusion of other points of view, educational institutions, media, large corporations, and many large city and state governments, minimizing social, cultural, and economic checks and balances on its power and authority.

Another admonition of *The Federalist Papers* applicable to the Overclass is the following: "The aim of every political constitution is, or ought to be, first to obtain for rulers men who possess most wisdom to discern, and most virtue to pursue, the common good of the society; and in the next place, to take the most effectual precautions for keeping them virtuous whilst they continue to hold their public trust."[3] Members of the Overclass are not trained in and do not possess the charism of virtue, and their powers of discernment become stunted by the credentialing process that results in their professionalization. They are not disposed to hold well a public trust for the common good. To benefit their faction, yes, they can use their offices well. Thus, Lord Acton's axiom about the human ethos, a source of daimons inspiring many of our managers, applies willy-nilly to members of the Overclass: power tends to corrupt, and absolute power corrupts absolutely.

The institutionalized power of bureaucracy, beloved of Hegel's God-State, was not authorized by the American Constitution. In his inaugural and farewell addresses, President George Washington did not mention administrators or agencies as essential or even desirable for the work of safeguarding the well-being of the new republic and all its citizens.

So we may rightly ask how the Overclass came to have the authority over the lives of Americans, which it so freely exercises today. The question can be asked of the federal government and of all state and local governments that today hire managers and administrators to supervise innumerable aspects of American lives and livelihoods. Who gave the Overclass the right to manage—to regulate—American citizens in their rights to life and liberty and in their search for happiness as they best see fit to believe themselves happy?

Briefly, the Overclass came to power through politics and law. The colleges, professional schools, and universities that trained Overclass managers and professionals could not authorize them to assume offices in the government—or in any other institution for that matter. Another social force was needed to bring them to the helm of legitimate public regulatory administration of our economy and society. To learn why the Overclass became so prominent and powerful in our lives, we need to ask who hired them and who paid them.

Politics Legitimizes the Overclass

The first step in legitimizing the Overclass came in 1883, with the Pendleton Act establishing a civil service to administer the executive branch of the federal government. After his election to the presidency, Rutherford B. Hayes had pressed the Congress for a law to end the spoils system, under which employees of the federal government were mostly hired on a partisan basis with recommendations from loyal party organizers who could "deliver" votes on Election Day. A law was only passed after the assassination of James Garfield during the presidency of Chester Arthur. Garfield had been killed by Charles Guiteau, who felt Garfield had blocked his appointment to a government position on partisan grounds.

Very much in line with Hegel's vision of public administration by and through a professionally trained elite, the Pendleton Civil Service Reform Act authorized selection of a few government employees through the administration of competitive exams and made it illegal to fire or demote some administrators for political reasons. The act allowed future presidents to increase the number of federal employees who would be hired as part of the civil service. Further, the act established an agency to administer the civil service examinations and outlawed the payment of "fees" paid by political appointees as the "purchase price" for their appointments.

Then came the Interstate Commerce Act of 1887, which permitted only "reasonable and just" rates to be collected by interstate railroads. It did not set prices, only an ethical standard but one that could be used to challenge rates set by the private companies before a government agency that had the last word in what was fair—the Interstate Commerce Commission. The authority to review and reject private sector decisions given to appointed professional experts was a significant initial step in legitimizing the role of the Overclass in supervising the American economy.

Thus, the point of entry of the Overclass into our system of constitutional governance was to act as a check on the discretion of private companies. Members of the commission, as it were, gave a second opinion while looking down on the tensions and rival interests among buyers and sellers in a free market from the higher perspective of an objective, disinterested observer investigating rationally and scientifically facts and other evidence, all in the educated manner promoted for humankind by the European Enlightenment and its avatars such as Hegel.

Railroads were accused of abusing their market power—power created not through competition but through the restriction of competition with cartel arrangements known as pools and trusts that would fix rates at higher than marginal cost. The Grange, officially the National Grange of the Order of Patrons of Husbandry, had mobilized farmers to lobby for laws restricting the freedoms of railroads to set prices.

In 1890 Congress passed the Sherman Antitrust Act to confront directly the legal arrangements used by many companies across many industries to concentrate market power for their benefit. A monopoly has the market power to charge customers a price higher than its marginal cost, thereby denying customers the benefit of lower costs of production coming from expansion of supply.

The act made it law that

> every contract, combination in the form of trust or otherwise, or conspiracy, in restraint of trade or commerce among the several States, or with foreign nations, is hereby declared to be illegal.
>
> Every person who shall monopolize, or attempt to monopolize, or combine or conspire with any other person or persons, to monopolize any part of the trade or commerce among the several States, or with foreign nations, shall be deemed guilty of a misdemeanor.[4]

Like the Interstate Commerce Act, the Sherman Antitrust Act sought to impose a standard of fairness on markets, preventing private power from indulging in extremes of selfishness. It did not seek to regulate businesses that competed with fairness. Senator George Hoar of Massachusetts, another author of the Sherman Act, said that "[a person] who merely by superior skill and intelligence . . . got the whole business because nobody could do it as well as he could was not a monopolist . . . (but was if) it involved something like the use of means which made it impossible for other persons to engage in fair competition."[5]

The act authorized the Department of Justice to, if it decided that monopoly power was operative in a market, ask the courts to enjoin such conduct. In addition, the act allowed private parties injured by conduct violating the act to bring suits for monetary damages.

So with respect to the Overclass, the Sherman Antitrust Act created in a department of the federal government the need to hire experts on what were illegal monopolistic market behaviors and what were non-abusive market prices and contract arrangements. In time, courts would adjudicate many cases under the act and so create a body of law—precedents and rulings on different sets of facts providing analyses of what is or is not an illegitimate monopoly practice. Law schools would then create courses to teach this new antitrust law to their students, who would graduate, become lawyers, and be newly minted members in good standing of the Overclass. In time, the federal government, company legal departments, and law firms would seek to hire the best students from the best law schools who had been taught antitrust by the most respected expert legal scholars in that subfield of the law. Thus would the social legitimacy of the Overclass came to be enhanced by the Sherman Antitrust Act and similar legislation.

The Sherman Act was followed in 1914 by the Clayton Antitrust Act, which outlawed more specific and creative abuses of market power designed to enhance the profitability of companies such as "price discrimination" between different purchasers if such discrimination tends to create a monopoly, "exclusive dealing" agreements, "tying" arrangements restricting another company from dealing with one's competitors, and mergers and acquisitions that substantially reduce market competition. In 1936 the Robinson-Patman Act added to the prohibitions of the

Clayton Act certain practices in which manufacturers would discriminate in their sales prices between equally situated distributors.

In August 2024 Google was found by a federal judge to have established illegal monopoly dominance of internet searches. In July 2024 Google took 91.04% of the internet search market. Microsoft Bing had 3.86%.

The *New York Times* reported,

> Justice Department officials are considering what remedies to ask a federal judge to order against the search giant, said three people with knowledge of the deliberations involving the agency and state attorneys general who helped to bring the case. They are discussing various proposals, including breaking off parts of Google, such as its Chrome browser or Android smartphone operating system, two of the people said.
>
> Other scenarios under consideration include forcing Google to make its data available to rivals, or mandating that it abandon deals that made its search engine the default option on devices like the iPhone, said the people, who declined to be identified because the process is confidential. The government is meeting with other companies and experts to discuss their proposals for limiting Google's power, the people said.
>
> The deliberations are in their early stages. Judge Amit P. Mehta of the U.S. District Court for the District of Columbia, who is overseeing the case, has asked the Justice Department and Google to come up with a process for determining a fix.[6]

So in America in 2024, who was running the market for searches on the web—members of the Overclass working for the government or entrepreneurs? An irony enclosed within the question is that the employees and owners of Google are not less Overclass in status and social orientation than those employed by the federal government. It was the right hand touching fingers with the left hand from a social class perspective, one interconnected elite deciding how the market will function for Americans, who thereafter must live with the dictated result.

The Overclass could not have been established with authority to manage the American economy and more unless money could be found to pay the salaries of such administrators. In 1894 the Congress passed an act permitting the federal government to collect a tax on the earnings of Americans. That act was declared unconstitutional by the Supreme Court in 1895. In 1909 the Congress would recommend an amendment to the Constitution to permit the collection of taxes on incomes. In 1913 that amendment would be ratified and become part of the Constitution. Thereafter the federal government enjoyed a revenue stream sufficient for the growth in size and addition of agencies and the expansion of their competencies and regulatory responsibilities.

An additional milestone came in the presidential election of 1896 when a Democrat candidate for the presidency, William Jennings Bryan, gave his "Cross of Gold" speech at his party's nominating convention. He focused attention on economic inequality in alignment with the Progressive movement. Bryan came neither from the North nor the South but had his views shaped by growing up in midwestern Nebraska. That year Bryan was nominated for the presidency by both the Democrats and the Progressive Party, building a coalition between the two. Bit by bit the Democrats would open up to include Progressives and their agenda, which was to elevate the Overclass and its educated professionalism to greater importance in American life.

Another financial panic, this time in 1893, had sharpened the policy debate about whether to base the currency on the price of gold—expensive but stable—or the price of silver—cheap because of plentiful supply. The monied class preferred a gold standard; farmers and the less well-to-do wanted cheaper money.

Bryan spoke to the Democrat convention as a champion of silver as a legal standard for money. He began softly,

> I would be presumptuous, indeed, to present myself against the distinguished gentlemen to whom you have listened if this were a mere measuring of abilities; but this is not a contest between persons. The humblest citizen in all the land, when clad in the armor of a righteous cause, is stronger than all the hosts of error. I come to speak to you in defense of a cause as holy as the cause of liberty—the cause of humanity.

He said he spoke for the supporters of a silver standard.

> It is for these that we speak. We do not come as aggressors. Our war is not a war of conquest. We are fighting in the defense of our homes, our families, and posterity. We have petitioned, and our petitions have been scorned. We have entreated, and our entreaties have been disregarded. We have begged, and they have mocked when our calamity came.
>
> We beg no longer; we entreat no more; we petition no more. We defy them!

He challenged the delegates of his party.

> Upon which side will the Democratic Party fight. Upon the side of the idle holders of idle capital, or upon the side of the struggling masses? That is the question that the party must answer first; and then it must be answered by each individual hereafter. The sympathies of the Democratic Party, as described by the platform, are on the side of the struggling masses, who have ever been the foundation of the Democratic Party.

He concluded,

> Having behind us the producing masses of this nation and the world. Having behind us the commercial interests and the laboring interests and all the toiling masses, we shall answer their demands for a gold standard by saying to them, you shall not press down upon the brow of labor this crown of thorns. You shall not crucify mankind upon a cross of gold.[7]

Bryan lost the election. William McKinley, the Republican, won. The gold standard was adopted four years later.

But the Progressive movement did not disappear. Progressives called for social reform, for improving the "natural order" of society as it had become under capitalism and a culture of "unenlightened ordinaryism." Progressives promoted the German model of a welfare state. They believed in better governance through the use of reason and a focus on efficiency in all areas of society. They supported worker compensation, improved child labor laws, minimum wage legislation, a limited workweek, a graduated income tax, and the right to vote for women.

Parts of the Progressive agenda appealed to upper-class Republicans such as Theodore Roosevelt and to Democrats. As president, Roosevelt would break up trusts and also supported an eight-hour workday, improved health and safety standards and factory working conditions, workers' compensation laws, and minimum wage laws for women.

Overclass intellectuals emerged to advocate Progressive approaches to management of the economy, culture, and society. Harvard Law School–trained lawyer Louis Brandeis used "scientific principles" and data produced by social scientists documenting the high costs of long working hours for both individuals and society. In *The Jungle* (1906), socialist Upton Sinclair described Chicago's meatpacking plants to the shock of his readers. His exposé led to food safety legislation. Thorstein Veblen took issue with conspicuous consumption by the well-off as essentially unbecoming and unproductive waste in his *Theory of the Leisure Class* (1899). In 1913 Walter Lippmann, Herbert Croly, and Walter Weyl became the founding editors of the *New Republic*, which thereafter until today has provided influential Overclass thought leadership in public policy. In his influential *Drift and Mastery* (1914), stressing the "scientific spirit" and "discipline of democracy," Walter Lippmann called for a strong central government guided by experts rather than public opinion.

John Dewey argued for a universal and comprehensive system of education, reasoning that a democratic society needed citizens conversant with Enlightenment thinking. Progressives turned to educational researchers to evaluate the reform agenda by measuring numerous aspects of education, later leading to standardized testing.

Jane Addams of Chicago's Hull House professionalized charitable engagement with the poor and the distressed. Muckraking journalists publicized abuses of economic privilege, political corruption, and social injustice.

In the 1912 presidential election, Woodrow Wilson, the Democrat candidate, had won at his party's nominating convention the support of William Jennings Bryan. Wilson won the election as the Republican Party split into two factions, each running a candidate for the presidency. Wilson appointed Bryan as his secretary of state. The Wilson-Bryan alliance brought Progressive thought, energy, and followers into the Democratic Party.

Thus, the Democratic Party thereafter would legitimize and institutionalize the Overclass as America's ruling elite. Republicans then would respond with sometimes strident opposition to Overclass policies and its demands for more and more management authority over American lives and fortunes.

The expansion of federal government authority delegated to Overclass agencies and so placed under expert control can be easily tracked from Woodrow Wilson's presidency down to Joe Biden's, with

Democratic presidents scaling up that authority and Republican presidents scaling it back or opposing further augmentation, modestly adding new programs, or just lethargically accepting the status quo put in place by the Democrats.

The growth trajectory of expanding legitimate and legal Overclass authority in supervising and regulating Americans can quickly and reliably be documented in the Wikipedia entries for the different presidencies. These entries list without making judgments the documented official actions of various presidents and congresses.

Here we can read that from Wilson's administration until the election of Richard Nixon in 1968, the Democratic Party would put in place on a national scale professional management of social, economic, and cultural outcomes by members of the Overclass. The Democrats secured legitimacy for this ever-expanding policy regime by sustaining a workable, supportive electoral coalition of three social structures: the Democratic Party in big cities such as Boston, New York, Philadelphia, Chicago, and Kansas City; the Southern Jim Crow states core to the failed Confederacy; and the rising Overclass of educated managers and professionals.

As Southern Whites then turned away from the Democrats toward the Republicans, something of an equilibrium between the two parties emerged, and with the baby boomers coming to mature positional advancement, the growth of the Overclass shifted more to bureaucracies in the private sector, both in business and with nonprofits. Educational institutions trained and certified ever more other-directed professionals, providing sufficient private sector legitimation for the employment of those in the Overclass. The more hubristic members of the Overclass tended to adopt Progressive politics and innovations in culture and seek employment in the media, consulting, education, finance, high tech, and government.

Importantly, Woodrow Wilson was the first American president from the Overclass. He obtained a bachelor's degree from the College of New

Jersey (now known as Princeton University), where he joined the Phi Beta Kappa fraternity. A southerner, he then studied law at the University of Virginia. Most importantly, in 1883 he enrolled at Johns Hopkins University to earn a PhD in history and government. Johns Hopkins was the leading activist in adopting the German Hegelian model of higher education, and Wilson proved to be an eager and apt student of the new approach to governing a society. Of note, he also studied German. While at Johns Hopkins, he wrote *Congressional Government: A Study in American Politics*, which was published in 1885 by Houghton Mifflin.

Wilson became a college professor and, in 1902, was chosen as the president of Princeton University. He was a member of academic professional associations, the American Academy of Arts and Letters and the American Philosophical Society. As president of Princeton, he aspired "to transform thoughtless boys performing tasks into thinking men."[8] He tried to raise admission standards and to replace the "gentleman's C" with serious study.

Then he went into politics. In 1911 and 1912, he was governor of New Jersey.

In his 1912 campaign for the presidency of the United States, Wilson spoke out for social justice. In 1913 he published a book of selections from his campaign speeches, *The New Freedom: A Call for the Emancipation of the Generous Energies of a People*, to memorialize, as a professor might want to do, his social philosophy.[9] He wrote,

There is one great basic fact which underlies all the questions that are discussed on the political platform at the present moment. That singular fact is that nothing is done in this country as it was done twenty years ago.

We are in the presence of a new organization of society. Our life has broken away from the past. . . .

There is a sense in which in our day the individual has been submerged. In most parts of our country men work, not for themselves, not as partners in the old way in which they used to work, but generally as employees,—in a higher or lower grade,—of great corporations. There was a time when corporations played a very minor part in our business affairs, but now they play the chief part, and most men are the servants of corporations.

You know what happens when you are the servant of a corporation. You have in no instance access to the men who are really determining the policy of the corporation. If the corporation is doing the things that it ought not to do, you really have no voice in the matter and must obey the orders, and you have oftentimes with deep mortification to co-operate in the doing of things which you know are against the public interest. Your individuality is swallowed up in the individuality and purpose of a great organization. . . .

Yesterday, and ever since history began, men were related to one another as individuals. To be sure there were the family, the Church, and the State, institutions which associated men in certain wide circles of relationship. But in the ordinary concerns of life, in the ordinary work, in the daily round, men dealt freely and directly with one another. To-day, the everyday relationships of men are largely with great impersonal concerns, with organizations, not with other individual men.

. . . There is something very new and very big and very complex about these new relations of capital and labor. A new economic society has sprung up, and we must effect a new set of adjustments. We must not pit power against weakness. The employer is generally, in our day, as I have said, not an individual, but a powerful group; and yet the workingman when dealing with his employer is still, under our existing law, an individual. . . .

So we must put heart into the people by taking the heartlessness out of politics, business, and industry. We have got to make politics a thing in which an honest man can take his part with satisfaction because he knows that his opinion will count as much as the next man's, and that the boss and the interests have been dethroned. Business we have got to untrammel, abolishing tariff favors, and railroad discrimination, and credit denials, and all forms of unjust handicaps against the little man. Industry we have got to humanize,—not through the trusts,—but through the direct action of law guaranteeing protection against dangers and compensation for injuries, guaranteeing sanitary conditions, proper hours, the right to organize, and all the other things which the conscience of the country demands as the workingman's right. We have got to cheer and inspirit our people with the sure prospects of social justice and due reward, with the vision of the open gates of opportunity for all.[10]

With advice from lawyer Louis Brandeis, Wilson formulated his New Freedom campaign platform and, as president, enacted most of it. To implement his proposals, he would need members of the Overclass as his administrators.

For reform of capitalism, Wilson established the Federal Trade Commission. For reform of finance, he established the Federal Reserve System and provided for federal loans to farmers. Pursuant to his Cotton Futures Act, the Department of Agriculture set enforceable physical standards for determining color grade, staple length and strength, and other valuable qualities and properties for cotton to minimize deceit in the cotton market, a failure of human integrity presumed beyond the power of markets to control. Wilson established extension services connected to land grant universities to help farmers learn new agricultural techniques by the introduction of home instruction. His administration established official quality standards for grains and oilseeds and required that exported grains and oilseeds be officially weighed and inspected to ensure quality and thereby validate prices.

Wilson provided federal funds for vocational education in "agriculture, trades and industry, and homemaking." The act was based largely on a report and recommendation from Charles Allen Prosser's *Report of the National Commission on Aid to Vocational Education*, an example of Overclass expertise in action.[11]

And so did Woodrow Wilson legitimately introduce Overclass management to American politics and government. There was a telling but, from a social justice perspective, very disappointing harmony between Wilson's class elitism with respect to professional management of social governance and his unwavering racial elitism with respect to African Americans. Barton Swaim has commented in reviewing a new study of Wilson's moral shortcomings that "at the core of progressivism, both in its original form and in the present day, is the belief that most people lack the wisdom to govern themselves and require a class of educated elites to organize society according to a shifting set of ideals. Wilson's warped ideas on race and sex weren't departures from progressivism but variant expressions of it."[12]

Most important for the ability of the Overclass to provide administrators for the federal government was the Revenue Act of 1913, which followed upon that year's ratification of the Sixteenth Amendment to the Constitution, facilitating the collection of taxes levied on the income of individuals and for-profit firms. The act imposed a 1% tax on personal incomes above $3,000, with a top tax rate of 6% on those earning more than $500,000 per year. Only 3% of Americans earned enough to be subject to the tax. The act also placed a 1% tax on the net income of all corporations.

My grandfather George Morris, a graduate of Dartmouth College and the University of Chicago Law School, returned from service in World War I and married my grandmother. Wondering how best to support his new wife, he asked a law school professor for advice. Famously in the family, the professor replied, "George, go to Washington and do tax!" He did just that, and during the 1930s as the federal income tax code became more and more technically complex and rates rose again and again, he enjoyed a very successful and remunerative law practice right through the Depression, becoming elected president of the American Bar Association during World War II.

History of Tax Monies Received by the Federal Government

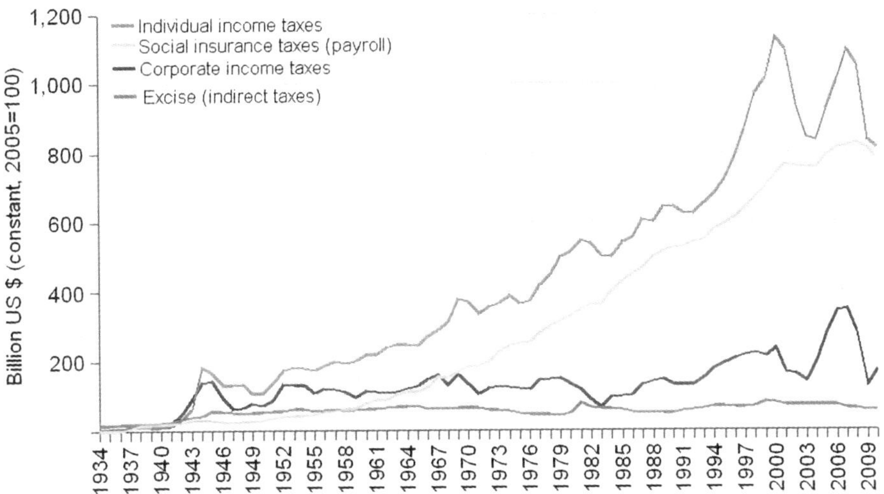

In 1929 Walter Lippmann wrote of his confidence in the Overclass rising to the occasion of achieving excellence in modern industry. He assumed that such a civilization rested on technology, machinery, and science. "The motives and the habits of mind which are thus brought into play at the very heart of modern civilization are mature and disinterested. . . . [Science] provides a body in which the spirit of disinterestedness can live . . . It is no exaggeration to say that pure science is high religion incarnate. . . . Scientific method can be learned. The learning of it matures the human character. . . . The scientific discipline has become . . . an essential part of our social heritage. For the machine technology requires a population which in some measure partakes of the spirit which created it."[13] In other words, a modern civilization needs the Overclass to prosper.

Lippmann found that capitalism was naive, with Adam Smith assuming that ordinary people pursuing their own interests would suffice. Rather, Lippmann wrote, "For the notion that an intricate and delicately poised industrial mechanism could be operated by uneducated men snatching competitively at profits was soon exposed as a simple-minded delusion."[14] He added, "The credo of naive capitalism is deeply at variance with the real character of modern industry. . . . To pursue his own interest his own way is a fairly certain way to disaster."[15]

He continued, "A mature industry, because it is too subtly organized to be run by naively passionate men, puts a premium upon men whose characters are sufficiently matured to make them respect reality and to discount their own prejudices."[16] Like Hegel, Lippmann preferred to live under a management elite of the trained, the talented, and the professional.

David Samuels very perceptively saw the important contribution of Walter Lippmann and his leadership in legitimating the Overclass.

> Lippmann was a progressive Harvard-educated technocrat who believed in engineering society from the top down, and who understood the role of elites in engineering social change to be both positive and inevitable. It was Lippmann, not Noam Chomsky, who coined the phrase "manufacturing consent," and in doing so created the framework in which the American governing class would understand both its larger social role and the particular tools at its disposal. "We are told about the world before we see it," Lippmann wrote. "We imagine most things before we experience them. And those preconceptions, unless education has made us acutely aware, govern deeply the whole process of perception." Or as he put it even more succinctly: "The way in which the world is imagined determines at any particular moment what men will do."[17]

Expansion of the Overclass would pause during the Republican presidential administrations of Warren Harding, Calvin Coolidge, and Herbert Hoover; the diversions of the Jazz Age and a moralistic Prohibition starting in 1919; and a rising stock market on Wall Street.

However, with the stock market crash of 1929 and the onset of a serious economic depression, the case for market failure was self-evident. Managers replacing markets was the acceptable alternative.

Or so proposed Franklin Roosevelt upon becoming president on March 4, 1933.

> Our greatest primary task is to put people to work. This is no unsolvable problem if we face it wisely and courageously. It can be accomplished in part by direct recruiting by the Government itself, treating the task as we would treat the emergency of a war, but at the same time, through this employment, accomplishing greatly needed projects to stimulate and reorganize the use of our natural resources. . . .
>
> Finally, in our progress toward a resumption of work we require two safeguards against a return of the evils of the old order; there must be a strict supervision of all banking and credits and investments; there must be an end to speculation with other people's money, and there must be provision for an adequate but sound currency. . . .
>
> We do not distrust the future of essential democracy. The people of the United States have not failed. In their need they have registered a mandate that they want direct, vigorous action. They have asked for discipline and direction under leadership. They have made me the present instrument of their wishes. In the spirit of the gift I take it.[18]

And so began the New Deal—a great expansion of government management of the economy to fill the void left by private market failures.

Roosevelt created new federal agencies: the National Recovery Administration, the Civilian Conservation Corps, the Works Progress Administration, the Civil Works Administration, the Farm Security Administration, the Social Security Administration, Federal Deposit Insurance Corporation, the Federal Crop Insurance Corporation, the Federal Housing Administration, the Tennessee Valley Authority, and the Securities and Exchange Commission.

Roosevelt passed the Securities Act of 1933 to require disclosure of material facts when selling financial securities, the Glass-Steagall Act to regulate banking, and the Fair Labor Standards Act of 1938, which set maximum hours and minimum wages for most categories of workers. Securities markets and employers now had to dance to tunes called by regulators.

Under the New Deal, the Overclass became fully legitimated as a part of America's governing order, providing direction through government for culture, society, the economy, and politics.

In 1935 the Supreme Court provided significant legitimacy to the claims of the rising Overclass to manage American lives and enterprises. In the case of *Humphrey's Executor v. United States*, the Supreme Court deferred to "experts" as a class that deserved privilege and accommodation in our politics and governance.

In its opinion, the court upheld the establishment by the Congress of an unelected regulatory agency—the Federal Trade Commission—taking into consideration the thinking of Woodrow Wilson (and Hegel before him) about the importance of professional expertise. The court said,

> The commission is to be nonpartisan, and it must, from the very nature of its duties, act with entire impartiality. It is charged with the enforcement of no policy except the policy of the law. Its duties are neither political nor executive, but predominantly *quasi*-judicial and *quasi*-legislative. Like the Interstate Commerce Commission, its members are called upon to

exercise the trained judgment of a body of experts "appointed by law and informed by experience."[19]

Therefore, the court continued,

The Federal Trade Commission is an administrative body created by Congress to carry into effect legislative policies embodied in the statute in accordance with the legislative standard therein prescribed, and to perform other specified duties as a legislative or as a judicial aid. Such a body cannot in any proper sense be characterized as an arm or an eye of the executive. Its duties are performed without executive leave and, in the contemplation of the statute, must be free from executive control. In administering the provisions of the statute in respect of "unfair methods of competition"—that is to say in filling in and administering the details embodied by that general standard—the commission acts in part quasi-legislatively and in part quasi-judicially. In making investigations and reports thereon for the information of Congress under §6, in aid of the legislative power, it acts as a legislative agency. Under §7, which authorizes the commission to act as a master in chancery under rules prescribed by the court, it acts as an agency of the judiciary. To the extent that it exercises any executive function—as distinguished from executive power in the constitutional sense—it does so in the discharge and effectuation of its quasi-legislative or quasi-judicial powers, or as an agency of the legislative or judicial departments of the government.[20]

The English economist John Maynard Keynes made another seminal contribution to the legitimation of Overclass economic management. In his 1936 book, *The General Theory of Employment, Interest, and Money*, Keynes provided the world with a new *Begriff* by which to understand modern industrialized economies and perhaps all economies. He amalgamated into one system of human action both the market and the government. He examined the flow of money and finance—money being a precapitalist driver of market prices and behaviors—and the aggregate demand for labor and products in an economy. Governments had become necessary for the creation and circulation of money. Interest rates on money influenced private sector decisions on investment and prices in general. Employment of workers depended on investment and market demand for goods and services. He provided a concept of aggregate demand that drove or did not drive prosperity and argued that government could stimulate demand with its spending and employment programs.

Keynes further provided a macro, top-down understanding of the welfare state partnership between private markets and government spending, which had been pioneered in Germany by Chancellor Otto von Bismarck in the 1880s. To deter Germans from giving their votes to the Social Democratic Party, Bismarck invented government programs to provide compensation for workers injured in their employment, subsidies for Germans in their old age, and, to some extent, funding for health care. Calling it "practical Christianity," Bismarck had Hegel's administrative state supplement market equilibriums where important opinion found them unsatisfactory with nonmarket alternatives managed by public administrators.

Keynes's theory intellectually legitimated Roosevelt's New Deal and justified the growth of the administrative state. It has guided professional economists until today.

But in the elections of 1938, opponents of the New Deal won seats in the Senate and the House of Representatives, bringing the explosive growth of government to a halt. World War II began for the United States on December 7, 1941, and absorbed the nation's energies and resources for four years.

After the war ended in victory, Presidents Truman and Eisenhower answered the challenge of the Soviet Union and a new Communist government in China with a foreign policy of containment during a cold war. The Central Intelligence Agency was created by the National Security Act of 1947. The act also created a unified military command known as the National Military Establishment, an independent United States Air Force (formerly the Army Air Forces), and the Joint Chiefs of Staff. The act placed the National Military Establishment under the control of a single secretary of defense. The National Military Establishment was renamed the "Department of Defense" on August 10, 1949.

My awareness of the need to constitutionalize and so legitimize federal agencies began in a meeting with William Colby, then director of the Central Intelligence Agency, in the fall of 1973. At the time, committees in the Senate and the House of Representatives were investigating alleged malfeasance by the agency and its employees in prior years. Colby was keen to cooperate with the committee to establish effective congressional oversight over an intelligence agency that operated in great secrecy. As a young officer in the U.S. Agency for International Development, I had been assigned to the Civil Operations Rural Development Support (CORDS) organization during the Vietnam War. CORDS was one part of the U.S. Military Assistance Command, Vietnam (MACV), and Colby was deputy to the MACV commander with the rank of ambassador. Colby had known my father when Dad had served as U.S. ambassador in Thailand and had brought me up from working as a deputy district adviser in Vinh Long Province to serve as chief of the Village Government Branch of CORDS.

That day in his office, Colby outlined why it was important for the CIA to work very cooperatively with the Congress. A secret intelligence agency had not been contemplated by the framers of the Constitution in 1787. There was no accepted process for the Congress to supervise such an agency thoroughly but safely as was the case with domestic agencies. Thus, Colby had in mind the evolution of a formal relationship for the agency with the Congress, befitting the constitutional requirement for checks and balances between the legislative and executive branches of the federal government. I left his office thinking that Colby was a pretty remarkable bureaucrat to think so deeply and faithfully about constitutional government.

Neither Truman nor Eisenhower repealed Roosevelt's New Deal, so the administrative state put in place by the Democratic Party in the 1930s remained powerful and fully engaged with running programs that regulated the economy or provided money, goods, and services to citizens in tandem with private market incentives. But with respect to government power to manage private enterprise, Truman had his secretary of commerce take over some steel mills in 1952 during a dispute between steel companies and their workers to maintain an uninterrupted flow of steel to the makers of munitions supplying combat units in battle in Korea during the Korean War. The Supreme Court invalidated Truman's use of executive authority as an unconstitutional violation of the separation of powers.

In November 1955 William F. Buckley Jr. founded the *National Review* to provide an intellectual alternative to Overclass narratives. Buckley cheekily said, "A conservative is someone who stands athwart history, yelling Stop, at a time when no one is inclined to do so, or to have much patience with those who so urge it."[21] James Burnham, the former Trotskyite who had written on the rise of a managerial class, joined him.

Those out of sorts with the Overclass also read Friedrich Hayek's *The Road to Serfdom* and *The Constitution of Liberty*. Hayek, an Austrian, represented the Austrian school of economics, which, in the tradition of Adam Smith, held that social outcomes resulted from the actions of individuals so that their motivations, including their self-interest, needed to be respected and taken into account as drivers of economic activity. Ayn Rand, a Russian émigré, offered objectivism, a moral philosophy defending egoism. Her 1957 novel *Atlas Shrugged* sold well.

Leading academic economics departments, say, at MIT and Harvard, blended Keynesian macroeconomics with the late-nineteenth-century microeconomics of marginal-utility supply and demand curves of Alfred Marshall to produce for the Overclass an establishment theory of economics. I was taught this framework as a Harvard freshman in 1963 using Paul Samuelson's famous textbook, which I still have on my shelf.

The Kennedy administration continued the Cold War policy emphasis, leaving the structure of domestic institutions in place. However, Robert McNamara, with a brilliant mind trained at MIT, brought Overclass administrative expertise to the work of war fighting. In particular, the game-theoretic rationality of Harvard's Thomas Schelling was used in setting strategy in the nuclear weapons competition with the Soviet Union and was applied in the 1962 confrontation over the Soviet Union's deployment of missiles in Cuba.

In Vietnam, McNamara confronted a village-based Vietcong insurgency with a Harvard Business School management-by-objectives approach, contemplating the number of operations completed, the number of enemy killed, and the number of weapons captured as the metrics for judging success. He would later rationalize his attrition tactic for defeating invading regular forces sent south from North Vietnam on the grounds that if we killed more of them, in time they would (1) be unable to attack the South Vietnamese, or (2) abandon their effort as futile. His efforts didn't turn out so well.

In October 1966 McNamara had to admit to his president that, with his current approach to the war, he had no confidence the United States could change the minds of Communist leaders in Hanoi so that they would end their aggression and that he had no better ideas. In November President Johnson decided on his own to change American strategy to a more political one of building up the South Vietnamese nationalists to assume the burden of combat.[22] In his book *The Best and the Brightest*, the noted journalist David Halberstam held up for criticism the self-confident pretentions of the Overclass war managers charged with helping the South Vietnamese nationalists, asking whether the best and brightest of Americans could actually win that war and whether their expertise provided only an illusion of competence.

Members of the Overclass in academia began to gain prominence in giving public advice to their peers in government. John Kenneth Galbraith of Harvard wrote on how to check the power of private companies. Richard Neustadt, also of Harvard, wrote on how presidents should use their power. Hans Morgenthau, Herman Kahn, and Henry Kissinger proposed theories of international relations and nuclear strategy.

In 1961 Kahn founded the Hudson Institute as a think tank and Overclass outpost to advise policymakers. Think tanks are private sector, nonprofit organizations mobilizing talent from the Overclass to make recommendations on reforms of society, culture, the economy, politics, and international affairs. The Carnegie Endowment for International Peace had been founded in Washington, DC, in 1910 by philanthropist Andrew Carnegie. The Brookings Institution had been founded in 1916, its mission to "provide innovative and practical recommendations that advance three broad goals: strengthen American democracy; foster the economic and social welfare, security, and opportunity of all Americans; and secure a more open, safe, prosperous, and cooperative international system."[23] The American Enterprise Institute, a conservative think tank, had been founded in 1938.

The next expansion of government management of social and economic outcomes came under President Lyndon Johnson. Johnson became president on the assassination of President Kennedy. In 1964 Johnson easily won election to the office in his own right after a campaign against the conservative Republican Barry Goldwater, who, in essence, ran against the dominance of Overclass Democrats and their policies and agencies over the lives and fortunes of ordinary Americans. Johnson's victory then constituted a popular vote of confidence in the Overclass, legitimizing its role in the American power structure.

Lyndon Johnson's activist Overclass augmentation efforts, which he called the "Great Society," resulted in impressive additions to the scale and scope of government management of social relations. After taking office, he won congressional passage of a major tax cut, a Clean Air

Act, and the Civil Rights Act of 1964. The Revenue Act of 1964 cut individual income tax rates by approximately 20%, cut the top marginal tax rate from 91% to 70%, and slightly reduced corporate tax rates, adding a monetary stimulus to the private economy. In April Johnson proposed the Economic Opportunity Act of 1964, which would create the Office of Economic Opportunity to oversee local Community Action Agencies charged with allocating financial support to citizens living in poverty. The act also founded the Job Corps and AmeriCorps VISTA to employ volunteers to work in local communities. Johnson also persuaded Congress to approve the Food Stamp Act of 1964, which made permanent the food stamp pilot programs that had been initiated by President Kennedy.

After his inauguration in January 1965, Johnson passed even more sweeping reforms: two government-run health-care programs, Medicare and Medicaid, and the Voting Rights Act of 1965, which prohibited racial discrimination in voting, finally breaking the back of Jim Crow in the Southern states. Johnson declared a "War on Poverty" and established the Department of Housing and Urban Development. He authorized major increases in federal funding to education.[24]

The term "Great Society" had been coined by Richard Goodwin and was drawn from an observation that the title of Walter Lippmann's book *The Good Society* best captured the scope of President Johnson's ambitions for his country, which included urban renewal, modern transportation, a clean environment, reducing poverty, health care, crime control, and improvements to education.

In August 1968 Johnson passed an even larger funding package designed for expanding aid to cities, the Housing and Urban Development Act of 1968. The program built on the 1965 legislation but created two new housing finance programs designed for moderate-income families, sections 235 and 236, and vastly expanded support for public housing and urban renewal. As a result of Johnson's War on Poverty, as well as a strong economy, the nationwide poverty rate fell from 20% in 1964 to 12% in 1974.

Buoyed by his landslide victory in the 1964 election, in early 1965 Johnson secured congressional passage of the Elementary and Secondary Education Act, which doubled federal spending on education from $4 billion to $8 billion.

Head Start was an early education program for children from poor families. It provided medical, dental, social service, nutritional, and psychological care for disadvantaged preschool children.

The Motor Vehicle Air Pollution Control Act empowered the federal government to establish and enforce national standards limiting the emission of pollutants from new motor vehicles and engines. In 1967 Johnson and Senator Edmund Muskie led passage of the Air Quality Act, which increased federal subsidies for state and local pollution-control programs. The National Traffic and Motor Vehicle Safety Act and the Highway Safety Act made the federal government responsible for setting and enforcing auto and road safety standards.

A new transportation department brought together the Commerce Department's Office of Transportation, the Bureau of Public Roads, the Federal Aviation Agency, the Coast Guard, the Maritime Administration, the Civil Aeronautics Board, and the Interstate Commerce Commission. Altogether, thirty-one previously scattered agencies were brought under the new department. In 1965 President Johnson signed legislation establishing the U.S. Department of Housing and Urban Development.

Given escalating protests against the war in Vietnam to assist the Nationalists in South Vietnam fight off an invasion from Communist North Vietnam, Johnson declined to run for reelection in 1968. The antiwar movement was an Overclass phenomenon. Its narrative of a war not worth fighting, a people not worth defending, was created by academics and intellectuals who neither spoke Vietnamese nor understood Vietnamese history correctly. Their sources for the "truth" about the Vietnam War were former French colonialists who, in 1946, had picked Ho Chi Minh as their preferred leader of all Vietnamese. The movement's social presence was manifest in college and university students, particularly young men of draft age who did not want to fight.

Years later, the Vietnamese Communist Party would make public once secret documents from November 1960 in which the party Politburo in Hanoi sent directives to its southern cadres and sympathizers to start an armed insurgency against the nationalist government in Saigon. These documents exposed the American Overclass antiwar narrative as having been false in every particular.[25]

After Johnson's effectual abdication, Robert Kennedy was assassinated, and Johnson's vice president, Hubert Humphrey, was nominated the Democratic Party's candidate for the presidency. Republican Richard Nixon won the election narrowly. A third-party candidate from Alabama, George Wallace, ran a campaign that separated many Southern White voters from their historic loyalty to the Democrats.

As had Republican president Eisenhower, Nixon focused on foreign affairs and ending American participation in the war to defend South Vietnam and did not seek to overturn the many programs authorized under Johnson's efforts to make America into a Great Society. But Nixon did establish the Environmental Protection Agency and reluctantly signed the Clean Water Act.

Unwittingly, Nixon changed government policy in a most significant way to enhance the overall functionality of the Overclass in American life. He ended the draft of young men to serve their country in the armed forces, thus fully professionalizing the American military as a cadre of specially trained personnel organized independently of civilian culture and society.

Nixon had adopted the idea of an all-volunteer army from two academics: Martin Anderson of Columbia University and Nobel laureate Milton Friedman. Friedman has been quoted in interviews as stating, "In the realm of policy, I regard eliminating the draft as my most important accomplishment."

Conscription was to expire at the end of June 1971, but the Department of Defense and the Nixon administration decided the draft needed to continue for at least some time. In September 1971 the draft renewal bill was approved. To prepare for recruiting volunteers to serve in the armed forces, military pay was increased, and the U.S. Army began advertising to stimulate volunteering. As the last American combat troops returned from South Vietnam, the last American men were conscripted for national service in December 1972.[26]

In 1972 the Overclass, acting through the movement to end the war in Vietnam, ran George McGovern as the Democratic candidate for president, taking over the Democrat Party pretty much lock, stock, and barrel. Southern Whites left the Democrats and voted for Nixon.

The process for taking over the party was led by George McGovern, then a senator from South Dakota, and Don Fraser, a congressman from Minnesota. In 1969 McGovern became chairman of the Commission on Party Structure and Delegate Selection, also known as the McGovern-Fraser Commission. The commission significantly reduced the role of party officials and insiders in the nomination process, creating a "power to the people" opening for single-issue, grassroots organizers to gain momentum in the nomination process.

The commission's 1970 report, "Mandate for Reform," was approved by the Democratic National Committee in 1971. It required that delegates be selected either by a party primary or by a state convention process where the first stage was open caucuses. It also mandated quotas for proportional Black, female, and youth delegate representation. The new rules had an immediate effect in promoting the Overclass within the decision-making structures of the Democratic Party. After his service in World War II, McGovern had attended college at Dakota Wesleyan University and earned a PhD in history from Northwestern University.

McGovern was influenced by the previous generation of "progressive" historians. His 450-page dissertation, "The Colorado Coal Strike, 1913–1914," was a sympathetic account of the miners' revolt against Rockefeller interests in the Colorado Coalfield War. Influenced by the Social Gospel movement, McGovern began divinity studies at Garrett Theological Seminary in Evanston, Illinois. He taught college history.[27]

As Johnson had overwhelmed the conservative Goldwater in 1964, Nixon turned the tables and overwhelmed McGovern in 1972. Nixon then resigned in 1974 as a consequence of Watergate and an impeachment proceeding.

Following Nixon, Presidents Ford and Carter made few additions to the sweep of federal government authority. Ford signed the Education for All Handicapped Children Act of 1975, which established special education throughout the United States. Ford expressed "strong support for full educational opportunities for our handicapped children" upon signing the bill. Carter focused on inflation and reducing the federal government's deficits. Responding to the 1973 international oil crisis with rising prices, Carter secured congressional approval for the creation of the Department of Energy.[28]

As a centrist Democrat, Carter deregulated prices and other government restraints on trucking, airlines, railroads, communications, and natural gas. Carter's orientation to individual lives in small towns and suburbs alerted him to the rising antagonism between the Overclass and the American people. In his "Malaise" speech of 1979, he said,

As you know, there is a growing disrespect for government and for churches and for schools, the news media, and other institutions. This is not a message of happiness or reassurance, but it is the truth and it is a warning.

. . . Looking for a way out of this crisis, our people have turned to the Federal government and found it isolated from the mainstream of our nation's life. Washington, D.C., has become an island. The gap between our citizens and our government has never been so wide. The people are looking for honest answers, not easy answers; clear leadership, not false claims and evasiveness and politics as usual. . . .

What you see too often in Washington and elsewhere around the country is a system of government that seems incapable of action. You see a Congress twisted and pulled in every direction by hundreds of well-financed and powerful special interests. You see every extreme position defended to the last vote, almost to the last breath by one unyielding group or another. You often see a balanced and a fair approach that demands sacrifice, a little sacrifice from everyone, abandoned like an orphan without support and without friends.

Often you see paralysis and stagnation and drift. You don't like it, and neither do I. What can we do?[29]

In the 1980 election, Carter lost to Ronald Reagan, governor of California.

Reagan sought to undo Overclass powers of administrative supervision of society and the economy. His famous quip was, "I think you all know that I've always felt the nine most terrifying words in the English language are: 'I'm from the Government, and I'm here to help.'"[30] Reagan kept himself attuned to the inner-directed values associated with rugged individualism more than Overclass elitism would ever countenance.[31]

His economic policies were called "Reaganomics" and were influenced by Arthur Laffer, a conservative intellectual with Overclass qualifications but without loyalty to the class. Reagan lowered taxes and sought to cut nonmilitary spending and eliminate federal regulations. Reagan's policy, called a New Federalism, sought to shift the responsibility for most social programs to state governments, but it garnered little support in the Congress.

Reagan's Economic Recovery Tax Act of 1981 cut the top marginal tax rate from 70% to 50%, lowered the capital gains tax from 28% to 20%, more than tripled the amount of inherited money exempt from the estate tax, and cut the corporate tax. Six million poor Americans were exempted from paying any income taxes, and there was a reduction of income tax liability at all income levels. But as deficits became a current and future drain on the federal budget, Reagan signed two bills that raised taxes. The net effect of Reagan's tax bills was that the overall tax burden remained at 19% of gross national product.

In August 1981 Reagan signed the Omnibus Budget Reconciliation Act of 1981, which cut federal funding for social programs such as food stamps, school lunch programs, and Medicaid. The Comprehensive Employment and Training Act, which had provided for the employment of three hundred thousand workers in 1980, was also repealed, and his administration tightened eligibility for unemployment benefits. Spending on programs such as Supplemental Security Income, Medicaid, the earned income tax credit, and Aid to Families with Dependent Children all increased after 1982.

The number of federal civilian employees rose during Reagan's tenure, from 2.9 million to 3.1 million. The national debt more than tripled from $914 billion to $2.7 trillion between fiscal year 1980 and fiscal year 1989 while national debt as a percentage of GDP rose from 33% in 1981 to 53% in 1989.

Reagan sought to loosen federal regulation of economic activities, and he appointed key officials who shared this agenda. According to historian William Leuchtenburg, by 1986 the Reagan administration eliminated almost half the federal regulations that had existed in 1981. The Federal Communications Commission aggressively deregulated the broadcasting industry. The 1982 Garn–St. Germain Depository Institutions Act deregulated savings and loan associations and allowed banks to provide adjustable-rate mortgages. Reagan also eliminated numerous government positions and dismissed numerous federal employees, including the entire staff of the Employment and Training Administration.

By the end of Reagan's first term, the Overclass had become very legitimate, a permanent part of American public governance of society and the economy. Nevertheless, Reagan won reelection in 1984 in a landslide of popular support. Again, the American people exhibited a mild schizophrenia in their embrace of the Overclass, which therefore had its detractors and its passionate advocates. There were those

Americans who liked it and those who resented it. After nearly one hundred years of growth under successive presidential administrations and congressional legislative initiatives, the Overclass had become legitimate but only partially so.[32]

Reagan was succeeded as president by his VP, George H. W. Bush, who easily won election over Democrat Michael Dukakis. The results of the 1980, 1984, and 1988 presidential elections could be interpreted as Americans putting a check on the power of the Overclass to manage the country through federal agencies and their regulation of private economic and social arrangements.

Bush could not win reelection. A southern Democrat, Bill Clinton, though well-credentialed by Georgetown University and Yale Law School and the winner of a Rhodes scholarship, ran as a centrist, not as a Progressive promoter of Overclass ideas and preferences for intentional social management in the Hegelian tradition of the God-State.

Clinton raised taxes and set the stage for future budget surpluses. The ratio of federal government debt—incurred to fund the build-out of Overclass programs and agencies—to GDP fell from 47.8% to 33.6% by 2000. Clinton's most ambitious legislative initiative—a four-square Overclass expansion of social management to provide universal health care—could not become law due to Republican opposition in the Congress. Constitutional checks and balances seeking an equilibrium between factions worked as intended by Madison.

Clinton hoped to forge a new consensus that did not totally reject government interventionism. In reaction to his party's 1994 electoral defeat, Clinton pursued a policy nicknamed "triangulation," filling the policy space between conservative Republicans and Progressive Democrats. He assembled a bipartisan coalition to pass welfare reform that imposed new work requirements on recipients of government payments to support their families and lifetime limits on the total amount a person could receive, and he successfully expanded health insurance for children. With triangulation, Clinton could achieve Overclass goals by shifting from direct social management by government agencies to transfer payments of money from taxpayers (and government borrowings) to those entitled, which private individuals could use in market transactions of their own choosing.

In 1993 AmeriCorps was established, a community service program that provided young people with an opportunity to serve their communities and earn money for college or skills training. In just five years, nearly two hundred thousand young people were enrolled in the program.

Republican George W. Bush, a graduate of Yale College and Harvard Business School, narrowly won election to the presidency in 2000. Like Clinton, he had excellent Overclass credentials and was another member of the Overclass who had avoided service in Vietnam.

The terrorist Islamist attack on the World Trade Center in New York City on September 11, 2001, diverted much of President Bush's attention to foreign affairs. In retaliation he declared a global war on terrorism and authorized wars to be fought in Afghanistan and Iraq, wars that the professional American military establishment, augmented by the highly educated officers of the State Department and the Central Intelligence Agency, did not win.

Before the 9/11 attacks, Bush had obtained passage of a $1.3 trillion tax cut program and the No Child Left Behind Act. In March 2002 Bush signed into law the Bipartisan Campaign Reform Act, which would ease the way of wealthy members of the Overclass to influence the outcomes of American elections with cash payments to parties, candidates, and special fundraising committees. Bush continued the transfer payment approach to government intervention in the private sector by expanding Medicare so that it would also cover the cost of prescription drugs, the largest expansion of Medicare since the program's 1965 creation under Lyndon Johnson.[33]

In 2008 Democrat candidate Barack Obama was elected president, the first biracial person so elected. He had graduated from Columbia University and Harvard Law School, where he had, most prestigiously, been editor of the *Harvard Law Review*. As a lecturer, he had also taught law at the Chicago University School of Law. In his autobiography, *Dreams from My Father*, Obama recounted a range of personal experiences in his other-directed search to find himself as a person.

Obama quickly obtained from the Congress a $787 billion economic stimulus package aimed at helping the economy recover from the collapse of credit markets due to irrational exuberance fueling unwise speculation in financial securities secured by subprime mortgage loans. He also used government means to revive troubled automobile companies, renewing loans for General Motors and Chrysler to continue operations while refining their business models, with the White House setting terms for the bankruptcies of both firms, including the sale of Chrysler to Italian automaker Fiat and the reorganization of GM, giving the U.S. government a temporary 60% equity stake in the company.

Obama signed the bipartisan Budget Control Act of 2011 to prevent the federal government from defaulting on its debt repayments. The debt had accumulated over many presidencies to fund Overclass administrative agencies and administrators and social engineering interventions in private lives and decision-making.

Obama called for Congress to pass legislation reforming health care in the United States by providing for more transfer payments to deserving recipients. The Affordable Care Act (nicknamed "Obamacare") made Medicaid accessible for individuals making up to 133% of the federal poverty level, subsidized insurance premiums for people making up to 400% of that income level so their maximum "out-of-pocket" payment for annual premiums would be no more than 9.5% of income, funded incentives for businesses to provide health-care benefits, prohibited denial of coverage and denial of claims based on preexisting conditions, established health insurance exchanges, prohibited annual coverage caps, and funded medical research. What had formerly been arrangements made privately by patients with their doctors, hospitals, clinics, and health maintenance organizations thereafter had to conform to federal law.

Obamacare was challenged in federal courts as not having legitimacy under the Constitution, as exercising authority that the federal government did not possess to mandate and regulate private transactions. However, the Supreme Court found the law to have legitimacy under the authority of the federal government to collect taxes.[34]

American advertisers brought their own insights and skills to the process of legitimating the Overclass through the facilitation of other-direction. As David Axelrod said in bringing his professional credentials from advertising to politics, thereby advancing the career of Barack Obama, the deployment of "permission structures" could shape mass opinion and behaviors. Permission structures can shift the size and orientation of Overton windows, "introducing new conversations into the mainstream that might previously have been considered marginal or fringe."[35]

In his most perceptive article, "Rapid-Onset Political Enlightenment," David Samuels conflated the Democrat Party with the Overclass and other-direction. As to the Democrats, he rightly wrote that "Obama's operatives shared the same character flaw as their master, a kind of brittle, Ivy League know-it-all-ness that demanded that they always be the smartest person in the room."

As to the Overclass, he wrote,

> With enough money, operatives could create and operationalize mutually reinforcing networks of activists and experts to validate a messaging arc that would short-circuit traditional methods of validation and analysis, and lead unwary actors and audience members alike to believe that things that [they] had never believed or even heard of before were in fact not only plausible, but already widely accepted within their specific peer groups. . . . In fact, the higher one climbed on the social and professional ladder, the more vulnerable to such techniques people turned out to be—making it easy to flip entire echelons

of professionals within the country's increasingly brittle and insecure elite.[36]

In the presidential election of 2016, Overclass Queen Bee Hillary Clinton (Wellesley, Yale Law School, author) won a majority of the total individual votes cast but, by a small margin of votes in a few states, lost the electoral college vote of the fifty states to Donald Trump. Even before his inauguration, Trump was put under siege from Overclass partisans in the government, the media, academia, finance, and high tech. For reasons not entirely clear even in retrospect, Trump was perceived by most in the Overclass as an existential threat to their way of life and to democracy, according to their narrative about who really counts in the American way of making decisions, or to put it in other-directed language—who deserves to sit at the table and be part of the conversation governing what Americans should think and do.

The election of Donald Trump did not sit well with the Overclass. An attempt was made by the federal government's investigative agencies, the CIA and the FBI, coordinated by its director of national intelligence, to delegitimize the votes of American citizens. President Obama ordered a comprehensive assessment of "Russia's election meddling." On December 9, 2016, the White House gathered top national security council principals for a meeting that included James Clapper, John Brennan, Susan Rice, John Kerry, Loretta Lynch, Andrew McCabe, and others to discuss Russia.

After the meeting, DNI Clapper's executive assistant sent an email to intelligence community (IC) agency leaders tasking them with creating a new IC assessment affirming that

> the IC is prepared to produce an assessment per the president's request, that pulls together the information that we have on the tools Moscow used and the actions it took to influence the 2016 election, an explanation of why Moscow directed these

activities, and how Moscow's approach has changed over time. … The Office of the Director of National Intelligence will lead the effort, with participation from CIA, FBI, NSA (National Security Agency) and DHS (Department of Homeland Security).

The goal of what would become a disinformation operation hostile to President-elect Trump was to produce a highly classified report and an unclassified version.[37]

The first public assertion of Russian efforts to influence the 2016 election had come before the November election in a joint statement on September 22, 2016, by Senator Dianne Feinstein and Representative Adam Schiff, the top Democrats on the Senate and House Intelligence Committees, respectively. Then, on October 7, 2016, the Department of Homeland Security and the Office of the Director of National Intelligence issued a joint statement claiming that the "U.S. Intelligence Community is confident" that Russia hacked the Democratic Party in order to "interfere with the U.S. election process."[38]

After Clapper confirmed that an assessment would be made of how the Russians had tried to fix the outcome of the election, the *Washington Post* told Americans that "the CIA has concluded in a secret assessment that Russia intervened in the 2016 election to help Donald Trump win the presidency, rather than just to undermine confidence in the U.S. electoral system, according to officials briefed on the matter."[39]

Reporters Adam Entous, Ellen Nakashima, and Greg Miller later received Pulitzer Prizes for their roles in creating a false narrative escalating political tensions and resentments among Americans. The objective of these Overclass operatives can be summarized as the management of democracy though the inculcation of correct thinking among voters, thinking nicely protected against doubts by affirming emotions. In such a democracy, voters have the right to express their views on election day—ballots are not filled out for them—but their views are not really their own but only what they have been taught by their intellectual "betters." Such a democracy is a kind of aristocracy where the "best" people—*aristoi* in Greek—hold the high ground socially, culturally, and politically while the little people—the *hoi polloi*—mind their manners and do what they are told.

The effort of Obama's intelligence agency managers was, in the jargon of modern American media-driven culture, to create and install a "permission structure" that would nullify Donald Trump's ability to serve as President of the United States.

On January 6, 2017, an assessment was released by DNI Clapper's office which asserted that Russian leadership had favored presidential candidate Trump over Hillary Clinton and that Russian President Vladimir Putin had personally ordered an "influence campaign" to harm Clinton's electoral chances and "undermine public faith in the US democratic process."

On January 17, Obama spoke—subconsciously on behalf of the entire Overclass—of "folks here" in the intelligence agencies, military, and State Department having acted as a "policing mechanism." In response to Obama's managerial paternalism, the very appropriate questions for the American people to ask would have been: Policing whom? For breaking what law? By whose authority?[40]

On May 17 of the same year, a special counsel was appointed to investigate Russian interference. After two years and $32 million spent, that investigation found no evidence that Trump or any of his aides had coordinated with the Russian government.[41]

Trump thus came into office encumbered and burdened by constant opposition, including the special counsel investigation for being a compromised Russian asset and an impeachment for asking the president of Ukraine questions about possible corrupt behavior on the part of a rival in the Democrat Party.

Trump was unsuccessful in his efforts to repeal the Affordable Care Act but rescinded the individual mandate. He sought substantial spending cuts to major welfare programs, including Medicare and Medicaid.

In 2020 his administration was confounded by the spread of COVID-19 among Americans. Much of his administration's response to the pandemic, notably personified by Dr. Anthony Fauci, was guided by Overclass approaches of how to use experts to manage contact with the virus. Schools were closed; masks were mandated and social distancing insisted upon. "Follow the science" was the rationale for these policy decisions. Contrary advice and views were disparaged and even censored. But a little debate was welcomed about which scientists deserved to have their opinions and recommendations obeyed.

On points of expertise, Trump was outclassed and therefore ridiculed. He was quickly ostracized by America's elite opinion leaders. Trump did, however, under Operation Warp Speed, quickly bring forth vaccines to protect people against the original virus and its variants.

Trump's economic policies centered on cutting taxes, deregulation, and trade protectionism. Deficit spending, combined with tax cuts for the wealthy, caused the U.S. national debt to sharply increase.

A tax bill was the first major legislation signed by Trump. The $1.5 trillion bill reduced the corporate federal tax rate from 35% to 21%, its lowest point since 1939. The bill also cut the individual tax rate, reducing the top rate from 39.6% to 37%. The bill doubled the estate tax exemption and allowed owners of pass-through businesses to deduct 20% of business income. The bill doubled the standard deduction while eliminating many itemized deductions.

In his public comments and policy decisions, Trump spoke against or challenged many of the virtue-signaling narratives accepted by most in the Overclass about what well-intentioned and well-educated other-directed people should think if they wanted to maintain their social standing as part of the country's most honorable elite.

Trump did not favor consumption of marijuana but did support longer sentences for drug users. He blamed wildfires in California on poor professional management of forests. He imposed tariffs on imports, raising prices for American purchasers and undercutting globalization of trade and production. The administration reversed Obama administration guidance on how schools and universities should combat sexual harassment and sexual violence. His administration favored school choice for parents as against acceptance of public schools as managed by teachers' unions.

His administration's "America First Energy Plan" did not mention renewable energy and instead focused on fossil fuels. Nearly all references to climate change were removed from the White House website, and the Environmental Protection Agency removed climate change material from its website, including detailed climate data. Trump had the U.S. withdraw from the Paris Agreement, a commitment made by two hundred nations to cut greenhouse gas emissions. Trump castigated illegal immigration and was partially successful in building a wall along the border between the United States and Mexico.

Trump presents a most unusual modal personality. Is he inner-directed and so dictatorial or other-directed in that he is so instinctively reactive to others and their take on him? I am tempted to say that he is a special case, that he is undirected and undirectable. I would not say that he has strong inner-direction other than a volatile egoism and a dynamic opportunism. Nor does his egoism permit him to incorporate the wishes and concerns of others into his persona; rather, he seeks to take personal advantage of those others, depending on how he can manipulate their wishes and concerns by playing what he calls his cards. He is more like the child who has temper tantrums every other moment when he doesn't get his way, a profound immaturity.[42]

Trump does desperately want to measure up in the eyes of others—to be bigger, even the greatest ever; to have in his hands the most cards; to hold the winning hand. Sadly, for him and for us, his algorithm for winning in life counts only things. Trump measures success in terms of quantity, not quality. He adds and subtracts the number of things possessed—like money and buildings—not their virtues. For him, therefore, people too are just things to be acquired, to be used—and to be abused if necessary. They are pawns or knights, rooks or bishops, in the chessboard game of life. Thus, he doesn't care what other people think, only what their moves might be. He lives to direct them, never to let them direct him, for that would make him a "loser" in his own eyes. Perhaps he is responding to an inner need—one not driven by ideals per se but only to make things his.

Joseph R. Biden, Obama's vice president, defeated Trump's reelection effort in 2020. Trump and many of his supporters challenged the results as unbelievable but could not meet the burden of proof ordinarily carried by plaintiffs in litigation.

Biden's loyalty to Overclass progressive social engineering resulted in very expensive public investments in infrastructure and clean energy industries and efforts to lower out-of-pocket health-care costs for consumers. His version of Overclass management of the economy was called industrial policy, where the government invested in innovations and enterprises it thought of as foundational for future growth but were too untested to attract private sector investment capital. Here the role of government was to supplement the market by assuming risks of failure, when financial markets and entrepreneurs found them to be unreasonable.

A cheerleader for the Biden administration opined, "Together, these laws represent American-style industrial policy: They make needed investments in growing industries that will drive future economic growth in a way that promotes quality American jobs, including by building electric vehicle (EV) charging stations and energy-efficient homes, manufacturing semiconductors, repairing crumbling roads and bridges, and closing the digital divide, among many other investments."[43]

The Biden legislation also funded clean water infrastructure and apprenticeship and workforce training programs in critical industries, "building a skilled domestic workforce in the critical semiconductor sector," and reducing the danger of excessive climate change in the years to come.[44]

Biden's administration energetically applied Overclass Gnostic *Begriffs* to American culture and society, particularly with a "whole of government approach" to installing Woke priorities in selecting and promoting those who would manage all federal bureaucracies, even the military charged with protecting our national security and those who supervised our foreign policy. Biden's executive order of June 25, 2021, said,

> On my first day in office, I signed Executive Order 13985 (Advancing Racial Equity and Support for Underserved Communities Through the Federal Government), which established that affirmatively advancing equity, civil rights, racial justice, and equal opportunity is the responsibility of the whole of our Government. To further advance equity within the Federal Government, this order establishes that it is the policy of my Administration to cultivate a workforce that draws from the full diversity of the Nation.
>
> As the Nation's largest employer, the Federal Government must be a model for diversity, equity, inclusion, and accessibility, where all employees are treated with dignity and respect.[45]

Another Biden policy, justified apparently only by the other-directed, feminized ethic of care, opened the southern border of the United States to entry by millions of people desperate to flee the failed states into which they had been born. A country that will not defend its heritage can only be understood as one spinning and spinning around in other-directed uncertainty about its rightful priorities.

Biden's noted capacity for empathy may only be his way of expressing other-direction. His identification with the feelings of others may be, instead of an intentionally cynical manipulation of their emotions, a need on his part to channel—but only for the moment—the emotions of others into himself and then play back what he then feels, moving on to other feelings and perceptions as he meets others.

The Biden administration fine-tuned the "permission structure machine" of playing off the vulnerabilities of the other-directed. As David Samuels observed,

Even more unusual, and alarming, was what followed Trump's defeat in 2020. With the Democrats back in power, the new messaging apparatus could now formally include not just social and institutional pressure but the enforcement arms of the federal bureaucracy, from the Justice Department to the FBI to the SEC. As the machine ramped up, censoring dissenting opinions on everything from COVID, to DEI programs, to police conduct, to the prevalence and the effects of hormone therapies and surgeries on youth, large numbers of people began feeling pressured by an external force that they couldn't always name; even greater numbers of people fell silent. In effect, large-scale changes in American mores and behavior were being legislated outside the familiar institutions and processes of representative democracy, through top-down social pressure machinery backed in many cases by the threat of law enforcement or federal action, in what soon became known as a 'whole of society' effort.[46]

As to inculcating more and more other-direction in American personalities, he added,

The effect of the permission structure machine is to instill and maintain obedience to voices coming from outside yourself, regardless of the obvious gaps in logic and functioning that they create. . . . What the permission structure machine seeks to do is . . . [to locate] consciousness outside of the self—but clothing it as an internal product via the mechanized propagation of what Marxists used to call 'false consciousness.' But where the progenitors of 'false consciousness' in the Marxist lexicon are villains, working on behalf of the capitalist order by preventing workers from being cognizant of their own interests, the mechanized permission structure machine offers the reverse: The 'false consciousness' it seeks to propagate is a positive instrument of the [Democrat] party's attempt to establish the reign of justice on earth.[47]

Julian Epstein, former Democratic chief counsel to the House Judiciary Committee, wrote for the *New York Post* that Overclass rule under President Biden rested on three hegemonic pillars of managerial power: (1) racial preferences ("DEI for African Americans and open borders for Hispanics"); (2) a class-based shadow government of "NGOs, consultants, activist groups, foundations and donors, public unions, and the increasingly politicized state and city bureaucracies in Democratic-run cities underwritten with gobs of COVID-relief and federal taxpayer dollars"; and (3) "massive cancel culture and accompanying online authoritarianism."[48]

Since the late 1800s, parallel to the institutionalization of Overclass management responsibilities at the federal level, in each of the fifty American states, to some degree or another, Overclass agencies and policies were legitimized by voters and legislatures.

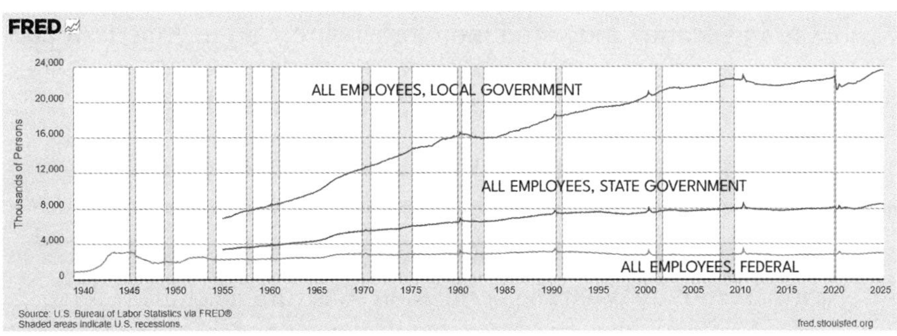

The Overclass and Theories of Constitutional Legitimacy

The legitimation of the Overclass as a major player in American governance has provoked two rival understandings of the Constitution. One seeks to follow the words of the Constitution literally understood. The other, crafted largely by law professors, proposes interpretation of the original text so that the literal words of the Constitution would take on an elastic quality of stretching to fit their meanings to the demands of the Overclass for modernizing our structures of governance and the super-imposition of public management over the economy and society. The first school of constitutional law became known as "originalism," for it's looking backward to discern what is now constitutionally permissible. The rival school of interpretation speaks of the Constitution as giving us a "living" text, one that is open, flexible, and expansive in its permissive-ness, which must keep up with the demands of the times and new under-standings of good and bad, right and wrong.

Both schools of interpretation focus on the role of judges in the federal courts, especially on the justices of the Supreme Court. Originalists want the courts to avoid innovation and leave to politics and amendments to the text of the Constitution any changes in governance seeking to adapt to new circumstances and changing popular understandings.

The core concern of originalists keeps faith with the cynicism expressed in *The Federalist Papers* about the inherent, and so everlasting, tendency for human persons to abuse their powers. Accordingly, Madison said, "If men were angels, there would be no need for government."[49] From this perspective, it is fundamental for justice and constitutional democracy to protect the people from the expansive ambitions of those given public authority, use of the police powers. This perspective looks with anxiety on expansions of Overclass authority to change the rights and customs of the people or impose new duties on them.

The concern of those who believe that the Constitution should accom-modate the plans and visions of the Overclass relies on Hegel's justifica-tion for rule by experts—those among us today who are expert should be listened to much more than anyone who lived in the late eighteenth century. Those who believe in a "living" Constitution also share the Overclass sensibility on the perfectibility of human nature. They trust that some people will reliably be wise, knowledgeable, and perceptive, without unconscious biases, generous, caring, selfless, and almost perfect in character and intentions all day, every day; that we can accurately discern such people and appoint them to offices; and that they will not disappoint us in the performance of their duties.

This jurisprudence echoes the politics of joy—all can be for the best in the best of all possible worlds, just as the savants of the eighteenth-century European Enlightenment believed and predicted to the best of their ability back then—if only we mortals tried hard enough to get things right in our hearts and minds by listening to them and their insightful peers.

But of course, the jurisprudence believing in a "living" Constitution does not much take into account the observations of Nietzsche, the psychology of Freud, and the study of history where, many times, it is the strong and the fittest who thrive. As Thucydides reported Athenian generals believing, "The strong do what they can. The weak suffer what they must."

One of the first major U.S. Supreme Court cases to check the ambitions of the Overclass was *Lochner v. New York* in 1905.[50] The court held that personal constitutional rights to contract freely prevented the Overclass from regulating the decisions of a baker. Under its police powers to regulate conduct, New York State had passed a law that prohibited employment in bakeries for more than sixty hours per week. Lochner had been fined for having an employee work more than sixty hours a week.

The court looked at the facts from the perspective of the employee who accepted the work contract with the baker, asking whether the police powers of the state should honor the decision of the employee to work those hours for compensation mutually agreed upon. A majority of justices thought that "it becomes of great importance to determine which shall prevail—the right of the individual to labor for such time as he may choose, or the right of the State to prevent the individual from laboring—or from entering into any contract to labor, beyond a certain time prescribed by the State."[51]

The majority asked, "Is this a fair, reasonable and appropriate exercise of the police power of the State, or is it an unreasonable, unnecessary and arbitrary interference with the right of the individual to his personal liberty?" In answer the majority worried that such use of the police powers of the State would create "an all pervading power" and concluded, "We think the limit of the police power has been reached and passed in this case. . . . It seems to us that the real object and purpose were simply to regulate the hours of labor between the master and his employees, in a private business, not dangerous in any degree to morals or in any real and substantial degree, to the health of the employees. Under such circumstances the freedom of master and employee to contract with each other in relation to their employment, and in defining the same, cannot be prohibited or interfered with, without violating the Federal Constitution."[52]

Thus, the U.S. Supreme Court held that management of private lives by the Overclass acting officially through government was illegitimate under the founding principles of the United States as a republic.

In dissent, Justice Oliver Wendell Holmes raised the question of how to interpret words in the Constitution, specifically the words "due process of law" found in the Fourteenth Amendment. Holmes argued,

General propositions do not decide concrete cases. The decision will depend on a judgment or intuition more subtle than any articulate major premise. . . . Every opinion tends to become a law. I think that the word liberty in the Fourteenth Amendment is perverted when it is held to prevent the natural outcome of a dominant opinion, unless it can be said that a rational and fair man necessarily would admit that the statute proposed would infringe fundamental principles as they have been understood by the traditions of our people and our law. It does not need research to show that no such sweeping condemnation can be passed upon the statute before us. A reasonable man might think it a proper measure on the score of health.[53]

Holmes made the case for a living Constitution, the words of which contained in his mind inherent flexibility to provide a zone of freedom for the State to exercise its police powers within reason.

In 1934 in the case of *Nebbia v. New York*, the Supreme Court upheld a New York law using the state's police powers to establish a milk control board to fix the minimum and maximum prices for milk to be charged consumers by stores.[54] To uphold the law, a majority of the justices brought forward the rationale of an older case from 1877 that had held that private property, if voluntarily put to a use that affected the public, so gave the public a legitimate interest in how that property was used. Property, then, is neither always absolutely private nor absolutely public but, at times, can be both a private good and simultaneously a public good. Economists talk about this understanding of property, contracts, and business as the problem of externalities—what are the impacts, good or bad, intended or unintended, of economic actions? We then judge the merits of the action by its consequences and expect responsible owners to take into account those consequences before they decide to act. The majority affirmed, "The Constitution does not guarantee the unrestricted privilege to engage in a business or to conduct it as one pleases."[55]

They added, "The guaranty of due process, as has often been held, demands only that the law shall not be unreasonable, arbitrary or capricious, and that the means selected shall have a real and substantial relation to the object sought to be attained. . . . So far as the requirement of due process is concerned, and in the absence of other constitutional restriction, a state is free to adopt whatever economic policy may reasonably be deemed to promote public welfare, and to enforce that policy by legislation adapted to its purpose . . . If the laws passed are seen to have a reasonable relation to a proper legislative purpose, and are neither arbitrary nor discriminatory, the requirements of due process are satisfied."[56]

In this opinion, the Supreme Court found an interpretation of "property" that permitted the Overclass to use the government to manage American society and its economy. The safe space provided to owners in which they could use their property as they might wish was reduced considerably. Individuals, after all, were part of society and thus had obligations to others. An old saying was, "Your right to swing your fist ends where my nose begins."[57]

In 1937 in *West Coast Hotel v. Parrish*, a majority of the Supreme Court again upheld the legitimacy of Overclass rights to manage the rest of us as long as such management provided us with due process of law. The majority opinion affirmed,

> "The Constitution does not speak of freedom of contract. It speaks of liberty and prohibits the deprivation of liberty without due process of law. In prohibiting that deprivation the Constitution does not recognize an absolute and uncontrollable liberty. Liberty in each of its phases has its history and connotation. But the liberty safeguarded is liberty in a social organization which requires the protection of law against the evils which menace the health, safety, morals and welfare of the people. Liberty under the Constitution is thus necessarily subject to the restraints of due process, and regulation which is reasonable in relation to its subject and is adopted in the interests of the community is due process."[58]

After World War II, the Congress adopted comprehensive legislation striking a balance between the autonomy of private rights of property and liberty and the police power of the state to condition and restrain those rights. This was the Administrative Procedure Act (APA), and it gave rise to the practice and teaching of a new legal discipline— administrative law.

Supreme Court Chief Justice John Roberts said in *Loper Bright Enterprises v. Raimondo* (2024), "Congress in 1946 enacted the APA 'as a check upon administrators whose zeal might otherwise have carried them to excesses not contemplated in legislation creating their offices.' It was the culmination of a 'comprehensive rethinking of the place of administrative agencies in a regime of separate and divided powers.' In addition to prescribing procedures for agency action, the APA delineates the basic contours of judicial review of such action."[59]

The APA specifies how federal government agencies will publicize information about an agency and its rules, opinions, orders, and public records. They must publicly give notice of any proposed rulemaking and give interested persons an opportunity to participate in the rulemaking and, in any adjudication, give interested parties an opportunity to present facts, arguments, settlement proposals, or proposals of adjustments. The APA thus specifically imposed on federal agencies the obligation to provide due process in making decisions.

In 1984 a unanimous Supreme Court had given Overclass administrators great leeway in deciding how they would regulate Americans. The court reasoned that, as professionals and experts who trained and studied in technical disciplines beyond the ken of citizens and judges and especially knowing about facts and the relevant science, regulators would have the last word on how their decisions would be understood and enforced.[60] In this *Chevron* case, a nonprofit environmentalist advocacy group, the Natural Resources Defense Council, challenged the definition of a source of pollution adopted by the Environmental Protection Agency. Since the plants of the Chevron company were affected by that definition, Chevron joined the litigation.

The issue in *Chevron* was somewhat arcane and procedural—the authority to decide on the validity of a regulation as between judges and agency administrators. The practical side of the issue was the right of those objecting to an agency decision to appeal that decision to a court and so try to persuade the court to overrule the agency.

The issue of authority arose only when the congressional statute was ambiguous in its wording, when the black-letter law did not provide a resolution one way or the other of who should decide a dispute over an agency's interpretation of a statute. The Supreme Court in *Chevron* decided that, when there was doubt about meaning, deference would be given to the agency's interpretation, and no appeal to the courts would be permitted.

The Clean Air Act passed by the Congress made reference to "a new or modified stationary source" of air pollution, and the Environmental Protection Agency had interpreted those words. The relevance was whether a company contributing to air pollution needed a permit if it installed a new, or modified an older, "stationary source" of such pollution.

The National Resources Defense Council sought a court judgment overruling the EPA's interpretation of what constituted such a "stationary source" of pollution. The federal court of appeals in Washington, DC, overruled the agency.

The Supreme Court then overruled the court of appeals and restored the agency's interpretation: "The basic legal error of the Court of Appeals was to adopt a static judicial definition of the term 'stationary source' when it had decided that Congress itself had not commanded that definition."[61]

In giving preference to the agency's thinking, the Supreme Court took expertise into account. Hegel would very much have approved.

First, the court noted the special function of administrative agencies: "The power of an administrative agency to administer a congressionally created . . . program necessarily requires the formulation of policy and the making of rules to fill any gap left, implicitly or explicitly, by Congress," adding, "Such policy arguments are more properly addressed to legislators or administrators, not to judges."[62]

In the *Chevron* case, the court concluded that "the Administrator's interpretation represents a reasonable accommodation of manifestly competing interests and is entitled to deference . . . Judges are not experts in the field, and are not part of either political branch of the Government. . . . The responsibilities for assessing the wisdom of such policy choices and resolving the struggle between competing views of the public interest are not judicial ones."[63]

Chevron became a frequently cited case in American administrative law. Over seventeen thousand lower federal court decisions and seventy decisions by the Supreme Court itself cited *Chevron*. Between 2003 and 2013, circuit courts of appeal applied *Chevron* in 77% of decisions in disputes over agency action.

And yet, as with presidential elections, the pendulum of American legitimation would later swing against the Overclass. In June 2024 a six-to-three majority of the Supreme Court overruled *Chevron*. The new case of *Loper Bright Enterprises v. Raimondo*, mentioned above, involved a regulation applicable to fishing boats in the Atlantic herring fishery waters.

The National Marine Fisheries Service (NMFS) required that "one or more observers be carried on board" domestic vessels "for the purpose of collecting data necessary for the conservation and management of the fishery."[64] With respect to the Atlantic herring fishery, the agency created an industry-funded program that aims to ensure observer coverage on 50% of trips undertaken by vessels with certain types of permits. Under that program, vessel representatives must "declare into" a fishery before beginning a trip by notifying the agency of the trip and announcing the species the vessel intends to harvest. "If NMFS determined that an observer is required, but declines to assign a Government-paid one, the vessel must contract with and pay for a Government-certified third-party observer. NMFS estimated that the cost of such an observer would be up to $710 per day, reducing annual returns to the vessel owner by up to 20 percent."[65]

The statute setting up the agency did not authorize the agency to require the owners of fishing boats to pay for the observers required by a government-imposed fishery management plan.

Chief Justice Roberts saw the case as an attempt to legitimate plenary Overclass power to regulate the private sector. He decided to return constitutional and administrative law to the original intentions of the Framers of the Constitution and so to limit the discretionary authority of Overclass bureaucrats. He wrote in his opinion, "Article III of the Constitution assigns to the Federal Judiciary the responsibility and power to adjudicate 'Cases' and 'Controversies'—concrete disputes with consequences for the parties involved. The Framers appreciated that the laws judges would necessarily apply in resolving those disputes would not always be clear. Cognizant of the limits of human language and foresight, they anticipated that '[a]ll new laws, though penned with the greatest technical skill, and passed on the fullest and most mature deliberation,' would be 'more or less obscure and equivocal, until their meaning' was settled 'by a series of particular discussions and adjudications.'"[66]

Citing *The Federalist Papers*, Roberts wrote,

> The Framers also envisioned that the final 'interpretation of the laws' would be 'the proper and peculiar province of the courts.' Unlike the political branches, the courts would by design exercise 'neither Force nor Will, but merely judgment.' To ensure the 'steady, upright and impartial administration of the laws,' the Framers structured the Constitution to allow judges to exercise that judgment independent of influence from the political branches.[67]

Thus, Roberts gave discretion to constitutional bodies—the courts—and not to congressionally created political bodies—bureaucratic agencies. He continued,

> As relevant here, [the APA] directs that '[t]o the extent necessary . . . the reviewing court shall decide all relevant questions of law, interpret constitutional and statutory provisions, and determine the meaning or applicability of the terms of an agency action.' It further requires courts to 'hold unlawful and set aside agency action, findings, and conclusions found to be . . . not in accordance with law.' The APA thus codifies for agency cases the unremarkable, yet elemental proposition reflected by judicial practice dating back to *Marbury* [a very famous case with an opinion written by Chief Justice John

Marshall] that courts decide legal questions by applying their own judgment. It specifies that courts, not agencies, will decide 'all relevant questions of law' arising on review of agency action—even those involving ambiguous laws—and set aside any such action inconsistent with the law as they interpret it. And it prescribes no deferential standard for courts to employ in answering those legal questions. . . . The deference that *Chevron* requires of courts reviewing agency action cannot be squared with the APA. . . . Perhaps most fundamentally, *Chevron's* presumption is misguided because agencies have no special competence in resolving statutory ambiguities. Courts do.[68]

Roberts insisted, "The very point of the traditional tools of statutory construction—the tools courts use every day—is to resolve statutory ambiguities. That is no less true when the ambiguity is about the scope of an agency's own power—perhaps the occasion on which abdication in favor of the agency is least appropriate."[69]

Associate Justice Elena Kagan dissented. She was an accomplished member of the Overclass, having graduated from Princeton University, Worcester College, Oxford, and Harvard Law School. She was a professor at University of Chicago Law School and later Harvard Law School, where she became its first female dean. She also had befitting Overclass administrative experience as an associate White House counsel.

In her dissent Kagan defended the legitimacy of Overclass bureaucrats holding discretionary power over the people, saying,

Congress knows that it does not—in fact cannot—write perfectly complete regulatory statutes. It knows that those statutes will inevitably contain ambiguities that some other actor will have to resolve, and gaps that some other actor will have to fill. And it would usually prefer that actor to be the responsible agency, not a court. Some interpretive issues arising in the regulatory context involve scientific or technical subject matter. Agencies have expertise in those areas; courts do not. Some demand a detailed understanding of complex and interdependent regulatory programs. Agencies know those programs inside-out; again, courts do not.[70]

Using the God-State approach of Hegel, she continued,

For one, because agencies often know things about a statute's subject matter that courts could not hope to. The point is especially stark when the statute is of a 'scientific or technical nature.' Agencies are staffed with 'experts in the field' who can bring their training and knowledge to bear on open statutory questions. Consider, for example, . . . [w]hen does an alpha amino acid polymer qualify as a 'protein'? I don't know many judges who would feel confident resolving that issue.[71]

Kagan accused Roberts and the other justices in the majority of having a political agenda to "roll back agency authority, despite congressional direction to the contrary."

In another case that similarly invalidated agency discretion, another justice from the Overclass, Sonia Sotomayor, with great annoyance, opposed the decision on the grounds that it was inimical to the interests of the Overclass: "Make no mistake: Today's decision is a power grab."[72]

Sotomayor had graduated summa cum laude from Princeton University and received a Juris Doctor from Yale Law School, where she was an editor of the *Yale Law Journal*. She later taught at the New York University School of Law and Columbia Law School. Nominated by President Barack Obama, Sotomayor was the first non-White woman, the first Hispanic, and the first Latina to serve on the Supreme Court, an appointment consistent with the other-directed and ethic of care ideals of the Overclass.

And so the two sides were drawn: on one side, a commitment to the Constitution's concern for abuses of power and checks and balances and, on the other, a commitment to the Overclass and its experts.

Supreme Court justice and former Harvard Law professor Stephen Breyer wrote a defense of constitutional jurisprudence promoting Overclass management of American society. Breyer had taught me administrative law at Harvard Law School. He was a well-intentioned, very decent person who put before us first and foremost the facts situating judicial opinions and drew connections between principles and the impact of judicial decisions. I got the impression that, in his mind, administrative decision-making in a modern state was enlightened and most beneficial for all.

In his 2024 book, *Reading the Constitution*, Breyer offered an other-directed jurisprudence for interpreting the Constitution and so for legitimating the social function of the Overclass. He provided a pick-and-choose buffet of different rational paths for judges to use in reaching their decisions about what was permitted under the Constitution and what was not. He called his recommended approach "pragmatism."

By other-direction in judicial decision-making, I am referring to an open-ended, flexible approach not committed to consistent logical rigor and formal structures of meaning. Breyer understands that, inherently, words come in shades of meaning and that language does not have the precision of Pythagorean geometry, wherein a ninety-degree angle always has ninety degrees, in a world where each degree is exactly equal in measurement to every other degree.

He writes that "law is not a science."[73] He quotes with approval the preface to the English Anglican Church Book of Common Prayer. "That happy mean between too much stiffness in refusing and too much easiness in admitting variation in things once advisedly established."

In other-directed jurisprudence, a judge's conclusions do not come from an inner commitment to principle or from a fixed standpoint about the ends of justice. Rather, they come from reaching out to externals and manipulating them until some inner psychic comfort with their realities is found. In such other-directed decision-making, relevant criteria chosen to justify the decision will vary from case to case, regulation to regulation, and statute to statute.

Breyer points out that judges have used various tools to help them determine "the proper interpretation of the language of statutes and of the Constitution." He then argues that, in any given case, "which of these many tools proves most helpful depends upon the particular case."[74]

He quotes the respected Harvard Law School professor and later Supreme Court justice Felix Frankfurter, saying, "Laws are not abstract propositions. They are expressions of policy arising out of specific situations and addressed to the attainment of particular ends."[75] Laws, said Frankfurter, "have an aim"; they seek "to obviate some mischief, to supply an inadequacy, to effect a change of policy, to formulate a plan of government." Thus did Frankfurter then and Breyer today think of courts and judges as an extension of the administrative state, solving our problems and leading us forward to better days.

Breyer's purpose-based approach to judging has three facets: (1) to go from case to case, focusing on the facts and not trying to set a rule for all times; (2) to see how a decision in one case will mesh or not with other legal rules and principles *and* affect the lives of those who fall within their scope; and (3) to consider what a fictional "reasonable legislator" would do in this case to determine how a statute serves broader democratic ends.[76] In this last way of reaching a decision—reaching out to a mythic honest and noble mind—Breyer proposes using other-direction: Take your cues from another; align your mind with theirs.

Breyer affirms the legitimacy of judges taking into account in their decision-making the practical effect on society or the economy of their preferred decision. A legitimately pragmatic judge, he writes, will seek to discern if the proposed decision will "have a positive effect upon those to whom it applies (or to Americans in general), taking account of the institutions, practices, and beliefs that make up our legal web of beliefs."[77] In this consideration, Breyer writes, the judge is seeking some degree of confidence that the proposed decision will work "better" or will help society function "better."

Thus can judges keep the Constitution alive and evolving and not just on display behind a glass window in a museum of American history for visitors to give the document glances over their shoulders as they walk by. For Justice Breyer, what once was does not now have to be. From this perspective, the rule of law becomes a progressive force in society.

As Marc J. Dunkelman, writing in 2025 in the *Atlantic*, observed, "From progressivism's founding in the late 19th century into the 1960s, the movement offered a simple answer to the question of who should decide. Scientifically driven expertise was, to the progressive mind, the key to good public policy. That meant authorizing expert public officials—the establishment—to stand up holistic solutions to big challenges. Let the engineers design good sewer systems. Let the social workers design proper social-safety nets. Let the medical professionals design the health-care system."[78]

The *Begriff* of a "living Constitution" has even been extrapolated into rejection of the Constitution itself. For example, in comments like this one from author and regular MSNBC contributor Elie Mystal: "We should replace our piece-of-crap Constitution."[79] Or this one from *New York Times* writer Jennifer Szalai: "Americans have long assumed that the Constitution could save us. A growing chorus now wonders whether we need to be saved from it."[80] Or books from Erwin Chemerinsky (dean of the UC-Berkeley Law School) and law professors Ryan D. Doerfler of Harvard and Samuel Moyn of Yale with titles like *No Democracy Lasts Forever: How the Constitution Threatens the United States* and *The Constitution Is Broken and Should Not Be Reclaimed.*

Also in 2024, Breyer's Supreme Court colleague Justice Neil Gorsuch wrote his own book, *Over Ruled: The Human Toll of Too Much Law,* taking the contrary point of view. Gorsuch wrote to deconstruct the modern Enlightened legitimacy narrative uplifting Hegel's *Begriff* about the God-State when such a state was actually not administered by God but only by more sinful creatures.

Gorsuch's critique of administrative law echoes the judgment of Paul that the letter kills, but the spirit gives life (2 Cor. 3:6). Gorsuch decided to write the book because he had seen too many cases where "the sheer volume and complexity of our laws had swallowed up ordinary people."[81]

He noted, "The man who is told he can't see the evidence officials are relying on to reject his application for Social Security benefits; the veteran who is denied disability benefits because he fails to apply quickly enough for the taste of the Department of Veterans Affairs; the immigrant who follows the law and is still refused a place in this country because the government changes the rules of the game on him retroactively."[82]

He is bothered by the culture of the Overclass because it focuses on "the greater good our laws and regulations seek to achieve and the collective social progress they promise" when the impact on a particular individual of those laws and regulations is most regrettable.[83] He refers to "a process" that has caused "our laws and regulations to [have exploded] in number and have come to reach much more deeply into our daily lives . . . Much [of our law] comes from administrative sources largely unresponsive to democratic elections."[84] He asks, "But what about everyday Americans and the rights promised them in our Declaration of Independence, Constitution, and Bill of Rights? . . . What does it say about our nation's promise of equal treatment when our laws become so numerous and so complex that only an affluent or connected few can navigate their way? . . . In our eagerness for quick solutions, we sometimes look to agency officials rather than our elected representatives."[85]

Gorsuch gives an example of how much law there is out there: The printed reports of only federal judicial decisions fill more than five thousand volumes of about one thousand pages each, for a total of five million pages of law. He reports that by federal decree, macaroni must have a diameter between 0.11 and 0.27 inches and that Virginia prohibits hunting a bear with the assistance of dogs on Sundays.[86]

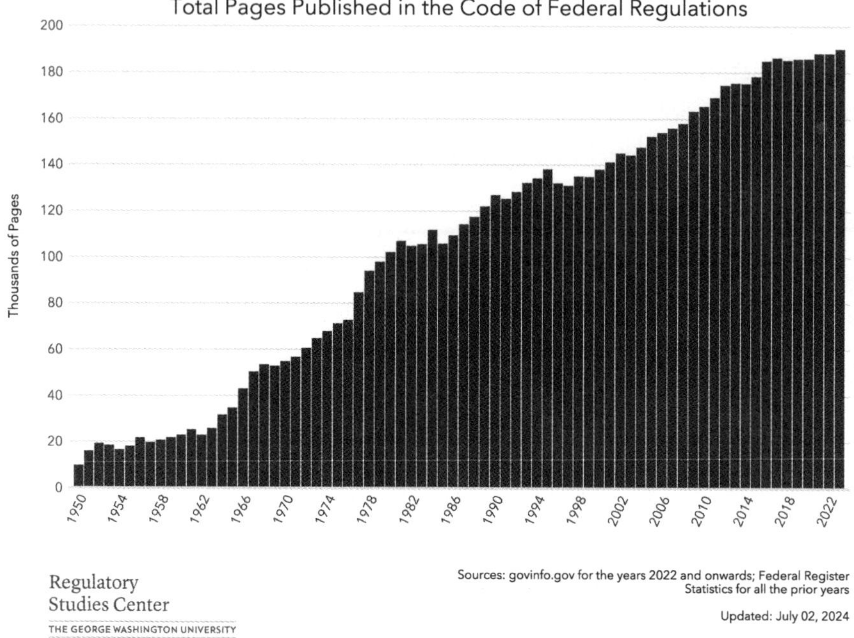

He also makes a causal connection between the proliferation of laws and regulations and the decline in citizen participation in civic associations along with the decline of trust in one another.[87] One may also ask if the decline in teaching civics in schools has reflected an awareness that, as we have more and more come to live under Overclass guidance and direction, the importance of citizens in our power structure is not what it once was.

He quotes James Madison, writing in *The Federalist Papers*, as still relevant.

> Another effect of public instability is the unreasonable advantage it gives to the sagacious, the enterprising, and the moneyed few over the industrious and uniformed mass of the people. Every new regulation concerning commerce or revenue, or in any way

affecting the value of the different species of property, presents a new harvest to those who watch the change, and can trace its consequences; a harvest, reared not by themselves, but by the toils and cares of the great body of their fellow-citizens. This is a state of things in which it may be said with some truth that laws are made for the FEW, not for the MANY.[88]

Gorsuch reprises the very important distinction between the rule *of* law and rule *by* law. The rule of law is a system of checks on rulers, legislators, officials, and the police. In our legal system, it takes its origin from the 1235 treatise of Henry de Bracton on English law, where he said that a "king must not be under man but under God and under the law, because law makes the king."[89] And similarly, Bracton also wrote that "the king has a superior, namely God. And also the law by which he is made king. Also his council, namely the earls and barons, because if he is without a bridle, that is without law, they ought to put the bridle on him."[90]

The motto *Non sub homine sed sub Deo et lege* (Not under man but under God and the law), taken from Bracton, is engraved over the main entrance to Langdell Hall at the Harvard Law School Library. When a student there, I would very favorably reflect for a second on that ideal of constitutionalism whenever entering the library through that door.

Rule *by* law, the regimes of dictators and tyrants, was well described by Shakespeare in a line from his play *Julius Caesar* when Marc Antony pledges, "When Caesar says 'Do this,' it is performed."[91]

Gorsuch ends his takedown of the Overclass and its jurisprudence of expertise with an appeal to individuals to show courage—"to labor courageously against great odds to sustain 'the fires of liberty.'"[92] This aligns him with admiration for inner-direction as the virtue needed to preserve the American constitutional republic.

In his 2024 book, *American Covenant,* Yuval Levin validates the analysis that Americans are divided between two inconsistent understandings of the purpose of their Constitution—one keeping to its original purpose of creating civic union through checks and balances and a process of compromise among factions who differ in their ideas and interests and the other centralizing power in a more autocratic government seeking to do good for the people as it defines their good. The first understanding of the Constitution seeks to achieve "an extraordinary balance between individual freedom and social order." The contrary understanding of the Constitution, says Levin, is "progressivism," a jurisprudence that "[insists] that every institution in our society, private and public, must be engaged in the same social crusade—no exceptions, no exemptions—and implicitly that there can be no society without a single, comprehensive common project."[93] This second understanding of the Constitution is defended by Breyer and forms the constitutional and regulatory preferences of the Overclass.

Levin adds that from the Progressive perspective, private interests "pursuing their own good at the expense of the good of the society . . . could only be overcome by an even more powerful champion of the public interest. This idea of the unifying leader clarifies the nature of progressive critique of the Constitution, because it combines two related conceptions of unity. One views unity as submission to a common authority, and the other a commitment to a shared understanding of the good."[94]

On both conceptions of unity, the Progressives could not in any way tolerate Donald Trump. As a unifying leader, he would destroy their "democracy," and he did not share their understanding of what was good for America. Thus, he had to be driven from politics with no regard for constitutional rights and procedures.

As if he wanted to prove the truth of Levin's thesis and enforce Breyer's open-ended theory of the Constitution, two days before stepping down as president—on January 17, 2025—Democrat Joe Biden issued a statement on his personal thinking intended to usurp the authority of the courts but dutiful to the Progressive, other-directed jurisprudence advocating a living Constitution. In other words, Biden advocated that constitutional law is what we here and now want it to be, thus not really law itself, but only whim and caprice or, as the courts say, when a decision-maker has exceeded their authority—"arbitrary and capricious," the very abuse of power that Bracton had rejected so many centuries ago at the birth of the common law of England.

President Biden's statement said, "On January 27, 2020, the Commonwealth of Virginia became the 38th state to ratify the Equal Rights Amendment. The American Bar Association (ABA) has recognized that the Equal Rights Amendment has cleared all necessary hurdles to be formally added to the Constitution as the 28th Amendment. I agree with the ABA and with leading legal constitutional scholars that the Equal Rights Amendment has become part of our Constitution. . . . In keeping with my oath and duty to Constitution and country, I affirm what I believe and what three-fourths of the states have ratified: the 28th Amendment is the law of the land."[95]

Appropriately, the American Bar Association, cited by President Biden as an authority on the Constitution, promotes the interests of a very important vanguard of the Overclass—law school graduates.

Only, the thirty-sixth, thirty-seventh, and thirty-eighth states to have approved the Equal Rights Amendment did so decades after the deadline for approval had passed, nullifying the legitimacy of their approvals. Moreover, six of the thirty-five other states that had once ratified the proposed amendment revoked their approval in subsequent years, leaving ratification of the amendment falling short by nine states.

A historic effort to squelch those fires of covenantal constitutional liberty, which Gorsuch and Levin are now once again stoking, occurred in a paradigm-shifting law review article written by Charles A. Reich in 1964, which boldly set forth a way of ensconcing Overclass social and economic management within the law. Reich proposed that entitlements resting on a promise of the state to transfer money or give permission to act should be considered as private property deserving of constitutional protection. Reich's article was called "The New Property."[96] He began with the recognition that "the institution called property guards the troubled boundary between individual man and the state" and then expanded the concept of property to move that boundary closer to the individual, thereby opening up more social space subject to the administrative prerogatives of the state.

For Reich, one person's expectations of benefits to be received from others were turned into legal rights in a proposed new legal culture of dependency on those others. The others Reich had in mind, of course, were the expert professionals working for the state who knew what was best for those under their care and control. Under the old law of property—the law of rightful ownership and personal agency to use your property however you saw fit within the law protecting the similar property rights of others—the inner-directed had a positive role to play in self-management. Under the new law of property, the inner-directed had less autonomy, while the other-directed had only a negative right to have others provide benefits.

In 1970 Reich wrote the book *The Greening of America*, full of praise for the success of the 1960s counterculture in breaking ranks with inner-direction and the traditional American covenant of personal responsibility. Reich was an outstanding member of the Overclass as editor in chief of the *Yale Law Journal* while in law school, being accepted by U.S. Supreme Court justice Hugo L. Black to work as his law clerk; working for the elite law firms Cravath, Swaine & Moore and Arnold & Porter; and becoming a professor at Yale Law School from 1960 to 1974.

Notable in its effort to legitimate the political superiority of the managerial state and denigrate the law as nothing more than a system "of the rulers, by the rulers, and for the rulers" was the critical legal studies movement. Critical legal scholars in academia sought to confound rules of law and judicial objectivity by pointing out inconsistencies in legal reasoning and convergences between rules of law and court decisions with the self-interests of the rich and the powerful, distancing the formal law from their Overclass ideals of social justice and sinking it into the icky muck of distasteful partisan politics and crass market decision-making. For critical legal scholars, the law should be flexible and ever changing to follow an ethic of care and was best left to the thinking of the well educated and the high-minded among us who would not make mistakes in reasoning or fall prey to selfish judgmental thinking. For these academicians, laws that embody the politics of the good—of properly guided other-directed persons—would be legitimate, and those laws that embodied the politics of the bad persons among us would be illegitimate and dismissed as morally null and void.

One of the founders of the critical legal studies movement was Harvard Law School professor Duncan Kennedy, who taught me contracts, sort of. When the casebook came to the doctrine of consideration, Duncan told us that such a doctrine was only a formalism, a fuddy-duddy conceptual heirloom passed down from premodern judges which we could ignore. But then he put a question about the doctrine in our final exam, which gave us our grade for the entire course.

Duncan was perhaps the most self-centered person I encountered as a student at the school. He was quite cynical, writing a law review article about the good that would come if we all elevated altruism in our lives and in the law. On one occasion, he advised a group of us planning on careers in legal education that, once we were on a tenure track, we should go Progressive left in our politics and teaching. That way, the school would not risk controversy by denying us tenure. Then after we had tenure and so were set for life, we could think any damn thing we pleased.

The Elections of 2024

In November 2024 the American people passed judgment on the Overclass, rejecting the legitimacy of its claims on their hearts, minds, and wallets. Donald Trump won reelection to the presidency, and the Republicans took control of the Senate and the House of Representatives. Trump's "Americanism," his "Make America great again" slogan, carried the most ethnically Hispanic county—Starr County, Texas—by 16% of the vote. Queens County voters in New York City moved 20% more toward the Republicans. Trump won the votes of 13% of African American men and of many women—44% of all women, 37% of Hispanic women, and 52% of White women.[97] Even in thoroughly Overclass-governed California, two Overclass prosecutors were turned out of office.

The Democratic candidate for president, Kamala Harris, positioned herself for that office on Woke criteria and failed to match Biden's voter support in the 2020 election in every state of the Union. Her campaign raised over $1 billion and spent hundreds of millions on advertising without success in converting a critical number of voters into supporting her.

The other-directed Overclass, manifesting its values in the Biden administration and the Harris campaign, did not—and could not—provide Americans with emotionally satisfying, steady, certain, uplifting, and enduring grounds for believing in themselves. If those Americans did not subscribe to the Gnostic management redemptions thrust on them by the Overclass, they were left on their own to flounder around inside a grab bag of hand-me-down identities. The alternative identities put before them by the Overclass were too frequently only based on race, sex, and resentment of others.

Bill Clinton's political mastermind, James Carville, offered this diagnosis of Kamala Harris's failure to attract a majority of American voters: "What killed the Democrats was a sense of disorder. And part of the disorder was the unfortunate events of what I would refer to as 'the Woke Era.'"[98]

After November 5, 2024, the Democratic Party cannot claim that it represents mainstream America. As the political party of the Overclass, it has become an invasive species seeking to change America into a more welcoming habitat for itself, just as Barack Obama once predicted, to "transform" America with policies and programs bringing "hope" and working "change." "Hope and change for whom exactly?" we may quite properly ask in retrospect.[99]

The day after the election, all serious commentators understood the election to have been a referendum on the Overclass. Democrats, bewildered by their losses, immediately took to ad hominem arguments that too many voters were racist or sexist or just "garbage." Their intellectual inability to understand the American people revealed the other-directedness that had encased them in an infantile need to manipulate their perceptions of reality into superficial self-validation.

One fierce opponent of Trump wrote that the election results were a damning condemnation of the American people themselves, both ignorant and spiteful toward their betters: "The media, it must be said, did not fulfill its role in educating the public and advancing truth as their primary objective. Refusal to explore Trump's manifest defects and place him and his movement in the context of fascist strongmen and their cults had the effect of normalizing and legitimizing a candidate utterly unfit for office. But the facts nevertheless were there for anyone who cared to look. At some point, voters are responsible for their own decisions."[100]

Others chimed in, sharing in the fragility of this Overclass other-directed ego-identity:

> Susan Glasser, a writer for *The New Yorker*: "It [Trump's election] is a disastrous revelation about what the United States really is, as opposed to the country that so many hoped that it could be."
>
> John Harwood, a journalist: "If you're accustomed, as I am, to believing that a critical mass of Americans embraces the values of freedom, pluralism, and common sense, the choice voters made defies comprehension."
>
> Jill Filipovic, a feminist author and columnist: "In the coming days there's gonna be a lot of opining about what the Harris campaign did wrong, but this election was not an indictment of Kamala Harris. It was an indictment of America."
>
> Peter Wehner, a fellow at the Trinity Forum: "This election was a CAT scan on the American people, and as difficult as it is

to say, as hard as it is to name, what it revealed, at least in part, is a frightening affinity for a man of borderless corruption. Donald Trump is no longer an aberration; he is normative."

George T. Conway, a never-Trumper: "America did this to itself. And now we must all suffer through it."[101]

David Ignatius of the *Washington Post*: "The Presidential election is a character test . . . also for the country, and this election makes me realize how little I understand the American character in 2024 . . . I am mystified by the outcome."[102]

Such would-be cultural overlords voice the superiority appropriate for their self-affirming Gnostic learning when suddenly and unexpectedly they are forced by events to confront the upsetting fact that there is, from their narrative's perspective, real evil in the world.

Chris Lehmann, in the *Nation*, perceived very correctly that the 2024 election was a referendum on the Overclass, a referendum won by Donald Trump:

[A] deliberate trashing of the model of impartial and impersonal governance handed down in the liberal tradition from the goo-goos and Mugwumps of the late 19th century. Appalled by the self-dealing excesses of Gilded Age governance, these crusading reformers promoted civil service reforms and the abolition of the party bosses' spoils system, while also extolling extensions of voter sovereignty via measures like ballot initiatives and the popular election of senators.

But behind many of these innovations was a covert bid for a more high-minded brand of class rule, in which experts and educated elites would lay claim to the public weal on grounds of general enlightenment . . . This Progressive model of reform gained broader popular traction during the New Deal, when FDR and his brain trust engineered a new battery of government programs to redistribute resources and work opportunities to workers left behind in the Great Depression.

Today, however, on the far side of this meritocratic social contract, Trump and his cronies have driven home the claim that all government operations are definitionally self-dealing ones, and that the meritocracy has always been a farce.

In the face of the Trumpian assault on meritocracy, Democratic Party elites continue to mistakenly cling to the core precepts of meritocratic rule.[103]

Noted pollster Nate Silver wrote that the 2024 election "was in some ways more shocking than 2016—and much more of a middle finger to the expert class." For roughly the past twenty years, Democrats have become increasingly the party of the educated. Silver calls the social composition of this political party the "Indigo Blob."

[A] merger between formerly nonpartisan institutions like the media, academia, and public health on the one hand—institutions that draw almost exclusively from the ranks of college graduates—and expressly partisan and political instruments of the Democratic Party and progressive advocacy groups on the other hand.

The Indigo Blob has control of the "means of moral production": it writes the story, at least as supposedly respectable people are expected to read it. It runs the newspapers and writes the Hollywood scripts. It awards the BAs, MDs and PhDs. And it seeks to shut out and shut up dissenters—it can be absolutely vicious toward [those who think differently].

The Indigo Blob can weave superficially compelling narratives . . . [It] just lost an election to Donald Trump. And it's losing the battle of ideas, the one thing that it's supposed to win.[104]

Astute Democrats understood that their party had become the vanguard of an elite class, though they had no understanding of the sociology and history of their own class—the Overclass: "If you think about sociological base of the Democratic Party today—the combination of demographic, geographic, and occupational backgrounds of the institutional leaders, donors, base voters, and activists that make up the party—it's stocked mainly with college-educated people from big cities and coastal states who work in non-profit organizations, universities, knowledge economy jobs, the media and entertainment, public sector unions, some parts of big tech, and in traditional professions such as the law."[105]

Just so, immediately after their soul-crushing electoral defeat, Democrats began to look for a new way forward for their party, a different politics that would gain the support of more Americans than had voted for their candidates in 2024. One strategy proposed with some conviction was for the party to return to its traditional role of representing the interests of "working class" Americans against the "malefactors of great wealth." This cannot happen and will not happen. In the real world, there is no going back in time. The Democrat Party is the party of the Overclass. To abandon the Overclass will leave it in a shambles without money and without a social power structure legitimating its programs and policies. Like tigers trapped in a cage, the Democrats can't just peel off their stripes. If they change their message, switch out their narrative, and abandon the other-directed managerial class, who will vote for them?

If they decide to no longer represent the Overclass, they will automatically lose support from those less well-to-do Americans who are their clients, economically dependent on their class—a more servile underclass of Americans who need rent transfers of money from the government for housing, personal income, education, and health care, those earning under $30,000 a year. These Americans have become wards of the God-State: without agency, lacking remunerative skills, poorly educated, and with little hope for improving their lives.

The argument that Mikhail Bakunin made against Marxist Communism applies again today to the dreams of those Democrats who want their party to be the party of the "working class." Bakunin understood that an elite party of managers—no matter how well intentioned—could only "boss around" and impose life circumstances on their inferior, dependent clients—the workers, who would not have personal agency to speak or act for themselves. Had anything changed in 150 years that would now invalidate Bakunin's prediction?

One prominent Democrat, Rahm Emanuel, a former mayor of Chicago, said bluntly that Democrats "use language to feel good about ourselves, not to communicate. We all think we're applying to be adjunct professors at a small liberal arts college. We don't listen to people. We tell them how to eat their peas."[106]

The Democrats are dominated in cultural orientation by the Progressive activists, whose views do not align with moderate and conservative Americans. These Progressive Democrats have "no doubts" that White privilege and sexism prevail in America. They are three times more likely to believe that people's life outcomes are the result of "luck and circumstance" (75%), to be ashamed of being an American (69%), and to be very proud of their political ideology (64%).[107] With their minds so fixed on these *Begriffs*, these Progressive activists cannot provide leadership for a covenantal people.

On June 24, 2025, a Democratic Socialist, Zohran Mamdani, won the Democratic primary to run for mayor of New York City. In late July 2025, State Senator Omar Fateh, another Democratic Socialist, was endorsed by the Democratic Party as its chosen candidate for mayor of Minneapolis.

Even before all of that happened, a former Democrat lashed out,

They're officially the party of Ivy League snobs, self-absorbed race grievance fools, unabashed elitists & unlikable nerds. . . .

But now, the Democrats are the party of dogma. There is nothing inquisitive or reflective about the party. They are verbal one-trick ponies, twisting their words to validate their end-goal ambition regardless if it works or not.

They're no longer the party of ideas but the party of a singular idea: Use identity to shield criticisms and make our upper-class overlords appear like good people.

And any moron can repeat an idea over and over and the louder you repeat it, the more you get elevated. Oh, and it doesn't hurt if your parents are well-connected or rich.

Their slogans are lame and have no substance to them. It's just drivel married to nothing substantive in the real world. But worst, their ideas always end up benefiting the wealthiest and most privileged Americans.

I've seen these people revel in the idea of being "educated" and everyone else who didn't earn a useless degree in bullshit studies as being "uneducated." Some of the trust fund children who got everything in life because someone handed it to them think they are better than the rest of us.

I ultimately left the Democrats because they abandoned classical liberal principles to kiss the ring of ideological elites.[108]

Sasha Stone, with appropriate realism, rebuked these Democratic mandarins for their inability to outgrow their needy fixation on other-direction. "No, this is a moment to allow the empire [the Overclass] to collapse completely and rebuild from scratch, to think about what the party stands for and what direction they wish to take this country. They've lost their way and lost their purpose."[109]

But after extreme and, from their point of view, heroic Overclass efforts to destroy Donald Trump's ability to run for the presidency and, further, his ability to win the support of Americans using an "all of government approach," supplemented with accusations of fascism, insurrection, racism, and lawbreaking (rape and fraud) and use of the courts to disqualify him as a citizen in good standing, a majority of American voters, nevertheless, turned on the Overclass. These Americans rejected Overclass guidance. Further, they refused to accept the good-faith legitimacy of its various malicious persecutions of Donald Trump.

Opinionated and frankly speaking commentator Tucker Carlson said, "People know in a country that has been taken over by a leadership class that actually despises them and their values and their history and their culture and their customs—really hates them to the point that it is trying to replace them—when someone actually has affection for them . . . and that is Donald Trump."[110]

One Democratic loyalist was more observant, writing,

> But because of their own class-inflected blind spots, that continues to be the basic message liberals send to the American people: "You don't get it." And the message in return was, "No, *you* don't get it." A political party is meant, among other things, to be a system of feedback between the populace and the governing classes. Among Democratic Party leaders this cycle, the feedback mechanism broke—or worse, was deliberately ignored. . . .
>
> The Democrats, in retreat from any meaningful mandate of popular accountability, have transformed themselves into the party of the establishment: wonks, statisticians, professionals, hectoring nonprofit advocates, celebrities, reformers, lecturers (in all senses of the word), assistant professors, and corporate beancounters. They worship G-men, spooks, and generals as minor deities. In a postelection piece for *The New Yorker*, Rachel Maddow lamented that the American people didn't listen to the 'experts.' That sentence alone tells you everything you need to know.[111]

A July 2025 *Wall Street Journal* poll revealed that 63% of Americans rejected Overclass management of their society, economy, and politics. Only 8% of voters had a "very favorable" view of the Democratic Party, which provides the Overclass with its political leadership. A Democratic pollster who worked on the *Journal* survey, John Anzalone, said "Until [the Democrats] reconnect with real voters and working people on who they're for and what their economic message is, they're going to have problems."[112]

After his election, acting on a primal instinct to check the Overclass, Donald Trump immediately set about taking away from that class its privilege of imposing its particular Gnostic *Begriffs* on the American people. Trump appointed to the most senior positions in his forthcoming administration persons who would deconstruct culturally the *Begriffs* of the Overclass and also disestablish its managerial power to deploy agencies of the federal government in furtherance of its class interests. In general Trump's first appointees, both men and women, appeared to be inner-directed in ways aligned with America's covenantal tradition. A precursor to his postelection personnel decisions had been his selection of J. D. Vance as his vice presidential running mate. Though a graduate of Yale Law School, Vance retained an ability to think and speak out for himself as he described his struggle to find an ego-identity of substance in his autobiography, *Hillbilly Elegy.*

Then for his secretary of defense, Trump selected Pete Hegseth—by no means a baron of the Washington power elite but rather a more lowly combat veteran and outspoken critic of the Overclass doctrine of Woke social justice as applied to the armed forces, who are charged with winning wars. Most creatively, Trump appointed Elon Musk, an immigrant always following his own genius to make the federal government more efficient and smaller.

In perhaps the pièce de résistance of his appointments—and as a smack in the face of the Overclass—Trump named Robert F. Kennedy Jr., nephew of an assassinated president and son of an assassinated candidate for president, as secretary of the Department of Health and Human Services. Upon maturing, Kennedy developed very independent, even idiosyncratic, thinking that was very inner-directed. His intellectually perfect quip on Hegel's design of the God-State was, "Trusting the experts is a function of religion and totalitarianism . . . In democracy, we question everybody."[113]

In this reorientation of federal leadership, Trump was acting as if he had read several of *The Federalist Papers* on the needs for checks and balances. The moral premise of those essays on constitutionalism is that if men were angels, no government would be necessary, and therefore, in human hearts and minds, power has an "encroaching nature" and so must be "effectually restrained from passing the limits assigned to it."[114] "The genius of Republican liberty seems to depend on one side, not only that all power should be derived from the people, but that those intrusted with it should be kept in dependence on the people."[115] Further, "you must first enable the government to control the governed, but in the next place oblige it to control itself. A dependence on the people [as happened in the 2024 elections] is, no doubt, the primary control on government, but experience has taught mankind the necessity of auxiliary precautions."[116]

The means to keep power from encroachment is to provide checks and balances on its exercise: "ambition must be made to counteract ambition."[117] Thus, when Trump appointed inner-directed persons to counteract the cultural aspirations of the other-directed Overclass, he was simply putting to work the wisdom of James Madison and Alexander Hamilton.

The Second Trump Presidency

Donald Trump's second presidency began on January 20, 2025, with an address to the nation and the signing of numerous executive orders to set policy and establish programs for his incoming administration. In his inaugural address, Trump dedicated himself to overthrowing, or at least marginalizing, the Overclass. He asserted that Americans were mired in a crisis of trust—or rather lack of trust. "We now have a government that cannot manage even a simple crisis at home while at the same time stumbling into a continuing catalog of catastrophic events abroad."[118]

He excoriated the Overclass for management failures: a public health system that does not deliver, an educational system that teaches our children to be ashamed of themselves and to hate their country, a southern border that provides no defense against illegal entry, failure to protect free speech, destroying wealth for the middle class and the real value of incomes through inflation by massive overspending, and failure to "forge a society that is colorblind and merit-based." He pledged to create a Department of Government Efficiency to "restore competence and effectiveness to our federal government," taking a policy axe to hack away at the central fortifications empowering the Overclass, a vast management structure 150 years in the making.[119]

He also committed to devalue the cultural capital accumulated by the Overclass in its commitment to discriminating among Americans based on their race, gender, or sexuality. He rather sophomorically tried to associate his new administration with "truth" rather than with elite, socially constructed *Begriffs* and narratives, saying, "This week, I will also end the government policy of trying to socially engineer race and gender into every aspect of public and private life. . . . As of today, it will henceforth be the official policy of the United States government that there are only two genders, male and female."[120]

He claimed a mandate to "completely and totally reverse a horrible betrayal" and to end American dysphoria. "To give the people back their faith . . . From this moment on, America's decline is over. . . . For American citizens, January 20, 2025, is Liberation Day. . . . [Americans will] once again act with courage, vigor, and the vitality of history's greatest civilization. . . . In America, the impossible is what we do best. . . . we will be proud. . . . we will not be broken and we will not fail."[121]

As he framed his vision, we can infer that his MAGA movement, seeking to "make America great again," is an instinctively insightful alternative to the identity dysphoria that has disheartened so many Americans.

An appropriate historical precedent for Trump's agenda was the taking of the Tennis Court Oath on June 20, 1789, by representatives of France's new middle class—the Third Estate—"not to separate and to reassemble wherever necessary until the Constitution of the Kingdom is established." Members of the Third Estate had already called themselves the "National Assembly"—representing the French people—not the king, the aristocracy, or the Catholic clergy.[122] The French Revolution thus began with identity politics answering the question of who was "French."

A week after Trump's inauguration, a comment in *The New Yorker* perfectly encapsulated the myopia of the Overclass about the reasons for its fall from grace—it found a new way to blame the American people, namely, "the way much of the country emerged from the pandemic—frustrated with rules, strictures, and instructions of all types, and with the principles behind them. What was once a niche campaign against diversity-equity-and inclusion programs has metastasized into a general anti-idealism."[123] This was only a way of saying that many Americans had finally turned against the legitimating conceits of Overclass *Begriffs*.

On February 18, 2025, Trump took official action to roll back the legitimation of unelected Overclass administrative agencies, reversing the concentration of its class power, which had commenced with President Woodrow Wilson. Trump issued an executive order that brought those agencies under the constitutional authority of the presidency.[124] The order said,

> By the authority vested in me as President by the Constitution and the laws of the United States of America, it is hereby ordered:
>
> <u>Section 1</u>. <u>Policy and Purpose</u>. The Constitution vests all executive power in the President and charges him with faithfully executing the laws. Since it would be impossible for the

President to single-handedly perform all the executive business of the Federal Government, the Constitution also provides for subordinate officers to assist the President in his executive duties. In the exercise of their often-considerable authority, these executive branch officials remain subject to the President's ongoing supervision and control. The President in turn is regularly elected by and accountable to the American people. This is one of the structural safeguards, along with the separation of powers between the executive and legislative branches, regular elections for the Congress, and an independent judiciary whose judges are appointed by the President by and with the advice and consent of the Senate, by which the Framers created a Government accountable to the American people.

However, previous administrations have allowed so-called independent regulatory agencies to operate with minimal presidential supervision. These regulatory agencies currently exercise substantial executive authority without sufficient accountability to the president and, through him, to the American people. Moreover, these regulatory agencies have been permitted to promulgate significant regulations without review by the president.

These practices undermine such regulatory agencies' accountability to the American people and prevent a unified and coherent execution of federal law. For the federal government to be truly accountable to the American people, officials who wield vast executive power must be supervised and controlled by the people's elected president.

Therefore, to improve the administration of the executive branch and to increase regulatory officials' accountability to the American people, it shall be the policy of the executive branch to ensure presidential supervision and control of the entire executive branch. Moreover, all executive departments and agencies, including so-called independent agencies, shall submit for review all proposed and final significant regulatory actions to the Office of Information and Regulatory Affairs (OIRA) within the Executive Office of the President before publication in the *Federal Register*.[125]

Then, as if inspired by some intuitive instinct to seek out ways to delegitimize and disempower the Overclass, President Trump issued executive order after executive order marginalizing the Overclass and uprooting its sources of power and authority. He focused his incoming administration on attacking (1) the Department of Education, (2) bloat and waste in the bureaucracies of the federal government, and (3) wokeness and DEI (diversity, equity, and inclusion). Trump's instincts for where power comes from and how it is used guided him to attack the funding of the Overclass and its moral justification for managing Americans and their individual lives. On the one hand, Trump proposed to hollow out or eliminate the "permission structures" used by the Overclass to maintain assent to its policies and narrative and, on the other, to deny it rent transfers and other sources of income.

Education

The Department of Education was created by President Jimmy Carter as a political reward to the National Education Association for its support of his election in 1976. The department proceeded to fund education with transfers of funds collected from taxpayers (rents) conditioned on compliance with department mandates about what was to be taught, to whom, by whom, and how. Thus was a partnership launched uniting the government and the Overclass in a common cause: recruiting, training, and certifying new members of the Overclass to staff the nation's public and private white-collar bureaucracies.

Thus was Hegel's vision of a managerial elite implementing without fear—but with very high-minded and specific favoritism—an American

God-State of progressive good intent systematically put into practice in the postmodern United States.

On March 20, 2025, Trump issued an executive order stating:

> Our Nation's bright future relies on empowered families, engaged communities, and excellent educational opportunities for every child. Unfortunately, the experiment of controlling American education through Federal programs and dollars— and the unaccountable bureaucracy those programs and dollars support—has plainly failed our children, our teachers, and our families. . . . Closing the Department of Education would provide children and their families the opportunity to escape a system that is failing them. Today, American reading and math scores are near historical lows. This year's National Assessment of Educational Progress showed that 70 percent of 8th graders were below proficient in reading, and 72 percent were below proficient in math. The Federal education bureaucracy is not working. . . . The Secretary of Education shall, to the maximum extent appropriate and permitted by law, take all necessary steps to facilitate the closure of the Department of Education and return authority over education to the States and local communities while ensuring the effective and uninterrupted delivery of services, programs, and benefits on which Americans rely.[126]

Trump indicted the Overclass for management failure in education. His effort to reduce Overclass dominion over American culture and politics through its control over identifying, educating, and certifying as suitable for class membership, new recruits for the Overclass extended to private universities.

In the cultural rivalry between the Overclass and American covenantal individualism, Harvard University has great symbolic importance, beginning as a covenantal Puritan college but later transforming itself after the Civil War into a citadel of the Overclass. Thus, for Trump's "Make America great again" rhetoric, continuous attacks on Harvard's status and cultural power provide strategic advances in narrative. If the citadel falls, the "deplorables" can bask in the sunshine of social victory.

So on April 11, 2025, the acting general counsels of the Department of Education and the Department of Health and Human Services wrote a letter to the president of Harvard University demanding certain reforms. The letter implied that, should Harvard not meet the standards set by the federal government, it would lose federal funding:

> Harvard has in recent years failed to live up to both the intellectual and civil rights conditions that justify federal investment. But we appreciate your expression of commitment to repairing those failures and welcome your collaboration in restoring the University to its promise. We therefore present the below provisions as the basis for an agreement in principle that will maintain Harvard's financial relationship with the federal government.[127]

The private university was instructed to do the things listed below, among others:

- By August 2025, the university must adopt and implement merit-based hiring policies and cease all preferences based on race, color, religion, sex, or national origin throughout its hiring, promotion, compensation, and related practices among faculty, staff, and leadership.
- By August 2025, the university must adopt and implement merit-based admissions policies and cease all preferences based on race, color, national origin, or proxies thereof, throughout its undergraduate program, each graduate

program individually, each of its professional schools, and other programs.

- By August 2025, the university shall commission an external party, which shall satisfy the federal government as to its competence and good faith, to audit the student body, faculty, staff, and leadership for viewpoint diversity, such that each department, field, or teaching unit must be individually viewpoint diverse. . . . Every department or field found to lack viewpoint diversity must be reformed by hiring a critical mass of new faculty within that department or field who will provide viewpoint diversity. [Viewpoint diversity would ring a death knell for the Overclass, which cannot survive without the cultural and political power to maintain and inculcate its legitimating *Begriff*.]

- The university must immediately shutter all diversity, equity, and inclusion (DEI) programs, offices, committees, positions, and initiatives, under whatever name, and stop all DEI-based policies, including DEI-based disciplinary or speech control policies, under whatever name; demonstrate that it has done so to the satisfaction of the federal government; and demonstrate to the satisfaction of the federal government that these reforms are durable and effective through structural and personnel changes.

The Trump administration then proposed to reconsider federal funding of research at American universities through the payment of overhead expenses allocated by the schools to the costs included in the budgets of individual research endeavors. Taxpayer funding of such overhead expenses is a rent transfer from citizens to the schools through the good offices of the federal government using its authority to levy taxes and then spend the proceeds as it sees fit. Overhead expenses have run up to 70% of the grants awarded. The Trump administration preferred to cap such payments at 15% of grant monies disbursed, saving the taxpayers more than $4 billion annually.

On April 23, 2025, President Trump went for the umbilical cord between higher education and the Overclass. He questioned the system for accrediting colleges and universities and so permitting them to play God in recruiting and training generations of entrants into the Overclass of managers and other professional experts. Being an accredited educational institution is a gift of great social power. Who should deserve to be so trusted with such control of our future?

Trump's executive order on accreditation put the issue this way:

A group of higher education accreditors are the gatekeepers that decide which colleges and universities American students can spend the more than $100 billion in Federal student loans and Pell Grants dispersed each year. The accreditors' job is to determine which institutions provide a quality education—and therefore merit accreditation. Unfortunately, accreditors have not only failed in this responsibility to students, families, and American taxpayers, but they have also abused their enormous authority.

Accreditors routinely approve institutions that are low-quality by the most important measures. The national six-year undergraduate graduation rate was an alarming 64 percent in 2020. Further, many accredited institutions offer undergraduate and graduate programs with a negative return on investment—almost 25 percent of bachelor's degrees and more than 40 percent of master's degrees—which may leave students financially worse off and in enormous debt by charging them exorbitant sums for a degree with very modest earnings potential.

The Order added:

Some accreditors make the adoption of unlawfully discriminatory practices a formal standard of accreditation, and therefore a condition of accessing Federal aid, through "diversity, equity, and inclusion" or "DEI"-based standards of accreditation that require institutions to "share results on diversity, equity, and inclusion (DEI) in the context of their mission by considering . . . demographics . . . and resource allocation."

To realign accreditation with high-quality, valuable education for students, the Secretary of Education shall, consistent with applicable law, take appropriate steps to ensure that:

(i) accreditation requires higher education institutions to provide high-quality, high-value academic programs free from unlawful discrimination or other violations of Federal law.

Thus, President Trump ordered:

The Secretary of Education shall, as appropriate and consistent with applicable law, hold accountable, including through denial, monitoring, suspension, or termination of accreditation recognition, accreditors who fail to meet the applicable recognition criteria or otherwise violate Federal law, including by requiring institutions seeking accreditation to engage in unlawful discrimination in accreditation-related activity under the guise of "diversity, equity, and inclusion" initiatives.[128]

On May 1, 2025, President Trump issued another executive order to impede the work of two private Overclass organizations that produce radio and television journalism—National Public Radio and the Public Broadcasting Service. Both organizations are prestigious and influential operations of the Overclass, directed and staffed by members of the Overclass and broadcasting their productions principally to other members of that class.

Trump's order stood on the premise that the government's Corporation for Public Broadcasting under law may not "contribute to or otherwise support any political party." Trump then asserted that the corporation "fails to abide by these principles to the extent it subsidizes NPR and PBS. Which viewpoints NPR and PBS promote does not matter. What does matter is that neither entity presents a fair, accurate, or unbiased portrayal of current events to taxpaying citizens."

Trump therefore instructed the corporation's board of directors and all executive departments and agencies to cease federal funding for National Public Radio and the Public Broadcasting Service.[129]

On August 1, 2025, the Corporation for Public Broadcasting itself announced that it is beginning to close down given that President Trump had signed into law a bill passed with a party-line vote in the Congress clawing back $1.1 billion in funding for public broadcasting through fiscal year 2027.

DOGE

Then Trump smashed his way into the *sanctum sanctorum* of the Overclass: tenured civil service careers in the federal government.

On January 20, 2025, Trump created a new, temporary executive department agency, renaming the United States Digital Service as the United States Department of Government Efficiency (DOGE) Service and establishing it in the Executive Office of the President.

He appointed Elon Musk, a most opinionated entrepreneur, to lead the DOGE effort to investigate all government programs, seeking to eliminate those considered ineffective or redundant or too wasteful. Over the next three months offices would be closed, including the Agency for International Development, and thousands of employees would be discharged. In the first three months of DOGE efforts to prune back the size of the Overclass funded by the federal government, at least 121,000 federal workers were fired or laid off.[130] Lawsuits were brought to challenge the legality of such somewhat impulsive discharges from civil service employment.

On February 11, 2025, President Trump ordered that: "Agency Heads shall promptly undertake preparations to initiate large-scale reductions in force (RIFs), consistent with applicable law, and to separate from Federal service temporary employees and reemployed annuitants working in areas that will likely be subject to the RIFs."

DEI

In recent years antiracism, or rather neoracism, where discrimination is turned in un-traditional directions, has been given the elevated social and cultural function—noted by Antonio Gramsci and critical theorists—of providing legitimation for a hegemonic ruling class of "right thinking" managers. Criteria of race (defined as resulting from genetically determined skin color) and gender (determined at birth by DNA or in practice by choice) have been used to favor some Americans over others regardless of individual merit, hard-earned experience, or determined self-mastery. DEI legitimated entitlement orientations toward life for some and caused resentment over unfair exclusion for others.

On January 21, President Trump signed an executive order insisting that:

> Longstanding Federal civil-rights laws protect individual Americans from discrimination based on race, color, religion, sex, or national origin. These civil-rights protections serve as a bedrock supporting equality of opportunity for all Americans. As President, I have a solemn duty to ensure that these laws are enforced for the benefit of all Americans.
>
> Yet today, roughly 60 years after the passage of the Civil Rights Act of 1964, critical and influential institutions of American society, including the Federal Government, major corporations, financial institutions, the medical industry, large commercial airlines, law enforcement agencies, and institutions of higher education have adopted and actively use dangerous, demeaning, and immoral race- and sex-based preferences under the guise of so-called "diversity, equity, and inclusion" (DEI) or "diversity, equity, inclusion, and accessibility" (DEIA) that can violate the civil-rights laws of this Nation.
>
> Illegal DEI and DEIA policies not only violate the text and spirit of our longstanding Federal civil-rights laws, they also

undermine our national unity, as they deny, discredit, and undermine the traditional American values of hard work, excellence, and individual achievement in favor of an unlawful, corrosive, and pernicious identity-based spoils system. Hardworking Americans who deserve a shot at the American Dream should not be stigmatized, demeaned, or shut out of opportunities because of their race or sex.[131]

This is a broadside against the presumption of the Overclass that only a certain kind of merit—the merit of having a special class identity and values-orientation—can qualify one for recognition and preferment in our culture, society, economy, and institutions exercising political authority.

In his frantic efforts to depose the Overclass of its authority, power, and hegemonic presumption, Trump applied the discretionary prerogative powers given to the president by Article II of the Constitution. The response of the Overclass to his strategic onslaught was to double down on the narrative that Trump was an authoritarian, an autocrat. Such an accusation made great sense to members of the Overclass. One who rejected Overclass direction, one who was not other-directed with respect to the Overclass, looking to it as the source of right-minded ideas and ideals, policies and programs, seeking the "best interests" of the American community, had to be authoritarian, contumacious, and so a threat to democracy.

Democracy, of course, for the Overclass as its shepherd, had to be defined substantively as what would be—in the thinking of that class—beneficial for those Americans subject to its stewardship—not what the American people wanted for themselves, following their own ingrown ideas of what they thought would be in their best interests. Progressive—Overclass—Democracy is substantive—outcome driven and by outcome justified. Real Democracy, however, is procedural—an inclusive process of decision-making accepting diversity of opinion and a multiplicity of self-interests.

Trump was indeed a full-throated antagonist to this self-centered Overclass perception of self and other. Indeed, Trump and his administration were not at all directed by Overclass sentiments and suppositions. Thus, from the perspective of the Overclass, Trump and his appointees were very improperly directed and so had to be shunned for impudently standing outside the paradigm of acceptable "democratic" behaviors.

The other-directed, therefore, are, by *a priori* assertion, chosen to be the genuine democrats among the American people. They possess the virtue of seeking credentialed influencers to wisely guide them toward "real" truth and personal happiness. This reliance on the other-directed explains neatly why Democratic party activists concentrate their attention on "messaging" as the key to obtaining and keeping political power in America. Messaging provides direction to the other-directed, keeping them supportive of Overclass privileges.

Challenges to Trump's use of presidential prerogative were quickly brought to federal courts demanding the application of law to his decisions. The courts were thus empowered by litigants, as intended by the Constitution, to determine who had what authority to direct the republic going forward.

The revelations in 2025 of Jeffrey Epstein's sprawling sex trafficking operation and the alleged participation of many Overclass darlings like former President Clinton and former president of Harvard University and Treasury Secretary Larry Summers, among others, are emblematic of the selfish dysfunction, decadence, and moral taint distinguishing their ethic of presumption of power to be abused without consequence—something like the robber barons of the 1890s.

The September 2025 assassination of Charlie Kirk by a twenty-two-year-old unhappily dysphoric young Mormon triggered an identity crisis for Americans: Who are we and who are they? It was immediately apparent to me that Kirk's young assassin was, with some rationality, defending the right of the Overclass to impose its new thinking on Americans.

A consensus immediately emerged after Kirk's death, among commentators and on social media, that there was no consensus to be had among Americans. To invoke the 2016 prejudice of Hillary Clinton, Americans suddenly woke up to the fact that they are divided either/or into the Overclass and the Deplorables. As an American, one now had to choose sides in what was becoming a kind of religious war of "us" against "them." As a Christian accepting a Covenantal America, Kirk reached out to college-age Americans still in the process of forming their personal identities. He still dreamed, following Calvinist John Winthrop, of America as a "City Upon a Hill." Kirk's success in building a cultural movement rejecting the Hegelian *Begriffs* and the Rousseauist General Will of a ruling Overclass was a knife-to-the-throat threat to the legitimacy of that Overclass.

Many Americans ascribing to Overclass status and narratives spoke of Kirk as having been deplorable in mind and heart and so to have been an "other," not deserving membership among the righteous or a safe space for his ideas (or even for his life). The more sophisticated Overclass politicians and commentators tried to have it both ways: Kirk's death was unacceptable, but he was not one of us, so . . .

The "Deplorables" spoke up by the thousands on X, TikTok, and YouTube for themselves and their America, castigating the Overclass for its rejection of a core American principle—liberty of speech and thought balanced by respect for a similar liberty in others. E pluribus unum, as the founding Covenantal motto has it. On the side of the Overclass, there was intolerance; on the side of the "Deplorables," there was rejection— "you don't speak for me or my country."

Even within the Overclass doubts emerged as to its legitimacy as a culturally superior social force. A very forthright member of the Overclass, Professor Musa al-Gharbi admits in his recent book *We Have Never Been Woke* that the Overclass has "a unique moral culture . . . oriented around words, numbers, ideas, and other abstractions" which tells them that they deserve to manage society for the good of all, especially the marginalized—all of which Hegel would approve. Al-Gharbi continues:

"Consolidated into the Democratic Party," the Overclass isn't "anywhere close to being on the right track." In short, their claim to elite status and privilege has become fraudulent.

Such a thoroughgoing confrontation between irreconcilable identities exposed a reality: Covenantal America had failed under Overclass supervision—right on schedule, on the 249th anniversary of its birth.

CHAPTER 9

SQUARING THE CIRCLE: RESTORING A COVENANTAL AMERICA

Let your light so shine before men,
that they may see your good works.

Matthew 5:16

If to do were as easy as to know what were good to do,
chapels had been churches,
and poor men's cottages princes' palaces.

Shakespeare, *The Merchant of Venice*

Politics will not conquer America's cultural neurosis brought on by identity dysphoria. American politics responds to that dysphoria as ice melts in hot weather. Our dysphoria will drive our politics, for politics, as they say with good reason, is downstream from culture. Politics will not bring about a healthy and constructive balance between the Overclass and the American people sufficient to restore the proper dynamics of the constitutional order. Politics will not revive the American covenant to provide the American people with inner-direction and once again bless them with a covenantal grace.

The political pretensions of the Overclass were rejected by 73.6 million Americans in the 2024 presidential election. However, the candidate of the Overclass, Kamala Harris, received 69.2 million votes. The long-term legitimacy of the Overclass and the future of America are still in play. What may be done to square the circle among so many Americans in bitter disagreement?

Only virtue in a people can sustain a republic, and too many Americans have lost their virtue. Our other-directed Overclass has no virtue. It cannot provide the American people with virtuous leaders.

Charlie Kirk's assassination gave Americans a new truth—they no longer lived with confident self-assurance pursuant to an implicit Covenant with one another. Their aspirational Republic had become not much more than a narrative, no longer a real community—just a fiction, if that suited your fancy; only an unhappy and unforgiving story of intersectional oppression. In this coming apart of modern America, the insights of Lord Acton had become most applicable: 1) "Power corrupts, and absolute power corrupts absolutely" and 2) "Where you have a concentration of power in a few hands, all too frequently, [people] with the mentality of gangsters get control."

To regain virtue—a special charism—Americans must once again become inner-directed. That inner work must be carried on day and night by individuals and their families. It is quite beyond the agency of politicians and bureaucrats. It is a work of fiduciary stewardship and the empowering acceptance of personal responsibility. It is the work of commitment, not the enjoyment of entitlements. It is a work of "us" and not "me."

A Broken Politics

With the rise to social power of an other-directed Overclass, Americans have bifurcated their politics into two extremes of right and left at the expense of the sensible center. This graph represents the distribution of opinion in a normal industrialized society, one without identity dysphoria. Those on the far left and the far right are few in number, with the majority of citizens seeking a balanced point of view on life. The drive of political activists is to the center, where the most votes are.

Voter Viewpoints Normal Distribution

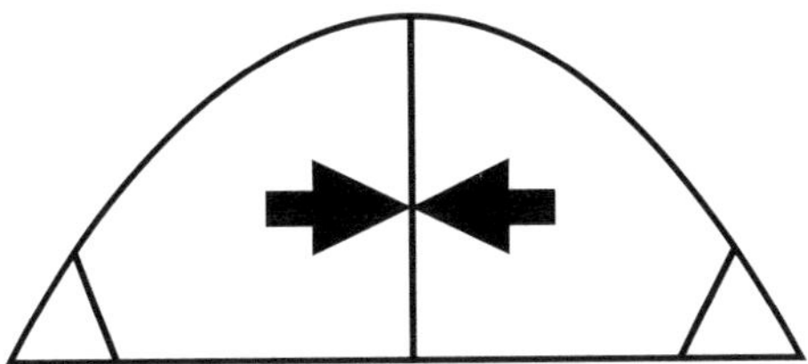

Extreme Left (3%); Left (22%); Center (50%);
Right (22%); Extreme Right (3%)

Voter Participation after Collapse of the Center: Bimodal Distribution

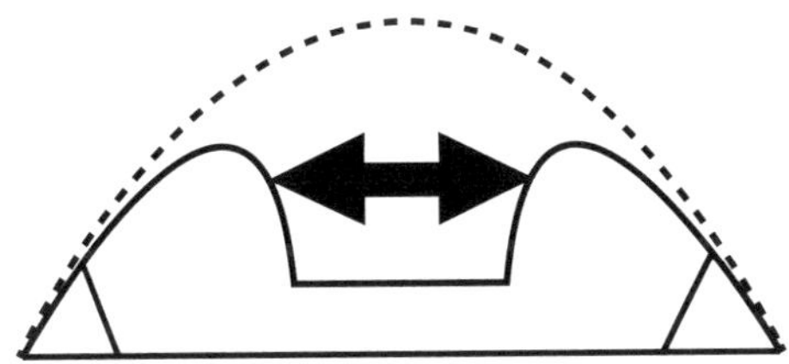

Left (25%); Center (15%); Right (25%);
Passive/Non-Party/Disengaged (35%)

The second graph represents the distribution of opinion in today's America. The center has collapsed, with many no longer participating in politics or voting in elections. The distribution has become bimodal with most political energies at the poles and most political activity directed at pulling voters from the center to one or the other of the poles.

The American cultural divide sustaining its bimodal politics can be delineated by a study of who buys and reads which books. Americans in one political modality do not read what other Americans read who identify with the opposite modal orientation. Only a few books are read by both camps. According to the *Economist*, those on the left, but not those on the right, read *White Trash* by Nancy Isenberg, *Strangers in Their Own Land* by Arlie Russell Hochschild, *The Once and Future Liberal* by Mark Lilla, *How the Right Lost Its Mind* by Charles Sykes, and *What*

Happened by Hillary Clinton. To the contrary, those on the right, but not those on the left, read *Rediscovering Americanism* by Mark R. Levin, *The Swamp* by Eric Bolling, *In Trump We Trust* by Ann Coulter, *Dangerous* by Milo Yiannopoulos, and *The Big Lie* by Dinesh D'Souza. These books attract readers on both the right and the left: *The Vanishing American Adult* by Ben Sasse, *Democracy* by Condoleezza Rice, and *Shattered* by Jonathan Allen and Annie Parnes.[1]

American media also have business models that sell to one narrow band or another within the distribution of political opinion. AllSides is a rating agency that assesses the systemic political and cultural biases of different publications and other sources of news and opinions based on surveys of consumers and the judgment of experts. Depending on their score, AllSides places a source of news and opinions in one of five categories: passionate left, moderate left, center, moderate right, and passionate right.[2]

In the passionate left customer category are the *Atlantic*, the *Daily Beast*, the *Guardian*, MSNBC, *The New Yorker*, *Slate*, *Vox*, and the *Nation*.

Assigned to the moderate left market niche are ABC News, Axios, CNN, NBC News, NPR, *Politico*, the *Washington Post*, and *TIME*.

Categorized as selling to the center category of consumers are BBC News, *Forbes*, *The Hill*, Reuters, the *Wall Street Journal*, and RealClear Politics.

Marketing to the moderate right category are Fox Business, The Free Press, Just the News, *National Review* (news), *Wall Street Journal* opinion pages, the *Washington Examiner*, and the *Washington Times*.

Last, but by no means least, are the media outlets selling to an audience on the passionate right: the *American Conservative*, the *American Spectator*, Blaze Media, Breitbart, the *Daily Mail*, Daily Wire, Fox News, The Federalist, the *New York Post*, and *National Review* (opinion).

The following chart displays how, over the years, members of the House of Representatives have separated into two mutually antagonistic factions, one supporting the Overclass and the other rejecting its claim to legitimacy.

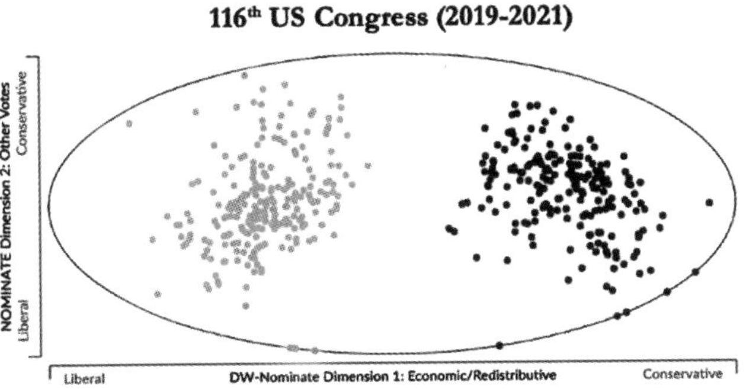

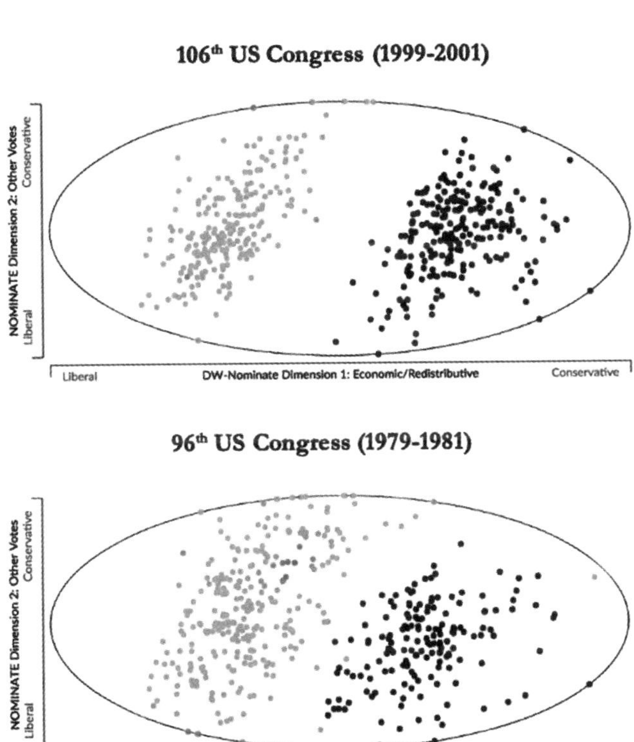

In 2018 an important contribution was made to the understanding of what was happening in American culture and politics with the report

Hidden Tribes: A Study of America's Polarized Landscape. The authors concluded,

> Our research . . . finds seven groups that are defined by their core beliefs, rather than by their political opinions, race, class or gender. In talking to everyday Americans, we have found a large segment of the population whose voices are rarely heard above the shouts of the partisan tribes. These are people who believe that Americans have more in common than that which divides them. While they differ on important issues, they feel exhausted by the division in the United States. They believe that compromise is necessary in politics, as in other parts of life, and want to see the country come together and solve its problems.
>
> In the era of social media and partisan news outlets, America's differences have become dangerously tribal, fueled by a culture of outrage and taking offense. For the combatants, the other side can no longer be tolerated, and no price is too high to defeat them. These tensions are poisoning personal relationships, consuming our politics and putting our democracy in peril.
>
> Once a country has become tribalized, debates about contested issues from immigration and trade to economic management, climate change and national security, become shaped by larger tribal identities. Policy debate gives way to tribal conflicts. Polarization and tribalism are self-reinforcing and will likely continue to accelerate.[3]

The seven tribal identity clusters noted by the researchers are as follows:

- **Left Wing**
  - Progressive activists: 8%

- **Exhausted Majority**
  - ◆ Traditional liberals: 11%
  - ◆ Passive liberals: 15%
  - ◆ Politically disengaged: 26%
  - ◆ Moderate: 15%

- **Right Wing**
  - ◆ Devoted conservatives: 6%

George Packer, a respected writer for the *Atlantic*, divided Americans into four narrative communities: the Free Americans—those who are inner-directed and subscribe to the traditional covenant in their personal lives; the Smart Americans, who belong to the Overclass; the Real Americans, who are the less couth, inner-directed traditionalists; and the Just Americans, who are younger than the Smart Americans but also part of the Overclass who find older members of that class too complacent and meritocratic and for whom justice and America can never rhyme.[4]

Packer noted that the Smart Americans had become associated with the Democratic Party while, under the watchful eye of parents, their children "devote exhausting amounts of energy to extracurricular activities and carefully constructed personal essays that can navigate between boasting and humility. The goal of all this effort is a higher education that offers questionable learning, dubious fulfillment, likely indebtedness, but certain status." There you have the ethos of the Overclass in a very few words.

The following graphics provide a snapshot of the largely irreconcilable value orientations and preferred behaviors of the left, center, and right, the three independent identity coalitions into which Americans have divided themselves.

The core value of the center derives from the traditional American covenant. I call it acting from the moral sense that we each receive at birth or acting naturally and comfortably from inner-direction. The core value of a culture, or a moral community held together by some social contract,

The American Covenantal Ethic

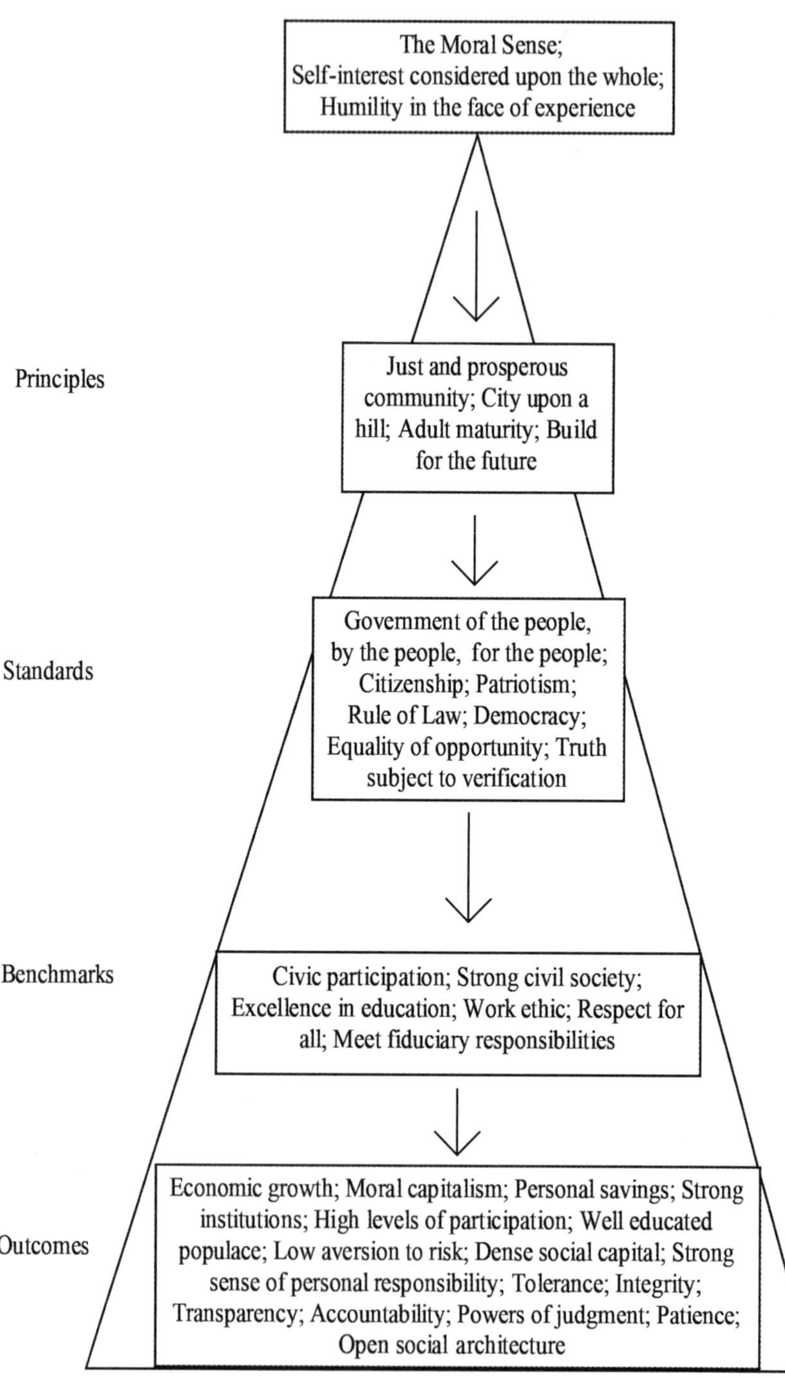

acts as an axis around which revolve the values, behaviors, and life outcomes of the people making up that culture or moral community. The moral sense then generates more specific and actionable principles that, in their turn, suggest even more specific standards by which to measure social justice as that culture or community imagines social justice. Metrics can then be proposed by which the culture or community can measure its success or failures in living up to the applicable standards. The effects of seeking to live by the standards are revealed in specific outcomes in the existential realm of facticity, or the "real world."

The core value, or dominant axis, for the American left is, to me, an unquestioned, and definitely unquestionable, desire to center one's life on an infantile individualism. The Hegelian *Begriff* legitimating such a desire is the thought that humans can hope to experience perfection, the best of times in the best of all possible worlds. Whatever gets in the way of such hopes is a worldly Gnostic evil in the minds of those who hold this core value, an evil thing or presence to be shunned and extirpated if possible.

The corresponding, and offsetting, core value at the other end of the American cultural spectrum on the right is a commitment to success in life as a struggle wherein only the fittest survive. This social Darwinism was dignified by associating its inequalities with a supposed Old Testament belief that those who succeed have walked righteously in the way of the Lord God, who gave a covenant to Abraham, the Ten Commandments to Moses, and sacrificed his son, Jesus. Today the precepts of Christian nationalism embody this *Begriff*.[5] Libertarianism privileges personal success without restraint from government but is secular in its moral foundations. More generally, this approach has been rejected by the Overclass as "neoliberalism" for its economics of beggar-thy-neighbor policies, self-interest, and private wealth creation.

The two *Begriffs* used to anchor the competing worldviews of the right and the left are irreconcilable. There can be no compromise between these moral communities. The core values of one deny the legitimacy of the core values of the other. The culture war between believers in these

The Left

Infantile Individualism
(perfectibility of humanity)

Principles

Entitlement to desires;
No authority over self;
No moral sense;
Authenticity define the elect

Standards

Sensual pleasure; Freedom of
thought; Material comfort; No
social standards for behavior;
Truth revealed

Benchmarks

Feminism; Equality of results; Wealth transfers;
Government subsidies; Political correctness;
Multiculturalism; GLBTism;
Weak law enforcement

Outcomes

Moral relativism; Society subservient to government;
Class warfare; Philosophical nihilism;
Culture of addiction; Codependency; Reality TV;
Internet porn; Shallow culture; Let government do it;
Socialism; Closed social architecture

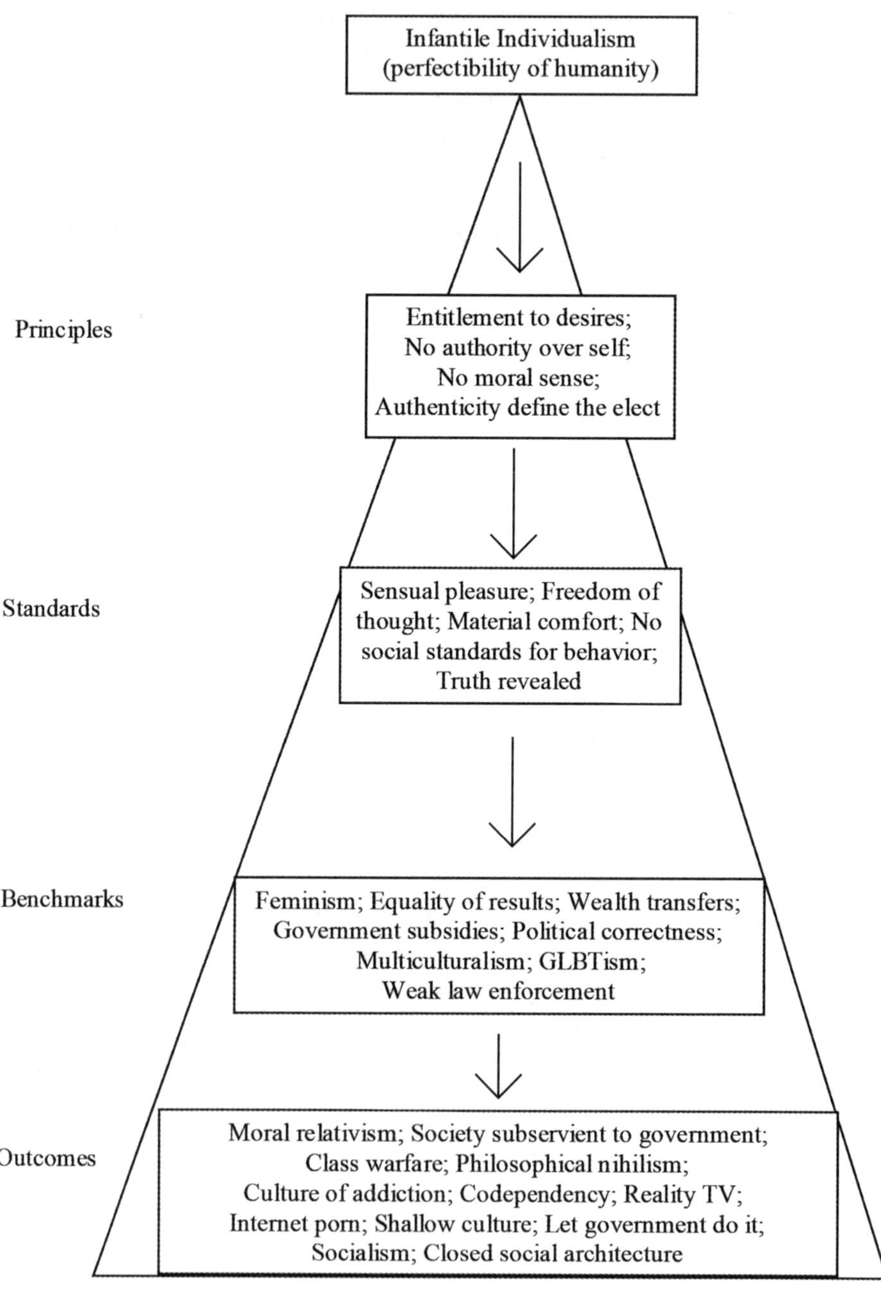

Neoliberalism

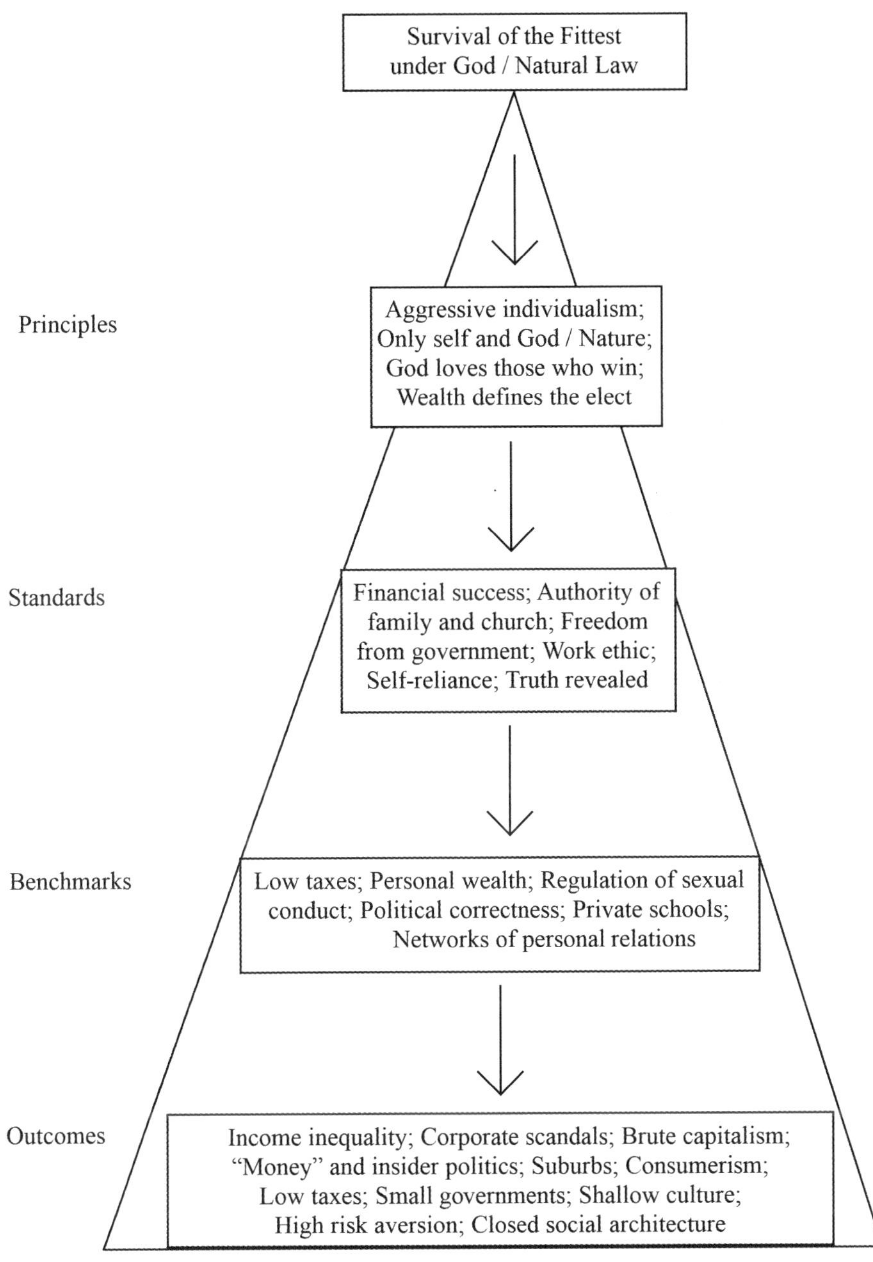

two *Begriffs* is deadlocked in a Darwinian ethos where only one can survive to become the victor who will rule the national roost.

Moreover, each polarizing *Begriff* simultaneously also finds itself at odds with the center which has its own *Begriff* privileging the moral sense. Americans are now stuck in a three-way deadlock.

In recent decades American politics has given primacy to the left and its Overclass agenda and the right with its advocacy of private wealth and individualism. The center has been eclipsed and has failed to produce leaders of quality and distinction.

The point of contention between the parties and their patrons has been the agenda and the discretionary power of the Overclass. The Democrats have evolved to become the party of the Overclass, while the Republicans have opposed the introduction of Overclass values and programs. Those who support the Overclass are supposedly "Progressives," while those who seek to curb Overclass enthusiasms and regulatory powers are castigated as closed-minded traditionalists or conservatives who just want to continue living with handed-down injustices and imperfections, with the devil taking the hindmost.

One commentator noted that President Biden's political narrative evoked "a sense of future possibility, a rebirth of social and racial justice, and a bold adaptation of the economy to meet the climate crisis." This essentialized the mission of the Overclass as savior.[6]

Conservative columnist Gerard Baker similarly noted about the Democrats, "Once in office they act as if they have a mandate to remake a benighted country, to reorder an unjust system, to replace American exceptionalism with European social democracy, and to rewrite the nation's values with the precepts of their cultural Marxism."[7]

The Democrat candidate for president in 2024, Kamala Harris, was quite accurately described by another conservative, Joel Kotkin, as a denizen of other-directed Overclass politics.[8]

> Harris may be many unpleasant things, but being a serious Stalinist is not one of them. Throughout her career she has

been one thing—an ambitious operative of the oligarchs, government bureaucrats and urban warlords who dominate today's Democratic Party.

Harris was introduced to the San Francisco elite in the 1990s by her former lover, California's longtime assembly speaker and former San Francisco mayor. She has never been a grassroots candidate with a strong working-class or minority base. Rather, she is the creation of a cabal of elite capitalists, their media megaphones and a network of nonprofits capable of producing hundreds of millions of dollars for progressive causes.

Harris has enjoyed consistent support from those who inhabit the Hamptons, Hollywood, and Silicon Valley. California donors collectively contributed over $500 million to her 2016 Senate race. The largest benefactors to Harris's 2020 presidential campaign included employees at Alphabet (the parent of Google), Cisco and Apple, as well as many prominent media and entertainment interests.

Now, as a recent Politico article breathlessly reports, Harris is now the "favorite daughter" of the powerful Bay Area political cabal. Her base lies with Bay Area law firms and tech mavens, such as Facebook's Sheryl Sandberg and Sean Parker, Marc Benioff of Salesforce, former Yahoo managing director Marissa Mayer, venture capitalist John Doerr, Steve Jobs's widow, Laurene Powell, and various executives at tech firms like Airbnb, Google and Nest.

Harris's husband, attorney Doug Emhoff, was a managing partner with Venable, whose clients include Microsoft, Apple, Verizon and trade associations opposing strict internet regulations.

If this is socialism, it is certainly a strange variant. No threat to big property—like Lenin's Bolsheviks—but a form of collectivism that more resembles the pro-big-business approach of fascist Italy and contemporary China. In these systems, massive private accumulation is permitted so long as they submit to what Mussolini described as "formal adherence to the regime".

Harris, if elected, is likely to usher in a new era of collusion between the wealthiest and most powerful with an increasingly powerful state, run by a federal bureaucracy that mostly feels Americans have too much freedom already. These elites, not surprisingly, have also shown a China-like willingness to censor opponents, acting increasingly in sync with state power.

On October 4, 2019, then Senator Harris, on behalf of the managerial class, took on the right of free speech as an intrusion on the rights of that class to order and manage American culture and society. She publicly and repeatedly called on the private corporation Twitter to ban a president of the United States from using its platform to present his feelings and ideas before the American people.

Calling Donald Trump's tweets "blatant threats," Harris invoked the assumed right of the Overclass, acting through members of the class working for a private corporation subordinate to class interests, to censor speech. Later a television host asked Harris, "How is that not a violation of free speech? The president has the same rights that you have, that I have. How would that not be a slippery slope to ban half the people on Twitter?"[9]

Harris defended her class: "I've heard that argument, but here's the thing, Jake. A corporation—which is what Twitter is—has obligations and in this case, they have terms of use policy. Their terms of use dictate who receives the privilege of speaking on that platform and who does not. And Donald Trump has clearly violated the terms of use, and there should be a consequence for that," she said. "Not to mention the fact that he has used his platform, being the president of the United States, in a way that has been about inciting fear and potentially inciting harm against a witness to what might be a crime against our country and our democracy."

She added, "And I am asking that Twitter does what it has done on previous occasions, which is revoke someone's privilege because they have not lived up to the advantages of the privilege."

Harris insisted, "[T]here has to be a responsibility placed on social media sites to understand their power. They are directly speaking to millions of people without any level of oversight or regulation and that has to stop."[10]

As they campaign for office in recent elections, most national Democrats have presented to the electorate a muted version of themselves as mainstream Americans, as good people seeking merely to bring a little unity and compassion to a fundamentally great country in need of reform. All this said with a straight face, though in truth, it is just another scripted narrative, words easily spoken when one chooses to live in a culture of other-directed make-believe.[11]

Few leaders have spoken out for the center and its moral sense, its covenantal tradition of idealism and acceptance of personal responsibility for self and the common good.

Surprisingly, in the 2024 presidential campaign, there occurred a move toward the center. Robert F. Kennedy Jr., son of an assassinated candidate for president and nephew of an assassinated president, dropped out of the race to become president and endorsed the controversial Donald Trump.

In explaining his decision to end his campaign and to justify his endorsement of the Republican nominee, Kennedy spoke out specifically in opposition to the Overclass and its power over Americans.

> As you know, I left that party [the Democrats] in October because it had departed so dramatically from the core values that I grew up with. It had become the party of war, censorship, corruption, big pharma, big tech, big AG, and big money.
>
> In the name of saving democracy, a Democratic Party set itself to dismantle it. . . .
>
> It deployed DNC-aligned judges to throw me and other candidates off the ballot and to throw President Trump in jail.

It ran a sham primary that was rigged to prevent any serious challenge to President Biden. Then, when a predictably awful debate performance precipitated a palace coup against President Biden, the same shadowy DNC operatives appointed his successor, also without an election. They installed a candidate who was so unpopular with voters that she dropped out in 2020 without winning a single delegate. . . .

What alarms me is the resort to censorship, media control, and weaponization of the federal agencies. When a U.S. president colludes with, or outright coerces, media companies to censor political speech, it's an attack on our most sacred right of free expression. And that's the very right upon which all of our other constitutional rights rest. . . .

The mainstream media was once the guardian of the First Amendment and democratic principles, but has since joined this systemic attack on democracy. Also, the media justifies their censorship on the grounds of combating misinformation, but governments and oppressors don't censor lies, they don't fear lies. They fear the truth, and that's what they censor.[12]

Just days after Robert F. Kennedy Jr. endorsed Donald Trump for the presidency in the 2024 election, a major figure in the Overclass and a high-tech billionaire, Mark Zuckerberg, provided confirmation for one of Kennedy's accusations of Overclass manipulation of public opinion. Zuckerberg then wrote to Congressman Jim Jordan, chairman of the House Committee on the Judiciary, affirming,

In 2021, senior officials from the Biden Administration, including the White House, repeatedly pressured our teams for months to censor certain COVID-19 content, including humor and satire, and expressed a lot of frustration with our teams when we didn't agree. . . . I believe the government pressure was wrong, and I regret that we were not more outspoken about it. I also think we made some choices that, with the benefit of hindsight and new information, we wouldn't make today.

In a separate situation, the FBI warned us about a potential Russian disinformation operation about the Biden family and Burisma in the lead up to the 2020 election. That fall, when we saw a New York Post story reporting on corruption allegations involving then-Democratic presidential nominee Joe Biden's family, we sent that story to fact-checkers for review and temporarily demoted it while waiting for a reply. It's since been made clear that the reporting was not Russian disinformation, and in retrospect, we shouldn't have demoted the story.[13]

Politics will not by itself put an end to its dysfunctions. It needs guidance from outsiders, the right kind of outsiders, those who are inner-directed. By cutting politics off from the center, our culture has increased the entropy or the amount of energy diverted away from productive projects to chaotic, spasmodic, tit-for-tat bursts that quickly dissipate, leaving the universe on track.

Politics has no capacity to design how we can prevent the collapse of our republic after 2026. We need design thinking.

Thomas Fisher of the University of Minnesota College of Design and a colleague wrote that we need to "reaggregate the world," to put it back together.[14] We need, he says, to think holistically—to put parts together, to connect dots, to interconnect as nature does.

The mental approaches we need are finding analogies, using metaphors to see problems in new ways, juxtaposing ideas and feelings to discover connections, rearranging, reinterpreting, diagramming relationships, and suggesting prototypes.

The centered, inner-directed person is best able to bring forth those mental tools. The best designers combine genius with humility, each bringing the other to greater authority so that genius serves truth and humility does not overreach and bend us toward withdrawal and inaction.

As the Lord Protector Oliver Cromwell said to some contumacious Scots, "I beseech you, in the bowels of Christ, think it possible that you may be mistaken." Design thinking requires an open mind and a becoming self-confidence. Then the charism of leadership will fill our souls with resolve, making us trustworthy to others.

In our time the reaggregation necessary to restore the dynamics of a constructive equilibrium in our culture and its politics must embrace individual ego-identities, families, cultures and subcultures, social structures, economics, and politics.

Acquiring a Charism

If not politics, then what? How can the American people bring an end to their identity dysphoria and put a constitutional "bridle" on the Overclass?

The task ahead of us will be best addressed by those individuals who can find a charism within themselves and put it to work in the world.

The inner-directed are more likely than others to be suitable hosts for such charisms. They are equipped emotionally to become psychosocial containers in which the needed charisms can find a safe space from which to speak and give guidance.

The task facing each of us then is acquiring a personal charism. How can that be done?

In Greek thinking and in Christian teachings over the centuries, and as adopted by German sociologist Max Weber, a personal charism is a gift of grace from a divine patron. In the New Testament, however, Jesus graced those who sought to approach God through him with special favor. He handed down to supplicants a gift from God. The apostle Paul wrote that "[f]or by grace you have been saved" and that through faith that grace can be activated in your life.[15]

It is very likely that, in acts of personal faith, each of us can use our inner power of conscience to bestow grace on others and, in so doing, to assume the office of steward, to enter upon a vocation by voluntarily responding to an inner call of moral purpose or to the call of a higher authority. The New Testament tells us that Jesus "did not come to be served, but to serve."

A commitment to service, to others, to a cause, and to community creates a charism. That creative process starts with an act of will, not Nietzsche's will to power but a will to grace our world with love and contribution. To create a charism by ourselves for ourselves takes an act of graceful caring, an act of noble character. We find a virtue within us that makes us virtuous.

The assumption of commitment is simple: Pledge yourself, make a promise to do good, assume responsibility, and take an oath. As you define yourself, you free up a charism that empowers you and supportively engages others in your life. The test of your charism will then be your dedication and skill in living up to your commitment, to walking your talk.

Adam Smith not only wrote about capitalism and its capacity to build our modern civilization based on education, technology, and ever-higher standards of living; he also gave good advice on how to be an admired, successful person. For him, resting your sense of self on an inner ideal of purpose would produce a charism. Each of us, he said, has within us a conscience, a somewhat spiritual guide to decision-making, acting as a fair and impartial judge of our emotions, intentions, and actions.

The person "of real constancy and firmness, the wise and just [person] who has been thoroughly bred in the great school of self-command . . . has been in the constant practice . . . of modeling, or of endeavoring to model, not only his outward conduct and behaviour, but as much as he can, even his inward sentiments and feelings, according to those of this awful and respectable judge. . . . [H]e almost becomes himself that impartial spectator, and scarce even feels but as that great arbiter of his conduct directs him to feel."[16]

Smith connects self-approbation with self-command. When fully synchronized, the two become a charism that ennobles the personality. Smith puts great emphasis on "objectivity," not self-love, guiding us correctly to self-empowerment and happiness with ourselves. Taking our stance from a higher "objectivity" of moral purpose in the service of others is our charism: "Our sensibility to the feelings of others, so far from being inconsistent with the [personhood] of self-command, is the very principle upon which that [personhood] is founded. . . . The [person] of the most perfect virtue . . . is [one] who joins, to the most perfect command of [their] own original and selfish feelings, the most exquisite sensibility . . . to the original and sympathetic feelings of others."[17]

Ralph Waldo Emerson, the American transcendentalist, believed in the charismatic capacity of each individual. He wrote, "Has he not a calling in his character? Each man has his own vocation. The talent is the call. The talent is the mode in which the general soul incarnates itself in [each of us]. . . . What has he done?' is the divine question which searches men and transpierces every false reputation. . . . By doing his own work, he unfolds himself. . . . What a man does, that he has . . . in himself is his might."[18] Man is a stream whose source is hidden. Our being is descended into us from we know not whence. . . . Within [each] is the soul of the whole; the wise silence, the universal beauty, to which every part and particle is equally related, the eternal ONE."[19]

For Emerson, those of us who do not seek out our charism are only "[c]ommon men . . . apologies for men; they bow the head, excuse themselves with prolix reasons, and accumulate appearances because the substance is not."[20]

The building up of a personal charism comes more from practice than from reasoning. This is the lesson taught by the Buddha and the Greek and Roman Stoics. Heraclitus proposed that our inner ethos—the rock-solid core values that give us inner-direction—becomes a daimon, an indwelling spirit that gathers and concentrates our physical, mental, and psychic energies for outward deployment in the world.

Our daimon serves as our anchor, holding us in position as the upsetting winds and waves of life flow over and under us.

By working on our character—what Adam Smith called our moral sentiments and what Erik Erikson called our ego-identity—we can infuse with power and grace that inborn possibility of becoming charismatic.

The Quran tells us that we are born with an indwelling capacity to serve as God's steward in his creation. The Buddha presumed that with diligent mindfulness we can experience right concentration, giving us the right intentions and views that will lead us to right speech and right action.

Cicero insisted that "no phase of life whether public or private, whether in business or in the home, whether one is working on what concerns oneself alone or dealing with another, can be without its offices; on the execution of which depends all that is morally right, and on its neglect all that is morally wrong in life."[21] Nature, Cicero insisted, provided that every human person could possess *honestum*, or moral goodness. So he said, "[W]e ought to follow Nature as our guide, to contribute to the general good by an interchange of acts of kindness, by giving and receiving, and thus by our skill, our industry, our talents, to cement human society more closely together, person to person."[22]

Here we might say that Cicero is speaking of the office of a person, the obligations of personhood to be carried out not to please others but to be honest with the daimon within us as to who we really are. Following Aristotle, Cicero also wrote of our virtues, powers within us not dependent on others, enabling us to accomplish deeds in the world. The roads on which we dutifully move forward are where we live out the virtues of wisdom, courage, justice, fortitude, and prudence. Greatness of spirit in a person regarded *honestum* as consisting of deeds that reveal virtues, not thoughts or words.[23] By our fruits shall we be known, said Jesus. Our thoughts, said Cicero, should be used to ascertain our duties.[24] He stated, "Everyone should . . . make a proper estimate of his own natural ability and show himself a critical judge of his own merits and demerits."[25] He added in another work, "[B]ut above all, we must decide what manner of person we wish to be and what calling in life we would follow."[26]

Confucius also advised that inner-directed character, or lack thereof, was a fundamental in how we should esteem others: "See what a person does. Mark their motives. Examine in what things they rest. How can they conceal their character?"[27] He affirmed that what a person of upright character seeks is in themselves, while what a person of weak character seeks is in others.[28]

He, too, believed that we are born "for uprightness," that the virtuous person is "satisfied and composed," while the mean-spirited person without virtue is "always full of distress."[29] He said, "To see what is right and not do it is want of courage."[30] One who abandons virtue cannot fulfill the duties incumbent upon those in the office of a gentleman.[31] Confucius would agree that the mind of an inner-directed person is conversant with righteousness, while, conversely, the mind of an other-directed person is conversant with gain.[32]

Marcus Aurelius pithily advised us all, "Dig within. There lies the wellspring of good: ever dig and it will ever flow."[33] He added, "Treat with respect the power you have to form an opinion."[34] In other words don't surrender your conscience to others. He stated, "Nowhere can a person find a quieter or more untroubled retreat than in their own soul. . . . Avail yourself often, then, of this retirement and so continually renew yourself."[35]

He did not advise us to copy others and use them as measurements of our own good and capabilities.

Likewise, the Buddhist *Dhammapada* advises, "The person who can restrain anger that has arisen like a reckless chariot—that one I call a driver. Other people just hold on to the reins; Irrigators guide the water. Fletchers shape an arrow's shaft. Carpenters shape wood. The virtuous tame themselves; It is better indeed to conquer yourself rather than other people."[36]

As for creating a charism, the *Dhammapada* instructs, "With drops of falling water even a water pot is filled. The wise person is full of virtue gathered day by day"; "If a person does something of value, he should do it again and again. He must create that impulse in himself"; "It is good to tame the mind, alighting as it does, wherever it desires—swift, resistant to restraint. A tamed mind gives rise to ease."[37]

That ease of mind releases the psychosocial energy that vitalizes a charism.

Roman emperor Marcus Aurelius, a Stoic, advised, "Hour by hour resolve firmly, like a Roman and a man, to do what comes to hand with correct and natural dignity, and with humanity, independence, and justice."[38]

There was no need, he wrote, to depend on help from without or crave the ease of inner tranquility from others.[39] The "deity which dwells within you" well directed your every impulse, weighed each impression coming from the outside, rejected sensual temptations, and had compassion for humanity.[40]

In our secular, enlightened, scientific culture, some might wonder whether finding one's charism is right for our times. That the very premodern Stoics, Buddhists, and Christians sought to live by an inner spirit, deity, daimon, or activated mindfulness directing our sense of who we are and what we should do with our lives may be no longer relevant to a culture that has nuclear weapons and artificial intelligence at its command. Our watchword for today and tomorrow, especially as we are taught by the Overclass, is said to be "reason" as the age of faith is long over and done with.

Contrary to the great thinkers of the European Enlightenment and their acolytes in our Overclass, rational thought alone is not the best way forward. As Nietzsche saw so insightfully, reason ends up twisting itself into a crude and brute, self-seeking, and often self-destructive will to power, a cruel persona wandering about causing trouble and sadness. Reason, therefore, cannot generate charisma all by itself.

Thus, when Hegel and, later, Max Weber looked only to reason and legal organizational structures of roles and responsibilities as the highest and best expression of progressive human activity and belief, they steered us toward an entropic secularism, a chaotic spinning of greed and oppressions, an endless misuse of our energies.

Adam Smith, who came from the very Protestant Scottish Enlightenment, in his design theory for human happiness, anchored reason in what he called a "moral sense."

"Our reason was constrained by a conscience, an observer living within the breast," he wrote, looking at our thoughts and actions and talking to us about right and wrong, short-term self-interest, and enlightened self-interest, or self-interest considered upon the whole. Our enlightenment, our capacity to see things objectively "upon the whole," was made possible by a moral filter screening our powers of reason.

One practice of adding thrust and scope to our insight is to take time to reflect. Buddhists are not alone in recommending meditation for the empowerment of our inner-direction and the refreshment of our charism.

Reflective thinking is both an "open sesame" doorway to rich inner resources of insight and courage and an underused action-oriented discipline. Developing our responsive and creative reflective thinking will increase our ability to make the most of opportunities, circumstances, and decisions.

How many times have we all said, hours or even minutes after a conversation, "I wish I had spoken up. It might have made a difference"? One goal of reflective thinking is to eliminate such self-imposed silences and to help us give the best response at the time it is needed.

We all take or make time to listen inwardly. It may be when on a walk in nature or when in the shower. Many dialogue within; others just think. Sometimes at an unexpected instant, an intuition comes. These insights or intuitions often point to great truths. So usually such creative reflective thinking is very helpful, but sadly we do not normally make an effort to develop a regular practice of cultivating them.

Practice disciplined listening to oneself: (1) make time for reflection—start with ten to fifteen uninterrupted minutes a day, (2) try to take time for this at the start of the day or at a time when you feel fresh and can best free yourself for a while from the pressures of life's demands, and (3) as well as dedicating time, try finding a special place for these moments of quiet concentration.

Prepare yourself properly: (1) Spend a few minutes with a book or article that inspires your thinking; some people meditate, pray, or do breathing exercises or physical exercise to prepare; (2) take a hot drink to a comfortable place to sit and think; (3) if your mind on its own comes up with a list of things you need to do, just write them down to take them out of your mind and thus free up time for thinking; and (4) be open to unexpected thoughts.

Keep at it until reflective thinking, which accesses your inner resources, is part of your normal thinking all the time. With practice it will also develop in you the ability to listen inwardly all the time, even while interacting with others: while speaking on the phone, in the midst of a conversation at home or school or the office, during an argument, and at a meeting discussing an important issue.

Also use this practice of reflective listening at points in your day when extra thoughtfulness is most needed and helpful, regardless of time and location, such as when you face a decision, when you are starting a task, when you read or hear something that challenges or inspires you, when you recognize a crisis, when you want to create something, or before meetings and important phone calls.

The result of such a practice is to stimulate your capacity for inner-direction, thereby giving birth to a good daimon within you.

Reflective thinking makes one more alert to differing facets of the same truth, as interpreted through the lenses of different cultural, regional, and historical perspectives. And we rather easily find ourselves able to explore, without prejudice, fear, or superficiality, the wisdom of the great religious and spiritual traditions. And we discover that we not only learn from history—its legacy of thoughts, feelings, and behaviors—we also become shapers of history, building a better legacy for those who come after.

For centuries Jesuit priests have made time each day to examine what they had done or said the day before, looking to learn from what they had done successfully or lovingly and from their shortcomings of anger, intolerance, and self-serving manipulations. In his *Spiritual Exercises*, Ignatius of Loyola, founder of the Order of Jesuits, described the frequent examination of one's conscience as the most important spiritual exercise.

Those who work in managed, bureaucratic structures can nevertheless find inspiration through reflection. In a research experiment, three thousand employees of a consumer goods firm were assigned to take part in workshops that help them reflect on pivotal moments in their lives to articulate what mattered to them and to consider how much their work for the company aligned with their sense of personal purpose. Those who concluded that their jobs and their values were aligned put more effort into their work, adding significant productivity to the firm's intangible human capital account.[41]

A second anchor, giving us resolute inner-direction and giving our daimon good work to do in the world through us, is assuming responsibility, entering an office, and taking on powers in trust to provide for and protect others.

When we are responsible, we have duties. When we have duties, we are in relationship. Others depend on us; our identity is not dependent on them but on our stepping forward, letting others witness our purpose and feel the reality of what is meaningful to us. We walk our talk step by step with our own feet listening to our own inner voice. The purpose we present to the world and the meaning that gives us that sense of purpose become our charism that others discern and respect.

A simple way to initiate taking on a responsibility, to commit to a relationship, and to assume duties is to make a promise or take an oath.

As we noted in chapter 1, generations of American boys took the Scout's Oath, committing themselves to duty and service. Any person spontaneously capable of so behaving without a second thought is likely to be inner-directed. And the Declaration of Independence famously ends with an oath in which its signers pledge their lives, fortunes, and sacred honor.

A story has it that when my collateral ancestor Lewis Morris, a rich man with expensive properties subject to confiscation by the English, was about to sign the Declaration, his half brother, Gouverneur, another of the other delegates, quipped, "What about your estate?" Lewis allegedly replied, "Damn the consequences, give me the pen!" During the ensuing war, Lewis Morris's lands were torched and his house ransacked.[42]

There are consequences, though, of leaving your charism stillborn. A charism left on its own wastes and withers away like a grape unpicked and left to rot on the vine, leaving its host prey to dysfunctional other-direction. An uncharged charism works no better than a dead battery. Alternatively, other-direction can be the fruit of a potential charism angered and gone awry, turning on its host in disappointment and out of disapproval, reaching out to others for reassurance and direction.

The Protestant Ethic

A third anchor for inner-direction, a cast of mind and heart that acts as a charism, was recommended by the two famous founders of the Protestant faith—Martin Luther and John Calvin.

In the United States, the Protestant Ethic was long associated with the American covenantal tradition.

There is a Protestant hymn—"Lift Up Your Heads, Ye Mighty Gates"—that encourages us to nourish and raise up our inborn spirit.

> Fling wide the portals of your heart;
> make it a temple, set apart

> from earthly use for heaven's employ,
> adorned with prayer and love and joy.
> Redeemer, come, with us abide;
> our hearts to thee we open wide;
> let us thy inner presence feel;
> thy grace and love in us reveal.

The first Protestant reformer, Martin Luther, recommended that each of us should seek a personal vocation, as doing so would bring us into an empowering and sustaining spiritual relationship with God.

Luther interpreted the Christian scriptures to encompass two kingdoms—a spiritual kingdom of heaven and a materialist kingdom of earth. While our aspiration for eternal life directs our attention to heaven, our present life on earth directs our attention to its own separate reality, which is only our interim concern. But while living in the earthly kingdom, we have our special spiritual work to do, and that is to find a personal calling, a vocation, or *Beruf*. On finding our *Beruf* and living it out in public with inward spiritual devotion, we find joy and affirmation in responsibility.[43] In secular terms our *Beruf* is known as a station in life, a role to fulfill (*stand* in German). But importantly for our gaining access to a charism, just having a station is pedestrian and without much meaning. When we invest our responsibilities in this world—father, mother, farmer, king—with spirit, we convert the station into a *Beruf* (a vocation) and give ourselves a charism. Luther thought we could and should transform an earthly station into a ministry of love.

For Luther spirit is a habitation for faith and the Word of God, both of which can be part of us, of our being and our ego-identity; we can bring ourselves to have faith, and we can hear the Word of God in scripture and prayer.[44]

Luther realized that our stations in life are oriented to serve others. Stations are relationships, not solitudes. Having a vocation is one way we fulfill Jesus's injunction to treat others kindly and thoughtfully, as we would want to be treated ourselves, and to love our neighbor. Luther pointed to the mother who cares for her children and a father who must arise in the morning and labor to support his family.[45] These two tasks are godly works in this fallen world of sin and woe, the faithful performance of which lifts us spiritually as a person who rightly matters in God's sight. In our relationships with others, we hold "offices" sustaining God's creation; we become agents of the Lord, an honorable estate.

One who inquires effectively into his neighbor's real welfare has faith and so becomes a child of God in good standing.[46]

Luther wrote, "If you are a craftsman, you will find a bible placed in your workshop, in your hands, in your heart. . . . Only look at your tools, your needle, your thimble, your beer barrel, your article of trade, your scales, your measures, and you will find this saying written on them. . . . 'My dear use me toward your neighbor as you would want him to act toward you with that which is his.'"[47]

For Luther, in vocation there is a direct connection between God's work in sustaining creation and our work for him in our offices of responsibility. Care for one's office in this earthly realm is participation in God's own mission of care for human beings.[48] In our vocations we don't reach up to God but rather bend ourselves down into the world around us as we find it.[49] In prayer and with faith, we turn ourselves up to God; in earthly service, we focus ourselves on where we stand to fulfill his Providence.

One who assumes one of God's "offices," the early Protestants thought, thereby assumes covenantal functions in God's creation.

(There is an analogous basis for taking personal responsibility for God's creation in the Talmudic tradition of the Jews—*tikkun olam*, Hebrew for "repairing the world."[50] Similarly in the Abrahamic tradition, the Quran placed on persons stewardship duties as trustees superintending the well-being of creation as the successor of God.[51])

For all his pessimism on the inherent self-destructive qualities of our human nature, given the sinfulness of our primal ancestors Adam and Eve, Protestant theologian John Calvin praised his God for the gift of creation, which, as God said in Genesis, was "good." Thus God, said Calvin, "sustains, nourishes, and cares for everything he has made even to the last sparrow."[52] He added, "To taste God's special care, by which his fatherly favor is known," brings to the devoted one a special grace—in other words, a charism. To obtain that feeling of grace, Calvin recommended attending to the world as a steward to honor creation and contribute to its well-being and fruitfulness. A steward has duties to serve. A steward contributes thoughtful labor and well-advised initiatives but does not take undue personal advantage of circumstances or extract rents to fund irresponsible personal indulgences.

Calvin wrote,

> . . . the Lord enjoins every one of us, in all the actions of life, to have respect to our own calling. He knows the boiling restlessness of the human mind, the fickleness with which it is borne hither and thither, its eagerness to hold opposites at one time in its grasp, its ambition. Therefore, lest all things should be thrown into confusion by our folly and rashness, he has assigned distinct duties to each in the different modes of life. And that no one may presume to overstep his proper limits, he has distinguished the different modes of life by the name of callings. Every man's mode of life therefore is a kind of station assigned him by the Lord, that he may not be always driven about at random. . . . [I]n following your proper calling, no work will be so mean and sordid as not to have a splendor and value in the eyes of God.[53]

Thus, thought Calvin, each of us has duties to discharge every day to every part of God's creation. We are to live lives of responsibility to something far greater than ourselves.

Confucius had similar advice: the lord should lord, the minister should minister, the father should father, and the son should son. And so on, the mother should mother, the daughter should daughter, the farmer should farm.[54] In accordance with this admonition to be in relationship with others, Confucius thought that the only word we need to live by is "reciprocity."[55]

In his 1981 encyclical *Laborem Exercens*, Pope John Paul II affirmed the assumption of responsibility by each person born into God's earthly creation. He wrote,

> Work is one of the characteristics that distinguish man from the rest of creatures. . . . Man has to subdue the earth and dominate it, because as the "image of God" he is a person, that is to say, a subjective being capable of acting in a planned and rational way, capable of deciding about himself, and with a tendency to self-realization. As a person, man is therefore the subject of work. As a person he works, he performs various actions belonging to the work process; independently of their objective content, these actions must all serve to realize his humanity, to fulfill the calling to be a person that is his by reason of his very humanity. . . . In carrying out this mandate, . . . every human being reflects the very action of the Creator of the universe.[56]

In other words the responsibility to work is the God-given office of each person.

The Protestant Ethic also promoted resilient self-assurance and the building out of one's abilities to swim successfully the tides of fortune and never sink beneath the waves of fate. Benjamin Franklin perhaps was the first to provide instruction to individuals with self-help advice in his *Poor Richard's Almanack*. He offered easy-to-follow, very practical ways of using time and personal effort to better one's condition in life: "Early to bed, early to rise, makes a man healthy, wealthy and wise"; "A penny saved is a penny earned"; "Lost Time is never found again"; "Speak little, do much"; "Search others for their virtues, thyself for thy vices"; and "What you would seem to be, be really."

The American tradition of self-help advice manuals, such as the rags-to-riches young adult novels of Horatio Alger (1868–1899) about poor boys rising from poverty through their own efforts and good works to middle-class security and comfort, gave credence to the possibility of living the "American Dream," of building up and then living in a "city upon a hill." Alger's most famous novel was *Ragged Dick*. This American self-help *Begriff* is that individuals, through their own efforts and mental discipline, can accumulate capital—first human, then social, and finally financial. The self-help journey to comprehensive well-being—worldly grace, if you will—can be thought of as consistently making small deposits into a savings account where the compound interest after twenty or thirty years makes you quite well-to-do. But in this savings account, your deposits are more than money; they are increments of your own human capital (skills, education, experience) and your social capital (the trust of others, good reputation, friendships).

Recently in this tradition, Canadian Jordan Peterson notably wrote *12 Rules for Life: An Antidote to Chaos.*

Stephen R. Covey followed in Ben Franklin's footsteps in providing Americans with self-help advice on how to live more productive lives. His first book of what he called "powerful lessons in personal change" was *The 7 Habits of Highly Effective People: Restoring the Character Ethic*, published in 1989.

In 2004 Covey published another self-help book responding to the rise of the Overclass. Covey wrote the book, he says, to solve a problem. What he saw as a problem was the spread of modern management practices based on the belief that "you have to control and manage people."[57] The modern management philosophy is to manage people as we do things. In modern bureaucracies "people think that only those in positions of authority should decide what must be done. They have consented, perhaps unconsciously, to being controlled like a thing. Even if they perceive a need, they don't take the initiative to act. They wait to be told what to do by the person with the formal title, and then they respond as directed. Consequently, they blame the formal leader when things go wrong and give him or her the credit when things go well."

Covey continues, "This widespread reluctance to take initiative, to act independently, only fuels formal leaders' license to direct or manage their subordinates. This, they believe, is what they must do to get followers to act. And this cycle quickly escalates into co-dependency. Each party's weakness reinforces and ultimately justifies the other's behavior."[58]

Covey's description of modern American organizational culture shows that Bakunin and Trotsky's observations and predictions of inevitable institutional failure on the part of progressive elites have been realized.

Covey's proposed solution, again, has historical antecedents. He looks to individuals, not to organizations. He calls on individuals to build themselves up from the inside out, to "find their personal voice" and then use that voice to "inspire" others to also find their individual voice.[59] Covey thus turns to the realm of spirit, to the spirit he believes we each can bring forth in our living, to the daimon waiting inside us to be validated and energized.

Optimistically, Covey believes, "Deep within each of us there is an inner longing to live a life of greatness and contribution—to really matter, to really make a difference."[60] Covey's advice therefore is to find your special voice, to activate your daimon, and to expose your charism by (1) "coming to understand your true nature," and (2) "cultivating the highest manifestations of vision, discipline, passion, and conscience."[61]

Here, Covey, without saying it, calls on all Americans, one by one, to find their inner-direction. He quotes the Roman Stoic Seneca: "Most powerful is he who has himself in his powers."[62]

Remoralizing America

A personal charism is not found. It is birthed. The soul is its parent; the moral sentiments are its nourishment. But like any other fortifying and encouraging part of our identity, it needs to be recognized and appreciated, never ignored or abandoned.

But no charism is conferred when you get a college degree, no matter how much you have paid.

If we consider the word "morale," we immediately see a connection between our charism and our moral sentiments. Morality governs our disposition, which hosts our charism. Those with high morale possess an indwelling charism, akin to what Adam Smith called the advisor "within the breast," a kindly mentor and cheerleader. Or what Aristotle and Cicero called "virtue." Those with high morale are confident, live with enthusiasm, are loyal to principle, and are motivated to act and get results.

Perhaps that is why John Adams was convinced that "[o]ur Constitution was made only for a moral and religious people. It is wholly inadequate to the government of any other."

We need to take ownership of that which both distinguishes us as special and unites us with the eternal. Our charism lives or dies on the inside but also works through us on the outside as we assume or reject responsibility. Uniting the inside with the outside invigorates our charism, empowering our agency, our capacity for inner-direction.

Gandhi, the Mahatma, understood how to activate a charism. He simply said, "We but mirror the world. All the tendencies present in the outer world are to be found in the world of our body. If we could change ourselves, the tendencies in the world would also change. As a man changes his own nature, so does the attitude of the world change towards him. This is the divine mystery supreme. A wonderful thing it is and the source of our happiness. We need not wait to see what others do."[63]

Our charisms thrive with work, or rather with vocation, responding to that which has efficacy with respect for the good, the true, and the beautiful.

In Christian terms our charism permits us to build that city upon a hill.

There has long been something of this truth in the American soul.

Emily Dickinson spoke of this in a poem.

> To make a prairie it takes a clover and one bee,
> One clover, and a bee,
> And revery.
> The revery alone will do,
> If bees are few.[64]

Walt Whitman put it this way:

> Afoot and light-hearted I take to the open road,
> Healthy, free, the world before me,
> The long brown path before me leading wherever I choose.
> Henceforth I ask not good-fortune, I myself am good-fortune,
> Henceforth I whimper no more, postpone no more, need nothing,
> Done with indoor complaints, libraries, querulous criticisms,
> Strong and content I travel the open road.[65]

And for Robert Frost,

> Not only sands and gravels
> Were once more on their travels,
> But gulping muddy gallons
> Great boulders off their balance
> Bumped heads together dully
> And started down the gully.
> Whole capes caked off in slices.
> I felt my standpoint shaken
> In the universal crisis.
> But with one step backward taken
> I saved myself from going.

A world torn loose went by me.
Then the rain stopped and the blowing,
And the sun came out to dry me.[66]

Carl Sandburg, the middle-class poet from middle America, wrote this about the American charism:

Lincoln?
He was a mystery in smoke and flags
Saying yes to the smoke, yes to the flags,
Yes to the paradoxes of democracy,
Yes to the hopes of government
Of the people by the people for the people,
No to debauchery of the public mind,
No to personal malice nursed and fed,
Yes to the Constitution when a help,
No to the Constitution when a hindrance,
Yes to man as a struggler amid illusions,
Each man fated to answer for himself:
Which of the faiths and illusions of mankind
Must I choose for my own sustaining light
To bring me beyond the present wilderness?
Lincoln? Was he a poet?
And did he write verses?
"I have not willingly planted a thorn
in any man's bosom."
I shall do nothing through malice: what
I deal with is too vast for malice."
Death was in the air.
So was birth.[67]

Great poets live close to their charisms.

Julia Ward Howe's "Battle Hymn of the Republic" (mentioned in chapter 1), verses 4 and 5, provides a covenantal anthem for Americans to sing together in a moment of shared community charism.

> He has sounded forth the trumpet that shall never call retreat;
> He is sifting out the hearts of men before His judgment-seat:
> Oh, be swift, my soul, to answer Him! be jubilant, my feet!
> Our God is marching on.
> In the beauty of the lilies Christ was born across the sea,
> With a glory in His bosom that transfigures you and me:
> As He died to make men holy, let us die to make men free,
> While God is marching on.
> Glory, glory, hallelujah!
> His truth is marching on.[68]

And unattributed folk songs like this one:

> I'm just a poor wayfaring stranger, I'm trav'ling through this world with woe;
> There is no sickness, toil, nor danger, In that bright world to which I go.
> I'm going there to see my father, I'm going there no more to roam;
> I'm just a going over Jordan, I'm just a going over home.

More universally, we can find instruction in the way of charisms in the *Tao Te Ching*.

> We make a vessel from a lump of clay.
> It is the empty space within the vessel that makes it useful.
> We make doors and windows for a room,
> But it is the empty spaces that make the room livable.[69]

> Cultivate virtue in your own person,
> And it becomes a genuine part of you.
> Cultivate it in the family,
> And it will abide.
> Cultivate it in the community,
> And it will live and grow.
> Cultivate it in the world,
> And it will flourish abundantly.[70]
>
> A tree as big as a man's embrace springs from a tiny sprout.
> A tower nine stories high begins with a heap of earth.
> A journey of a thousand miles starts from where your feet stand.[71]

Our charism gains strength and acquires centrality in our lives through our practice. Thinking and feeling are not enough to give birth to a charism, though they can point us in the right direction. Ritual, then, brings a charism to fruition.

The ritual can be private—meditation and prayer—the experience of solitude.

Or it can be public—speaking out, caring for loved ones, affirming our beliefs, making decisions, and assuming risks.

In the covenantal American tradition, in our civil religion, holidays were instituted to provide rituals animating our charisms. Just as Christians practice in the Eucharist or by singing Christmas carols and observing Lent, Americans gathered by families and in communities for Thanksgiving and the Fourth of July.

When calling for the first national Thanksgiving ritual, George Washington framed the event solemnly as participating in a relationship with the transcendent.

> . . . that we may then unite in most humbly offering our prayers and supplications to the great Lord and Ruler of

Nations and beseech him to pardon our national and other transgressions—to enable us all, whether in public or private stations, to perform our several and relative duties properly and punctually—to render our national government a blessing to all the people, by constantly being a Government of wise, just, and constitutional laws, discreetly and faithfully executed and obeyed.[72]

Abraham Lincoln followed Washington's example of proposing solemn ritual as part of his crusade to save the Union when he, too, asked Americans to give thanks to the Almighty.

. . . the Most High God, who while dealing with us in anger for our sins, hath nevertheless remembered mercy. It has seemed to me fit and proper that [His gifts] should be solemnly, reverently, and gratefully acknowledged as with one heart and one voice by the whole American people. I do, therefore, invite my fellow-citizens in every part of the United States, and also those who are at sea and those who are sojourning in foreign lands, to set apart and observe the last Thursday of November next as a Day of Thanksgiving and Praise to our beneficent Father who dwelleth in the heavens. And I recommend to them that, while offering up the ascriptions justly due to Him for such singular deliverances and blessings, they do also, with humble penitence for our national perverseness and disobedience, commend to His tender care all those who have become widows, orphans, mourners, or sufferers in the lamentable civil strife in which we are unavoidably engaged, and fervently implore the interposition of the Almighty hand to heal the wounds of the nation, and to restore it, as soon as may be consistent with the Divine purposes, to the full enjoyment of peace, harmony, tranquility, and union.[73]

To restore our national covenant, we must resolemnize Thanksgiving and the Fourth of July. In doing so we would welcome all to partake of Americanization, the way some Christians partake of bread and wine at the Eucharist, with participation and an open heart.

Perhaps this entering into a common national covenant is the best hope we have for finally giving full due to the dignity and honor of those among us descended from slaves.

This was precisely Martin Luther King Jr.'s aim when he explicitly sought to widen America's covenantal community via the inclusion of African Americans in his 1963 speech at the Lincoln Memorial.

> I have a dream that one day this nation will rise up and live out the true meaning of its creed: "We hold these truths to be self-evident, that all men are created equal."

Restoring the Covenant

The original American covenant passed down from the Pilgrims and the Puritans provided roughly seven generations of Americans with an identity of responsibility leading to great achievements unprecedented in human history. That covenant was for self-management of individuals, families, and communities—for government of the people, by the people, and for the people.

It lost its credibility under assault from postmodernism and its viability with the rise of the Overclass.

It was a birthright covenant of citizenship made by and to be faithfully executed by inner-directed citizens of both sexes and all ages and was open for implicit subscription by new arrivals from across the seas who accepted its terms, promises, and obligations.

There was an unwritten cultural covenant, a construct called American exceptionalism, America aspiring to become a city upon a hill, Americanism as an ethos of assimilation. Its cultural symbolism included songs—"The Star-Spangled Banner" and "America the Beautiful"; speeches by George Washington, Abraham Lincoln, and John F. Kennedy; pledging allegiance to a flag; pastimes—baseball and football, summer family picnics, holidays with parades in small towns as on the Fourth of July, and eating turkey on Thanksgiving; images—Washington crossing the Delaware, Grant Wood's *American Gothic*, soldiers running up Omaha Beach, Normandy, France, on D-Day 1944, Norman Rockwell's heartwarming *Four Freedoms*, and Martin Luther King Jr. speaking before the Lincoln Memorial; and a house in the suburbs with a yard.

That cultural covenant has lost its appeal. It no longer governs our commitments to one another and to a beloved community. Too few Americans have time for covenantal responsibilities or recognize themselves as signatories to any such agreement.

The amorphous cultural covenant was supplemented by a governing covenant adopted by representatives elected by the people in the several colonies upon their winning independence from the British Crown and assuming national sovereignty under the accepted conventions of the Law of Nations. The purpose of that written covenant was expressed rather well by Gouverneur Morris when he wrote the Preamble to the Constitution of 1787.

> We the People of the United States, in Order to form a more perfect Union, establish Justice, insure domestic Tranquility, provide for the common defense, promote the general Welfare, and secure the Blessings of Liberty to ourselves and our Posterity, do ordain and establish this Constitution for the United States of America.

The traditional American covenants—cultural and constitutional— were community covenants more than oaths of obligations taken by individuals in good faith on their personal honor.

Today the dysfunctions brought upon us by the Overclass, by other-directed managers of our culture and society, and by identity dysphoria—

dysfunctions that have laid a foundation for a future of gloom, anxiety, and subversion of our republic—need to be corrected.

If politics is not up to the task, then individuals must take over the work of reviving covenantal inner-direction.

Those men and women with inner-direction need to come forward in families, religious communities, local governments, education, media, and business to reboot our moral heritage of respect for one another, hard work, and proud self-discipline.

It is not managers we need but leaders, those with charisma, those who will not shy away from decision-making and the assumption of personal responsibility.

In this new American covenant, we choose ourselves—not the Overclass—to set the course for our nation.

Just as in the Abrahamic tradition, where Jesus brought forth his new covenant for individuals, one by one, to pledge their faith in God's ministry and commit themselves to vocations of service in his earthly kingdom as stewards of the common good, so too can Americans, one by one, pledge themselves to serve their national commonwealth.

The terms of the new American covenant must insist on privileging the moral sense that resides in each of us, on politics and economics being centered and balanced, on avoiding the chaotic entropy implicit in ideologies.

Very importantly, the new American covenant will not exclude the descendants of slaves. The new Moses for African-Americans will appear as a charism in each and every individual African-American who accepts Covenantal responsibilities.

Such acts of covenanting need not exclude anyone of faith—whether Jew or Muslim, Confucian or Buddhist, atheist or indigenous.

A general covenant for all Americans could be drafted and presented for signature in every town and city. More specialized covenants could also be drafted for ethnic communities, political parties, companies, social clubs and fraternal organizations, and sports teams.

Making personal commitments with individual charisma behind them would be the dawn of a new and better day for the United States of America.

**Ask not what your country can do for you—
ask what you can do for your country.**

John F. Kennedy

YOUR INNER-DIRECTION SELF-ASSESSMENT

S can the QR code that follows to reach my website and then, on the website, complete the short Inner/Other Directedness Indicator self-assessment questionnaire. An individualized report will then be sent to you. Knowing your results and reflecting on them will better position you to identify and energize your charism.

The self-assessment contrasts an inner-directed orientation of personhood with an other-directed orientation of personhood. The inner-directed ideal is inspired by self-confident individualism in every social contest, highlighting those who look inward for their guiding principles, governing core values, beliefs, answers, and self-approval.

Inner-directedness is activated by those who know what they stand for. Basically, with them, "what you see is what you get." As they live out their values and beliefs, they can be nonconformist. They do not shy away from truth. They keep an open mind and are resilient, as they are settled in their appreciation of the commons and the common good. They are courageous.

The self-assessment also measures an other-directed perspective, in which you would look to others for values, beliefs, guidance, direction, and approval. The other-directed readily adjust to the ways and values of influencers and peers. They are performative in presentation of self in public. They tend to be poseurs, impostors, narcissists, and fitfully absorb others into the self. They borrow confidence from others, are easily upset, need constant reassurance, and expect to be given a safe space. While they tend to be conformist, they can fall back on passive-aggressive manipulations.

Inner-directedness can be internalized while understanding and knowing the elements of the other-directedness but not succumbing to "other" pressures.

To identify how closely you would come to practicing a high degree of inner-direction and low levels of other-direction, just scan the QR code at the beginning of this section and fill out the Inner/Other Directedness Indicator questionnaire. Your resulting scores will help you learn how to become a more self-confident person, better leader, and appreciated community contributor.

The two perspectives of inner-direction and other-direction are often thought of as opposites, when they are actually closely related. Inner-directed and other-directed ought to be experienced together in optimal alignment: **high** inner-directed and **low** other-directed. A close metaphor may be a dynamic equilibrium or a fulcrum, a pivot point, being centered, balanced among different radii going off in different directions. It is at the "center" or where high meets low. Here is where you say, "Upon reflection, taking into account all important facts, truths, what I believe: here I stand. I can do no other."

The "centered" person is more capable of choosing wisely among alternatives, not simply following what shines and glitters at any moment or seems most advantageous at the time. The "centered" person is neither overbearing and demanding nor uncertain and grasping for reassurance.

To be centered is to be aware of surroundings but not beholden to any particular point of view or thought.

The center is where trust is high and covenants are made and honored.

To be centered allows the mind to reflect, supporting a judicious temperament that compares alternatives and looks out for what is persuasive. To be centered is to be resistant to exaggerations, delusions, entreaties, manipulations, stupidities, extreme emotions, unsupported generalizations, and unrealistic wishes and hopes.

NOTES

Chapter 1: Once a Covenantal People

1 David Remnick, "'An Oligarchy Is Taking Shape,'" *New Yorker*, January 16, 2025, https://www.newyorker.com/news/the-lede/joe-biden-farewell-speech-warns-about-oligarchy.

2 John Bagot Glubb, *The Fate of Empires and Search for Survival* (Edinburgh, Scotland: William Blackwood & Sons, 1976), https://people.uncw.edu/kozl-offm/glubb.pdf.

3 Rick Marin, "The Anti-Woke King of Hollywood Lets Loose," *Commentary*, January 2025, https://www.commentary.org/articles/rick-marin/taylor-sheri-dan-anti-woke-director/.

4 Daron Acemoglu and James A. Robinson, *Why Nations Fail* (New York: Crown Business, 2012).

5 "Mayflower Compact Text," Teach Democracy, https://teachdemocracy.org/online-lessons/foundations-of-our-constitution/mayflower-compact-text-3.

6 "John Winthrop: A Model of Christian Charity (1630)," Gilder Lehrman Institute of American History, 2012, https://www.gilderlehrman.org/sites/de-fault/files/inline-pdfs/A%20Model%20of%20Christian%20Charity.pdf.

7 "Journals of the Continental Congress—the Articles of Association; October 20, 1774," Yale Law School Avalon Project, https://avalon.law.yale.edu/18th_century/contcong_10-20-74.asp.

8 "First Inaugural Address of Abraham Lincoln," Yale Law School Avalon Project, https://avalon.law.yale.edu/19th_century/lincoln1.asp.

9 "The Battle Hymn of the Republic," Wikipedia, https://en.wikipedia.org/wiki/Battle_Hymn_of_the_Republic.

10 "John F. Kennedy's Inaugural Address, 1961," The Gilder Lehrman Institute of American History, https://www.gilderlehrman.org/history-resources/spot-light-primary-source/john-f-kennedys-inaugural-address-1961.

11 David Hackett Fischer, *Albion's Seed: Four British Folkways in America* (New York: Oxford University Press, 1989).

12 James Webb, *Born Fighting: How the Scots-Irish Shaped America* (New York: Broadway Books, 2004).

13 *Plessy v. Ferguson*, 163 U.S. 537 (1896).

14 Martin Luther King Jr., *A Testament of Hope: The Essential Writings and Speeches* (New York: HarperOne, 2003).

15 Gen. 9:16 (New International Version—used throughout).

16 Gen. 15:18.

17 Gen. 22:12.

18 Deut. 28:1–14.

19 Deut. 10:12–13.

20 Ezek. 34:1–2, 10.

21 John 14:6.

22 Matt. 4:10.

23 Matt. 5.

24 Matt. 25.

25 John Locke, *Second Treatise on Civil Government*, from *The English Philosophers from Bacon to Mill* (New York: Random House—the Modern Library, 1929).

26 Ibid., 411.

27 Ibid., 438.

28 Max Weber, *The Protestant Ethic and the Spirit of Capitalism*, trans. Talcott Parsons (New York: Scribner, 1958).

29 Benjamin Franklin, *Autobiography of Benjamin Franklin*, Project Gutenberg, December 28, 2006, https://www.gutenberg.org/files/20203/20203-h/20203-h.htm.

30 Ibid.

31 Alexis de Tocqueville, *Democracy in America* (New York: Anchor Books, Doubleday & Company, 1969), 287, 525.

32 Thomas Reid, *Essays on the Intellectual Powers of Man* (1788).

33 Adam Smith, *The Theory of Moral Sentiments* (Indianapolis: Liberty Classics, 1976; originally published in 1759).

34 de Tocqueville, *Democracy in America*, 514.

35 Ibid., 515.

36 Ibid., 291.

37 Ibid.

38 Ibid., 295.

39 "What Are the Scout Oath and Scout Law?" Scouting America, https://www.scouting.org/about/faq/question10/.

40 Alice Liles, "Perhaps It's Time to Revisit Roy Rogers' Rules to Live By," *Muleshoe Journal*, February 7, 2019, https://www.myplainview.com/muleshoe/article/perhaps-its-time-to-revisit-roy-rogers-rules-to-live-by-19527500.php.

41 "Gene Autry's Cowboy Code," Gene Autry Entertainment, https://www.geneautry.com/geneautry/cowboycode.pdf.

42   Stephen R. Covey, *The 7 Habits of Highly Effective People: 30th Anniversary Edition* (Simon & Schuster, 2020).

43   Jordan B. Peterson, *12 Rules for Life: An Antidote to Chaos* (Random House Canada, 2018).

44   Lyndon Johnson, "The President's News Conference," American Presidency Project, July 28, 1965, https://www.presidency.ucsb.edu/documents/the-presidents-news-conference-1038; Robert Jewett, *The Captain America Complex* (Philadelphia: Westminster Press, 1973).

45   John Roach, presidential special assistant, to author.

46   Adam Sabes, "Johns Hopkins Medicine Chief Diversity Officer Resigns after 'Poorly Worded' Email about Men, 'White People,' and 'Christians,'" March 7, 2024, https://www.campusreform.org/article/johns-hopkins-medicine-chief-diversity-officer-resigns-poorly-worded-email-men-white-people-christians/24983.

47   "Diversity, Equity, and Inclusion Glossary of Terms," College of the Siskiyous, siskiyous.edu/committees/diversity/documents/8-dei-glossary-of-terms.pdf.

48   Ibid.

49   Marina Watts, "In Smithsonian Race Guidelines, Rational Thinking and Hard Work Are White Values," *Newsweek*, July 17, 2020, https://www.newsweek.com/smithsonian-race-guidelines-rational-thinking-hard-work-are-white-values-1518333.

50   Lindsay Ellis and Aaron Zitner, "Americans Lose Faith That Hard Work Leads to Economic Gains, WSJ-NORC Poll Finds," *Wall Street Journal*, September 1, 2025, https://www.wsj.com/economy/wsj-norc-economic-poll-73bce003?st=VzqhN5&reflink=article_gmail_share.

Chapter 2: The Unraveling of a Free Society

1   Derived from "Evil appears as good in the minds of those whom god leads to destruction" (lines 620–623).

2   Marcus Tullius Cicero, *Letters to Atticus*, trans. D. R. Shackleton Bailey (Cambridge: Harvard University Press, 1977), Letter 38.

3   Ibid., Letter 161.

4   Echelon Insights tweet, October 1, 2025, https://x.com/EchelonInsights/status/1973378389416280395.

5   63% of Voters Disapprove of the Trump Administration's Handling of the Jeffrey Epstein Files, Quinnipiac University National Poll Finds; Nearly Half of Voters Would Consider Joining a Third Party, Just Not One Created by Elon Musk," Quinnipiac University poll, July 16, 2025, https://poll.qu.edu/poll-release?releaseid=3928.

6   Cory Smith, "Polls Say We're on the Wrong Track as a Nation; Understanding Why Is More Complicated," ABC News Channel 9, April 11, 2024, https://newschannel9.com/news/nation-world/polls-say-were-on-the-wrong-track-as-a-nation-understanding-why-is-more-complicated-political-polarization-surveys-american-communities-project-michigan-state-university-american-life-public-opinion-differences-from-place-to-place-in-united-states.

7	Lance Morrow, "America Feels like a Codependent Household," *Wall Street Journal*, December 25, 2023, https://www.wsj.com/articles/america-feels-like-a-codependent-household-division-polarization-politics-303c8c9a.

8	Jimmy Carter, "Crisis of Confidence" speech, July 15, 1979, https://www.pbs.org/wgbh/americanexperience/features/carter-crisis/.

9	Aaron Zitner, "Voters See American Dream Slipping Out of Reach, WSJ/NORC Poll Shows," *Wall Street Journal*, November 24, 2023, https://www.wsj.com/us-news/american-dream-out-of-reach-poll-3b774892.

10	Rachel Wolfe, "The American Dream Feels Out of Reach for Most," *Wall Street Journal*, August 28, 2024, https://www.wsj.com/economy/consumers/american-dream-poll-us-economy-e5ddf640?utm.

11	Chart from the National Institutes of Health, https://meta.m.wikimedia.org/wiki/File:US_timeline._Number_of_overdose_deaths_from_all_drugs.jpg.

12	Roni Caryn Rabin, "Overdose Deaths Reached Record High as the Pandemic Spread," *New York Times*, November 17, 2021, https://www.nytimes.com/2021/11/17/health/drug-overdoses-fentanyl-deaths.html.

13	"Drug Abuse Statistics," National Center for Drug Abuse Statistics, https://drugabusestatistics.org/.

14	Press release, "Unprecedented Gen Z Research Panel to Track Behavior, Sentiments on Education and More Over Time," Walton Family Foundation, September 14, 2023, https://www.waltonfamilyfoundation.org/about-us/newsroom/unprecedented-gen-z-research-panel-to-track-behavior-sentiments-on-education-and-more-over-time.

15	Andrea Diaz, "Study: Less Than Half of Gen Z Thriving, Lowest among All Generations," Scripps News, September 14, 2023, https://www.scrippsnews.com/science-and-tech/study-less-than-half-of-gen-z-thriving-lowest-among-all-generations#:~:text=In%20general%2C%20today%2047%25%20of,%2C%20with%2045%25%20considered%20thriving.

16	"National Teddy Bear Day Survey Finds More Than Half of Adult Americans Still Have Their Teddy Bear from Childhood," PR Newswire, September 5, 2017, https://www.prnewswire.com/news-releases/national-teddy-bear-day-survey-finds-more-than-half-of-adult-americans-still-have-their-teddy-bear-from-childhood-300512770.html.

17	U.S. Department of Health and Human Services, Parents Under Pressure (Washington, DC: U.S. Government Publishing Office, 2024).

18	Colleen Seto, "Mom Rage Is a Real Thing—Here's How to Deal with It," Today's Parent, updated January 20, 2025, https://www.todaysparent.com/family/family-health/mom-rage-is-a-real-thing-heres-how-to-deal-with-it/.

19	Dr. Laura Markham, *Peaceful Parent, Happy Kids: How to Stop Yelling and Start Connecting* (New York: Tarcher, 2012).

20	Jeffrey M. Jones, "Confidence in U.S. Institutions Down; Average at New Low," Gallup, July 5, 2022, https://news.gallup.com/poll/394283/confidence-institutions-down-average-new-low.aspx.

21	Jamie Ballard, "Millennials Are the Loneliest Generation," YouGov, July 30, 2019, https://today.yougov.com/society/articles/24577-loneliness-friendship-new-friends-poll-survey.

22 Daniel De Visé, "A Record Share of Americans Is Living Alone," *The Hill*, July 10, 2023, https://thehill.com/policy/healthcare/4085828-a-record-share-of-americans-are-living-alone/.

23 Paulina Cachero and Claire Ballentine, "Nearly Half of All Young Adults Live with Mom and Dad—and They Like It," *Wall Street Journal*, September 20, 2023, https://www.bloomberg.com/news/articles/2023-09-20/nearly-half-of-young-adults-are-living-back-home-with-parents?embedded-checkout=true.

24 Dan Witters, "U.S. Depression Rates Reach New Highs," Gallup, May 17, 2023, https://news.gallup.com/poll/505745/depression-rates-reach-new-highs.aspx.

25 Jessica Dickler, "Amid Persistent Inflation, 54% of Americans Are Using Savings to Pay for Everyday Expenses," CNBC, February 16, 2023, https://www.cnbc.com/2023/02/16/54percent-of-americans-are-dipping-into-savings-to-pay-for-everyday-expenses.html.

26 Lorie Konish, "63% of workers unable to pay a $500 emergency expense, survey finds. How employers may help change that," CNBC, August 31, 2023, https://www.cnbc.com/2023/08/31/63percent-of-workers-are-unable-to-pay-a-500-emergency-expense-survey.html.

27 Erika Giovanetti, "Survey: 42% of Americans Don't Have an Emergency Fund," *U.S. News & World Report*, January 22, 2025, https://www.usnews.com/banking/articles/2025-financial-wellness-survey#:~:text=Most%20(62%25)%20said%20their,a%20financial%20goal%20for%202025.

28 Charlotte Morabito, "Here's Why Even Americans Making More Than $100,000 Live Paycheck to Paycheck," CNBC, December 11, 2023, https://www.cnbc.com/2023/12/11/why-even-americans-making-more-than-100000-live-paycheck-to-paycheck.html.

29 "Families and Living Arrangements," U.S. Census Bureau, https://www.census.gov/topics/families.html.

30 Aleks Phillips, "Americans Don't Want to Fight for Their Country Anymore," *Newsweek*, November 10, 2023, https://www.newsweek.com/american-military-recruitment-problems-public-apathy-1842449?utm.

31 "Them vs. U.S.: The Two Americas and How the Nation's Elite Is Out of Touch with Average American," The Committee to Unleash Prosperity, January 2024, https://committeetounleashprosperity.com/wp-content/uploads/2024/01/Them-vs-Us_CTUP-Rasmussen-Study-FINAL.pdf.

32 John R. Lott Jr., "Law Enforcement Collapse Masks Rising Crime Rates," RealClearPolitics, August 28, 2024, https://www.realclearpolitics.com/articles/2024/08/28/law_enforcement_collapse_masks_rising_crime_rates_151529.html.

33 Diana Nerozzi, Chris Nesi, and Patrick Reilly, "Minneapolis School Shooter Robin Westman Confessed He Was 'Tired of Being Trans': 'I Wish I Never Brain-Washed Myself,'" *New York Post*, August 28, 2025, https://nypost.com/2025/08/28/us-news/minneapolis-school-shooter-robin-westman-confessed-he-was-tired-of-being-trans.

34 Derek Thompson, "The Anti-Social Century," *Atlantic*, February 2025, 26, https://www.theatlantic.com/magazine/archive/2025/02/american-loneliness-personality-politics/681091/.

35 Ibid., 29.

36   Ibid., 30, 32.

37   Louis Hartz, *The Liberal Tradition in America* (Cambridge: Cambridge University Press, 1955).

38   Fischer, *Albion's Seed.*

39   Kathleen Kassel, "Agriculture and Its Related Industries Provide 10.4 Percent of U.S. Employment," USDA, November 3, 2023, https://www.ers.usda.gov/data-products/chart-gallery/gallery/chart-detail/?chartId=58282&utm.

40   Daniel Bell, *The Cultural Contradictions of Capitalism* (New York: Basic Books, 1976).

Chapter 3: The Psychosocial Orientation of the Overclass

1   David Riesman, *The Lonely Crowd: A Study of the Changing American Character* (New Haven: Yale University Press, 1961).

2   Matt. 4, *The New Jerusalem Bible* (New York: Doubleday, 1985).

3   Confucius, *The Analects of Confucius (from the Chinese Classics)*, Project Gutenberg, II:I, https://www.gutenberg.org/ebooks/3330.

4   Confucius, *The Analects*, XV:XX.

5   Ibid., II:X.

6   Ibid., II:XXIV.

7   Mencius, *The Works of Mencius*, book 1, part 1, chap. 1, http://nothingistic.org/library/mencius/mencius01.html.

8   "Queen Elizabeth I's Famous Speech to the Troops at Tilbury," Royal Museums Greenwich, https://www.rmg.co.uk/stories/topics/queen-elizabeth-speech-troops-tilbury.

9   Women Fight for the Vote, Library of Congress, https://www.loc.gov/exhibitions/women-fight-for-the-vote/.

10   "Notable & Quotable: Bull Run," *Wall Street Journal*, July 20, 2025, https://www.wsj.com/opinion/notable-quotable-bull-run-america-sullivan-ballou-b0644c3d?mod=Searchresults_pos1&page=1.

11   William Ernest Henley, "Invictus," Poetry Foundation, https://www.poetryfoundation.org/poems/51642/invictus.

12   Rudyard Kipling, "If—," Poetry Foundation, https://www.poetryfoundation.org/poems/46473/if—.

13   Robert Frost, "The Road Not Taken," Poetry Foundation, https://www.poetryfoundation.org/poems/44272/the-road-not-taken.

14   Riesman, *The Lonely Crowd*, 15.

15   Max Weber, "Politics as a Vocation," in *From Max Weber: Essays in Sociology*, edited and translated by Hans H. Gerth and C. Wright Mills (New York: Oxford University Press, 1946), 77–128.

16   Charles Murray, *In Pursuit of Happiness and Good Government* (New York: Simon and Schuster, 1988), 125.

17   Ibid., 120.

18   Ibid., 131.

19   Alexander Bick, Adam Blandin, Richard Rogerson, "Hours Worked and Life-time Earnings Inequality," National Bureau of Economic Research, working paper 32997, September 2024, https://www.nber.org/papers/w32997.

20   Confucius, "Great Learning," in *The Chinese Classics: Vol. 1. The Life and Teachings of Confucius*, trans. James Legge (Hong Kong: Hong Kong University Press, 1960).

21   Riesman, *The Lonely Crowd*, 19.

22   Ibid., 20.

23   Ibid., 21–22.

24   Alissa Quart, "How Insecurity Became the New Inequality", *TIME*, January 30, 2025, https://time.com/7210680/insecurity-is-the-new-inequality-essay/.

25   Ibid., 48.

26   Ibid., 63.

27   Ibid., 72.

28   Ibid., 75.

29   David Brooks, "The Sins of the Educated Class," *New York Times*, June 6, 2024, https://www.nytimes.com/2024/06/06/opinion/elites-progressives-universities.html.

30   Riesman, *The Lonely Crowd*, 72.

31   David Horsager, *Trust Matters More than Ever* (Savage, MN: Broadstreet Publishing Group, 2024).

32   Ingrid Clayton, *Fawning: Why the Need to Please Makes Us Lose Ourselves—and How to Find Our Way Back* (G. P. Putnam's Sons, 2025); Meg Josephson, *Are You Mad at Me?: How to Stop Focusing on What Others Think and Start Living for You* (Gallery Books, 2025); see also Katy Waldman, "How to Recover from Caring Too Much," *The New Yorker*, January 12, 2026, https://www.newyorker.com/magazine/2026/01/19/fawning-ingrid-clayton-book-review-are-you-mad-at-me-meg-josephson.

33   Marsha M. Linehan, *Cognitive-Behavioral Treatment for Borderline Personality Disorder* (The Guilford Press 1993); Theodore P. Beauchaine and Sheila E. Crowell, eds., The Oxford Handbook of Emotion Dysregulation (Oxford University Press, 2020); Peggilee Wupperman, Treating Impulsive, Addictive, and Self-Destructive Behaviors (The Guilford Press, 2019).

34   Riesman, *The Lonely Crowd*, 89.

35   "Remarks by President Biden on the Continued Battle for the Soul of the Nation," The White House, September 1, 2022, https://www.whitehouse.gov/briefing-room/speeches-remarks/2022/09/01/remarks-by-president-bidenon-the-continued-battle-for-the-soul-of-the-nation/#:~:text=And%20here%2C%20in%20my%20view,results%20of%20a%20free%20election.

36   Ibid., 181.

37   Ibid., 184.

38   "Kennedy Library & Museum Rededication Film (1993): Source of Quotation, 'We Enjoy the Comfort of Opinion . . . ,'" John F. Kennedy Presidential Library and Museum, June 11, 1962, https://www.jfklibrary.org/about-us/about-the-jfk-library/kennedy-library-fast-facts/rededication-film-quote.

39   Riesman, *The Lonely Crowd*, 239–40.

40   Friedrich Nietzsche, *The Birth of Tragedy and the Genealogy of Morals*, trans. F. Goffling (New York: Anchor Press, 1956; originally published in 1872, *The Birth of Tragedy*, and 1887, *The Genealogy of Morals*), 172.

41   David Brooks, "I Should Have Seen This Coming," *Atlantic*, April 7, 2025, https://www.theatlantic.com/magazine/archive/2025/05/trumpism-maga-populism-power-pursuit/682116/.

42   Jordan Kisner, "Who Needs Intimacy?," *Atlantic*, April 4, 2025, https://www.theatlantic.com/magazine/archive/2025/05/katie-kitamura-audition-book-review/682120/.

43   Covey, *The 7 Habits*.

44   Peterson, *12 Rules for Life*, 350.

45   Ibid., 27.

46   "The 34 CliftonStrengths Themes Explain Your Talent DNA," Gallup, https://www.gallup.com/cliftonstrengths/en/253715/34-cliftonstrengths-themes.aspx.

47   Confucius, *The Analects*, XIII:III.

48   Daniel Bell, *The Cultural Contradictions of Capitalism* (New York: Basic Books, 1976).

49   Ibid., 13.

50   Ibid., 52–53.

51   Ibid., 34.

52   "John F. Kennedy's Inaugural Address, 1961."

53   "Children in Progressive-Era America," Digital Public Library of America, https://dp.la/exhibitions/children-progressive-era/childhood-postwar-america/teenage-culture.

54   Erik H. Erikson, *Childhood and Society* (New York: W.W. Norton, 1963).

55   Ibid., 261.

56   Ibid.

57   "The Teenage Brain and You," Campbell County Health, October 1, 2022, https://www.cchwyo.org/news/2022/october/the-teenage-brain-and-you/.

58   Erik Erikson, "Identity and the Life Cycle," *Psychological Issues* 1, no. 1 (1959): 89, https://psycnet.apa.org/record/1994-97386-000.

59   Ibid., 93.

60   Stephen B. Young, *Kissinger's Betrayal* (Herndon, VA: Amplify, 2023).

61   Helen Andrews, *Boomers: The Men and Women Who Promised Freedom and Delivered Disaster* (New York: Sentinel, 2021).

62   Ibid., 4.

63   Ibid., 28.

64   Ibid., 30.

65   Ibid., 33.

66   Jennifer Wilson, "What Professional Organizers Know about Our Lives," *New Yorker*, December 16, 2024, https://www.newyorker.com/magazine/2024/12/23/more-than-pretty-boxes-carrie-m-lane-book-review.

67   Ibid., 127.

68   Ibid., 147.

69   Gerald F. Seib, "Will Debt Sink the American Empire?," *Wall Street Journal*, June 21, 2024, https://www.wsj.com/politics/policy/will-debt-sink-the-american-empire-8459096b.

70   Brooks, "The Sins of the Educated Class."

71   Rikki Schlott "Is it any wonder liberals are having a mental health crisis?," *New York Post*, June 3, 2025, https://nypost.com/2025/06/03/us-news/is-it-any-wonder-liberals-are-having-a-mental-health-crisis/.

Chapter 4: Theory of the Overclass: From Rousseau to Today

1   Isaac Schorr, "Trump the Myth-Buster: Wrecking the Left's Delusions Is His Superpower," *New York Post*, February 16, 2025, https://nypost.com/2025/02/16/opinion/myth-buster-wrecking-lefty-delusions-is-trumps-superpower/.

2   Jean-Jacques Rousseau, *Discourse on the Origin of Inequality*, from *The Social Contract and Discourses* (New York: E. P. Dutton, 1950; originally published in 1755), 234.

3   Ibid., 237.

4   Ibid., 248.

5   Ibid., 251.

6   Ibid., 15.

7   Ibid.

8   Ibid., 57.

9   Ibid., 57.

10   Ibid., 139.

11   "Declaration of the Rights of Man—1789," Yale Law School Avalon Project, https://avalon.law.yale.edu/18th_century/rightsof.asp.

12   G. W. F. Hegel, *Outlines of the Philosophy of Right*, trans. T. M. Knox (Oxford: Oxford University Press, 2008; originally published in 1820), 270.

13   Daniel Bell, *The Coming of Post-Industrial Society: A Venture in Social Forecasting* (New York: Basic Books, 1976), 10.

14   Roger Kimball, "Kamala Harris and the Masque of Magical Thinking," American Greatness, August 4, 2024, https://amgreatness.com/2024/08/04/kamala-harris-and-the-masque-of-magical-thinking/.

15   Hegel, *Outlines of the Philosophy of Right*, 229.

16   Ibid., 244, 258.

17   Ibid., 236–237.

18   Ibid., 264.

19   Ibid., 265.

20   Ibid., 283.

21   Ibid., 269.

22   Ibid., 280.

23   Karl Marx and Friedrich Engels, *The Communist Manifesto*, from *Marx & Engels: Basic Writings on Politics & Philosophy*, ed. Lewis Feuer (Garden City: Anchor Books, 1959), 7–9.

24   Ibid.

25   Ibid.

26   Ibid.

27   Karl Marx, Critique of the Gotha Programme, Marxists Internet Archive, 1875, https://www.marxists.org/archive/marx/works/1875/gotha/index.htm.

28   Marx and Engels, *The Communist Manifesto*.

29   Ibid.

30   1 Tim. 6:10 (New King James Version).

31   Lewis Carroll, *Through the Looking-Glass, and What Alice Found There* (Chapter 6), Project Gutenberg, originally published in 1871, https://www.gutenberg.org/cache/epub/12/pg12-images.html#link2HCH0006.

32   Fredrich Nietzsche, *Thus Spoke Zarathustra* (Germany: Ernst Schmeitzner, 1883), XXXVIII.

33   Oliver E. Williamson (citing Simon), "The Economics of Organization: The Transaction Cost Approach," *American Journal of Sociology* 81 (1981): 553.

34   Nietzsche, *The Birth of Tragedy and the Genealogy of Morals*, 151.

35   Ibid., 160.

36   Ibid., 171.

37   Ibid., 287.

38   Ibid., 288.

39   Ibid., 290.

40   Fredrich Nietzsche, *Beyond Good and Evil*, trans. Walter Kaufman (New York: Vintage Books, 1966; originally published in 1886), 99.

41   William Shakespeare, *Macbeth*, act 5, scene 5.

42   Nietzsche, *The Birth of Tragedy and the Genealogy of Morals*, 173.

43   Mozi, "Identification with the Superior," in Excerpts from Mozi, trans. Roberto Galentino, https://www.robertogalentino.com/wp-content/uploads/2017/10/Mo-Zi-Identification-with-the-Superior-Excerpts.pdf.

44   Mikhail Bakunin, *God and the State* (New York: Dover, 1970), 79.

45   Ibid., 15.

46   Ibid., 17.

47   Ibid., 31.

48   Ibid., 56.

49   Mikhail Bakunin, *Marxism, Freedom and the State* (New York: Dover Publications, 1970), chap. 3.

50   George Sorel, *Reflections on Violence* (Cambridge: Cambridge University Press, 2012; originally published in 1908), 101.

51   Ibid., xxi.

52   Ibid., 105.

53   Ibid., 107.

54   Ibid., 52, 60, 63.

55   Thorstein Veblen, *The Theory of Business Enterprise* (New York: Charles Scribner's Sons, 1927).

56   Ibid., 10.

57   Ibid., 37.

58   Ibid., 147.

59   Julien Benda, *The Treason of the Intellectuals* (New Brunswick: Transaction Publishers, 2007), 39.

60   Ibid., 40.

61   Ibid., 47.

62   Ibid., 81.

63   Ibid., 118.

64   Gramsci, Antonio, *Selections from the Prison Notebooks*, translators and editors, Quinto Hoare and Geoffrey Smith, (New York: International Publishers, 1971), 5.

65   Ibid., 9.

66   Ibid., 10.

67   Ibid., 12.

68   Ibid., 258, 259.

69   Ibid., 333.

70   Ibid., 334.

71   Ibid., 335.

72   Leon Trotsky, *The Revolution Betrayed* (Garden City: Doubleday, 2004; originally published in 1836) 73.

73   Ibid., 74.

74   Ibid., 76.

75   Ibid., 79.

76   Ibid., 81.

77   Ibid., 83.

78   Ibid., 85.

79   Ibid., 86–87.

80   Ibid., 100.

81   Ibid., 105.

82   Ibid., 188.

83   James Burnham, *The Managerial Revolution* (London: Lume Books, 2021; first published in 1941), 65.

84   Ibid., 66.

85   Ibid., 242.

86   Ibid., 254.

87   Friedrich August Hayek and Liberty Fund, Inc., "The Use of Knowledge in Society," *American Economic Review*, September 1945, 519–30, https://www.cato.org/sites/cato.org/files/articles/hayek-use-knowledge-society.pdf.

88   Milovan Djilas, *The New Class: An Analysis of the Communist System* (New York: Praeger, 1957), 38.

89   Ibid., 40.

90   Ibid., 46.

91   Ibid., 45, 46, 51.

92   Ibid., 61.

93   Ibid., 54.

94   Ibid., 69.

95   C. Wright Mills, *White Collar: The American Middle Classes* (New York: Oxford University Press, 1956), xii.

96   Ibid., 65.

97   Ibid., 81.

98   Ibid., 92.

99   Ibid., 93.

100   Ibid., 112.

101   Ibid., 243.

102   Ibid., 131.

103   Ibid., 142.

104   Ibid., 149.

105   Ibid., 68.

106   Ibid., 69.

107   Ibid., 77.

108   Ibid., 71.

109   Ibid., 219.

110 Ibid., 232.

111 Ibid., 255.

112 Ibid., 263.

113 C. Wright Mills, *The Power Elite* (New York: Oxford University Press, 1957), 3.

114 Ibid., 289.

115 Ibid., 4.

116 Ibid., 9.

117 Ibid., 361.

118 Ibid., 314.

119 Tom Hayden, "The Port Huron Statement," Students for a Democratic Society, June 15, 1962, https://images2.americanprogress.org/campus/email/PortHuronStatement.pdf.

120 Robert McNamara, *In Retrospect: The Tragedy and Lessons of Vietnam* (New York: Times Books, 1995), 254–56; Stephen B. Young, "Saving Robert McNamara," *Harvard Magazine*, 2017, https://www.harvardmagazine.com/sites/default/files/inline_images/2017-MarchApril/Young_Letter.pdf.

121 Ibid., 2.

122 Ibid., 3.

123 Ibid., 4.

124 Ibid., 47.

125 Ibid., 51.

126 Ibid., 85.

127 Ibid.,147.

128 Bell, *The Coming of Post-Industrial Society*, 112.

129 Ibid., 118.

130 Ibid., 127.

131 Ibid., 362.

132 Ibid., 246.

133 Ibid., 358.

134 B. Bruce-Briggs, ed., *The New Class? America's Educated Elite Examined* (New York: McGraw-Hill, 1979), ix.

135 Bruce-Briggs, *New Class*, 8.

136 David Lebedoff, *The New Elite: The Death of Democracy* (New York: Franklin Watt, 1981), 18.

137 "Hillary Clinton's 'Basket of Deplorables' Remarks (Transcript)," *TIME*, September 9, 2016, https://time.com/4486502/hillary-clinton-basket-of-deplorables-transcript/.

138 Will Weissert, "Biden Calls Trump Supporters 'Garbage' in Puerto Rico Comic," Associated Press, September 19, 2024, https://apnews.com/article/biden-trump-supporters-garbage-puerto-rico-comic-e62ccf9108ba0ca8d1ee694f-91a6867e.

139 Lebedoff, *New Elite*, 140.

140 Ibid., 31.

141 Ibid., 66.

142 Ibid., 67.

143 Ibid., 96.

144 Ibid., 146.

145 Christopher Lasch, *The Revolt of the Elites and the Betrayal of Democracy* (New York: W. W. Norton, 1995), 6.

146 Ibid., 7.

147 Ibid., 17.

148 Ibid., 18.

149 Ibid., 180.

150 Richard Florida, *The Rise of the Creative Class* (New York: Basic Books, 2002), 5.

151 Ibid., 21.

152 Ibid., 9.

153 Ibid., 55.

Chapter 5: An Ideology of Decadence

1 Derived from "The Strong do what they can. The weak suffer what they must."

2 David Selbourne, *The Principle of Duty* (Notre Dame, Indiana: University of Notre Dame Press, 2001).

3 Thomas Hobbes, *Leviathan* (Project Gutenberg, originally published in 1651), chap. 13–14. https://www.gutenberg.org/files/3207/3207-h/3207-h.htm.

4 William H. Whyte Jr., *The Organization Man* (New York: Simon and Schuster, 1956), 46.

5 Ibid., 11.

6 Ibid., 51–52.

7 Ibid., 54.

8 Ibid., 57.

9 "The Executive's Reading List," McKinsey, July 14, 2024, https://www.mckinsey.com/featured-insights/themes/the-executives-reading-list.

10 Erving Goffman, *The Presentation of Self in Everyday Life* (New York: Anchor Books, 1959), 251.

11 Ibid., 17.

12 Ibid.

13 Ibid., 252.

14 1 Sam. 8:4–9.

15 Ibid., 95.

16 Francis Fukuyama, *Trust: The Social Virtues and the Creation of Prosperity* (New York: Free Press, 1995); see also Fukuyama, *Identity: The Demand for Dignity and the Politics of Resentment* (New York: Farrar, Straus, and Giroux, 2018).

17 Horsager, *Trust Matters.*

18 Chantal Delsol, *Icarus Fallen: The Search for Meaning in an Uncertain World* (Wilmington, DE: ISI Books, 2003), 27.

19 William Shakespeare, *As You Like It*, act 2, scene 7.

20 Erikson, *Childhood and Society*, 254.

21 Ibid., 255.

22 Ibid., 256.

23 Ibid., 263.

24 Abraham Maslow, *Toward a Psychology of Being* (New York: John Wiley & Sons, 1999; originally published in 1962), 27.

25 Ibid., 173.

26 Alan Jacobs, *The Essential Gnostic Gospels* (London: Watkins Publishing, 2006) 57–58, 76, 84.

27 Ibid., 85–86.

28 Glenn Hughes, *Transcendence and History* (Columbia, MO, University of Missouri, 2003), 91.

29 Ibid.

30 Ibid., 92.

31 Dayna Tortorici, "What Did the Pop Culture of the Two-Thousands Do to Millennial Women," *The New Yorker*, June 16, 2025, https://www.newyorker.com/magazine/2025/06/16/girl-on-girl-sophie-gilbert-book-review.

32 World Bank, "World Development Report 2015: Mind, Society, and Behavior," December 4, 2014, https://www.worldbank.org/en/publication/wdr2015, 4–5.

33 David McClelland, *The Achieving Society* (Princeton: Princeton University Press, 1961), and *Human Motivation* (New York: Cambridge University Press, 1987).

34 Daron Acemoglu and James A. Robinson, *Why Nations Fail: The Origins of Power, Prosperity, and Poverty* (New York: Crown Currency, 2012).

35 Zitner, "Voters See American Dream Slipping Out of Reach."

36 Carol Gilligan, *In a Different Voice: Psychological Theory and Women's Development* (Cambridge: Harvard University Press, 1982), xi.

37 Ibid., xiii.

38 Ibid., xix.

39 Ibid., 22.

40 Ibid., 29–33

41 Ibid., 33.

42 "Kamala Harris Shows Why She Can't Do Interviews," Redarchives, August 28, 2024, https://redarchives.net/kamala-harris-shows-why-she-cant-do-interview/.

43 Gilligan, *In a Different Voice*, 42.

44 Ibid., 48.

45 Ibid., 49.

46 Ibid., 62.

47 Ibid., 64–65.

48 Ibid., 73.

49 Ibid., 74.

50 Ibid., 79.

51 Mariann Edgar Budde, "'Contempt Is a Dangerous Way to Lead a Country': That Enraged Donald Trump," *Guardian*, January 24, 2025, https://www.theguardian.com/commentisfree/2025/jan/24/bishop-mariann-edgar-budde-sermon-that-enraged-donald-trump.

52 Kay Hymowitz, "The New Girl Order," *City Journal*, Summer 2024, https://www.city-journal.org/article/the-new-girl-order.

53 Young, *Kissinger's Betrayal*.

54 Ibid., 352.

Chapter 6: Seizing Power Through Higher Education

1 Forest Romm and Kevin Waldman, "Performative Virtue-Signaling Has Become a Threat to Higher Ed," *The Hill*, August 12, 2025, https://thehill.com/opinion/education/5446702-performative-virtue-signaling-has-become-a-threat-to-higher-ed/.

2 "United States Total Debt: % of GDP," CEIC Data, September 2024, https://www.ceicdata.com/en/indicator/united-states/total-debt--of-gdp.

3 Burton J. Bledstein, *The Culture of Professionalism: The Middle Class and the Development of Higher Education in America* (New York: W. W. Norton & Company, 1976), 135.

4 Ibid., 324.

5 "Morrill Act (1862)," National Archives, https://www.archives.gov/milestone-documents/morrill-act, Sec. 4.

6 Christina Metzger, "A Crisis in Education: Can We Make the Humboldtian Concept Sexy Again?," *Yale Distilled*, 2020, https://yaledistilled.sites.yale.edu/browse-issues/2020-issue/crisis-education-can-we-make-humboldtian-concept-sexy-again.

7 Bledstein, *Culture of Professionalism*, 324.

8 Ibid., 129.

9 Ibid., 132.

10 Ibid., 323.

11   Ibid., 84.

12   Ibid., 86.

13   Ibid., 88.

14   Ibid.

15   Milton Friedman, "A Friedman Doctrine: The Social Responsibility of Business Is to Increase Its Profits," *New York Times*, September 13, 1970, https://www.nytimes.com/1970/09/13/archives/a-friedman-doctrine-the-social-responsibility-of-business-is-to.html.

16   "Take the MBA Oath," https://mbaoath.org/take-the-mba-oath/.

17   Bledstein, *Culture of Professionalism*, 289.

18   Ibid., 90.

19   United States Attorney's Office, District of Massachusetts, "Investigations of College Admissions and Testing Bribery Scheme," https://www.justice.gov/usao-ma/investigations-college-admissions-and-testing-bribery-scheme.

20   Tovia Smith, "Mastermind of the Varsity Blues College Admission Scandal Is About to Learn His Fate," *NPR*, January 4, 2023, https://www.npr.org/2023/01/03/1146672235/varsity-blues-college-cheating-scandal-mastermind-rick-singer-sentence.

21   Milla Surjadi and Sara Randazzo, "The Cheating Scandal Rocking the World of Elite High-School Math," *Wall Street Journal*, August 15, 2024, https://www.wsj.com/us-news/education/math-competition-cheating-scandal-acb0cde9?mod=Searchresults_pos1&page=1.

22   Lincoln Caplan, "Academic Freedom and Free Speech," *Harvard Magazine*, October 11, 2024, https://www.harvardmagazine.com/2024/09/harvard-academic-freedom-free-speech.

23   Bledstein, *Culture of Professionalism*, 312.

24   Ibid., 311.

25   "Hillary Rodham's Student 1969 Commencement Speech," Wellesley College, https://www1.wellesley.edu/events/commencement/archives/1969commencement/studentspeech.

26   Victor Davis Hanson, "From 'Clingers' to 'Garbage': Why the 16 Years of Vilification?," *American Greatness*, November 4, 2024, https://amgreatness.com/2024/11/04/from-clingers-to-garbage-why-the-16-years-of-vilification/.

27   "Exit Polls of the Presidential Election in the United States in 2024, Share of Votes by Household Income," Statista, November 12, 2024, https://www.statista.com/statistics/1535295/presidential-election-exit-polls-share-votes-income-us.

28   Erica Pandey, "America's Diploma Divide: States with Fewer Grads Went for Trump," *Axios*, November 11, 2024, https://www.axios.com/2024/11/07/college-degree-voters-split-harris-trump.

29   Miranda Devine, "Rise of Kamala Harris Solidifies Dems' Full Embrace as the Party of 'Preachy Females,' Scolding Shrews," *New York Post*, August 1, 2024, https://nypost.com/2024/07/31/opinion/rise-of-kamala-harris-solidifies-dems-full-embrace-as-the-party-of-preachy-females-scolding-shrews/.

30 Anthony Gockowski, "Gov. Walz Calls Trump a 'Bastard,' Likens Socialism to 'Neighborliness' at Event for 'White Dudes,'" *Alpha News*, July 31, 2024, https://alphanews.org/gov-walz-calls-trump-a-bastard-likens-socialism-to-neighborliness-at-event-for-white-dudes/.

31 Roger Kimball, "Kamala Harris and the Masque of Magical Thinking," *American Greatness*, August 5, 2024, https://amgreatness.com/2024/08/04/kamala-harris-and-the-masque-of-magical-thinking/.

32 Education Healthcare Public Services, "AFT votes to endorse Kamala Harris for president," https://www.aft.org/news/aft-votes-endorse-kamala-harris-president.

33 "Endorsement of Kamala Harris for President," American Federation of Teachers, July 31, 2024, https://www.aft.org/resolution/endorsement-kamala-harris-president.

34 "Fighting the Harmful Impacts of Private Equity on Our Economy, Public Pension Funds and Healthcare System," American Federation of Teachers, August 1, 2024, https://www.aft.org/resolution/fighting-harmful-impacts-private-equity-our-economy-public-pension-funds-and-healthcare.

35 Hymowitz, "The New Girl Disorder."

36 Lauren Weber and Stephanie Stamm, "40% of Lawyers Are Women. 7% Are Black. America's Workforce in Charts," *Wall Street Journal*, February 9, 2024, https://www.wsj.com/economy/jobs/workers-america-jobs-demographics-charts-94a5ff6c?st=w6u53nu2f6rh4n4&reflink=desktopwebshare_permalink.

37 Lom3z, "What Is the Longhouse?," *First Things*, February 16, 2023, https://www.firstthings.com/web-exclusives/2023/02/what-is-the-longhouse.

38 Hanna Rosin, "The End of Men," *Atlantic*, accessed July 20, 2023, https://www.theatlantic.com/magazine/archive/2010/07/the-end-of-men/308135/.

39 Louis Nelson, "Clinton: 'The Future Is Female,'" *Politico*, February 7, 2017, https://www.politico.com/story/2017/02/hillary-clinton-video-message-future-is-female-234723.

40 Max Eden, "Trauma-Deformed Pedagogy," American Enterprise Institute, July 24, 2023, https://www.aei.org/op-eds/trauma-deformed-pedagogy/.

41 S. Mac Healty and Angelina J. Parker, "Harvard Launches New Intro Math Course to Address Pandemic Learning Loss," *Harvard Crimson*, September 3, 2024, https://www.thecrimson.com/article/2024/9/3/new-math-intro-course/.

42 Tom Sarrouf Jr., "What's Wrong with Boys at School?," Institute for Family Studies, June 5, 2024, https://ifstudies.org/blog/whats-wrong-with-boys-at-school.

43 Rachel Wolfe, "America's Young Men Are Falling Even Further Behind," *Wall Street Journal*, September 28, 2024, https://www.wsj.com/lifestyle/careers/young-american-men-lost-c1d799f7.

44 Miles J. Herszenhorn and Claire Yuan, "'I Am Sorry': Harvard President Gay Addresses Backlash over Congressional Testimony on Antisemitism," *Harvard Crimson* December 8, 2023, https://www.thecrimson.com/article/2023/12/8/gay-apology-congressional-remarks/.

45 Thomas B. Edsall, "The Gender Gap Is Taking Us to Unexpected Places," *New York Times*, January 12, 2022, https://www.nytimes.com/2022/01/12/opinion/gender-gap-politics.html.

46 John Tierney, "DEI v. Science," *City Journal*, August 27, 2024, https://www.city-journal.org/article/dei-v-science?skip=1.

47 Lom3z, "What Is the Longhouse?"

48 Abigail Shrier, *Bad Therapy: Why the Kids Aren't Growing Up* (New York: Sentinel, 2024), 46–47.

49 Ibid., 43.

50 Ibid., 77.

51 Ibid., 87.

52 Ibid., 158.

53 Ibid., 247.

54 Jenny Anderson, "The New Must-Have for Overwhelmed Kids: An Executive Function Coach," *Wall Street Journal*, November 8, 2024, https://www.wsj.com/health/wellness/the-new-must-have-for-overwhelmed-kids-an-executive-function-coach-13feb5b3.

55 Ibid.

56 Ibid.

57 Tierney, "DEI v. Science."

58 Wendy M. Williams and Stephen J. Ceci, "National Hiring Experiments Reveal 2:1 Faculty Preference for Women on STEM Tenure Track," *Proceedings of the National Academy of Sciences* 112, no. 17 (April 13, 2015): 5360–65, https://doi.org/10.1073/pnas.1418878112.

59 Lin Zhang et al., "Gender Differences in the Aims and Impacts of Research," *Scientometrics* 126, no. 11 (October 12, 2021): 8861–86, https://doi.org/10.1007/s11192-021-04171-y.

60 Gerard Baker, "Just When We Need Them, the Media's Credibility Hits Bottom," *Wall Street Journal*, March 3, 2025, https://www.wsj.com/opinion/just-when-we-need-them-the-medias-credibility-hits-bottom-79b11b8f.

61 Susan Faludi, "All the News That's Fit to Feel," *New York Review of Books*, July 25, 2024, https://www.nybooks.com/articles/2024/08/15/all-the-news-thats-fit-to-feel-girls-on-the-bus/.

62 Deborah Chambers, Linda Steiner, and Carole Fleming, *Women and Journalism* (London and New York: Routledge, 2004).

63 Gabrielle Gurley, "Celebrity Fatigue," *American Prospect*, January 31, 2025, https://prospect.org/culture/2025-01-31-celebrity-fatigue-democrats/.

64 "About Us," Creative Artists Agency, https://www.caa.com/about-us.

65 David Brooks, "How the Bobos Broke America," *Atlantic*, September 2021, https://www.theatlantic.com/magazine/archive/2021/09/blame-the-bobos-creative-class/619492/.

66 Kelefa Sanneh, "The Fight to Redefine Racism," *New Yorker*, August 12, 2019, https://web.archive.org/web/20190813211634/https://www.newyorker.com/magazine/2019/08/19/the-fight-to-redefine-racism.

67 Jonathan Haidt, *The Anxious Generation: How the Great Rewiring of Childhood Is Causing an Epidemic of Mental Illness* (New York: Penguin, 2024), 17.

68   Ibid., 28.

69   Ibid., 54.

70   Ibid., 73.

71   Ibid., 85.

72   Jonathan Haidt and Greg Lukianoff, *The Coddling of the American Mind: How Good Intentions and Bad Ideas Are Setting Up a Generation for Failure* (New York: Penguin, 2018), 32.

73   Adam Kirsch, *On Settler Colonialism: Ideology, Violence, and Justice* (New York: W. W. Norton, 2024).

74   Naomi Schaefer Riley and James Pierson, "And We Do Classes, Too!," *City Journal*, Spring 2024, https://www.city-journal.org/article/and-we-do-classes-too.

75   Erin Loh, "Behind Stanford's doubled staff-to-student ratio," Stanford Daily, March 13, 2024, https://stanforddaily.com/2024/03/13/behind-stanfords-doubled-staff-to-student-ratio/.

76   Yascha Mounk, "College Grades Have Become a Charade. It's Time to Abolish Them," *Wall Street Journal*, September 6, 2024, https://www.wsj.com/us-news/education/college-grades-have-become-acharade-its-time-to-abolish-them-ee4eb3fe.

77   Peter Berkowitz, "The Press, the Professors, and Postmodern Progressivism," RealClearPolitics, September 15, 2024, https://www.realclearpolitics.com/articles/2024/09/15/press_professors_and_postmodern_progressivism_151610.html.

78   David Brooks, "How the Ivy League Broke America," *Atlantic*, November 14, 2024, https://www.theatlantic.com/magazine/archive/2024/12/meritocracy-college-admissions-social-economic-segregation/680392/.

79   Nathan Honeycutt, "Silence in the Classroom: The 2024 FIRE Faculty Survey Report," Foundation for Individual Rights and Expression, 2024, https://www.thefire.org/research-learn/silence-classroom-2024-fire-faculty-survey-report.

80   The Nation's Report Card, https://www.nationsreportcard.gov/.

81   Brenda Wineapple, "In Search of the Real Hannah Crafts," *New York Review of Books*, August 15, 2024, https://www.nybooks.com/articles/2024/08/15/in-search-of-the-real-hannah-crafts-gregg-hecimovich/?srsltid=AfmBOopM6tirTzSsN3-KzhtcAzsagUekBLhIoh3Rg6VYLOtOP0bWzU4U.

82   W. E. B. Du Bois, *The Souls of Black Folk* (New York: Penguin Signet Classic, 1995; originally published in 1903), 108.

83   Ibid., 118–19.

84   Martin Robison Delaney, "The Condition, Elevation, Emigration, and Destiny of the Colored People of the United States," 1852, https://www.gutenberg.org/files/17154/17154-h/17154-h.htm.

85   Joy DeGruy Leary, *Post Traumatic Slave Syndrome* (Milwaukie: Upton Press, 2005).

86   Ibid., 117.

87   Ibid., 133.

88   LittleJerryFan92, "Sesame Street—I Am Somebody," YouTube, July 1, 2007, https://www.youtube.com/watch?v=iTB1h18bHlY.

89   Jason L. Riley, "The Tragedy of Affirmative Action," *Wall Street Journal*, May 2, 2025, https://www.wsj.com/opinion/the-tragedy-of-affirmative-action-black-mobility-racial-preferences-merit-b1ca70e3?mod=author_content_page_1_pos_2.

90   de Tocqueville, *Democracy in America*, 690.

Chapter 7: Rule Through Management Rather Than Leadership

1   Chester Barnard, *The Functions of the Executive* (Cambridge: Harvard University Press, 1938), 284.

2   Ezek. 34.

3   Philip Selznick, *Leadership in Administration* (Berkeley: University of California Press, 1957), vi.

4   Ibid., 3.

5   Ibid., 4.

6   Kevin Cashman, *Leadership from the Inside Out* (San Francisco: Berrett-Koehler, 2017), 2.

7   Ibid., 3.

8   Ibid., 29.

9   Daniel Kahneman, *Thinking, Fast and Slow*, (New York: Farrar, Straus and Giroux, 2011).

10   Tom Rosentiel, "What Brain Science Tells Us About Religious Belief," Pew Research Center, May 5, 2008, https://www.pewresearch.org/science/2008/05/05/what-brain-science-tells-us-about-religious-belief/; Dr. Ernie, "The Amygdala Gospel: Rewiring How We Grow Closer to Jesus," *Radically Happy*, January 1, 2022, https://2transform.us/2022/01/01/the-amygdala-gospel-rewiring-how-we-grow-closer-to-jesus/.

11   Selznick, *Leadership in Administration*, 74.

12   Ibid., 146–47.

13   Ibid., 25.

14   Barnard, *The Functions of the Executive*, 82.

15   Ibid., 215–16.

16   Ibid., 259.

17   Ibid., 260.

18   Winston Churchill, "We Shall Fight on the Beaches" speech, June 4, 1940, https://winstonchurchill.org/resources/speeches/1940-the-finest-hour/we-shall-fight-on-the-beaches/.

19   Winston Churchill, "Some Chicken! Some Neck!" speech, December 30, 1941, https://winstonchurchill.org/publications/churchill-bulletin/bulletin-043-jan-2012/winston-churchill-70-years-ago-some-chicken-some-neck/.

20 Alan Axelrod, *Patton on Leadership* (Saddle River: Prentice Hall Press, 1999), 55–57.

21 Ibid., 157.

22 Alex Horton, "Top U.S. Military Leader: 'I Want to Understand White Rage. And I'm White,'" *Washington Post*, June 23, 2021, https://www.washington-post.com/powerpost/republicans-joint-chiefs-chairman-critical-race-theory-congress/2021/06/23/84654c34-d451-11eb-9f29-e9e6c9e843c6_story.html.

23 Biography of General Mark Milley, Department of Defense, https://www.defense.gov/About/Biographies/Biography/Article/614392/retired-general-mark-a-milley/#:~:text=While%20serving%20as%20the%20Commanding,Commanding%20General%2C%20U.S.%20Forces%20Afghanistan.

24 Barnard, *The Functions of the Executive*, 263.

25 Ibid., 279.

26 Ibid., 283.

27 David Callahan, *The Cheating Culture: Why More Americans Are Doing Wrong to Get Ahead* (New York: Houghton Mifflin Harcourt, 2004), 110–16.

28 Ibid., 19.

29 Ibid., 23.

30 Hiranmayi Srinivasan, "What Is Joe Biden's Net Worth?," Investopedia, June 17, 2024, https://www.investopedia.com/joe-biden-net-worth-8655652#:~:text=Key%20Takeaways,2024%20by%20the%20White%20House.

31 David Nadelle, "What Is Hillary Clinton's Net Worth?," GOBankingRates/Nasdaq, November 9, 2023, https://www.nasdaq.com/articles/what-is-hillary-clintons-net-worth.

32 Becky Yerak and *Chicago Tribune* staff, "Straddling the Worlds of High Finance and Community Activism," *Chicago Tribune*, June 19, 2018, https://www.chicagotribune.com/2013/04/01/straddling-the-worlds-of-high-finance-and-community-activism-2/.

33 Sean Neumann, "Barack & Michelle Obama Just Bought a $11.75M, 7-Bedroom Martha's Vineyard Estate: Reports," *People*, December 6, 2019, https://people.com/home/barack-michelle-obama-buy-marthas-vineyard-mansion/.

34 Hillary Hoffower and Joshua Nelken-Zitser, "The Obamas' Net Worth: How Michelle and Barack Obama Make Their Money," *Business Insider*, February 22, 2023, https://www.businessinsider.com/barack-obama-michelle-obama-net-worth-2018-7.

35 Isabel Vincent, "The Obamas Are 'Becoming' a Billion-Dollar Brand," *New York Post*, November 17, 2018, https://nypost.com/2018/11/17/the-obamas-are-becoming-a-billion-dollar-brand.

36 Daniel Goleman, "What Makes a Leader?," *Harvard Business Review*, November–December 1998, https://helenagmartins.wordpress.com/wp-content/uploads/2015/09/what-makes-a-leader-d-goleman-hbr-1998.pdf, 3.

37 Ibid., 17.

38 Jim Collins, *Good to Great: Why Some Companies Make the Leap . . . and Others Don't* (New York: Harper Business, 2001), 20.

39 Ibid., 21.

40 Ibid., 30.

41 Ibid., 20.

42 Ibid., 51.

43 Ibid., 70.

44 Ibid., 72.

45 Ibid., 87.

46 Ibid., 91.

47 Ibid., 183.

48 Kevin Cashman, *Leadership from the Inside Out: Becoming a Leader for Life* (San Francisco: Berrett-Koehler, 1998), 28.

49 Ibid., 39–40.

50 Ibid., 82.

51 Robert Spitzer, *The Spirit of Leadership: Optimizing Creativity and Change in Organizations* (Provo: Executive Excellence Publishing, 2000), 32.

52 Paul Graham, "Founder Mode," PaulGraham.com, September 2024, https://paulgraham.com/foundermode.html.

53 Mary C. Gentile, *Giving Voice to Values: How to Speak Your Mind When You Know What's Right* (New Haven, CT: Yale University Press, 2012) 27.

54 Robert Terry, *Authentic Leadership: Courage in Action* (San Francisco: Jossey-Bass, 1993), 123.

55 Ibid., 116.

56 "Narcissistic Personality Disorder—Symptoms and Causes," Mayo Clinic, n.d., https://www.mayoclinic.org/diseases-conditions/narcissistic-personality-disorder/symptoms-causes/syc-20366662.

57 Susan H. Gebelein et al., *Successful Manager's Handbook* (Personnel Decisions International, 1992), 299.

58 Goleman, "What Makes a Leader?"

59 Anne-Laure Fayard et al., "Nurturing Innovation," *Harvard Business Review*, March 12, 2024, https://hbr.org/2024/03/nurturing-innovation.

60 Jamil Zaki, "How to Sustain Your Empathy in Difficult Times," *Harvard Business Review*, December 13, 2023, https://hbr.org/2024/01/how-to-sustain-your-empathy-in-difficult-times.

61 Julia Binder and Michael D. Watkins, "To Solve a Tough Problem, Reframe It," *Harvard Business Review*, April 1, 2024, https://hbr.org/2024/01/to-solve-a-tough-problem-reframe-it.

62 Harvard Kennedy School, "About," https://www.hks.harvard.edu/more/about.

63 Harlan Cleveland, *Nobody in Charge* (Jossey-Bass, 2002).

64　Natalie Daher, "41% of Young Voters Say UnitedHealthcare CEO Kill-ing 'Acceptable': Poll," *Axios*, December 17, 2024, https://www.axios.com/2024/12/17/united-healthcare-ceo-killing-poll.

65　Zoe Hussain, "AOC Sympathizes with Those Celebrating UnitedHealthcare CEO's Murder, Says Denied Claims Are 'Acts of Violence," *New York Post*, December 13, 2024, https://nypost.com/2024/12/13/us-news/aoc-sparks-criticism-defending-those-who-dont-have-sympathy-for-unitedhealthcare-ceo-brian-thompson-killing/.

66　Ted Kaczynski, *The Unabomber Manifesto* (Jolly Roger Press, 1995), https://www.thetedkarchive.com/library/ted-kaczynski-industrial-society-and-it-s-future-2nd-edition.

67　Ibid., 5–6.

68　Ibid., 9.

69　Ibid., 51.

70　Ibid.

71　Ibid., 50.

72　James Alan Fox, "Mass Killing Database," Northeastern University, https://cssh.northeastern.edu/sccj/mass-killing-database/.

73　Joel Kotkin, "The Great Dumbing Down of American Education," *American Mind*, January 16, 2025, https://americanmind.org/salvo/the-great-dumbing-down-of-american-education/.

74　Ibid.

75　Hiranmayi Srinivasan, "What Is Nancy Pelosi's Net Worth?," Investope-dia, August 15, 2024, https://www.investopedia.com/nancy-pelosi-net-worth-8690668.

76　Edward Heckman, "How Rich Is Willie Brown and His Ties to Kamala Har-ris," *Wealth Tax*, August 25, 2024, https://www.lawyersclubindia.com/wealth/willie-brown-net-worth-kamala-harris/.

77　"Kristin Crowley," Transparent California, https://transparentcalifornia.com/salaries/2023/los-angeles/kristin-crowley/.

78　"Notable & Quoteable: Fire," Wall Street Journal, December 30, 2025, https://www.wsj.com/opinion/notable-quotable-fire-d8437af2?gaa_at=eafs&gaa_n=AWEtsqfhH2JUFFo62PLKig8BgoE-3oTyurFmVVcx__3GxR0HBz91oJUE9GnER0LYev0%3D&gaa_ts=696f97c2&gaa_sig=v9QekOtCiECeXYxziv4RuFTjtN4KU7DUl92_l8nLLeQDtxaLq6v5Xks6MFyCkkzYzv7E-hvB7OZ1fayUG13CVg%3D%3D.

79　Tom McClintock, "Bad Policy Served as Kindling for California's Wildfires," *Wall Street Journal*, January 12, 2025, https://www.wsj.com/opinion/bad-poli-cy-served-as-kindling-for-californias-wildfires-forest-water-management-social-justice-c5b94a4f.

80　Steve Malanga, "L.A.'s Total Leadership Failure," *City Journal*, Janu-ary 10, 2025, https://www.city-journal.org/article/la-mayor-karen-bass-budget-wildfires; National Weather Service, https://web.archive.org/web/20250109140408/https://www.weather.gov/wrh/TextProduct?product=afdlox&id=d967ebab-a397-491d-9fea-1c676839775c.

81 Marissa Wenzke, "Mayor Bass, LAFD Chief Put on United Front After Speculation of Chief's Firing," CBS News, January 11, 2025, https://www.cbsnews.com/losangeles/news/mayor-bass-lafd-chief-put-on-united-front-after-speculation-of-chiefs-firing/.

82 Allysia Finley, "How the Left Turned California into a Paradise Lost," *Wall Street Journal*, January 12, 2025, https://www.wsj.com/opinion/how-the-left-turned-california-into-a-paradise-lost-government-policy-wildfires-48b88d6a.

83 Ryan Bourne and Sophia Bagley, "California Insurance Market: Another Victim of the War on Prices," Cato Institute, January 10, 2025, https://www.cato.org/blog/california-insurance-market-another-victim-war-prices.

84 Ibid.

85 Edward Ring, "The Politicization of Wind and Fire," California Policy Center, January 22, 2025, https://californiapolicycenter.org/the-politicization-of-wind-and-fire/.

86 Jake Tapper and Alex Thompson, *Original Sin: President Biden's Decline, Its Cover-Up, and His Disastrous Choice to Run Again* (New York: Penguin Press, 2025).

Chapter 8: Legitimizing the Overclass

1 James Madison, "Federalist No. 10," in *The Federalist Papers* (New York: Random House, 1937; originally published in 1788).

2 Ibid., 339.

3 Ibid., 370.

4 "Sherman Anti-Trust Act (1890)," National Archives, https://www.archives.gov/milestone-documents/sherman-anti-trust-act.

5 "Sherman Antitrust Act," Wikipedia, https://en.wikipedia.org/wiki/Sherman_Antitrust_Act.

6 David McCabe and Nico Grant, "U.S. Said to Consider a Breakup of Google to Address Search Monopoly," *New York Times*, August 13, 2024, https://www.nytimes.com/2024/08/13/technology/google-monopoly-antitrust-justice-department.html.

7 "Bryan's 'Cross of Gold' Speech: Mesmerizing the Masses," History Matters–George Mason University, https://historymatters.gmu.edu/d/5354/.

8 "President Woodrow Wilson ('79) Campaigns for Preceptorials," *Princeton Alumni Weekly*, first published December 13, 1902, https://paw.princeton.edu/article/president-woodrow-wilson-79-campaigns-preceptorials.

9 Woodrow Wilson, *The New Freedom: A Call for the Emancipation of the Generous Energies of a People* (New York and Garden City: Doubleday, Page, and Company, 1913).

10 Ibid.

11 Charles Allen Prosser, "Report on the Commission on National Aid to Vocational Education," https://onlinebooks.library.upenn.edu/webbin/book/lookupid?key=ha001974151.

12   Barton Swaim, "'Woodrow Wilson' Review: Liberty Limited," *Wall Street Journal*, November 8, 2024, https://www.wsj.com/arts-culture/books/woodrow-wilson-liberty-limited-759dbf0e.

13   Walter Lippmann, *A Preface to Morals* (New York: Macmillan Company, 1929), 237, 239.

14   Ibid., 243.

15   Ibid., 245.

16   Ibid., 257.

17   David Samuels, "Rapid-Onset Political Enlightenment," *Tablet*, December 20, 2024, https://www.tabletmag.com/feature/rapid-onset-political-enlightenment.

18   "First Inaugural Address of Franklin D. Roosevelt," Yale Law School Avalon Project, https://avalon.law.yale.edu/20th_century/froos1.asp.

19   *Humphrey's Executor v. U.S.*, 295 U.S. 602 (1935), https://tile.loc.gov/storage-services/service/ll/usrep/usrep295/usrep295602/usrep295602.pdf.

20   Ibid.

21   William F. Buckley, "Our Mission Statement," *National Review*, November 19, 1955, https://nrinstitute.org/wp-content/uploads/2020/05/Our-Mission-Statement.pdf.

22   Stephen B. Young, *Theory and Practice of Associative Power: CORDS in the Villages of Vietnam, 1867–1972* (Lanham, Maryland: Hamilton Books, 2017).

23   "Brookings Institution," Wikipedia, https://en.wikipedia.org/wiki/Brookings_Institution.

24   "Presidency of Lyndon Johnson," Wikipedia, https://en.wikipedia.org/wiki/Presidency_of_Lyndon_B._Johnson.

25   Young, *Kissinger's Betrayal*.

26   "Conscription in the United States," Wikipedia, https://en.wikipedia.org/wiki/Conscription_in_the_United_States.

27   "George McGovern," Wikipedia, https://en.wikipedia.org/wiki/George_McGovern.

28   Ibid.

29   Carter, "Crisis of Confidence" speech.

30   "The President's News Conference," Ronald Reagan Presidential Library & Museum, August 12, 1986, https://www.reaganlibrary.gov/archives/speech/presidents-news-conference-23.

31   Ronald Reagan Presidential Library, "President's News Conference #23," https://www.reaganlibrary.gov/archives/speech/presidents-news-conference-23.

32   "Presidency of Ronald Reagan," Wikipedia, https://en.wikipedia.org/wiki/Presidency_of_Ronald_Reagan.

33   "Presidency of George W. Bush," Wikipedia, https://en.wikipedia.org/wiki/Presidency_of_George_W._Bush.

34   "Barack Obama," Wikipedia, https://en.wikipedia.org/wiki/Barack_Obama.

35   Samuels, "Rapid-Onset."

36   Ibid.

37 Press Release, "New Evidence of Obama Administration Conspiracy to Subvert President Trump's 2016 Victory and Presidency," Office of the Director of National Intelligence, July 18, 2025, https://www.dni.gov/index.php/newsroom/press-releases/press-releases-2025/4086-pr-15-25.

38 Aaron Maté, "Russiagate's Architects Suppressed Doubts to Peddle False Claims," RealClearInvestigations, July 22, 2025, https://www.realclearinvestigations.com/articles/2025/07/22/russiagates_architects_suppressed_doubts_to_peddle_false_claims_1124060.html.

39 Adam Entous, Ellen Nakashima, and Greg Miller, "Secret CIA assessment says Russia was trying to help Trump win White House," *Washington Post*, December 9, 2016, https://www.washingtonpost.com/world/national-security/obama-orders-review-of-russian-hacking-during-presidential-campaign/2016/12/09/31d6b300-be2a-11e6-94ac-3d324840106c_story.html.

40 "Notable Quotable: Obama on 'Policing' the Russia Problem," *Wall Street Journal*, July 29, 2025, https://www.wsj.com/opinion/notable-quotable-policing-obama-russia-state-department-af9e33d8?mod=opinion_feat2_commentary_pos1.

41 Katelyn Polantz, "Mueller Investigation Cost $32 Million, Justice Department Says," CNN, August 2, 2019, https://www.cnn.com/2019/08/02/politics/mueller-report-cost.

42 "Presidency of Donald Trump," Wikipedia, https://en.wikipedia.org/wiki/Presidency_of_Donald_Trump.

43 Aurelia Glass and Karla Walter, "How Biden's American-Style Industrial Policy Will Create Quality Jobs," *American Progress*, October 27, 2022, https://www.americanprogress.org/article/how-bidens-american-style-industrial-policy-will-create-quality-jobs/.

44 Glass and Walter, "How Biden's American-Style Industrial Policy Will Create Quality Jobs".

45 "Executive Order on Diversity, Equity, Inclusion, and Accessibility in the Federal Workforce," White House, June 25, 2021, https://www.whitehouse.gov/briefing-room/presidential-actions/2021/06/25/executive-order-on-diversity-equity-inclusion-and-accessibility-in-the-federal-workforce/.

46 Samuels, "Rapid-Onset."

47 Ibid.

48 Julian Epstein, "The End of the 'Obama Era' Has Officially Arrived—with a Deep Sense of Betrayal among Dem Voters," *New York Post*, January 4, 2025, https://nypost.com/2025/01/04/opinion/the-end-of-the-obama-era-has-officially-arrived/.

49 *The Federalist Papers*, "Federalist No. 51," 335.

50 *Lochner v. New York*, 198 U.S. 45 (1905).

51 Ibid.

52 Ibid.

53 Ibid.

54 *Nebbia v. New York*, 291 U.S. 502 (1934).

55 Ibid.

56   Ibid.

57   Ibid.

58   *West Coast Hotel v. Parrish*, 300 U.S. 379 (1937).

59   *Loper Bright Enterprises v. Raimondo*, 603 U.S. (2024).

60   *Chevron USA, Inc., v. Natural Resources Defense Council, Inc.*, 467 U.S. 837.

61   Ibid.

62   Ibid.

63   Ibid.

64   *Loper v. Raimondo*.

65   Ibid.

66   Ibid.

67   Ibid.

68   Ibid.

69   Ibid.

70   Ibid.

71   Ibid.

72   *SEC v. Jarkesy*, 803 F.3d 9 (D.C. Cir. 2015).

73   Stephen Breyer, *Reading the Constitution: Why I Choose Pragmatism, Not Textualism* (New York: Simon & Schuster, 2024), xxv.

74   Ibid., 3.

75   Ibid.

76   Ibid., 5.

77   Ibid., 11.

78   Marc J. Dunkelman, "The Question Progressives Refuse to Answer," *Atlantic*, April 2, 2025, https://www.theatlantic.com/ideas/archive/2025/04/democrats-need-to-want-to-build/682264/.

79   Jonathan Turley, "The liberals' license: How the left finds release in an age of rage," *The Hill*, April 5, 2025, https://thehill.com/opinion/education/5233594-counter-constitutional-movement.

80   Jennifer Szalai, "The Constitution Is Sacred. Is It Also Dangerous?," *New York Times*, August 31, 2024, https://www.nytimes.com/2024/08/31/books/review/constitution-secession-democracy-crisis.html.

81   Neil Gorsuch, *Over Ruled: The Human Toll of Too Much Law* (New York: Harper, 2024), 3.

82   Ibid.

83   Ibid.

84   Ibid.

85   Ibid., 4–5.

86   Ibid., 18.

87   Ibid., 24.

88   *The Federalist Papers*, "Federalist No. 62," 400.

89   Henry de Bracton, *De legibus et consuetudinibus Angliae (On the Laws and Customs of England)*, vol. 11, p. 22, https://amesfoundation.law.harvard.edu/Bracton/Unframed/English/v2/33.htm?utm.

90   Ibid.

91   William Shakespeare, *Julius Caesar*, act 1, scene 2.

92   Gorsuch, *Over Ruled*, 212.

93   Yuval Levin, *American Covenant: How the Constitution Unified Our Nation—and Could Again* (New York: Basic Books, 2024), 277.

94   Ibid., 282–83.

95   "Statement from President Joe Biden on the Equal Rights Amendment," White House, January 17, 2025, https://bidenwhitehouse.archives.gov/briefing-room/statements-releases/2025/01/17/statement-from-president-joe-biden-on-the-equal-rights-amendment/.

96   Charles A. Reich, "The New Property," *Yale Law Journal* 73, no. 5 (April 1964): 733–87, https://doi.org/10.2307/794645.

97   Katharina Buchholz, "The Trump-Harris Gender Gap," Statista, November 6, 2024, https://www.statista.com/chart/33408/female-male-us-voters-exit-polls/.

98   Gerald F. Seib, "The Democrats Need Another Bill Clinton," *Wall Street Journal*, November 8, 2024, https://www.wsj.com/politics/the-democrats-need-another-bill-clinton-21fe5cb1.

99   Victor Davis Hanson, "Obama: Transforming America," *National Review*, October 1, 2013, https://www.nationalreview.com/2013/10/obama-transforming-america-victor-davis-hanson/.

100 Jennifer Rubin, "A 'Republic If We Can Keep It.' Perhaps We Cannot," *Washington Post*, November 6, 2024, https://www.washingtonpost.com/opinions/2024/11/06/trump-election-americans-blame-democracy/.

101 The Glasser, Harwood, Filipovic, Wehner, and Conway quotes all appear in an article by James Pierson, "Democrats & Never-Trumpers Blame the Voters," *New Criterion*, November 8, 2024, https://newcriterion.com/dispatch/democrats-and-never-trumpers-blame-the-voters/.

102 Matt Bai, "Where Did Kamala Harris's Campaign Go Wrong?," *Washington Post*, November 6, 2024, https://www.washingtonpost.com/opinions/2024/11/06/trump-harris-election-2024-prompt/.

103 Chris Lehmann, "Somehow, Americans Are Liking Trump Better Every Day," *Nation*, November 26, 2024, https://www.thenation.com/article/politics/trump-approval-ratings.

104 Nate Silver, "The Expert Class Is Failing, and So Is Biden's Presidency," *Silver Bulletin*, December 2, 2024, https://www.natesilver.net/p/the-expert-class-is-failing-and-so.

105 John Halpin, "The Sociology of Party Decline," *The Liberal Patriot*, March 26, 2025, https://www.liberalpatriot.com/p/the-sociology-of-party-decline.

106 John Opdycke, "The Democratic Party Is Pushing Away Independents," *Hill*, December 21, 2024, https://thehill.com/opinion/campaign/5050531-dems-independent-thinking/.

107   Michael Baharaeen, "The Left-Flank Albatross," *Liberal Patriot*, December 3, 2024, www.liberalpatriot.com/p/the-left-flank-albatross.

108   Adam B. Coleman, "It's Official: The Democrats Have Learned Nothing," *Speaking Wrong at the Right Time*, February 2, 2025, https://www.adamb-coleman.com/p/its-official-the-democrats-have-learned.

109   Sasha Stone, "Sorry, Democrats, America Is Just Not Ready for You," *Free Thinking through the Fourth Turning*, November 16, 2024, https://sashastone.substack.com/p/sorry-democrats-america-is-just-not.

110   Philip Wegmann, "Final MAGA Rally: Trump Surveys Empire from Madison Square Garden," RealClearPolitics, October 28, 2024, https://www.realclearpolitics.com/articles/2024/10/28/trump_surveys_empire_from_madison_square_garden_151849.html.

111   John Ganz, "Party Under Country: Dissecting the Democratic Malaise," *Nation*, https://www.thenation.com/article/politics/party-under-country-dissecting-the-democratic-malaise/.

112   Aaron Zitner, "Democrats Get Lowest Rating from Voters in 35 Years, WSJ Poll Finds," *Wall Street Journal*, July 25, 2025, https://www.wsj.com/politics/elections/democratic-party-poll-voter-confidence-july-2025-9db38021?gaa_at=eafs&gaa_n=ASWzDAjMs0Cz0qSjOGtfuwA6lbABuAovdJ0gz4WFYd5deuxMaAhl81qkTEUAUZVmvSE%3D&gaa_ts=68894897&gaa_sig=h4DNcBgvRV8feyXlKScuNxdvgBwCgIWD_ETTMBal6Vn51iAzt6m9PNHllIsf08Fs2Jqi-yj4Izzq-limkMxk0pMA%3D%3D.

113   Scott Adams, "Coffee with Scott Adams #2195: Biden's Mental Tics, Speaker Vote Fun, A.I. and the Woke Hall of Fame," YouTube, October 6, 2023, https://www.youtube.com/watch?v=184t7UoXMEk.

114   *The Federalist Papers*, "Federalist No. 48" and "Federalist No. 51."

115   Ibid., "Federalist No. 37."

116   Ibid., "Federalist No. 51."

117   Ibid.

118   Melissa Quinn and Caitlin Yilek, "Read the Full Transcript of Trump's Inauguration Speech," CBS News, January 20, 2025, https://www.cbsnews.com/news/transcript-trump-inauguration-speech-2025/.

119   Ibid.

120   Ibid.

121   Ibid.

122   John Hall Stewart, *A Documentary Survey of the French Revolution* (New York: Macmillan Company, 1959), 88.

123   Benjamin Wallace-Wells, "Trump's Attempt to Redefine America," *New Yorker*, February 3, 2025, https://www.newyorker.com/magazine/2025/02/03/trumps-attempt-to-redefine-america.

124   "Ensuring Accountability for All Agencies," The White House, February 18, 2025, https://www.whitehouse.gov/presidential-actions/2025/02/ensuring-accountability-for-all-agencies/.

125   Ibid.

126 "Improving Education Outcomes by Empowering Parents, States, and Communities," The White House, March 20, 2025, https://www.whitehouse.gov/presidential-actions/2025/03/improving-education-outcomes-by-empowering-parents-states-and-communities/.

127 "Letter Sent to Harvard," Harvard University, https://www.harvard.edu/research-funding/wp-content/uploads/sites/16/2025/04/Letter-Sent-to-Harvard-2025-04-11.pdf.

128 "Reforming Accreditation to Strengthen Higher Education," The White House, April 23, 2025, https://www.whitehouse.gov/presidential-actions/2025/04/reforming-accreditation-to-strengthen-higher-education/.

129 "Ending Taxpayer Subsidization of Biased Media," The White House, May 1, 2025, https://www.whitehouse.gov/presidential-actions/2025/05/ending-taxpayer-subsidization-of-biased-media/.

130 Annette Choi and Danya Gainor, "Analyzing the scale of Trump's federal layoffs in his first 100 days," CNN Politics, April 29, 2025, https://www.cnn.com/2025/04/26/politics/federal-layoffs-trump-musk-dg/index.html

131 "Ending Illegal Discrimination and Restoring Merit-Based Opportunity," The White House, January 21, 2025, https://www.whitehouse.gov/presidential-actions/2025/01/ending-illegal-discrimination-and-restoring-merit-based-opportunity/.

Chapter 9: Squaring the Circle: Restoring a Covenantal America

1 "Many Writers Try to Span America's Political Divide," *Economist*, September, 30 2017, https://www.economist.com/culture/2017/09/30/many-writers-try-to-span-americas-political-divide?fsrc=scn%2Ftw%2Fte%2Fbl%2Fed%2F manywriterstrytospanamericaspoliticaldivide.

2 "AllSides Media Bias Chart," AllSides, https://www.allsides.com/media-bias/media-bias-chart.

3 Stephen Hawkins et al., *Hidden Tribes: A Study of America's Polarized Landscape*, Hidden Tribes, 2018, https://hiddentribes.us/media/qfpekz4g/hidden_tribes_report.pdf.

4 George Packer, "The Four Americas," *Atlantic*, August 1, 2023, https://www.theatlantic.com/magazine/archive/2021/07/george-packer-four-americas/619012/.

5 Scott A. Leadingham, "What Is Christian Nationalism? The Complete Guide," Freedom Forum, accessed July 11, 2024, https://www.freedomforum.org/what-is-christian-nationalism/.

6 Fintan O'Toole, "Savior Complexes," *New York Review of Books*, August 15, 2024, https://www.nybooks.com/articles/2024/08/15/savior-complexes-joe-biden-fintan-otoole/.

7 Gerard Baker, "Democrats' Deception May Win the Presidential Election Again," *Wall Street Journal*, August 26, 2024, https://www.wsj.com/opinion/democrats-deception-may-be-enough-to-win-again-dnc-kamala-harris-election-8572df67.

8   Joel Kotkin, "Kamala Harris: Creature of the Oligarchy," *Spiked*, September 4, 2024, https://www.spiked-online.com/2024/08/23/kamala-harris-creature-of-the-oligarchy/.

9   Abigail Shrier, "Elon Musk, Mark Zuckerberg, and Our Government Censors" (quoting Jake Tapper interview on CNN), The Truth Fairy, September 5, 2024, https://www.thetruthfairy.info/p/elon-musk-mark-zuckerberg-and-our.

10   Shrier, "Elon Musk, Mark Zuckerberg"; Ian Schwartz, "Jake Tapper Interviews Kamala Harris: How Would Banning Trump on Twitter Not Be a Slippery Slope?," RealClear-Politics, October 4, 2019, https://www.realclear-politics.com/video/2019/10/04/jake_tapper_interviews_kamala_harris_how_would_banning_trump_on_twitter_not_be_a_slippery_slope.html#!.

11   Baker, "Democrats' Deception."

12   IM Editors, "RFK Jr. Address to the Nation: Full Transcript," IM—1776, August 23, 2024, https://im1776.com/2024/08/24/rfk-address-to-the-nation/.

13   Kelly Wynne, "Read Mark Zuckerberg's Full Statement on Blocking Trump From Facebook and Instagram," *Newsweek*, January 7, 2021, https://www.newsweek.com/read-mark-zuckerbergs-full-statement-blocking-trump-facebook-instagram-1559750.

14   Thomas Fisher, *Designing Our Way to a Better World* (Minneapolis: University of Minnesota Press, 2016), 14.

15   Eph. 2:8.

16   Smith, *The Theory of Moral Sentiments*, 146–47.

17   Ibid., 152.

18   Ralph Waldo Emerson, "Spiritual Laws," from *The Portable Emerson* (New York: Penguin Books, 1946), 193–94, 203.

19   Ibid., "The Oversoul," 210–11.

20   Ibid., 204.

21   Marcus Tullius Cicero, *De Officiis*, trans. Walter Miller (Cambridge: Harvard University Press, 1913; originally published in 44 BC), 7.

22   Ibid., 25.

23   Ibid., 67.

24   Ibid., 109.

25   Ibid., 117.

26   Ibid., 119.

27   Confucius, *The Analects*, II:X.

28   Ibid., XV:XX.

29   Ibid., VI:XVII; VII:XXXVI.

30   Ibid., II:XXIV.

31   Ibid., IV:V.

32   Ibid., IV:XVI.

33   Marcus Aurelius, *Meditations*, Internet Classics Archive, 7:59, https://classics.mit.edu/Antoninus/meditations.html.

34 Ibid., 3:9.

35 Ibid., 4:3.

36 Buddha, *Dhammapada* (New York: Random House—The Modern Library, 2007), 23, 31, 48.

37 Ibid., 10, 26, 27.

38 Marcus Aurelius, *Meditations*, 2, 5.

39 Ibid., 3, 5, 6.

40 Ibid., 3, 6.

41 Bartleby, "How to Inspire People," *Economist*, December 5, 2024, https://www.economist.com/business/2024/12/05/how-to-inspire-people.

42 Mark Alden Branch, "Damn the Consequences. Give Me the Pen," *Yale Alumni Magazine*, July 3, 2014, https://yalealumnimagazine.org/blog_posts/1831-damn-the-consequences-give-me-the-pen.

43 Gustaf Wingren, *Luther on Vocation*, trans. Carl C. Rasmussen (Eugene: Wipf & Stock ,1957), 2.

44 Ibid., 39.

45 Wingren, *Luther on Vocation*, 5.

46 Ibid., 73.

47 Ibid., 72.

48 Ibid., 9.

49 Ibid., 10.

50 "The Place of Tikkun Olam in American Jewish Life," Jerusalem Center for Security and Foreign Affairs, July 11, 2019, https://jcpa.org/article/place-tikkun-olam-american-jewish-life.

51 Quran, verses 2:29; 33:72.

52 John Calvin, *Institutes of the Christian Religion, Book 1*, ed. John T. McNeill (Philadelphia: The Westminster Press, 1960), 197.

53 Ibid., *Book III*, chap. 11, section 6, 724.

54 Confucius, *The Analects*, XII:XI.

55 Ibid., XV:XXII.

56 Pope John Paul II, *Laborem Exercens*, September 14, 1981, sections 1, 4, and 6, https://www.vatican.va/content/john-paul-ii/en/encyclicals/documents/hf_jp-ii_enc_14091981_laborem-exercens.html.

57 Stephen R. Covey, *The 8th Habit: From Effectiveness to Greatness* (New York: Free Press, 2004), 16.

58 Ibid., 17.

59 Ibid., 27.

60 Ibid., 28.

61 Ibid., 30.

62 Ibid., 64.

63   Mahatma Gandhi quotes, Goodreads, https://www.goodreads.com/quotes/760902-we-but-mirror-the-world-all-the-tendencies-present-in.

64   Emily Dickinson, Poem 572, in *Final Harvest: Emily Dickinson's Poems*, ed. Thomas H. Johnson (Boston: Little, Brown, 1961), 319.

65   Walt Whitman, *Leaves of Grass and Selected Prose*, ed. John Kouwenhoven (New York: Modern Library, 1950), 118.

66   Robert Frost, "One Step Backward Taken," in *Selected Poems of Robert Frost*, ed. Robert Graves (New York: Holt, Rinehart and Winston, 1965), 251.

67   Carl Sandburg, "The People, Yes," Poetry Foundation, https://www.poetryfoundation.org/poems/51748/the-people-yes.

68   Julia Ward Howe, "Battle Hymn of the Republic," Poetry Foundation, 2024, https://www.poetryfoundation.org/poems/44420/battle-hymn-of-the-republic.

69   Lao Tzu, *Tao Te Ching*, trans. John C.H. Wu (New York: St. John's University Press, 1961), 35, #11.

70   Ibid., 77, #54.

71   Ibid., 93, #64.

72   George Washington, "Thanksgiving Proclamation, 3 October 1789," *The Papers of George Washington*, Presidential Series, vol. 4, 8 September 1789–15 January 1790, ed. Dorothy Twohig (Charlottesville: University Press of Virginia, 1993), 131–32; also, *Founders Online*, https://founders.archives.gov/documents/Washington/05-04-02-0091.

73   "Lincoln and Thanksgiving," National Park Service, last modified November 25, 2020, https://www.nps.gov/liho/learn/historyculture/lincoln-and-thanksgiving.htm.

ACKNOWLEDGMENTS

Above all else, I acknowledge the supportive patience of my wife, Pham Thi Hoa, in accepting with grace the hours of my being distracted with reading and typing.

My teachers at Harvard College gave me the concepts that brought forth the thesis of this story of America and demonstrated for me the intellectual skills, the faith in truth, the skepticism needed before coming to conclusions, and the integrative sensitivity to the interplay of culture, society, psychology, economics, and politics, which are needed for any well-founded understanding of human successes and failures.

Professor David Riesman accepted me as a peer in discussions about politics, sociology, and human nature when I was only an undergraduate. It is to him that I owe an intellectual debt of being able to think coherently about inner- and other-direction.

Professor Evon Vogt, founder of the Harvard Chiapas Project, selected me as a summer fellow for field research in cultural anthropology in Zinacantán, a Highland Maya community in Chiapas, Mexico. He gave advice on best practices in learning about others from participant observation and in writing up notes daily, always making a spare copy kept separately just in case.

Professor Samuel Beer put before us big questions about how modernity arrived for us in the shape it has, contrasting Max Weber with Karl Marx.

Professor Samuel Huntington supervised my writing of a senior thesis and so focused my attention on the foundations provided for human communities by institutions.

Walter Slote, a stunningly insightful psychotherapist in the school of Harry Stack Sullivan, and friend, anchored me convincingly in learning how to respectfully delve into the human psyche and so relate the individual to the social as a joint venture with reciprocal duties one to the other.

But first perhaps was Ms. Parsons, my fifth-grade teacher, who insisted that learning history made for right action. My great-grandmother Etta Ross Hubbard and then my grandfather George Morris and his wife, my grandmother Miriam Hubbard Morris, modernized two eighteenth-century houses and furnished them with eighteenth-century furniture, both American and English Chippendale. History thus was made contemporaneous for my siblings, cousins, and me.

My father was a teacher by example in his deft cultivation of Asian cultural and interpersonal dynamics, from his friendship with the king of Thailand to charming villagers in northeastern provinces. His example was that one could constructively participate in a culture on the other side of a language barrier and also bring into the present learning from the other side of time.

And I am so grateful for the wise advice and generous support of my editors at RealClear Publishing.

ABOUT THE AUTHOR

Stephen B. Young is the global executive director of the Caux Round Table for Moral Capitalism. He is the author of *Moral Capitalism: Reconciling Private Interest with the Public Good* and *The Road to Moral Capitalism.*

In 2008 Professor Sandra Waddock of the Carroll School of Management at Boston College listed Young in her book *The Difference Makers* among the twenty-three people who created the corporate social responsibility movement.

Young has served as an assistant dean at Harvard Law School and dean and professor of law at Hamline University School of Law. He is a graduate of the International School in Bangkok, Harvard College, and Harvard Law School and has taught corporate social responsibility at the Carlson School of Business, University of Minnesota, and the Sasin School of Management, Chulalongkorn University, Thailand.

He is also a recipient of the Albert Nelson Marquis Lifetime Achievement Award, the highest honor extended by Marquis Who's Who, and was included in the 2023–2024 Who's Who Commemorative Edition book for Lifetime Achievement.

His 1968–1971 service in Vietnam for the U.S. Agency for International Development in village development and counterinsurgency was highly praised by President Richard Nixon, Central Intelligence Agency Director William Colby, and ambassador to Saigon Ellsworth Bunker.

In 1966 Young discovered the Bronze Age culture of the village of Ban Chiang in Northeast Thailand, which is now a UNESCO World Heritage site. In 1989 he proposed the formation of a United Nations interim administration for Cambodia to finally put an end to the Killing Fields in that country.

Young is also a non-Catholic member of the Advisory Council to the Papal *Fondazione Centesimus Annus Pro Pontifice*, established by Pope (now Saint) John Paul II as a lay organization to promote Catholic social teachings. With encouragement from Pope Francis, Young coordinated a study group of Christian and Muslim scholars to recover knowledge about the covenants of the Prophet Muhammad to respect and protect Christian communities.

He founded the Minnesota Character Council to promote character education in Minnesota public schools.

His other books include *Kissinger's Betrayal: How America Lost the Vietnam War*, *The Tradition of Human Rights in China and Vietnam* (with Nguyen Ngoc Huy), *The Theory and Practice of Associative Power: CORDS in the Villages of Vietnam 1967–1972*, and *Qur'anic Guidance for Good Governance* (coeditor with Abdullah Al-Ahsan).

He and his wife, Pham Thi Hoa, translated from Vietnamese the novel about Ho Chi Minh published as *The Zenith*, a behind-the-scenes look at the real Ho Chi Minh.

He has published articles on corporate social responsibility, enterprise valuation, public and private goods, Chinese jurisprudence, the culture and politics of Vietnam and Thailand, Native American law, the history of negligence, and the law of war. His commentaries have been published in the *Washington Post*, the *New York Times*, the *Wall Street Journal*, the *Asia Times*, RealClearPolitics, RealClearDefense, the *American Thinker*, American Greatness, and the *Minnesota Star Tribune*. He also has an author's site on Substack.